D1226675

TENTACLES OF POWER

TENTACLES

The Story of

THE WORLD PUBLISHING COMPANY

OF POWER

Jimmy Hoffa

by CLARK R. MOLLENHOFF

Cleveland and New York

PUBLISHED BY The World Publishing Company
2231 West 110th Street, Cleveland 2, Ohio

Published simultaneously in Canada by
Nelson, Foster & Scott Ltd.

Library of Congress Catalog Card Number: 65-23359

FIRST EDITION

Copyright © 1965 by Clark Mollenhoff

No part of this book may be reproduced in any form without
permission in writing from the publisher, except by a reviewer
who wishes to quote brief passages in connection with a review
written for inclusion in a magazine, newspaper, or broadcast.
Printed in the United States of America.

HD
6515
T3M6
.

CITATION FOR A PULITZER PRIZE
IN JOURNALISM FOR NATIONAL REPORTING
1958

Awarded to Clark Mollenhoff of The Des Moines
Register and Tribune for his persistent inquiry into
labor racketeering, which included investigatory reporting of wide significance.

May 5, 1958

102584   EMORY AND HENRY LIBRARY

To
Richard L. Wilson, Kenneth MacDonald,
Frank Eyerly and the late Gideon
Seymour. They made it possible.

CONTENTS

I

The Great Investigation

Room 160 of the old Senate Office Building contains 50 file drawers, each packed with two rows of 3 by 5 cards that serve simply as the index to files on The Great Investigation. These files line the walls of the huge room on the first floor of the building and overflow into the National Archives Building at Ninth Street and Constitution Avenue.

Nearly every week investigators for the Federal Bureau of Investigation, the Internal Revenue Service or other law-enforcement agencies go to the office of chief counsel Jerome Adlerman, requesting access to these files of the Select Committee on Improper Activities in the Labor or Management Field. The committee was more popularly known as the "McClellan labor racket committee."

The investigation was one that many said could not be made because of the power of organized labor in Congress. Yet it was made. It exploded across the front pages of the nation's newspapers for more than three years, making and breaking reputations. It was surely The Great Investigation of our time. Perhaps it was one of the greatest in our history.

It was great in length, in scope, and in its impact on the national political and economic scene. Starting in September, 1956, and extending into 1960, it was the longest such special Congressional investigation ever conducted. It rocked the power of organized labor; exposed the corruption and compromises of top men in the most powerful labor unions; made headline figures of the chairman and chief counsel of the committee, and was a springboard for Presidential nominations for two of its members—Senator John F. Kennedy of Massachusetts and Senator Barry M. Goldwater of Arizona.

It was an investigation that exposed corruption in city, county, and state governments in nearly every section of the United States. Before completion it had exposed corruption and brutality in the International Brotherhood of Teamsters, Chauffeurs, Warehousemen and Helpers of America, from Seattle, Washington, to Miami Beach, Florida, and from Long Island, New York, to San Diego, California. Improper activities were uncovered in New York City, Chicago, Los Angeles, Cleveland, Kansas City, Minneapolis, Detroit, Pittsburgh, Philadelphia, Scranton, Salt Lake City, Portland, Omaha, Indianapolis, Louisville, St. Louis, Chattanooga and Nashville.

The testimony traced perversion and attempted perversion of the whole democratic process through political string-pulling on governors, former governors, judges, prosecutors, and law enforcement officials. Local and state government officials, ranging from policemen to governors, were subverted by some Teamsters union officials to serve as their tools. Efforts were made to buy or intimidate the press. The same methods were tried, with varying degrees of success, on federal officials and institutions—the National Labor Relations Board, the Labor Department, the Congress, and even the federal courts.

Union money was available to pay legal fees or consultant's fees to former governors, associates or political cronies of governors, relatives of judges, or to former members of the United States House of Representatives or the Senate.

Workers could always be recruited for political campaigns, and the Teamsters' organizations could raise "voluntary" contributions from union members for political activity at all levels —to help a friendly sheriff in the state of Washington, a prosecutor in Michigan, a judge in Tennessee or a mayor in Oregon.

Before their convictions, two of the most prominent labor leaders in America—Teamsters boss Dave Beck and Carpenters Union chief Maurice Hutcheson—had entree to the White House for conversations with the President. The Great Investigation brought the conviction of Beck and Hutcheson, and contained a drama of personal rivalry that has become a classic in American history. The bitterness that developed between committee counsel Robert F. Kennedy and Teamsters president James R. Hoffa caught the public fancy and helped usher in the Kennedy Administration. The acrimonious duel between them provided the impetus necessary to accomplish a successful prosecution of Hoffa.

This was the investigation that put Senator John F. Kennedy on page one of the newspapers. It made him part of a brother act in a fight against the most sordid types of illegal and brutal corruption of the power of organized labor. Until 1957, the bright young Massachusetts senator was one of the glamour boys in Congress. He was characterized by society columnists as a gay bachelor in the House of Representatives and in his first years in the Senate. If his marriage to pretty Jacqueline Bouvier made him a more serious and more effective legislator, it was not obvious in his legislative record up to 1957.

In the Democratic party's 1956 national convention, Senator Kennedy was able to capitalize on the "stop Kefauver" sentiment in many southern delegations to pile up 648 votes for the Democratic vice-presidential nomination. He was only 38 votes short of the nomination as the running mate to Adlai Stevenson, but this was not a true indication of pro-Kennedy sentiment at that time.

The biggest bloc of Kennedy support came from the South. It included the Texas delegation, where House Speaker Sam Rayburn and Majority Leader Lyndon Johnson, neither of them admirers of John Kennedy, were intent on using every available trick to stop Senator Estes Kefauver of Tennessee. Kefauver paid little attention to "Mr. Sam" or Lyndon. Some delegates regarded Kefauver as a traitor to the South because of his progressive views on civil rights.

Out of that convention loss, Senator Kennedy gained his first exposure on national television. He and his brother Robert learned by direct experience that a crime and racket prober who used television properly could have potent grassroots appeal even five years after the Kefauver crime probe had ended. This was no little factor in the Kennedy decision to take on the politically explosive labor racket investigation—an investigation that had been killed more than a half-dozen times between 1953 and 1956 by the tremendous political power of organized labor within both parties in Congress. While the investigation had the potential for making the Kennedy name well known, it also contained great risks. It could just as easily destroy the political careers of those who meddled with it.

Within a month after that Democratic convention in Chicago in August, 1956, Bob Kennedy started work on The Great Investigation of labor rackets.

At the time, he expected the job to cover a few months. Before he resigned as committee counsel in 1960 to run his brother's campaign for the Presidency, Bob Kennedy's crusade had made the crime investigations by Tom Dewey and Kefauver seem pale by comparison.

Through their own investigations, Jack and Bob Kennedy made personal contact with reporters and editors on nearly every large newspaper in the country. They did not have to seek television coverage, but were sought for appearances on "Meet the Press," "Face the Nation," and similar nationwide shows. Both Kennedys became cover boys on national publications which would not have given them space a few months earlier.

Through his efforts to pass labor reform legislation, Senator Kennedy compiled his only concrete record as a legislator. Though the Kennedy-Ives labor reform bill failed to get through Congress in 1958, Senator Kennedy was a key figure in the successful passage of the Landrum-Griffith labor reform bill in September, 1959. The effort on this legislation brought him in working contact with men who were later to play top roles in his political campaign and in the Kennedy Administration. These were such men as Arthur Goldberg, former counsel for the A.F.L.-C.I.O., former Secretary of Labor, later a Justice of the Supreme Court and now U.S. Ambassador to the U.N.; Archibald Cox, the Harvard law professor who became Solicitor General for the Justice Department in the Kennedy Administration, and Stewart L. Udall, a member of the House Education and Labor Committee who worked closely with Kennedy on labor legislation and was named as Kennedy's Secretary of the Interior.

Many other Kennedy Administration appointments were of

men who had developed close political associations with Jack or Bob Kennedy during the labor-racket investigations. They included Carmine Bellino, the accountant-investigator who was named as a special assistant to President Kennedy; Kenneth O'Donnell, President Kennedy's appointment secretary at the White House, and Pierre Salinger, the White House press secretary.

Paul Tierney, as assistant counsel on the Senate's McClellan committee, became a member of the Interstate Commerce Commission. An investigator for the committee, James McShane, was named United States Marshal. Investigator Walter Sheridan became a special assistant to Attorney General Robert Kennedy and headed a unit that specialized in investigating Hoffa. Herbert J. (Jack) Miller, lawyer for a board of Teamsters monitors appointed by a Federal Court, was named Assistant Attorney General in charge of the Criminal Division of the Justice Department. Lester P. Condon, one of those who advised Bob Kennedy on Hoffa's background, was named Inspector General for the Department of Agriculture.

Edwin O. Guthman, Pulitzer-Prize-winning Seattle *Times* reporter, met the Kennedys through the Beck investigation and became Bob Kennedy's top press man at the Justice Department. John Seigenthaler, who investigated Teamsters for *The Nashville Tennessean* and won a Nieman Fellowship at Harvard, served as administrative assistant to Attorney General Kennedy. Wallace Turner and William Lambert, a Pulitzer-Prize-winning team of reporter-investigators for *The Portland Oregonian,* served for a time as top-level press consultants in the Department of Health, Education and Welfare.

The Senate labor-racket inquiry was almost as beneficial to the political career of Senator Goldwater. He was only one of four Republicans on the eight-member special committee, but his strong views on the abuse of power by organized labor gained wide attention and produced a significant national following.

The Arizonan had been in the Senate only four years when the McClellan investigation started. He was low in seniority and came from one of the least populous states. His ideas on the power of labor officials had virtually no possibility of serious consideration by the Senate before the McClellan investigation.

As a member of a Senate labor and public welfare subcommittee, Senator Goldwater had a small role in a 1955 investigation of loose and corrupt handling of union pension and welfare funds. He had taken part in several abortive attempts to stimulate a major labor-racket probe prior to 1957.

Between January, 1957, and 1960, the McClellan committee's inquiry created a nationwide demand for Senator Goldwater as a speaker before business organizations and conservative groups. Television and radio producers of public-affairs shows were eager to include Senator Goldwater in their programs as an outspoken Republican member of a most exciting and newsworthy investigation. He became the anti-union symbol in the eyes of the A.F.L.-C.I.O. leadership. He was "Mr. Conservative" and the hero of many who believed in passing stringent laws to curb the power of union officials.

While the political advantages of investigating big labor are obvious today, it is often forgotten that pitfalls were there for committee members or staff investigators who tackled the job. It meant risking the bitter enmity of the A.F.L.-C.I.O. and the possibility of being characterized as "anti-labor."

The wreckage of a dozen futile efforts to start the much-needed investigation of labor racketeering cluttered the period between January, 1953, and January, 1957. The political power of the Teamsters union combined with the power of other corrupt unions to kill several inquiries before they were started. Where investigations and hearings could not be stopped, union influence was used to cripple the investigators by sharply limiting their funds or curtailing their jurisdiction.

Committee members were threatened with political reprisal. Aggressive staff members were harassed and in some cases forced to resign. One of the finest investigators to tackle the labor rackets was out of a job for more than six months in 1956 because he was blackballed by union-influenced Congressmen who resented his effective role in an investigation of the Teamsters.

The heroes of that 1953 to 1957 period were Republicans and Democrats, liberals and conservatives. Some had their investigations ended by political pressure; some gave up in frustration.

Senator Charles W. Tobey, the crusading New Hampshire

Republican, had completed most of the New York waterfront hearings and had authorized an investigation of Minneapolis Teamsters before he died in the summer of 1953. His plan to probe the Teamsters was encouraged by Senator Hubert Humphrey, a Minnesota Democrat, and Senator Karl Mundt, a South Dakota Republican.

Representative Clare Hoffman of Michigan and Representative Wint Smith of Kansas, both Republicans, were spearheads of investigations of the Teamsters union that included Kansas City, Detroit, `Minneapolis, Chicago, Pittsburgh and Cleveland. Senator Paul Douglas, a liberal Illinois Democrat; Senator Irving M. Ives, a New York Republican, and Senator Gordon L. Allott, a conservative Colorado Republican, were key figures in a Senate labor subcommittee investigation of corruption in two satellites of the Teamsters union—the Laundry Workers International Union and the old A.F.L. United Automobile Workers Local 286, in Chicago.

Investigator Lester Condon provided most of the energetic sleuthing in the first investigations of James R. Hoffa in 1953 by Representatives Hoffman and Smith. A small team including Downey Rice and Francis X. Plant, both former F.B.I. agents, and George Martin and Stanley Fisher did the basic work in Minneapolis, Pittsburgh and Cleveland.

House Labor Committee counsel Edward McCabe and investigator-accountant Carmine Bellino provided the drive in the first inquiries into the handling of Teamsters pension and welfare insurance in Dave Beck's eleven-state Western Conference of Teamsters. William Leece, Paul Cotter and Frank Plant, all former F.B.I. agents, came up with proof of a $900,000 embezzlement from the pension funds of the Laundry Workers International Union.

These lawyers and investigators received little public attention in the 1953-57 period, but they made a substantial record under most difficult circumstances. It was this record, compiled by experienced and able men, that paved the way for the success of Robert F. Kennedy and his huge staff. Without the testimony and reports produced by these earlier and unsung committee investigators there would have been no McClellan committee created by the Senate in January, 1957.

As a newspaper reporter on assignment for the Cowles Publications, I started making inquiries into the activities of the Minneapolis Teamsters Local 544 in January, 1953. From that time, I literally lived with the labor-racket investigations in the Congress and in the courts.

I attended the first Congressional hearings on Hoffa's activities in 1953. In 1964, I attended the trials that resulted in his conviction on charges of attempted jury-fixing and on charges of engaging in fraudulent practices in lending millions of dollars from the Teamsters union pension funds. Ironically, the 1964 convictions resulted partly from some of the material on Hoffa's actions that was first developed by a House subcommittee in November, 1953.

In 1956, I convinced Robert Kennedy of the need for an investigation of Hoffa, Dave Beck, and other labor officials. After that probe began, I was in daily attendance at most of those hearings. I also attended all of the six Hoffa trials. I was present for the rowdy revelry of Teamsters business agents when Hoffa was acquitted or won a hung jury. I saw the sullen defiance when he was finally convicted and sentenced for the first time in March, 1964.

I became aware, through these experiences, of the massive power of the Teamsters union, with its tentacles reaching into nearly every business and every community in the United States. Not only was it the wealthiest union in the country, boasting of the most members, but it had a strategic position in transportation that gave it a lever against other unions. Its leaders claimed jurisdiction over every product or personal possession moved on wheels, including milk and other foods, clothing, furniture, appliances, coal, oil, automobiles, steel, lumber, construction materials, and daily newspapers. This formidable strength could reach into every household in the land, affect every life.

This is the story of the dramatic eleven-year fight to sever the corrupt tentacles of the huge octopus that is the Teamsters union. It was a drama that made and broke great reputations.

This is a brutal story, but it is a factual story. It is a more fantastic story than would have been possible for me to imagine when I landed at the Minneapolis airport in January, 1953, to look at what I believed was a local union scandal.

While the Teamsters union is a major focal point of this book, it is not my intention to indicate that all the officers of this huge union are corrupt or that the rank-and-file union members are supporters of corruption. The members of this union are working men who must have a union card to hold their jobs. They have been caught under leadership dominated by Dave Beck and Jimmy Hoffa. In some instances, the local union officers have been ruthless racketeers and brutal wielders of union power for their own benefit.

Many Teamsters officers and many union members have fought courageously to throw out the corrupt elements. Others have simply submitted to bad leadership because they felt it was futile to fight the power lodged in the Teamsters hierarchy by the law and through the union constitution. It has been this feeling of futility that has caused many otherwise honest Teamsters officials to cooperate with the Hoffa administration or simply remain silent.

The story told in this book is based largely upon hearings and reports of Senate and House committees, or is from state and federal court proceedings or reports filed with government agencies.

II

A Helpful Hand from Hoffa

A rough-looking group of Teamsters crowded into the dingy little office in St. Paul on January 26, 1953, to tell me what they knew about labor rackets. It was bitter cold that day in Minnesota, but these union officials and members had poured in from all parts of the state—from the Iron Range country in the far north around Virginia, from St. Cloud and the head-high drifts of snow near Duluth, and from the windswept farm country around Mankato and Rochester.

Most of these men were thick-bodied and muscular former truck drivers, padded further with the clothing necessary for sub-zero January weather.

Some hadn't shaved. Most of them wore heavy caps with the flaps down over their ears. Some were officers of county seat locals with small memberships. Others were former officers of Teamsters locals in Minneapolis and St. Paul who had been shoved aside by associates of Sidney L. Brennan, top Teamsters boss in Minnesota. Brennan was third vice president of the International Brotherhood of Teamsters, Chauffeurs, Warehousemen and Helpers of America.

Sid Brennan was a pal of Dave Beck, the Seattle Teamsters boss who a few months earlier had snatched the presidency of the International Teamsters from ailing Dan Tobin. Brennan was making a power grab of his own to consolidate his control in Minnesota.

There was resentment against Brennan among the heads of the small union locals. They objected to the tight control over contracts and operations. A great deal of local autonomy had been possible under the loose operations of the Tobin regime. Declaring that Brennan was trying to institute a dictatorship, they said they were ready to talk. Their fury was aimed at Brennan and his top associates—Eugene Williams, a surly, rusty-haired business agent for Teamsters Local 544, and Gerald P. (Jerry) Connelly, a mysterious, cold-eyed muscle man from Chicago who had become active in the Minneapolis Teamsters within the previous few months.

The insurgent Teamsters were so eager to talk to me that day in St. Paul that frequently they were all talking at once. When one had spilled about half of his story on a racketeering incident, another would break in to declare, "I know one better than that."

There were decent, hard-working men in the group who raised legitimate complaints about underworld infiltration of the Teamsters, about payoffs, misuses of funds, soft "sweetheart" arrangements with some employers, and the brutal stifling of union democracy. But there were also some tough and calloused former union officials. They were simply irritated because they had been shouldered off the gravy train by the Brennan forces and made to go to work.

All these men had one thing in common: an intense dislike for Sid Brennan, whom they blamed for the activities of Jerry Connelly.

At first, I tried to question each of the men in the room while the others were present. It was helpful to have someone to fill in the name of a union member, the number of a local, or some other detail. But a few minutes of it convinced me we would never make progress that way. There were constant interruptions with extraneous detail. One older Teamster insisted on turning the talk back to the late 1930's and the internal fights and corruption of that period.

I wasn't interested in ancient history. The tobacco smoke thickening in the small room and the distraction of interruptions resulted in nearly total confusion. I took my yellow legal pad to a corner of another room and asked the men to come in one at a time, except where two of them had direct knowledge of the same incident.

Arriving in Minneapolis a week earlier, I had been unenthusiastic about the assignment to investigate reports of racketeering by Teamsters officials. I was cooled by more than the frigid winter wind whipping up Nicollet Avenue, tugging at my light topcoat and leaving my ears numb.

Gideon Seymour, then executive editor of the Minneapolis *Star* and *Tribune,* had called the Cowles Publications bureau in Washington, D.C., with a request to bureau chief Richard Wilson that I be sent to Minneapolis to conduct an investigation of alleged "Teamsters racketeering." I thought the idea of an investigation probably was inspired by some labor-baiting employers who were trying to exaggerate a little incident into a union-busting campaign.

Before that call from Gid Seymour, I hadn't followed labor matters closely. I accepted the basic thesis put forth by high labor officials, most politicians, and the labor press: The top leadership of major unions was honest and dedicated to fair play, better wages, and better working conditions. I knew that Republican Senator Charles Tobey of New Hampshire was investigating racketeering in the International Longshoremen's Association (I.L.A.). This corrupt union was considered a rare exception, and there were indications that the American Federation of Labor would ostracize the I.L.A.

Many labor officials had police records, but most assault convictions were explained as the result of picket-line fights. It was easy to excuse minor assault convictions in the light of the "goon squads" which management had used to crush union efforts to organize twenty, thirty, or forty years earlier.

Political scientists, labor reporters, and most politicians in 1953 would have described labor scandals as insignificant. All but a few of these opinion moulders accepted the idea that labor unions had come of age and were honest, responsible organizations.

Unions had consolidated their power during the administration of Franklin Delano Roosevelt, using the broad provisions of the Wagner Act, passed in 1937. The Taft-Hartley labor law, enacted in 1947, was attacked by unions as a "slave labor act," but it had made no noticeable difference in the political and social prestige labor had gained under the New Deal.

Old Dan Tobin, for thirty-five years president of the sprawling International Brotherhood of Teamsters, was the darling of the Democratic party. He was on a "Dan" and "Franklin" basis with President Roosevelt. William Hutcheson, president of the International Carpenters Union, was the big union wheel in the Republican party of 1948, when New York Governor Tom Dewey was the Republican Presidential candidate, and Hutcheson was still the big man at the time of the nomination of General Dwight D. Eisenhower as Republican standard-bearer in 1952.

There were a few conservatives who grumbled about "union power" and "union racketeers," but most of them did it in private. Representative Clare Hoffman, a Michigan Republican, was one of the few who spoke out sharply on the floor of Congress. His bitterness and extreme viewpoint made it possible to discredit him as merely "anti-labor." His following was such a small right-wing group that it had virtually no influence.

I had been talking to Teamsters in Minnesota only about a week in January of 1953, but luck was with me. Sam Romer, labor reporter for the Minneapolis *Star* and *Tribune,* introduced me to a few of his Teamster friends. They led me to more union members, to a couple of union lawyers, and soon it seemed everyone wanted to talk. The mass meeting was arranged by a St. Paul Teamsters official as an accommodation.

But even before those interviews started, it became clear there was more than luck involved in this spirited cooperation. Some truly powerful person was helping me. During the interviews the identity of my helper emerged. An International Teamsters vice-president named Jimmy Hoffa had passed the word that he was siding with the dissident group in the fight against Sid Brennan. A union organizer told them that Hoffa was behind them, and it was okay to tell this reporter all they knew about Brennan.

James Riddle Hoffa was only a name to me. I could not recall if what I'd heard had been favorable or derogatory. He was on my side, I was told, and there was no reason for questioning it as long as the cooperation continued.

"Jimmy is a stand-up guy," is the way most of my Minnesota informants put it. "Jimmy put Beck in as president, and Jimmy is the number two man."

"Jimmy won't stand for the crooked deals Connelly is pulling," a St. Paul Teamster said with conviction. "Jimmy won't stand for these guys dipping into pension and welfare funds to fill their own pockets."

"It looks like you get along better with Sid Brennan if you got a police record," one declared as he listed a number of Brennan's subordinates who had arrests and convictions. "Jimmy Hoffa wouldn't stand for that."

The political situation in the Teamsters union started to emerge. Jimmy Hoffa was moving to establish full control over the thirteen-state Central Conference of Teamsters. Brennan stood in his way. Years earlier, Brennan had cooperated with Beck in a union fracas involving a boycott on apples from the Yakima Valley. The resultant friendly relationship between them had persisted.

Young and aggressive, Hoffa was powerful enough to grab the title of chairman of the Central Conference of Teamsters. At thirty-nine, he had been in the union organizing business more than twenty years. His promotion by Beck to head the Central States organization was made over the heads of many older Teamsters. Now it was proving hard for Hoffa to get Brennan to submit to the control of a vice-president with less seniority. Yet, as Brennan tried to tighten his control over Minnesota locals in order to hold his own territory, he was driving the small locals into Hoffa's hands.

John Lisowski, president of Teamsters Local 615 at Virginia, Minnesota, figured he was fighting with his back to the wall against Brennan's subordinates. So did men like Ovid (Shorty) Moran, president of Local 329 at St. Cloud. They wanted autonomy—the local control of union affairs they had always had in the past. They resisted moves to incorporate their operations in a huge statewide plan.

The business agent for the local at Winona said he was approached by one of Brennan's subordinates from Minneapolis and offered a bribe in the form of wages to cooperate in throwing the local into trusteeship. The Winona man replied that his salary was $90 a week, and this was as much as the local could afford to pay. The Minneapolis Teamsters official called him "a sucker."

"Go along on the trusteeship, and we can boost your pay to $150 a week plus expenses," the Winona man quoted Jerry Connelly as saying.

An official of a Teamsters local at Red Wing told me Connelly had made a similar attempt to bribe him with a higher salary. He would have no part of it.

These men weren't talking because they liked the color of my eyes or the way I parted my hair. It wasn't because they wanted to expose Teamsters corruption. They disliked Brennan, they feared Connelly and other thugs, and Hoffa had passed the word: It was okay to talk.

They looked to Hoffa to save them from Sid Brennan's control, and they painted an attractive picture of Hoffa. Jimmy was for union democracy. Jimmy was for local autonomy. Jimmy was against stealing union funds. Jimmy was against officials taking money from employers.

They talked of "Jimmy" as if he were a personal friend. The troubles he had had with police were excused as "just picket-line scuffles" that any true unionist might have.

Dave Beck was regarded in a different light. He wasn't warm and friendly, but his aloof and authoritarian air made them look up to him. They believed Beck to be a man of stern-principled honesty—a millionaire who could have earned millions of dollars in the business world. They accepted his explanation that he stayed in union office because of a desire to give them the benefit of his leadership.

"If Dave Beck ever finds out what is going on up here in Minneapolis, he'll put a stop to it," one old Teamster said.

They reasoned that letters written to him about Brennan and Connelly hadn't reached Beck personally.

"They probably aren't letting the Old Man have the story," the rebel Teamsters said. "If Beck knew what is going on up here there would be hell to pay."

These Teamsters wanted stories in the newspapers to help

Beck learn the sordid facts of union corruption in Minnesota—
facts they felt were being kept away from him by some unidentified assistants in league with the Brennan crowd.

One week in the Twin Cities had opened my eyes and
changed my viewpoint. In a number of unions there was misuse
of union funds, borrowing from pension funds, and gun-toting
by union business agents. A ruthless group of racketeers and
ex-convicts held offices in some Teamsters locals and in other
unions. There was evidence of violation of federal labor laws
and state labor laws. Why hadn't there been prosecution?

I asked Teamsters members and minor officers if they had
taken their stories to the police, the county attorney, or federal
officials.

"What good would it do?" one said.

"They've got the grand jury sewed up," a Teamsters official
from St. Paul added.

"How did they do that?" I asked.

"There's always some of that Minneapolis Teamsters crowd
on the grand jury," he answered. He ticked off the names of
several Teamsters who had been on the state grand jury recently,
and added that he had been told there was a grand jury spot
reserved for one of the Minneapolis Teamsters most of the time.

"You can't get convictions when Teamsters crooks or their
pals are in bed with the prosecutors, and are just as close to some
judges and a few members of the police department," he said.

The whole story seemed fantastic. If these things were true,
the story of union-political corruption was similar to the cynical
business-political corruption that Lincoln Steffens had written
about at the turn of the century. For the time being, the union
corruption alone was enough to keep me busy. I made a note to
check the allegation of grand-jury packing later.

I was glad I had not received my evidence of labor racketeering in Minneapolis from business sources. A few truck-line
operators discussed aspects of the problem, but most of my
dozens of interviews had been with Teamsters officials, Teamsters union members, and Teamsters lawyers. My information
came from union men talking frankly about the perversion of
the power of unionism into something evil. They explained how
the Teamsters union used its power over business, and how it

used its central position in transportation to control the effectiveness of the strikes of other unions. Strikes were successful or unsuccessful depending on Teamsters' cooperation.

Most businesses are dependent upon trucks to bring supplies and to haul away finished products. A strike by truckers could wreck a business, even if employees of the place would cross the picket line. Other unions had little chance of making a strike successful if the Teamsters continued to make deliveries.

I had not realized the full strength of this giant union and until I talked to a number of employers I did not realize how fearful they were of that power.

Few truck-line operators were strong enough to put up a struggle. Most of them were heavily mortgaged, and a few weeks' strike would be disastrous. Payments had to be met. They were at the mercy of Teamsters officials who interpreted and enforced the union contract. Those interpretations often meant the difference between profit and loss for the truck-line owner.

Some owners said flatly that they would pay off to a Teamster official if they were squeezed. Some would have taken the initiative to bribe a union official, if it meant the difference between a loose or tight enforcement of the labor-management contract. Some employers considered union corruption none of their concern, as long as it didn't interfere with their operations.

Veteran union members were outraged when they learned that Teamsters business agent Eugene Williams of Local 544 was getting seven per cent of one Teamsters union pension fund for administering it. Furthermore, they did not think it right that Williams had borrowed $10,000 through the pension fund to start a night club, nor did they like seeing relatives of the union business agent on the payroll of the union, or of the pension or welfare funds administration. Independent trade unionism appeared to them to be distorted when Williams borrowed approximately $85,000 from employers who hired Teamsters and from persons with underworld connections.[1]

Veteran Teamsters union officials fumed over reports—later

[1]"Investigation of Welfare Funds and Racketeering," report of special subcommittee to the Committee on Education and Labor, 83d Congress, 2d Session, 1954, pages 9 and 10. See also, "Investigation of Racketeering in the Minneapolis, Minn., Area," pages 207-226.

proved accurate—that the Red Truck Line in Minneapolis had given several thousand dollars in checks to Sid Brennan. The payments were concealed on the company's books by entries stating the checks were for "parts," "repairs," "advertising," and "sales expenses."[2]

Muscle-man Connelly was a particularly sharp irritant to these long-time union members. An outsider, the Chicagoan had in a few months become a power through his association with Brennan. Connelly was the bullying, bribing labor hoodlum who ruthlessly threatened to put locals into trusteeship if they did not cooperate. As a side line, he was shaking down business firms. In fact, it appeared that Connelly's actions were the reason for most of the general discontent with Brennan.

Many local union members had written letters of complaint to Beck. Some of these letters were produced for me to examine. The writers knew about Beck's speeches denouncing labor racketeering, and they were sure there would be swift and drastic action if he ever learned the truth. They excused Beck's lack of action by saying he was busy, an important man—the general president of the union which was such a big part of their lives. They believed him to be a wise, even a brilliant man. Above all, they were sure he was honest.

Beck was to be in Minneapolis for the Sidney Brennan testimonial dinner on Wednesday, January 28, 1953. Some of my informants were trying to make arrangements to see Beck privately. If they could reach the Teamsters leader, they were sure they would make this a testimonial dinner that Brennan would remember a long time. The mere idea of attending a testimonial for Brennan made them angry, but they hoped it might be the break they needed. All they wanted was an opportunity for a few minutes with the big man from Seattle. They believed that would be all the time they would need to convince Dave Beck of the sorry state of the Teamsters union in Minnesota.

[2]"Investigation of Welfare Funds and Racketeering," report, page 4. See also, hearings, pages 369-377.

III

Beck's Boy—Sid Brennan

It was a strange assortment of men and women that jammed the ballroom of the Radisson Hotel the night of January 28, 1953, to pay tribute to the power of Sid Brennan—third vice-president of the International Brotherhood of Teamsters, vice-president of Teamsters Joint Council 32, secretary-treasurer of the huge drivers Local 544 and trustee of several union health and welfare funds.

Present were more than one thousand of the most respected and the least respected men in the state of Minnesota. They ranged from Governor C. Elmer Anderson down to Salvatore (Rocky) Lupino, a convicted safe cracker and a pal of Teamsters business agent Tony Schullo of Minneapolis Local 638.

Governor Anderson, naïve and genial, and Minneapolis Mayor Eric Hoyer posed for pictures with the guest of honor and added to the impression of Sid Brennan as a pillar in the community who had top officials among his friends. There were judges, aldermen and a host of others. Some knew what the Minneapolis Teamsters officials were, but others attended as a routine procedure to keep a friendly contact with just another political pressure group.

In the gathering that night were underworld cronies of the Minneapolis Teamsters bosses—criminals who had been arrested along with key Teamsters in past years. They reveled in the impression of Teamsters union power at city hall, at Hennepin County courthouse, and at the state capital in St. Paul.

But there were present those who hated Brennan, business agent Williams, and Connelly, and had nothing but contempt for the crude way the Teamsters union threw its weight around. These foes came only because they feared the political and economic power of the huge union with its bulging treasury and its power to cripple or bankrupt nearly any firm in the city.

"I've got to get along with the Teamsters," said a warehouse and truck-line operator, justifying his presence. "They can be life or death for my business. That union contract is only part of it—it's the interpretation they put on it that can ruin us."

"I don't like Sid Brennan or that racketeer Connelly he associates with," snapped one out-of-state Teamster. "I'm in here because I want to avoid trouble."

One Teamsters official, who had talked with me secretly a day earlier to tell me what he knew about Williams and Connelly, gave me only a quick wink of recognition and avoided any open acknowledgment that he knew me.

Gid Seymour, executive editor of the Minneapolis *Star* and *Tribune,* was with me, and we shook hands with his friends and acquaintances as we made our way across the ballroom. Newspaper executives don't usually go on such assignments, but Gid was personally interested in this testimonial dinner. He was busy surveying the room, and commenting under his breath on how many of his friends in the business community were swallowing their pride to bow at the throne of Teamsters power. As a local labor reporter, Sam Romer of the Minneapolis *Star* and *Tribune* was acquainted with most Teamsters officials. He could also identify underworld figures, racket attorneys, and thieves. He pointed them out to us, and Gid asked a *Star* and *Tribune* photographer to concentrate on a few pictures of the mobsters.

Although Brennan had become a major interest in my investigation, I had not yet met him. It was a big disappointment when I saw him. I had expected a sinister-looking and aggressive figure, or possibly a gregarious, back-slapping Irish type who had built his power on personality. Brennan was a paunchy six-footer with blank eyes and an unimpressive manner. He seemed uncertain and even weak, and I wondered how this man had become Mr. Big among the Minneapolis Teamsters. He might be careless, but he did not seem an aggressive, power-hungry official.

Connelly was different. One look was enough to tell you that this cold-eyed man was aggressive, a racketeer who made his own rules in going after what he wanted. Connelly could be a personality kid, patting backs, shaking hands, and beaming a smile that exploded across his face. But behind the smile were the icy and cunning eyes, looking for a weakness to exploit. Connelly had worked with labor-gangster groups in Chicago, Detroit, and Florida. Only a year earlier, Connelly had fled Miami while law-enforcement officials sought to subpoena him for questioning in connection with violence in a laundry union strike and in connection with an attempted murder.[1]

This was Jerry Connelly, the mysterious 42-year-old labor operator who in September, 1952, had been granted a Minneapolis local union charter by the Building Service Employees Union.

Gene Williams was about what I had expected. He was young, less than forty, and there was an alert and tough quality about him as he moved into the ballroom, shaking hands and whispering a private word to acquaintances.

"Williams is twice as smart as Brennan," one of my Teamsters informants had told me several days earlier. Several employers concurred.

Confident in manner, big and muscular, although he was developing a paunch, it was easy to imagine how the husky, red-haired Teamster had sold employers and union trustees on the idea of giving him seven per cent of a Teamsters pension fund for administering it. He had also convinced the employer trustees they should approve a loan to him of $10,000 through the pension fund for use in starting a night club, Williams' Bar and Cafe, in Minneapolis.[2]

Nathan W. Shefferman was there, too. But the presence of the 65-year-old Chicago labor-relations consultant went almost unnoticed. Grey-haired and long-winded, he was known only as a close personal friend of Dave Beck. He was also a friend of

---

[1]McClellan committee, Interim Report No. 1417, 85th Congress, 2d session, March 24, 1958, pages 234 and 240.

[2]"Investigation of Welfare Funds and Racketeering," report, pages 9 and 10.

Brennan. Shefferman knew when to stay in the shadows and when to move to the center of the stage. At private dinners he was a raconteur who could amuse Dave Beck and please him with praise. Beck, the poor boy who quit school to drive a laundry truck, liked to associate with the erudite-appearing Shefferman who lectured before college groups on labor relations.

Shefferman was more than theoretical in his labor relations. He was practical. He knew it was of benefit to his firm to send a $750 check to Sid Brennan as a "referral fee" in connection with a Minneapolis employer who had been steered to Shefferman's firm by Brennan.[3]

Shefferman operated a firm called Labor Relations Associates, with offices in Chicago, Detroit, and New York, and with clients from coast to coast. The firm specialized in charging big fees for settling labor problems for employers. It was obvious why Shefferman wanted to curry the favor of high Teamsters union officials. Local Teamsters officials in Minneapolis questioned the ethics of Shefferman's operations, but I tended to disregard the questions. Shefferman was a former federal labor relations expert, and was reputedly a learned lecturer. Possibly he was more influential with Beck than he should have been, but this could be just the result of friendship. There would be difficulty in proving anything wrong, so I crossed Shefferman off as a subject for serious study at that time.

Dave Beck was shaking hands on his way along the head table at the Brennan testimonial banquet when I first saw this round-bodied prima donna who was boss of the Teamsters empire. He oozed confidence and importance as he extended his short arm, and his pudgy, freckled hand honored those he met. I recognized the 58-year-old Teamsters boss from newspaper pictures, but I had had the impression he was bigger and more rugged in appearance.

The chunky man from Seattle would have had to stretch to reach the height of five feet seven inches he claimed. His bulging one hundred ninety pounds made him seem much shorter.

[3]"Investigation of Racketeering in the Minneapolis, Minn., Area." 83rd Congress, 2d session, hearings before the Subcommittee of the Committee on Government Operations, House of Representatives, April 9 and 10, 1954, pages 234 and 235.

His face was moon-shaped and pink, and a few wisps of reddish-brown hair fringed his bald head. His most striking characteristic—the palest blue eyes I had ever seen—were marked with eyebrows so light they were hardly visible.

Except on the West Coast, Dave Beck was not a well-known figure in 1953. Pouring out Teamsters funds for a personal public relations buildup had not yet accomplished its end.

Less than four months earlier, at a Teamsters convention, Beck had maneuvered to grab the presidency of the union by kicking the infirm 76-year-old Dan Tobin upstairs to the post of president emeritus.

Governor Earl Warren welcomed the delegates to that convention in Los Angeles on October 13, 1952, by declaring his "increasing admiration for the Teamsters union." He emphasized that the Teamsters union was "not only something great of itself, but splendidly representative of the entire labor union movement."[4]

That October convention had been highly successful from Beck's standpoint. He had boosted the pay for the president from $30,000 to $50,000 a year, increased membership dues to bring an additional one and one-half million dollars into the treasury annually, and had increased the number of vice-presidents from nine to eleven. This addition made it possible for Jimmy Hoffa of Detroit to become a vice-president as a reward for helping Beck to oust Tobin.

That conventon also buoyed Beck's confidence in his ability to manage big things. As executive vice-president and chairman of the eleven-state Western Conference of Teamsters, he had nominated Tobin for the presidency. Tobin, under some tough pressure from Beck and Hoffa, had accepted an ovation from the two thousand delegates but had declined to run. Tobin then nominated Beck, who was elected by acclamation.

Beck had promised big things. He pledged he would stay in office no more than ten years, but would boost the Teamsters membership to ten million members in that time. Teamsters headquarters were to be moved from Indianapolis to Washington, D.C., and Beck planned an impressive new building.

He said the $50,000 annual salary was not important to him

---

[4]*New York Times,* October 14, 1952.

and left the impression he was so well-to-do that the Internal Revenue Service received much more of his union salary than he did.

"I don't need the money. I've been very successful in business investments," Beck told the delegates.

This was the Dave Beck who bellied up to the speaker's table at the Sid Brennan testimonial dinner—a goodwill ambassador from Big Labor to the Big Business of the Twin Cities.

During the introductions and the dinner, Beck had the appearance of a mild-mannered, even gentle person. But when he rose to speak he was a changed man. His face flushed red. He energetically flailed the air with his arms and beat the table with his fat fists.

He told the business community he believed in free enterprise and was totally opposed to any form of socialism. He preached cooperation with management, but made it clear that the strength of the Teamsters could, of course, determine what was proper cooperation.

"The day has not yet arrived when we can forego the right to strike," Beck said. "But the strike will be used only when all other means fail.

"The day of skull-and-knuckle alley rule is past. The employers no longer can bring in their strike breakers and armed thugs and guards.

"This means that labor must be led by men who will not forget that our tremendous economic power cannot be exercised in contradiction to fairness for invested capital."[5]

Beck, in that testimonial banquet speech, played to the business community as a millionaire who understood the problems of big money, and he played to their fears of the Teamsters. He also posed as a stern and consistent crusader against crooks, racketeers and Communists.

He piously castigated the International Longshoremen's Association with an evangelistic fury that would have done justice to a tent-and-sawdust crusader. The New York waterfront scandals investigation had implicated some minor Teamsters officials, and Beck assured the crowd he would take immediate action to suspend them.

---

[5]*Minneapolis Tribune,* January 29, 1953.

"The labor movement must not be a haven for thieves, racketeers and gangsters," Beck declared.

I looked to see what kind of an impression these words made on Brennan. It was impossible to tell anything about his thoughts from his expression. He seemed the happy guest of honor. Connelly, the terrorist, and Rocky Lupino, safe-cracker, listened with the attentiveness of choir boys, and they were no less enthusiastic than the business leaders or Governor Anderson in applauding Beck's speech.

John F. English, secretary-treasurer of the International Teamsters, then presented a gold plaque to Brennan for "outstanding service and devotion."

"Sidney Brennan is a man who is able, active and aggressive and whose honesty and integrity and sincerity never have been questioned," English declared.[6]

Brennan's face showed a small, self-conscious smile as he accepted the plaque. I wondered if he was thinking of the Internal Revenue agents who were at that time questioning the accuracy of Brennan's federal income tax returns. The IRS was contending he had fraudulently failed to report more than $20,000 income in the period from 1947 through 1950.[7]

I whispered to my editor, Gid Seymour, that if Sid hadn't been questioned, it was only because his lawyers wouldn't let him talk to the federal tax agents.

At that first exposure to Dave Beck, I was struck by his pompous, affected and ambitious personality. He seemed to be tightening his grip on the sprawling, undisciplined giant that was the Teamsters union. He planned to boost membership in a drive to organize every truck driver and workers at every auto wash rack, service station and parking lot in the nation. Such a tremendous concentration of power in any one group was to be feared, but I told Gid Seymour I felt Beck's ambitions would be an advantage in trying to clean house in Minneapolis.

"Beck sounds as though he means what he says about cleaning out the crooks and racketeers," I told Gid after the testimonial dinner. "No one could be hypocritical enough to make that

---

[6]*Minneapolis Tribune*, January 29, 1953.

[7]Sidney L. Brennan, petitioner, v. Commissioner of Internal Revenue, United States Tax Court, August 6, 1952, cases 43184 and 43185.

speech if he didn't mean it. Besides, I don't believe he can afford to keep any racketeers around if he wants his union to grow."

At that point in my preliminary inquiry, I had obtained a pretty good line on Jerry Connelly's background. He seemed the personification of the worst in labor, and I felt certain that Dave Beck would feel compelled to oust him.

Connelly had showed up in Minneapolis in the summer of 1952, only a little more than a year after his hurried exit from Miami. On February 28, 1951, Holston Newbold, a 23-year-old Negro, looked up from a bed in a Miami hospital and pointed to two of Connelly's associates, Dave Kaminski and Sol Isaacs, as the union terrorists who had shot him five times, tried to crack his skull with a rock and left him for dead. Later Newbold made a sworn statement that Connelly, then secretary-treasurer of a laundry drivers' local in Miami, had paid him to hire Negro boys to throw rocks at laundry trucks.[8]

Connelly had been present when Kaminski and Isaacs put Newbold in the car to take him on what was to have been his last ride, Newbold said. The union racketeers had accused Newbold of a "double-cross" for refusing to shoot a reluctant Miami laundry owner.

Connelly and Kaminski had been issued gun permits and Miami police cards under the sponsorship of a Miami city commissioner. Connelly and Kaminski were also identified as the purchasers of two guns similar to the one used in the attempt to kill Newbold. However, by the time the grand jury subpoena was issued for Connelly he had fled the state.

While Kaminski and Isaacs were being convicted and were serving time for attempted murder, Connelly returned to Chicago briefly before going to Minneapolis.

In the early fall of 1952, Connelly and James Azzone obtained a charter for Building Service Employees Local 194 in Minneapolis and started using it as a "catch-all" union.

"We plan to organize anything which is not organized—

---

[8]McClellan committee, Interim Report, No. 1417, 85th Congress, 2d session, page 234. See also the Holston Newbold affidavit of February 28, 1951, on file with the McClellan committee, and the hearings on "Investigation of Welfare Funds and Racketeering" in Detroit, pages 378-383.

except drivers, of course," said Azzone, who had been an organizer for Tony Schullo's Teamsters Local 638 in Minneapolis before throwing in with Connelly.

Connelly and Azzone operated their Building Service local out of the Teamsters headquarters office of Schullo's Local 638, and Connelly became a working associate of Sid Brennan.[9] Connelly had been accustomed to dealing with big men in the union business. Prior to 1950, he had worked with Paul (Red) Dorfman, from Chicago, an associate of Capone mob members and a union friend of Jimmy Hoffa. Dorfman had moved into control of a Chicago waste-handlers local after the murder of its former president.[10]

In Florida, Connelly had been employed by Eugene C. (Jimmy) James, the secretary-treasurer of the Laundry Workers International Union who was also the original organizer of the racket-ridden Teamsters juke-box local in Detroit. Connelly was also an acquaintance of the distinguished-looking, stentorian-toned Nathan W. Shefferman, the pompous and scholarly appearing labor consultant from Chicago.

On Thursday morning, the day after the testimonial dinner for Brennan, I went to the Hennepin County jail to talk with Mitchell Schwartz, a convicted burglar. I had heard there was a Teamster-engineered payoff in connection with a parole on another conviction Schwartz had received several years earlier. Al Woodruff, a *Minneapolis Star and Tribune* court reporter, accompanied me. We wanted two witnesses to what Schwartz said.

Schwartz was reluctant to talk to us at first, but he finally disclosed that his parents and wife had raised $2,800 in cash to give to two Minneapolis Teamsters officials to arrange his parole from the Minnesota penitentiary. His family had sold defense bonds and scraped together every bit of cash they had to make what was described as a $2,000 payoff, plus a payment of $800 to attorneys for fees.

The attorney had told me earlier that he billed Schwartz

---

[9]McClellan committee, Second Interim Report, No. 621, 86th Congress, 1st session, Part 1, page 176. See also hearings, Part 43, page 16083.

[10]McClellan committee, Second Interim Report, No. 621, 86th Congress, 1st session, Part 1, page 120.

for only $300, and that Mrs. Schwartz had come to the office to
protest. She said a fee of $800 in cash had been included with
the $2,000 payoff given to the two Teamsters officials. It was to
have been paid to the lawyer. The attorney said he hadn't
received a penny.

Schwartz told us he later went to the Teamsters officials.

"They insisted they spent $2,000 for the payoff, and they
laughed and said they used the $800 for a party," Schwartz
related. "There wasn't anything I could do about it."

Schwartz was a thief, but it made me boiling mad to think
of his family selling everything they had to raise $2,800 to try
to get him out of trouble, then see the money squandered by a
ruthless bunch of union crooks.

"Who got the money?" I asked.

"You know who it was, but don't ask me to say it," Schwartz
pleaded. "Those fellows have got a lot of pull with the police
and the courts, and they can make it tough for me. I could get
life for being a habitual criminal."

"I know who they are, because your attorney told me," I
said. "I just want to hear the names straight from you so there
isn't any doubt about it."

"The attorney probably told you right," Schwartz said. "He
knew them. Leave me alone. I want to be able to tell 'em I never
told you their names if they ever ask me."

I mentioned the names given to me by the attorney and
urged Schwartz to confirm them.

"You've got it right," Schwartz finally admitted, "but you
don't know what you're messing with. Those guys have got a lot
of influence."

When I got back to the offices of the *Minneapolis Star* and
Tribune I reviewed the whole situation with Gid Seymour.

"How soon can you get out a series on rackets in the Teamsters?" Gid asked. "Could we start it next week?"

I said that I could write part of it. But I cautioned him
that I didn't think we should try to expose anything except information from a record of a court or a Congressional committee.

"I've got the story straight from the witnesses who know
about most of these rackets, but we could still be subject to
losing a few million dollars in libel suits," I warned.

"Schwartz isn't a witness we could depend on in a squeeze, and I doubt that many of the Teamsters would stick with us under pressure," I said. "In fact, I wouldn't even be sure that all our employer-witnesses would remain firm on their stories unless we had them under oath."

Gid was anxious for us to get in print. I was equally eager to expose this rotten perversion of union power. But the power frightened me. For the first time in my life I was put in a position of urging an editor to go slow instead of hitting fast and hard.

I reminded Gid that Senator Charles Tobey was already engaged in an investigation of the labor rackets on the New York-New Jersey waterfront. The chief counsel for Tobey's Interstate and Foreign Commerce subcommittee was Downey Rice, the Washington lawyer and former F.B.I. agent who had demonstrated his ability during the Kefauver crime investigations.

All the Minneapolis labor rackets wouldn't be within the jurisdiction of the Tobey subcommittee, but I thought we could get our foot in the door.

Gid agreed that it was better to move slowly, and pull the story out through a Congressional committee or handle only what we could document on a public record. I cleaned up a few details in Minneapolis, then returned to Washington to discuss the story with Senator Tobey and Rice.

IV

Teamsters' Troubles and Senator Tobey

Senator Charles W. Tobey was his usual eager self as I was ushered into his office in the Senate Office Building. The bald, 72-year-old New Hampshire Republican was bubbling with enthusiasm over the progress his committee counsel, Downey Rice, was making in exposing the waterfront labor rackets. Senator Tobey's voice rang with indignation against waterfront gangsters who forced working men to pay tribute and shook down employers. The Republican Senator was equally critical of employers who played ball with labor crooks, and public officials who failed to enforce the law.

This was the man I hoped would head an investigation of labor rackets in the Teamsters union in Minneapolis. I had already discussed the Minneapolis Teamsters with Rice and Francis X. Plant, the chief investigator for Tobey's subcommittee of the Senate Interstate and Foreign Commerce Committee.

Senator Tobey was short on legal experience, but he was long on nerve and energy. What was equally important, he had reached the age where he had no fear of gangsters, the labor-political bloc, or the opposition of his colleagues in the Senate.

Tobey's fiery hatred of organized crime had blazed during his time on what had become known as the Kefauver crime committee, and I could see it had not subsided. He assured me he was interested in doing the investigation of the Minneapolis

Teamsters "as soon as we get through with the waterfront hearings."

He hoped two or three months would be sufficient to finish the inquiries into racketeering among the longshoremen. The outlook was good for a deep investigation into the Minneapolis Teamsters. I had already taken steps to make sure there was both liberal and conservative political support for the investigation.

William (Bill) Wilson, wealthy owner of the Wilson Trucking System, with headquarters in Sioux Falls, South Dakota, had been helpful in providing some of my first information on the Teamsters. He had followed through by talking to Republican Senator Karl Mundt of South Dakota, seeking Mundt's support in the event Tobey proved unenthusiastic. Wilson assured me that Mundt would talk to Tobey and urge fast action.

Meanwhile, I called on Senator Hubert Humphrey, the liberal Democrat from Minnesota, to determine whether there was any possibility that he would use Democratic pressure to block or hamper an investigation of the Teamsters.

I was surprised to hear Humphrey declare that he had "absolutely no time for Sid Brennan or any of his crowd."

"I haven't had any help from that Minneapolis Teamsters group since I ran for mayor of Minneapolis." Humphrey said. "I would welcome an investigation of the Minneapolis Teamsters, and I'll go around and ask Senator Tobey to do it. The Teamsters are a black mark on the labor movement."

It amazed me to have Humphrey volunteer help until he related some of the problems he'd had with other Teamsters when he was mayor.

"They had slot machines in the Teamsters headquarters, and they didn't like it when I insisted that the laws be enforced and closed them down," Humphrey said.

The fast-talking Minnesota Senator also revealed that one of the Minneapolis Teamsters officials (he named him) came to his office "to tell me who I had to name as chief of police, chief of detectives, and the middle captain of the uniformed division."

"I was shocked that he would make such a demand," Senator Humphrey said. "I tried not to show it. I asked him why he needed the middle captain. He told me the Teamsters might want to mess someone up, and that they wanted to arrange to delay the police a little."

"I told him that if he wanted to run the city he should run for mayor," Humphrey related. "I told him to get out of my office with his proposition. I haven't had the support of that group since then, and I don't want it."

There seemed no point in pushing to get stories into print at that stage, but there was one story in the United States Tax Court in Washington, D.C., involving Sid Brennan which could be written without danger of a law suit against the newspapers.

Internal Revenue agents had investigated Brennan's tax returns for the years 1947 through 1950 and concluded that the Teamsters boss had failed to report approximately $20,000 in income. The tax men had to overcome one barrier after another before gaining access to union books and bank records dealing with the Brennan case. They finally obtained enough information to satisfy themselves. Brennan fought back, filing in the Tax Court an answer to the allegation that he owed $15,000 in back taxes and civil fraud penalties.[1] (He later settled this case for about $7,000.)

The story I wrote was taken from the fully privileged records of the Tax Court, but Brennan and his attorney raised a furor about an "anti-labor smear" on the Teamsters. This was going to be a tough fight. The charge of "anti-labor" was to become familiar in later months. It was used against nearly every committee of Congress, committee counsel or writer who tried to expose the corruption.

The Minneapolis Teamsters were arrogant in their belief that they could frustrate local law enforcement and pull the political strings necessary to avoid exposure by Congress. Brennan's attorney was Elmer Ryan, who had been a Democratic Congressman from Minnesota and, in earlier years, a law partner of former Minnesota Governor Harold Stassen.

In those years, the Minneapolis Teamsters had friends with strength in both political parties. Some top Teamsters officials served as members of the Hennepin County grand jury. One

---

[1]United States Tax Court, petition filed by Sidney L. Brennan to contest a claim of tax deficiencies. See also, Internal Revenue action filed in United States District Court in Minneapolis, seeking access to Brennan's bank records.

dissident Teamsters informant told me there was an arrangement with the county political machine for the union to have a representative on the grand jury.

It would certainly be handy for any racket-ridden organization to have a man on the inside when the county grand jury went to work. I told my informant I couldn't believe there was such a deal. The law said members of the grand jury were to be selected by drawing names from a large panel. Normally, the names would be pulled from a large, closed barrel. The drawings had to be certified by several county officials as having been handled in a legal manner that would preclude a "fix.'"

"If it isn't a fix, then the Teamsters have been mighty lucky," my informant said.

A check of grand jury panels disclosed that the Teamsters have indeed been lucky; it was rare when the union did not have a representative on the Hennepin County grand jury.

Even in the weeks I was talking with Senators Tobey, Humphrey and Mundt, the Minneapolis Teamsters were engaging in more illegal activities. Jerry Connelly, the transient labor racketeer, was taken to the bosom of the Teamsters hierarchy.

Connelly arranged a $5,000 cash payoff from an official of the Archer-Daniels-Midland Co., grain milling operator of Minneapolis, for Teamsters' help in breaking a pending strike by the United Mine Workers at the A.D.M. processing plant.[2] The money was paid through Connelly's son, Gerald junior.

According to the trial testimony, Connelly parceled out the $5,000. There was $1,000 each for Brennan, business agent Eugene Williams and Jack Jorgenson, the president of Teamsters Joint Council 32 who had been active in politics and held city office as the Thirteenth Ward alderman.[3]

Those officials who weren't tainted when Connelly landed in Minneapolis were hooked into a conspiracy of illegal practices within a period of months. In less than a year, Connelly, a long-time pal of Detroit Teamsters boss Jimmy Hoffa, became an influential figure in the Minneapolis labor movement.[4]

---

[2]McClellan committee, Interim Report, No. 1417, page 240.

[3]On November 23, 1955, Connelly, Williams and Jorgenson were convicted on the charges of violating section 302 (b) of the Taft-Hartley labor law in the United States District Court for Minnesota.

[4]McClellan committee, Interim Report, No. 1417, pages 239, 240 and 241.

It was a strange maneuver—a Hoffa crony worming his way quickly and deeply into the camp of Hoffa's foe, Sid Brennan.

Although they were contemptuous of local law enforcement, the Teamsters had learned one lesson from Brennan's income tax troubles. That payoff to Connelly from an official of the Archer-Daniels-Midland Co. was reported on their income tax returns.

Minneapolis Teamsters were unaware that they were on Senator Tobey's schedule after he disposed of Longshoremen's union racketeers. But in Detroit it became apparent in late May, 1953, that there would be House committee hearings on the operations of Teamsters Local 985. A subpoena had been served requiring William Bufalino, a lawyer turned union boss, to produce financial records and other documents concerning the operations of the local, which was alleged to be responsible for shakedowns and protection rackets in the lucrative juke-box industry.

Representative Clare Hoffman, the conservative Michigan Republican, was the moving force behind the House investigating committee's thrust at the Teamsters in Detroit. The Hoffa organization there was not overly concerned. Representative Hoffman was an old foe, and his extremely conservative record on labor matters made him an ideal target for Teamsters, who shouted that it was an "anti-union investigation" aimed at crushing labor. Moreover, the Hoffa organization was experienced in dealing with local investigations. Financial records were destroyed periodically, as were most other papers that might be useful to inquisitive investigators.[5] Hoffa had also found it possible to get political figures, an attorney and a Teamsters business agent, to funnel information to him on evidence given in the supposedly secret confines of the grand jury room.[6]

In the first week of June, 1953, accountant-investigator Martin Uhlmann of the House committee went to Teamsters headquarters on Trumbull Avenue in Detroit to examine the financial records of Local 985. Uhlmann was a veteran govern-

---

[5]"Investigation of Welfare Funds and Racketeering," report of the special subcommittee, to the Committee on Education and Labor, 83d Congress, 2d session, page 12.

[6]McClellan committee, Interim Report, No. 1417, pages 244 and 245.

ment accountant, but this was his first experience with the Teamsters.

The secretary in the office of Local 985 said that William Bufalino was not in and would not be in for some time. She told Uhlmann that a Mr. Hoffa might be able to help him.

When a small, boyish-faced man in shirt sleeves entered the office Uhlmann was unaware that he was meeting a man of power in the Teamsters union. This dark-haired man had a pleasant grin and an open-faced appearance. Hoffa was accompanied by his attorney, George Fitzgerald, who had been a top figure in the Democratic organization in Michigan. (Jimmy had even dipped into union funds for $42,000 in an unsuccessful effort to elect Fitzgerald as governor of Michigan, according to later findings of a Congressional committee.[7])

The pleasant young man in shirt sleeves told Uhlmann he thought he knew the situation in Bufalino's local well enough to answer questions about the records.

Uhlmann politely asked for financial records for 1948, 1949, and 1950.

Hoffa said they weren't there, and Uhlmann inquired where they were.

After several minutes of fencing, Hoffa said the records had been destroyed.

When Uhlmann asked to see the records of the previous year Hoffa told him that they, too, had been destroyed; that under the policy of the Teamsters union the records could be destroyed at the end of every year.[8]

Uhlmann, an experienced accountant, was amazed that records only a few months old had been destroyed and questioned the policy.

"Our office was crowded and we needed the room," Hoffa replied.

Uhlmann called attention to the Internal Revenue regulation requiring records be kept for reasonable periods of time.

"They were destroyed on advice of counsel," Hoffa said. "It is done according to the International Teamsters constitution."

Uhlmann asked Hoffa if there was specific authority in the

[7]McClellan committee hearings, Part 39, September 10, 1958, page 14823.
[8]"Investigation of Racketeering in the Detroit Area," report, page 10.

Teamsters union constitution to destroy financial records each year.

Hoffa replied there was no specific authority to destroy records but neither was there a prohibition against such destruction. He said the Detroit unions exercised local autonomy with regard to the handling of financial records.

Uhlmann dryly remarked that he didn't think much of any Teamsters methods which made it difficult or next to impossible to pin down responsibility.

"None of your wisecracks," Hoffa replied in an irritated voice. "Apparently, you don't know who I am, Bud."

Hoffa reeled off his titles: ninth vice-president of the international union, chairman of the thirteen-state Central Conference of Teamsters, chairman of the Michigan Conference of Teamsters, president of Detroit Teamsters Joint Council 43, and president of Teamsters Local 299. It was the first time that Uhlmann realized the full power of the youthful-looking union official.

Upon request, however, Hoffa did produce financial records for the first six months of 1953.

Uhlmann examined them briefly and raised questions about the completeness of records which failed to document the expenditures of thousands of dollars of cash. He wanted to know what the business agents had done with this cash.

The suggestion that cash expenditures should be documented by bills brought only a scornful laugh from Hoffa. He said that even though the books might not satisfy a Congressional committee he was sure they would pass the inspection of the International Teamsters union, and that was the only group with which he was concerned.

"And, Brother, do they check us!" Hoffa said with emphasis.

"When were your books last checked?" Uhlmann said.

"A couple of years ago," Hoffa answered.

"How will they check on 1952 with those books already destroyed?" Uhlmann asked.[9]

Hoffa was furious at the questioning. He snapped that he

_____
[9]"Investigation of Racketeering in the Detroit Area," Joint Subcommittee Report of Special Subcommittee of the Committee on Education and Labor and the Committee on Government Operations, 83d Congress, 2d session, page 5.

was sure it would be possible to find enough records to satisfy the auditors for the international.

Although Hoffa was irritated at the questioning he was confident. "This committee doesn't bother me. They'll do about what the Kefauver committee did on the juke boxes, and they'll get the same damned answers."

The lack of records was an obstacle, but chief counsel William McKenna and his staff weren't stopped by it. Chief investigator Lester Condon, the former F.B.I. agent, Clyde Smith, and Uhlmann rounded up witnesses and seized records connected with the juke-box industry.

In the first months of 1953, my knowledge of Teamsters corruption was limited to Minnesota and a few problem locals in New York City. When the hearings opened in Detroit on June 8, 1953, it became apparent the pattern was widespread.

Chairman Wint Smith of the House subcommittee, a Kansas Republican, and Clare Hoffman took testimony on the terror tactics that accompanied organizing drives by Teamsters Local 985. The subcommittee members were told that Bufalino used his power as head of the union to maintain dictatorial control of the juke-box industry. Even employers were forced to join the union to avoid bombings and other terror tactics, witnesses said.

The emphasis in the four days of hearings· in room 859 of the Federal Building in Detroit was on William Bufalino, his background, his financial backing from his uncle, Angelo Meli, and his relations with Hoffa. Although Bufalino was a lawyer, he found it more lucrative to start in business as the owner of a juke-box distributing business, the Bilvin Distributing Co. Bufalino and his partners received much of their financing from the underworld, including $30,000 from the notorious Angelo Meli.[10]

One of Bufalino's foes, Eugene C. (Jimmy) James, first came to my attention during those hearings. By that time James was secretary-treasurer of the International Laundry Workers Union, and he was involved in an embezzlement of more than $900,000 from the pension and welfare funds of that union.[11]

---

[10]"Investigation of Racketeering in the Detroit Area," Joint Subcommittee Report, page 8. See also McClellan committee, Report No. 1139, pages 829-837.

[11]Welfare and Pension Plans Investigations, Interim Report, Committee on Labor and Public Welfare, by its Subcommittee on Welfare and Pension Funds, 84th Congress, 1st session, 1955, pages 36 and 37.

The hearings in Detroit showed that James had given up operating a pool hall in 1940 to take up the union business, and he
had made his first big money organizing the first juke-box local
in Detroit a few years later.

Jimmy James complained of having trouble with gangsters.
According to the record, Bufalino moved from the distributing
side of the juke-box business to the union side to help out
James. Soon, he had helped James all the way out and had
become boss of the juke-box local himself. James received what
the committee referred to as "installment payments" for several
years for the sale of the union.

This was strange union business. Bufalino the lawyer and
employer became Bufalino the union boss with jurisdiction over
juke boxes, auto wash racks, parking lots and garages. At the
same time, his cousin, Vincent Meli, dominated an association
of the juke-box owners who had a labor contract with Bufalino's
Teamsters local.

It was a "gigantic, wicked conspiracy to, through the use of
force, threats of force and economic pressure, extort and collect
millions of dollars" from union members, non-union members
and independent businessmen, the subcommittee found.[12]

"Local 985, through its president William E. Bufalino is
the principal offender and perpetrator of the racketeering, extortion, and gangsterism," the subcommittee report said.

Wages, working conditions, and hours had little or no part
in this union's activity.

The use of a Teamsters union local to create a business
monopoly was a new and interesting device to me. I read with
close attention the subcommittee's explanation of Bufalino's
operations:

". . . to create a monopoly, Bufalino forced certain members
of the union in good standing out of the union, and then pro-
ceeded to picket establishments where their juke-boxes were
located. He would first contact the owners of the establishments
where the juke-boxes were located and demand that they be
removed, at the same time suggesting that they be replaced by
juke-boxes owned by his favored few. He would threaten the

---

[12]"Investigation of Racketeering in the Detroit Area," Joint Subcommittee
Report, 1954, pages 2-4.

owners of the establishments, and indicate that if they did not comply with his demands a picket line would be established, and no member of the Teamsters Union would cross the picket line to make deliveries of beer, food, etc. In instances where these methods were not successful, a few weeks later the location would be bombed—this forced the owner to comply with Bufalino's demands."[13]

When Jimmy Hoffa was called to testify before that subcommittee, he declared defiantly that the financial records of his Local 299 were destroyed each year, the same as those of Local 985.[14]

Hoffa was equally defiant when the subcommittee tried to get an explanation of allegations that his wife, Josephine, had been on the payroll of Bufalino's juke-box local and had received money from hidden interests in trucking firms with which Hoffa's union had contracts.

Hoffa snapped that the questions were not pertinent to the inquiry. Then he clammed up. The subcommittee decided to initiate a contempt action against him for refusing to testify. In their report, the subcommittee labeled Hoffa the "brains" behind the shakedown and power grab by Bufalino. It said Hoffa was "virtually a dictator" over the Teamsters in certain areas despite convictions for violations of the Michigan state labor law and the federal anti-trust laws.[15]

When the subcommittee ended the hearings on June 13, Hoffa was growling with rage. The tough little Detroit labor boss was not accustomed to having public officials challenge him. In a few short days Jimmy and his pals had become embroiled in deep trouble. In addition to the threat of a contempt charge, the subcommittee laid the groundwork for indictments of many of Hoffa's top Teamsters subordinates. Local law enforcement officials were under newspaper and public pressure to take action.

---

[13]"Investigation of Racketeering in the Detroit Area," Joint Subcommittee Report, 1954, page 4.

[14]"Investigation of Racketeering in the Detroit Area," Joint Subcommittee Report, page 5.

[15]"Investigation of Racketeering in the Detroit Area," Joint Subcommittee Report, 1954, page 9.

Bufalino and six others were indicted in Wayne County on charges that they had used threats of physical violence and bombings to prey on juke-box operators, restaurant owners, and others.[16]

Five more Teamsters officials from the Detroit area were indicted on other charges of milking construction firms of hundreds of thousands of dollars. Included was Daniel J. Keating, president and business agent of Local 614, in Pontiac, Michigan.[17]

In all his brawling, violent days Jimmy Hoffa had never had so much trouble. It made the little Teamsters boss suspect he had some stool pigeons in his Detroit organization. Hoffa got in touch with New York labor racketeer Johnny Dioguardi. It was arranged by Dioguardi for Bernard Spindel of New York to go to Detroit to do a complete wiring job on the Teamsters headquarters on Trumbull Avenue. The system was installed with a control box in Hoffa's office. From the chair at Hoffa's desk it was possible to flip a switch and obtain either a recording or an amplified reproduction of any conversation on telephones or in any major rooms in the building. Installation was made at night so that employees would not be aware of it.[18]

(Rudolph L. Doeliche, a witness at the Hoffa wire-tapping trial, testified that he helped install the system in Hoffa's office in the Detroit Teamsters headquarters. He also testified that he instructed Hoffa and Brennan as to its use for listening to conversations in other rooms as well as on the telephones. Hoffa admitted such a system was installed, but denied knowing that it could be used for wire-tapping. He also denied that he had ever received instructions from Doeliche, and insisted that he believed it was a legal device for simply listening to conversations in other rooms.)

[16]William Bufalino was acquitted in 1954 in a trial in the court of Judge Joseph Gillis. McClellan Report No. 621, page 90.

[17]Daniel Keating, Mike Nicoletti, Louis Linteau and Samuel Marroso were convicted. Teamsters union funds were used to pay for their lawyers and to continue their salaries while in prison. McClellan Report No. 621, pages 89 through 93. "Keating, Linteau, Marroso and Nicoletti all pleaded guilty in order to protect Frank Fitzsimmons, vice-president of Hoffa's own local 299," according to Report No. 1417, page 244.

[18]U. S. v. James R. Hoffa, Bernard Spindel, and Owen Bernard Brennan, in The United States District Court for The Southern District of New York.

Meanwhile, a coalition of Democratic and Republican Congressmen was intent on depriving Representative Hoffman of power to conduct further investigations and hearings without first clearing with the full House Government Operations Committee. Such action to hamstring its chairman was unprecedented for a committee. Hoffman charged that some members were doing it to keep him from conducting further labor racket hearings. He said others on the committee simply didn't know what they were doing.

While electricians were busily wiring Hoffa's headquarters in late June, 1953, Chairman Hoffman overcame his opposition and sent his team of investigators to the Kansas City area. Target of the investigation was a pistol-packing Teamsters gang headed by Orville F. Ring, president of Local 541 and president of Teamsters Joint Council 56.[19]

The steam for the Kansas City investigation came from Republican Representative Smith of Kansas. He had a local interest and had received complaints from businessmen about jurisdictional disputes between unions that had cost the Kansas area millions of dollars. Some of these disputes halted work on large defense projects.

Jurisdictional disputes involving the Teamsters and some building trades locals had shut down construction for 90 days. Some of the disputes involved such questions as whether large saw horses should be carried by Teamsters or carpenters.

A strong-arm Teamsters crew of 100 men had threatened mass violence. Union members who disagreed with dictatorial methods were threatened. The Teamsters hierarchy had moved into a position of friendly cooperation with some law enforcement officials. Crimes involving union officials were not receiving proper attention. Teamsters thugs were given credentials as special deputy sheriffs, with authority to carry guns, which they did.

Edward Chevlin, a broken 130-pound former vice-president of Teamsters Local 838 in Kansas City, told of being beaten by Local 541 president Ring and a group of burly pistol-packing

---

[19]"Strikes and Racketeering in the Kansas City Area," Interim Report, special subcommittee of the Committee on Education and Labor, 83d Congress, 1st session, 1953, page 7.

Teamsters business agents. The slight, 50-year-old man told the committee that while the beating took place, the spectators included "Al Ross, secretary-treasurer of Local 953, and deputy sheriff of Jackson County, with a gun hanging on him."[20]

But Chevlin was like many others. He did not blame Dave Beck for the perversion of the Teamsters union in Kansas City.

"The methods being used in Kansas City I don't think are Dave Beck's methods," Chevlin testified.

Chevlin testified that after several threats on his life, and an attempt to shoot him, he yielded to his wife's plea and quit the union. He became an employee of the Kansas City, Missouri, welfare department.

The Kansas City man also testified that Jimmy Hoffa had been one of four men who "beat me up with chains" several years earlier when he was passing out leaflets for an organizing drive by the C.I.O. in Detroit which was opposed by the Detroit Teamsters.

"He (Hoffa) was hired by somebody to do a job on me, and he did it," Chevlin testified. But Chevlin hadn't had much contact with Hoffa in recent years, and he was charitable: "I think Jimmy's tactics have changed some in the last five or six years. I think he has outlived (it) ."

Brutality and political corruption were accompanied by misuse of union dues money, and union health and welfare funds. Orville Ring and his business agents drove air-conditioned Cadillacs paid for out of union funds, as were the gasoline and oil. To top off the whole preposterous arrangement, Ring and some of his boys charged the union for mileage on the union-financed cars.

The automobile expenses were small items individually, but they were symptomatic of the whole financial operation under Ring. It was the same combination of corruption and misman-agement that had been apparent to me in Minneapolis and Detroit.

"The Congress should look with deep concern at the sordid account of free men, afraid to work, terrorized by the gangster tactics of those (union officials) to whom the Congress itself

---

[20]"Strikes and Racketeering in the Kansas City Area," Interim Report, 1953, page 7. See also Kansas City hearings, pages 359 to 368.

has given privilege and authority," the subcommittee said in its report.[21]

Most members of Congress preferred to look in the opposite direction and pretend they did not see the cynical misuse of union power, and the ruthless assaults, kidnappings and extortion that were taking place in the name of organized union labor. Many members of Congress were as guilty by their lack of action as were the sheriffs, police officials and other local political figures who allotted deputy sheriff commissions to union figures or chose to overlook crimes where union officials were involved.

Most labor reporters for newspapers and magazines merely ignored the documented record.

---

[21]"Strikes and Racketeering in the Kansas City Area," Interim Report, 1953, pages 7, 8.

V
_____

Death Stops an Investigation

Finishing the waterfront investigations and hearings took longer than Senator Tobey had anticipated. Not until July 15, 1953, could I write the first story reporting that he had authorized investigation of the Minneapolis Teamsters. Elated that the Teamsters investigation was finally in motion, we who had been studying the unions and Congressional reaction to them realized it could be as big as the Kefauver crime probe if properly handled.

Nine days later, Senator Tobey died. The death of the colorful, Bible-quoting crime-fighter on July 24, 1953, delayed the big labor racket investigation more than three years.

"Senator Tobey couldn't be pressured to lay off the racketeers," said his committee counsel, Downey Rice. "I'm afraid it will be a long time before a chairman comes along who will have the courage to stay with the job. It gets into too many sensitive political areas."

None of us had any illusions about Senator Tobey as an investigator. He wasn't a lawyer, and often his questions could be highly irrelevant. But he hated organized crime, and during the Kefauver crime investigations thousands of Americans wrote to express their appreciation of those who challenged and exposed the crooks.

Tobey wasn't much on the fine points of the law, but he

was hell on the legal quibblers. Repeatedly during the investigation of the waterfront rackets he peered from under his green eye shade, poked an accusing finger at a witness and declared: "Man, surely you knew that what you were doing was wrong."

Senator John Bricker, the conservative Ohio Republican, assumed the chairmanship of the Senate Committee on Interstate and Foreign Commerce after Tobey's death. Because he was a conservative who owed nothing to union labor, I hoped he would seize this opportunity to expose labor racketeering.

Talking to Bricker curbed my optimism. He sounded like a real crusader against the evils of brutality, extortion, and bribery that existed under the label of trade unionism—until he came to the point of saying what he was going to do about it. He made no commitment to continue the Minneapolis probe.

Surprisingly, he authorized Rice, with the committee's chief investigator, Frank Plant, investigator George Martin and accountant Stan Fisher, to go to Minneapolis. But his lack of enthusiasm caused me to start looking for another Congressional committee chairman with more interest in the subject.

Representative Hoffman of Michigan was interested, particularly in the story that Local 544 business agent Gene Williams had borrowed from a union pension fund and from employers to start a night club in Minneapolis. Hoffman told me this episode might be used to dramatize the misuse of union funds.

However, Hoffman was having his own troubles. The Government Operations Committee, which he headed, had taken the unprecedented step of foreclosing the chairman's right to hold hearings. Hoffman had a small but skilled investigation staff, an adequate budget, and files bulging with evidence and information about Teamsters rackets, but a bipartisan bloc of Democrats and Republicans on his committee barred him from holding hearings.

"Some of them are intentionally protecting the labor racketeers from exposure," Hoffman said bitterly. "Some don't know what they are doing, and others are just afraid to investigate anything in the labor field."

Hoffman would have liked to blame his problem on the Democrats, but he had to admit his own party members had gone along with the curb on his power to expose the Teamsters.

It seemed hopeless, but the Congressman said he was going to keep the staff working "and find some way to get the scandals out in the open."

Hoffman could be the life preserver of the investigation in the event Bricker folded. Despite his 78 years he was wiry, tough and acid-tongued. I liked him, yet I had reservations about the advisability of his doing the Minneapolis investigation if there was a reasonable alternative. Clare Hoffman was as unpredictable as he was irrepressible. His extreme assaults on organized labor for its violence and political spending pegged him politically as "anti-labor" and "a reactionary."

A good legislator with a liberal reputation would be better for the job, but I concluded there was not much chance of it. With rare exceptions, most of the liberals in either party were beholden to union labor or blind to its faults. Many middle-of-the-roaders made a studied effort to know as little about labor rackets as they could, on the theory that what they didn't know wouldn't hurt them.

Only a few crusty old conservatives in Congress would speak out openly about the labor rackets, and the record showed that they produced mostly talk, little action.

The labor committees should have handled the rackets probe, but those committees seemed hopeless.

Those labor committees had received complaints about the racket-infiltrated Operating Engineers Union and its dishonest president, William Maloney,[1] but had buried them. I don't know whether the reason for "losing" such complaints was incompetence or connivance. Certainly there were plenty of complaints for the committees to follow had they displayed the courage or the ability.

Even without the use of subpoenas, Downey Rice and Frank Plant had been able to pin down most of the leads I had given them, and had turned up many new ones on the Minneapolis Teamsters. If Senator Bricker was interested we were going to score.

---

[1]Robert Greene, *Newsday's* able investigative reporter, had pointed out corruption in the Operating Engineers Union that was later the subject of hearings and criticism by the McClellan committee in Report No. 1417, pages 437-443.

At the Labor Department, I tried to obtain access to financial reports of the Minneapolis Teamsters union. Filing of the reports was required by the Taft-Hartley labor law, but I was told they were available only to members of the union. I learned also that the Labor Department informed officers of the union of any request for the reports, to make sure that any such request came from a member in good standing.

This meant that if a union member asked for the reports, the union officers were immediately notified. I found that this system discouraged union members from cooperating in obtaining reports.

Rice and Plant said the secret financial reports filed under the Taft-Hartley law didn't accomplish a thing toward keeping the unions honest. In fact, the evidence indicated that false financial reports were being filed with the Labor Department and nothing was being done about it. Labor racketeering and thefts of funds belonging to union members were bad enough, but it was infuriating to think that laxity by the federal government was partly responsible.

I tried to reach Labor Secretary Martin Durkin on October 1, 1953, but he was out. I was steered to Lloyd A. Mashburn, the acting Undersecretary of Labor who was running the department.

"What are the safeguards against unions filing false financial reports with the Labor Department?" I asked.

"There are none," he answered.

"Does the department ever attempt to examine the financial reports to determine if false or fraudulent reports are being filed?" I asked.

Mashburn said there was no such audit. The reports, he said, were merely filed, and notifications were sent to the National Labor Relations Board to indicate that the union had met its requirement under the Taft-Hartley law.

"Has there been any prosecution for filing false reports?" I asked.

Mashburn said he had been advised that the Labor Department was powerless to take action, even if it should find a false report. The financial reports, signed by the union officers, were not sworn statements. The Labor Department had no power to audit union books, even if it had reason to believe that a report was false, Mashburn explained.

He went on to say he thought the financial reports had done some good:

"They have made it necessary for many locals to go on record with some kind of a financial return. I know from experience that, although the returns were false, it did pin local leaders down to something, and it made it possible for the union itself to catch up with them."

Mashburn said the requirements for filing reports were meaningless:

"It is impossible to keep them up to date. Administratively it is a monstrosity. As far as I'm concerned it is just a big pile of paper that costs the unions to file, and it costs us to store."

Mashburn told me he believed the law requiring financial returns should be tightened, and that it should be made a crime to file a false report.

Mashburn's basic view was in agreement with mine: Lack of safeguards against filing false reports made the whole system a farce. It was obvious why crooked labor leaders did not feel that the financial reports were an effective barrier to wild spending.

Mashburn said the Internal Revenue Service made closer checks on union spending. I'm sure he believed it to be true, but it was contrary to what I had seen of the operations of the Internal Revenue Service on tax-exempt returns. And unions are tax-exempt organizations.

The tax department's major objective is collecting revenue, and tax-exempt organizations do not normally produce much revenue. Consequently, investigators work on tax-producing organizations first. Tax-exempt organizations are last to be examined. The result: Unions, churches, educational institutions and foundations are not investigated unless some pretty loud and persistent complaints are made.

VI

Hoffa's Detroit—Heart of a Hoodlum Empire

For weeks there were indications that Senator Bricker might kill the Minneapolis Teamsters investigation, and on October 6, 1953, he did. Rice and Plant were told they would be dropped from the Commerce subcommittee's payroll on November 30. There would be no hearings.

Bricker told me the documented reports by Rice and Plant showed "a bad situation" in the Teamsters union, but he questioned the subcommittee's jurisdiction. He was turning the investigation over to the Senate Labor Committee. My argument that this committee as constituted was the burial ground of labor racket inquiries was useless.

Bricker admitted that the resolution under which Senator Tobey had launched the Teamsters investigation was broad enough to cover it. He criticized Tobey, however, for not having kept the other committee members informed about what he was doing.

On October 15, the *Minneapolis Star* and *Tribune* lashed out at Bricker's decision, charging that he shouldn't be using such fine jurisdictional arguments to dodge hearings.

"Republican spokesmen have said repeatedly that their party is in favor of labor but against the racketeering that has infiltrated some unions," the independent Republican newspaper said. "This is the party's chance to prove that it means what it says."

It was excellent editorial support, but in the nine months since I had been called to Minneapolis I had written no more than a dozen cautiously worded stories. I had only touched upon corruption in the Teamsters union. It was frustrating.

With the possibility of an investigation by Bricker thus ended, I turned to Representative Hoffman. He had been blocked from conducting the Minneapolis Teamsters hearing with his Government Operations subcommittee, but now the wily Republican was trying to sell the House Labor Committee chairman, Sam McConnell, a Pennsylvania Republican, on authorizing a subcommittee of the Labor Committee to conduct the Detroit, Chicago and Minneapolis hearings.

McConnell established a subcommittee in the fall of 1953 with conservative Republican Wint Smith from Kansas as chairman. Hoffman was named a member of the subcommittee, but McConnell imposed sharp limitations on the unit's jurisdiction in an effort to keep the unpredictable Hoffman from widening it into a broad labor racket inquiry. I was disappointed because McConnell restricted the hearings to labor racketeering in Detroit and Chicago. It seemed every possibility for the Minneapolis investigation had been killed.

Jimmy Hoffa was bitterly opposed to even a limited investigation of his Detroit operations, and he was willing to spend Teamsters money to stop or neutralize it. The moment Wint Smith was named to head the Detroit hearing Hoffa went into action. He reached out to Kansas and hired a friend and political associate of Chairman Smith as one of his lawyers.

Payne Ratner, the former Republican governor of Kansas, was hired by Hoffa as a legal consultant. It was a typical Hoffa move. Ratner had been governor of Kansas at the time Chairman Smith was head of the Kansas Highway Patrol. Hoffa wanted Ratner to persuade Representative Smith to kill the investigation.[1]

Hoffa wasn't sure the gambit would work, but he was willing to try anything. Robert B. (Barney) Baker, a twice-convicted New York labor thug, and Richard Kavner, Team-

---

[1]McClellan committee hearings, Part 37, page 13754.

sters organizer from St. Louis, asked Ratner to intercede for Hoffa.[2]

Smith declined to postpone the hearings, but Ratner reported to Hoffa that he would continue to work on Chairman Smith. His fee was $200 a day plus expenses.[3]

"I hired every one I could get that I thought would do some good," said Hoffa later to justify hiring Ratner.

"Hoffa's use of former Governor Ratner of Kansas to ease his problems with the House Investigating Subcommittee headed by Congressman Wint Smith closely paralleled other testimony regarding Hoffa's relationship with judges and prosecutors in the Michigan area," another investigating committee reported years later.[4]

In the same week Hoffa hired former Governor Ratner to help protect his hoodlum empire in Detroit, Dave Beck made his first appearance before the National Press Club in Washington. It is a forum in which heads of state from all over the world have expounded their views, and on October 20, 1953, Dave Beck regarded himself as an emperor of the Teamsters world. He bragged about the 1,347,980 paid-up members in the International Teamsters union at the time, and commented that there were actually more than one and a half million members in what he called "the world's largest labor union."

Less than two months earlier, on August 13, Beck had been elected to the AFL Executive Council as the thirteenth vice-president. On September 26, he was named to a five-man A.F.L. committee to clean up corruption in the I.L.A.

Few persons present at the Press Club that day realized how ludicrous it was to have Beck as a member of a committee to clean up the rackets.

He told the press he had his eye on every auto service station, parking lot, wash rack or garage in the United States, and he expected to have two million members by 1956.

Beating his soft, round paw on the lectern, Beck yelled that labor didn't need any help from government, and could do its

---

[2]McClellan committee hearings, Part 37, pages 13744, 13748 and 13766.

[3]McClellan committee, Second Interim Report, No. 621, pages 86-87.

[4]McClellan committee, Second Interim Report, No. 621, page 88.

own job of cleaning out the Communists, muscle men, and racketeers.

However, he had done nothing about Orville Ring, the Kansas City Teamsters local president who had been labeled corrupt by a House subcommittee. Nor had Beck done anything about local president William Bufalino in Detroit, or Dan Keating, president of Local 614 in Pontiac, Michigan.

Beck did not mention the Congressional investigations that had touched his own union. He said there might be a certain amount of dishonesty in any group as large as the Teamsters union, but it was no greater than among similar groups in business.

"I believe in honesty in the labor movement," he bawled out to that National Press Club audience. But, he said, labor is a "tough game" and he had seen some of the tough side of it.

Beck beat his chest and took personal credit for the A.F.L. efforts to clean up the International Longshoremen's Association in New York and New Jersey. A.F.L. President George Meany had moved at his "insistence," Beck said, adding, "It is no job for ribbon clerks or hair stylists." He said the A.F.L. had the responsibility to move against the I.L.A. earlier, and that a similar responsibility lay upon the governor of New York and on city and federal officials.

Dave Beck was trying to sell himself as a champion of labor reform, even as he was doing nothing about evidence of racketeering in his own union.

He had hired a full-time public relations expert, Edward T. Cheyfitz. Cheyfitz had been a special assistant to Eric A. Johnston, a former president of the U. S. Chamber of Commerce and head of the Motion Picture Association of America, Inc.

The Teamsters president had also tried to hire Merlyn S. Pitzele, the labor editor of *Business Week* magazine, who was a top labor adviser to New York Governor Thomas E. Dewey and, in the 1952 campaign, to President Dwight D. Eisenhower.

Dave Kaplan, then chief economist for the Teamsters, said Pitzele could have named his own figure had he joined Beck on a full-time basis. Pitzele turned down the offer, but did accept a part-time job with Beck for a retainer of $5,000 a year plus expenses. The money was paid through Nathan Shefferman, the labor relations consultant.[5]

Beck had reason to be cocky during his Press Club speech. Senator Bricker had killed the Minneapolis investigation and there seemed little hope of getting any evidence of Teamsters corruption in Minnesota into the record.

As a last chance to get the facts on Minneapolis Teamsters into a Congressional hearing in 1953, I called Bill Wilson, my friend who operated a truck line at Sioux Falls, South Dakota. "We have to sell Smith and Hoffman on how urgent it is to get the Minneapolis story on the public record," I said. Wilson agreed.

He left immediately for Kansas to see Smith, made a special trip to Washington, D.C., to talk with Hoffman, and got in touch with as many political friends as he could think of who could encourage either of them. Meanwhile, I also talked with Smith and Hoffman, and with the investigators from Hoffman's sub-committee in the House.

"We haven't time to send investigators out to Minneapolis before the hearings in Detroit," Representative Hoffman said.

"You don't have to," I assured him. "I can furnish the investigators with the information they need to question the Minneapolis witnesses."

I suggested that Hoffman try to obtain copies of reports Downey Rice and Frank Plant had made for the Senate committee files, and indicated how copies might be obtained.

The hearing jurisdiction was limited to Chicago and Detroit. I found the prior activity of Gerald P. Connelly in Chicago and Detroit gave me grounds for arguing in favor of including this Minneapolis labor racketeer and his associates within the investigation's jurisdiction. It was stretching a bit, but it served its purpose.

The other witnesses subpoenaed were Eugene Williams, the business agent for Minneapolis Local 544, who doubled as opera-tor of a big night club, and James E. McNelis, who operated a trucking firm and was a pal of Sidney Brennan. Bill Wilson volunteered to give testimony if it was needed to reveal the way Brennan and Williams ran Local 544.

---

[5]McClellan committee, Report No. 1417, pages 295, 296 and 297.

The Minneapolis witnesses and documents allowed me to hit Brennan, Connelly, and Williams with four streamer headline stories in a row. Executive Editor Gid Seymour was delighted to get a substantial part of the story into print.

"Williams Admits Using Teamster Cash to Buy Bar," blared the headine in *The Minneapolis Star* and *Tribune* of November 5, 1953.

"Truck Line Head Bares Loan from Union Chief," the headline said on November 26, 1953, revealing "concealed" financial transactions between Brennan and McNelis.

"Gerald Connelly declined to testify about an attempted murder in Miami, Florida, on grounds that an answer might incriminate him," I wrote on November 26.[6]

"Rep. Wint Smith, chairman of the House labor subcommittee, announced he will seek committee approval for a full-scale hearing in Minneapolis on Minnesota A.F.L. Teamsters union affairs," I reported as the last of the Minnesota witnesses was heard.

Although the Minneapolis witnesses had been my real reason for going to Detroit, I became fascinated there by Jimmy Hoffa. Months earlier I had discarded the notion that he was a reformer who would purge the Minneapolis Teamsters of corrupt elements. However, I had to sit through the hearings, watch Hoffa in the corridor, and listen to him tongue-lash union business agents and lawyers before I realized the full brutality of his hoodlum empire.

There was no doubt that it was a hoodlum empire. Hoffa's subordinates included a versatile lot—convicted armed robbers, burglars, extortionists, narcotics peddlers, dynamiters, white slavers, gun men, and one business agent who had been convicted of sodomy.[7]

Hoffa was barred from the hearing room in Detroit as the special three-man Congressional subcommittee heard testimony about his manipulation of a multi-million-dollar health and welfare insurance plan. The insurance covered Teamsters union

[6]"Investigation of Welfare Funds and Racketeering," hearings before a special subcommittee of the Committee on Education and Labor, House of Representatives, 83d Congress, 1st Session, November 23, 24, 25, and 27, 1953, pages 279 and 280.

[7]McClellan committee, Report No. 1417, pages 448-449.

members in a twenty-two-state region, and was known as the Central States, Southeast, Southwest Area Health and Welfare Fund. Hoffman said there was no sense in letting Hoffa know the details of the testimony against him.

"If Hoffa plans on coming in and telling the truth about these things, he doesn't have to worry about what other witnesses say," Hoffman told me.

While Hoffa waited impatiently in the eighth-floor corridor of the Federal Courthouse, members of the subcommittee were exploring how a million dollars in insurance fees had been handed to Hoffa's friends, the Dorfmans.

Paul Dorfman, the Capone-connected boss of a Chicago Waste Handlers union, had no direct interest in the Union Insurance Agency of Illinois, which had collected heavy fees as agent. But Paul's wife, Rose, and a son, Allen Dorfman, were the recorded owners of this new and booming insurance business.[8]

The Taft-Hartley law required that decisions on placing union health and welfare insurance be made by a trustees' committee consisting of an equal number of employers and union representatives. But according to the testimony Jimmy Hoffa had overruled the employers and tossed the million-dollar plum to Union Casualty & Life Insurance Company, Mount Vernon, New York. This permitted Hoffa's friends, the Dorfmans, to pocket the agent's commissions and fees of a million dollars.[9]

This one transaction made Union Casualty & Life Insurance Company a flourishing business. It was apparent that Hoffa and his henchmen could make or break a small insurance company by placing or withholding business. It also became apparent that deposits of the million-dollar funds collected from union dues could be crucial to the banking community.

Many truck-line operators demonstrated their fear of Hoffa, and abdicated their responsibility as employer trustees of the Central States, Southeast, Southwest Health and Welfare Fund. Initially they preferred a better plan with an insurance firm of

[8]"Investigation of Welfare Funds and Racketeering," report of a special subcommittee to the Committee on Education and Labor, 83d Congress, 2d Session, 1954, pages 9 and 11.

[9]"Investigation of Welfare Funds and Racketeering," report of special subcommittee, page 9.

higher financial standing, but then they bowed when Hoffa insisted on his choice.

"The bulk of the industry representatives were opposed to Union Casualty and were in favor of one of several different companies that carry good ratings," testified Willis J. McCarthy, a Des Moines attorney who had represented trucking interests in meetings with Hoffa.[10]

"The companies, or the company representatives, are fully aware that if they diametrically oppose the union and refuse to go along, it will result in a deadlock and probably reprisals against their companies," McCarthy said.

"Is it your considered opinion . . . they feared that unless they did so they would have labor disputes, labor troubles, strikes, and that it was an effort to buy labor peace?" asked Representative Hoffman.

"In my mind there isn't any question about it," McCarthy answered.[11]

The picture of wealthy employers cringing before Hoffa's demands seemed inconsistent with the smiling, boyish-looking man who waited in the corridor for his chance to testify.

Testimony had depicted him as a man who ruthlessly crushed small truckers, then pressured them to sell out to his wife, Josephine, or his union associates. Other witnesses said Hoffa ousted honest members of the Teamsters union from office in Local 614 in Pontiac, Michigan, and restored corrupt officials under a Hoffa-administered trusteeship.[12]

"Hoffa doesn't look old enough or tough enough to do the things the witnesses say he does," I commented to chief investigator Condon.

"Don't let the looks fool you, Clark," Condon cautioned. "He can be a likeable little guy when he wants to be, but he can be tough. He can be tough enough to do about anything you can imagine."

"He doesn't look any older than twenty-five," I said.

---

[10]"Investigation of Welfare Funds and Racketeering," hearings of special subcommittee, page 210.

[11]"Investigation of Welfare Funds and Racketeering," hearings of special subcommittee, pages 211 and 212.

[12]"Investigation of Welfare Funds and Racketeering," report of special subcommittee, pages 4 and 5.

"Jimmy keeps in shape," Condon said. "He doesn't smoke, and he doesn't drink. He chops wood in northern Michigan to keep those muscles hard."

Hoffa was only about five feet five inches tall, but he was broad shouldered and muscular. There was no fat in the 180 pounds he carried easily.

Condon said Hoffa was then 39 or 40 years old and had been in the union organizing business about 20 years.

"Unless something stops him, he'll be the next president of the Teamsters," Condon predicted. "The title of ninth vice president doesn't mean a thing. He put Beck in as general president, and he is the real Number Two in the Teamsters now."

Condon explained that Hoffa had already been able to stretch his power over the 13-state Central States Conference of Teamsters. He had also gained rather firm control of the ten states in the Southern Conference through the health and welfare funds. Jimmy was already working through Paul Dorfman and labor racketeer Johnny Dioguardi to get a foothold in the Eastern State group, then dominated by Thomas (Honest Tom) Hickey, of New York.

Hoffa ran a transportation empire. And, as the vast power of his command became apparent, I viewed the little Detroit man with some respect for his achievements. Hoffa's father had died when Jimmy was seven. He lived in poverty in his early years, and went to work on the docks and in the warehouses in Detroit when he was only 14. He was a grade school drop-out, but he organized his own union and received a charter from the American Federation of Labor in 1931 when he was only 18.

The police record that Hoffa compiled in those early years was, in his own words, "maybe as long as your arm." Most of his arrests were a result of picket-line brawls, and there were few convictions. At 24, Hoffa was elected president of Local 299, the huge Teamsters local that continued to be the base of his operations. Three years later he was named chairman of the negotiating committee for the central states drivers, and he began to spread his power outside of Michigan.

Watching Jimmy in the corridor of the courthouse, I could see Napoleonic touches in his make-up. He had to be the center of attention. The Teamsters business agents and officers who crowded around him were totally subservient. They laughed at his jokes, nodded in agreement, and in carriage and facial expression told Hoffa he was their leader.

During one recess Hoffa seemed to be reprimanding a stocky, red-haired man. The man's effort to explain appeared futile for he found Hoffa and several business agents arrayed against him.

"Who is the redhead?" I asked Condon.

"That's Eddie Cheyfitz," Condon answered. "He's Dave Beck's public relations man."

"He doesn't seem to be getting along too well with Hoffa," I commented.

"He will," Condon answered. "Cheyfitz is about as smooth an operator as there is in Washington. Hoffa is a little suspicious of the Beck crowd, but if anyone can calm him Cheyfitz can."

Cheyfitz and Condon had gone to night classes together at the Georgetown Law School in the late 1940's. Occasionally, they had studied together and Condon was well acquainted with Cheyfitz' background.

Cheyfitz, a native of Toledo, Ohio, was a Communist for years, but quit the party about 1940. He was an organizer for the C.I.O. unions in the 1930's, and jumped from union work to the payroll of Eric Johnston, when Johnston was president of the U. S. Chamber of Commerce and also head of the Motion Picture Association of America, Inc. From there, Cheyfitz bounced to the Teamsters as a public relations adviser to Beck.

Condon introduced me to the friendly, eager-eyed young man.

"What's the problem with Hoffa?" I asked Cheyfitz.

"No problem," Cheyfitz answered. "Jimmy is a little suspicious about why I'm here. He thought Beck might be out to get him, but there isn't anything to it. I'm just down to see what happens, and to report back to Beck."

Cheyfitz said he was certain that he had been able to quiet Hoffa's fear that Beck was behind the committee investigation in an effort to cut Jimmy down to size.

"Have you met Jimmy?" Cheyfitz asked.

I answered that until now I had been limited to admiring Jimmy from afar.

"Come on over, and I'll introduce you to him," Cheyfitz said as if he and Hoffa were close friends.

"I'm glad to meet you, Mr. Hoffa," I said at the introduction. I kept it formal because I didn't know what kind of a reaction there would be.

"Hiya, Big Stuff." Hoffa was grinning up at me and applying a strong grip to my hand.

"You reporters are getting bigger every year," Hoffa quipped. He gave me a friendly but solid slug on the biceps, measured the 11 inches I towered over him, and added, "The bigger they come the harder they fall."

Without being antagonistic, I asked him about the allegations of payoffs, irregularities in the insurance program, the interest his wife had in a trucking line, and the throttling of union democracy.

"It's the testimony of a few disgruntled employers, and some union members who are mad because they can't run things," Hoffa said.

"Why did you insist that the insurance be given to the Dorfmans?" I asked. "The testimony is that Union Life was not the best qualified firm."

"It was the best policy for the membership," Hoffa said. "If it is the best policy, it shouldn't make any difference if the commissions go to some friends of mine. Businesses do it all the time."

"What about that interest you have in that truck leasing firm?" I asked.

From Condon and chief counsel McKenna of the subcommittee I had learned that Hoffa had balked at talking to investigators about Test Fleet Corporation—a firm that was incorporated in Tennessee. It was a company in which the wives of two Teamsters bosses had interests in their maiden names—Mrs. Hoffa as Josephine Poszywak, and Mrs. Owen Bert Brennan as Alice Johnson.[13]

"Let's get this straight," Hoffa replied to my question about Test Fleet. "I don't have any interest in Test Fleet. That is my wife's interest. What my wife does should be no business of this committee or anyone else."

---

[13]"Investigation of Welfare Funds and Racketeering," report of a special subcommittee, page 3.

Hoffa went on to explain that in his opinion there would be no "conflict of interest" even if he owned Test Fleet, since that concern hired no Teamsters union members but merely leased trucks to Commercial Carriers, a Detroit company that did hire Teamsters.

Hoffa's wife had shared in the $62,000 in dividends from leasing her Test Fleet equipment to Commercial Carriers, after Commercial Carriers had set up the truck leasing firm for her.[14] I asked Hoffa if, as a Teamster's official, he could deal objectively with a trucking firm that paid his wife such handsome profits.

"It would not influence me, and I don't think it would influence any real trade unionist," Hoffa said. "I will always do what is best for the membership."

Why should a proper transaction be hidden in a Tennessee corporation? Why should there be so many manipulations to make it difficult to trace the true owners?

McKenna and Condon suggested that if Hoffa and Brennan declined to talk about the organization of Test Fleet, subpoenas would be issued for Mrs. Hoffa and Mrs. Brennan. Hoffa was furious at the idea that a Congressional committee would sub-poena his wife. Under this pressure he told Condon the wives knew little or nothing about the operation of Test Fleet, and simply collected their profits from officials of Commercial Carriers, the trucking firm. Mrs. Hoffa and Mrs. Brennan had put only $4,000 into Test Fleet, he said, and in four years they had paid for the equipment and taken out $62,000 in dividends.[15]

Although Hoffa was barred from the hearing room, his attorneys were not barred. In addition, there was an almost steady stream of business agents in and out of room 859 of the Federal Building, keeping Jimmy posted as to what the witnesses were saying about him.

"He's a liar," Hoffa snapped about one witness.

"We'll take care of him when this is over with," he commented about another. "These hearings will be over in a few days."

---

[14]"Investigation of Welfare Funds and Racketeering," report of a special subcommittee, page 3.

[15]"Investigation of Welfare Funds and Racketeering," report of a special subcommittee, page 3.

He could smile one moment, and wink impishly, but bad news made him cloud up. Then he would clip out orders like a top sergeant. With a loud snap of his fingers he commanded lawyers and business agents to carry out his instructions.

He was irritated at being barred from the hearing room and wanted the press and the public to know that Hoffa wasn't bowing to a Congressional committee, or any other authority.

Jimmy Hoffa had a million-dollar treasury in Local 299. He knew how to buy or coerce politicians, and he had nothing but contempt for them.

When a one-man grand jury brought about his conviction on a state labor charge, he was infuriated, and put on a drive to get the law changed. It was successful, because of Teamsters power in the Michigan legislature.

For Hoffa's hoodlum empire there was almost complete protection. When grand juries got out of hand, Hoffa provided his subordinates with the best criminal lawyers. Often, they went to trial before judges who had been softened by Teamsters' political contributions.[16]

When these safeguards misfired, as they occasionally did, Hoffa paid the fines out of the union treasury and continued the salaries of the Teamsters officers and business agents who went to prison.

Some law enforcement officials in Wayne County, Michigan, were afraid of the Teamsters. Some were in collusion with union racketeers, or just weren't competent to deal with them.[17]

"The Wayne County prosecutor's office and the Detroit Police Department have taken no effective action with regard to any of the legal actions on the part of the Teamsters Union or its officials," a subcommittee had stated in an official report on the juke-box rackets.[18]

Hoffa poured $22,669 into a public relations firm which used a large part of the money to pay $100 a week to Michigan State Judge Joseph Gillis, and to sponsor television shows that

---

[16]McClellan committee, Report No. 621, pages 89 to 93.

[17]McClellan committee, Report No. 1417, pages 239-241 and 244-245.

[18]"Investigation of Welfare Funds and Racketeering," report of a special subcommittee, page 9.

publicized judges, including Gillis, who were in favor with Hoffa.

In the political atmosphere of Detroit at that time, Judge Gillis found no conflict of interest and no ethical problem in presiding as judge in criminal cases involving Hoffa's leading Teamsters associates.[19]

With regard to money paid to Judge Gillis through the public relations firm of Joe Schneiders Associates, Inc., Detroit, Hoffa said the ethics were up to the judge. He explained it this way:

"I think that if a judge, on his own time, could assist in a show and enterprise, of any description, and he could earn some money doing it, and he wasn't obligated to the individual who paid him for anything other than producing what he was paid for, there certainly wouldn't be anything immoral about it."[20]

Hoffa had used $42,000 of union funds in what was an unsuccessful attempt to elect his attorney, George Fitzgerald, as governor of Michigan on the Democratic ticket.

These were only samples of the way he tossed union funds into local and state political campaigns. He was careful to avoid direct contribution of union funds to federal campaigns because this could have been a violation of the Federal Corrupt Practices Act.

Hoffa was truly bipartisan. In fact, he seemed to consider himself above either the Democratic or Republican political parties.

On November 25, 1953, the Detroit hearings were interrupted while Chairman Smith left the room to take a long distance call. He said afterward that he was under strong political pressure to call off the Teamsters investigation.

"The pressure comes from away up there, and I just can't talk about it any more specifically than that," Smith said, pointing at the ceiling.

He would not tell reporters who was putting pressure on him, but he said it would be necessary to wind up the hearings quickly.

November 26 was Thanksgiving, but the subcommittee

---

[19]McClellan committee, Report No. 621, pages 92 and 93.

[20]McClellan committee, Report No. 621, page 93.

stayed in Detroit to finish up proceedings on Friday. When Hoffa took the witness chair Friday, it was almost all over, and he knew it. He was cocky and defiant, but he did answer the questions, in his own vague manner. He did it to purge himself of the contempt threat that had been hanging over him since his refusal to answer questions in June.

When he was questioned about the $100 a week his wife and Mrs. Bert Brennan each received from Local 985, Hoffa admitted the women did no work for that Teamsters local. It was only a device for paying back the $2,000 in cash he and Brennan had loaned Local 985, Hoffa said glibly.[21]

Members of the subcommittee then pointed out that $6,000 was repaid, or about 200 per cent interest.

Jimmy James, who was running the juke-box local at the time, had explained the $4,000 profit to Hoffa and Brennan as being paid from union funds "out of the goodness of my heart." James described Hoffa and Brennan as "big men—they could help me a lot."[22]

Chief counsel McKenna's effort to pin Hoffa down was only partly successful. Jimmy admitted being in several joint business operations with the Dorfmans, and he admitted receiving a few minor gifts. But he denied having received any of a mysterious $100,000 investigators reported had disappeared from the Dorfman insurance agency. Allen and Paul Dorfman had taken the Fifth Amendment on questions about the use of the $100,000, and it remained a mystery as the Detroit hearing ended.

Hoffa was even arrogant when he brushed by Condon, McKenna, and the other investigators in leaving the hearing room.

"I pay my business agents more than you guys make," he snarled contemptuously.

Immediately after the hearing, McKenna resigned as chief counsel to return to his law practice in Los Angeles. The next day, Representative Hoffman was quoted as saying that Mc-

---

[21]"Investigation of Welfare Funds and Racketeering," hearings, pages 435-436.

[22]Kefauver "Investigation of Organized Crime in Interstate Commerce," hearings, Part 9, Michigan, February 8, 9 and 19, 1951, pages 995, 998.

McClellan committee, Report No. 1417, pages 234 and 235.

Kenna was "humiliated in not getting more support from Smith in his attempt to get the truth out of Hoffa."[23]

On November 30, former Governor Ratner was back in Wichita writing to Hoffa:

"Dear Jimmy: I listened carefully to all of the evidence last week, and it is my considered opinion that you did nothing illegal or improper. I am proud to call you my friend . . . . Wint Smith told me today that he certainly got in bad with Hoffman and the staff by having gone along with me in his treatment of you Friday. I, of course, expressed appreciation to him and told him that I have always thought no one had to worry very much about doing the right thing."[24]

On December 9, 1953, Ratner received a check for $1,554.09 from the Teamsters union. It was the first of many he was to receive. Hoffa was well satisfied with his services, and said so in a letter to him.[25]

Chairman Smith denied that any favored treatment was given to Hoffa. On this he was defended by Representative Hoffman. Hoffman said there had been "disagreements" as to the scope of the hearings, but that he had faith in Smith and believed the Kansas Republican had done a conscientious job.[26]

But one point was undisputed: Beginning in June, 1953, Hoffa pulled every trick in the book in an attempt to crush or neutralize the hearings.

The juke-box hearings were just beginning in June when Hoffa brazenly approached his old foe, Representative Hoffman: "Don't you know, Clare, that I am a Republican?"

"Well, I didn't know you were," Hoffman answered.

Hoffa boasted that he was able to get votes for candidates he liked, and cited the case of a man supported by the Teamsters who was elected to the Supreme Court of Michigan by a large margin.

Hoffa pointed to his support of a Republican United States Senator from Michigan, hoping that his support of the Republican might help persuade Hoffman to drop the investigation.[27]

[23]McClellan committee report, No. 622, part 1, page 87.
[24]McClellan committee hearings, part 37, page 13768.
[25]McClellan committee hearings, part 37, page 13749.
[26]McClellan committee hearings, part 37, pages 13960 and 13841.
[27]McClellan committee hearings, part 37, page 13839.

"We are investigating, and that is what we intend to do," Hoffman said with finality.

Despite the brazen approach to Hoffman, and the hiring of lawyers with political connections in both parties, the basic pattern of rottenness in Hoffa's operations had been exposed. It gave me hope that we would finally get a thorough job done on the entire Teamsters hierarchy.

VII
_____

Defiance by Beck's Bad Boys

The Teamsters union's ostentatious multi-million-dollar palace had not yet been completed in December, 1953, but Dave Beck had established temporary headquarters on the northwest slope of Capitol Hill. It was almost close enough for Congressional leaders to hear Beck pound his desk and scream out his opposition to Congressional investigations.

"I want to keep my eye on Congress," Beck said with a smile, when he was in one of his better moods.

The dome of the nation's Capitol still loomed higher than Beck's office, but there were indications that Beck was bigger than some Congressional committees. Leaders in Congress made excuses for ducking or ignoring their responsibility to clean up the mighty Teamsters. They accepted Beck's assertion that he would handle any problem himself, or merely heeded his warning to keep their noses out of the union's finances.

Beck liked Representative Sam McConnell, the Pennsylvania Republican who headed the House Labor Committee. McConnell conducted investigations, and Beck praised McConnell as "responsible." He lauded McConnell for avoiding the "circus atmosphere" and keeping his probes on a "high level."

McConnell had authorized the hearings in Detroit and Kansas City, but he told me he had serious doubts about the propriety of investigations that dug into the personal finances of labor leaders, or anyone else.[1]

"I don't know whether that is the function of Congress," McConnell told me. "We are interested in getting enough facts for a proper study of the Taft-Hartley law."

Although McConnell spent months on an investigation of possible revision of the Taft-Hartley labor law, he avoided making anyone angry. There was testimony from persons with complaints about improper activities in the labor-management field, but McConnell did not run an investigation to embarrass anyone.

He prided himself on being a compromiser between the extreme groups in the labor and management area. He was a mild chairman, and a strong believer in avoiding controversy. He said, however, that he was willing to let Representative Smith go ahead in Minneapolis.

On December 10, I called on Beck to see what he was going to do about the documented evidence of improper activities involving Hoffa, Eugene Williams, Gerald Connelly, Orville Ring, and others.

"No union official can justify borrowing $10 or $10,000 through the employees' pension or insurance fund, or from a union's petty cash," Beck roared as he paced in his plush temporary office in the Letter Carriers Building.

"It is wrong and not in the best interest of the union members. I won't put up with it from the highest or the lowest union member," he declared.

Beck promised that he would examine the record on Jimmy Hoffa and would oust him if what I told him about Hoffa proved true. He said he wanted to read the transcript before saying whether he would take action against Williams, who had admitted using union cash and borrowing $10,000 through a union pension fund to start a night club.

Seldom has there been a more noisy display of indignation and righteousness than Beck treated me to that day. He wouldn't tolerate tampering with union funds, he bellowed. He brought his pudgy fist down on the custom-made executive desk for emphasis, and at the moment I believed him.

---

[1]McClellan committee hearings, part 37, page 13846.

Later developments showed that, at that time, Beck had used approximately $320,000 in Teamsters union funds to pay his personal bills and to build his home.[2] The money had been charged off on union books as "public relations" costs and "construction" expenses.

The very desk Beck was pounding was part of the custom-made furniture he had purchased with Teamsters money in a deal that paid $13,000 in commissions to Norman Gessert, a cousin of Mrs. Dave Beck. Another $13,000 profit on the furniture deal went to Shelton Shefferman, the son of Beck's good friend, Chicago labor relations consultant Nate Shefferman.[3]

The union money Williams and Connelly "borrowed" was negligible compared with the amounts that later investigations disclosed Beck had siphoned out of the treasury of the Western Conference of Teamsters.

I was accompanied by Jack Wilson, another correspondent for Cowles newspapers, when I made that visit to Beck's office. I wanted a witness for a twenty-minute interview, but it stretched into hours as I brought up the name of one racketeering Teamster after another.

While denouncing corruption generally, Beck always had an excuse for not taking action on specific cases. He fancied himself quite an authority on the United States Constitution, and on the Teamsters constitution. I was not familiar with the Teamsters constitution, but I knew enough about the U. S. Constitution to recognize Beck as a blow-hard and a phony.

His shallowness showed through in that interview. Before I talked to him I had accepted declarations that he was a brilliant man. The longer he stalked up and down, braying his views on crime, the Constitution and Congress, the more ludicrous he became. But, while it was comic, it was tragic; this man was a ruthless dictator.

He bragged of the "tremendous economic and political power" of the Teamsters, and he said he knew how to wield it.

There was an intense coldness in his light blue eyes and fervor in his voice as he blasted "the investigative circuses" that

---

[2]McClellan committee, Report No. 1417, page 85.

[3]McClellan committee, Report No. 1417, pages 69, 70, and 85.

had engulfed the Teamsters leadership in Detroit, Kansas City, and Minneapolis.

"What about the five indictments that were returned against Orville Ring and others in Kansas City?" I asked. "What about the twelve indictments returned against union officials following the Detroit hearings?"

"Indictments!" Beck exploded. "They were indictments by a one-man grand jury, and I think a one-man grand jury is a violation of the rights of the individual."

"Isn't the one-man grand jury legal in Michigan?" I asked.

"The one-man grand jury may be legal, but it is like tearing up the Constitution," he declared.

Beck added that he didn't want his comments construed as support of those who had stolen union money, or had otherwise engaged in racketeering.

"We have some problems, but in the over-all picture, I think we are pretty clean," he commented.

"You have to remember that I've only been in this office a year now. Sure, there is some cleaning up to be done, and I've said from the rostrum a hundred times that I'll tolerate no Communists and no racketeers in my union, if I find them.

"My record will speak for itself on the way I threw the Communists out. I'm sure there is no Communist in a position of leadership in the union today."

He said he had thrown some unions into trusteeship after receiving information indicating racketeering. He overlooked the fact that in some cases the trusteeships had been imposed to keep crooked union officials in office.

"I don't have the machinery to find out all about these rackets," he continued. "I don't have the power to issue a subpoena, or to bring a man in here and put him under oath. Those are jobs for the proper department of government."

"Don't you welcome some of the assistance that Congressional committees give you?" I asked softly. But Beck boomed out the reply:

"No. No is the answer. It should be done in the grand jury— and I don't mean any of those damned one-man grand juries. If the F. B. I. and the Internal Revenue and other enforcement authorities can't do it, I don't want it done by a bunch of labor-baiting Congressmen.

"They crucify a man, and down in Kansas City they even did it with television. It's a violation of our Constitution."

"Mr. Beck, do you believe a union official should be suspended from office if he refuses to answer questions on grounds of self-incrimination?"

"On Communism, yes, I got no time for those sons of bitches, and you've got to fight fire with fire as far as they are concerned. I'll bounce any man who won't tell whether he's a Communist."

"But what about those cases of terrorism and theft of union funds?" I asked.

"It's part of our Constitution." He slammed his hand on the desk for emphasis. "A man has a right to refuse to answer questions if it might incriminate him, and I won't be the one to fire him for it. I won't be a party to tearing up that Constitution of ours that has stood the test for more than 150 years."

Fighting Communism had been a useful device for Beck. In his home town of Seattle, Washington, he had often excused the extreme tactics of his earlier years by saying they were necessary to beat the Communists.

As head of the Western Conference of Teamsters Beck convinced many employers that if they didn't go along with him the Communists would get them.

There was no real logic to Beck, and no great wisdom. He had Teamsters power, and he would use it bluntly or cunningly. I imagined he would interpret his contracts with trucking concerns with the same poetic license he used in interpreting the U. S. Constitution.

When Jack Wilson and I finally brought the interview to a close, Jack had a headache from the racket Beck had created.

I didn't have a headache, but I felt sick at the thought of a man like Beck climbing to a position of such power. He had complete authority over the men who drove the taxis, hauled the furniture, picked up the garbage, and delivered the milk and the fuel. Beck's Teamsters were the life lines between other unionized industries, and Teamsters could cripple them merely by refusing to cross picket lines.

"Everything that is on wheels, or ever was on wheels," was the way Beck had described Teamsters jurisdiction.

My stories were critical of Beck, but I still hoped that his self-interest would make him get rid of the crooks. Ed Cheyfitz, Beck's public relations man, urged "understanding" of the problem. He said Beck would clean house, but he would have to move slowly. Cheyfitz had logical explanations for everything, and he sold me on using his reasoning in my story. I wrote.

"He (Beck) may not clean up his organization as fast as some Congressmen would say he should, but to understand that situation it is necessary to understand something about the politics of the Teamsters union.

"It was necessary for Beck to have the support of much-criticized James Hoffa...to take over the Teamsters organization.

"Beck also had the backing of Sidney L. Brennan, the international vice president from Minneapolis.

"It is understandable why Beck would be slow to reprimand Hoffa in the first year of his rule, particularly in view of the fact that Hoffa is still a power in Detroit, and, despite Congressional hearings, continues to be the greatest single threat to Beck's throne."

Beck, a millionaire businessman as well as a labor leader, was far too wealthy to be interested in this petty thievery or in protecting those who were dishonest, Cheyfitz assured me. It did seem logical.

My stories were not flattering to Beck, but they left room for the reader to believe that Beck might act against corruption. However, I was amazed to see that Beck's public relations organization had stimulated some highly flattering articles about the Teamsters president by some well-known labor writers.

When Jimmy Hoffa wrote to Payne Ratner that he was pleased with the treatment he had received at the Detroit hearings, it was by no means a general endorsement of Wint Smith by the Teamsters. The Detroit hearings were concluded, but Chairman Smith appeared to be headed for Minnesota under a full head of steam.

"The evidence justifies full-scale hearings in Minneapolis," he said. Smith and the Minneapolis *Star* and *Tribune* were the only major forces seeking continuation of the Teamsters hearings, but that was enough to make some Minnesota Teamsters panicky.

In mid-December, 1953, the F. B. I. reported to Smith that a group of Teamsters officials had held a meeting in Minneapolis to discuss ways of stopping the hearings.

"Let's bump off Wint Smith and pull a strike on the Minneapolis *Star* and *Tribune*," one Teamster suggested, according to an F. B. I. informant who was in the meeting.

Shooting a Congressman seemed rash to most of the Teamsters present, but the possibility of striking the newspapers was left open, according to the F.B.I. advice to Smith.

On December 21, the Teamsters struck the Minneapolis *Star* and *Tribune*. The dispute involved wages and a contract negotiation, but Executive Editor Gideon Seymour said he was sure the papers' effort to stimulate the investigation made the Teamsters more obstinate.

The week before Christmas was the most expensive week in the year for the newspapers to be shut down, and the cost was several hundred thousands of dollars. The strike was settled on Christmas Day, after Seymour had put in five tension-filled days trying to keep the paper moving. Two days later he had a severe heart attack.

December was a frustrating month. Chairman Smith was given authority to conduct hearings, but the committee staff failed to provide money or office space for the men he engaged. After arranging to hire Downey Rice and Frank Plant, he had to drop them because of a lack of funds.

"It looks to me as if someone around that Labor Committee staff is trying to sabotage the whole investigation," Rice said sharply.

The system of spies and counterspies in labor and business was dramatized to me one night that month. During the afternoon, I had been at the House Labor Committee for some discussions about the Minneapolis labor situation.

Later that evening, in a long distance call to Bill Wilson, my trucker friend from South Dakota, he remarked that I should be more careful about what I said around the committee.

"How do you know what I was saying over there?" I asked.

"I didn't get it from anyone in the Labor Committee," Wilson replied. "A report on what you'd said was telephoned to Teamsters headquarters."

"How do you know all this?" I questioned.

"I've got a fellow over in the Teamsters who has been keeping me posted on what they're doing," he explained.

This was a complicated intrigue, and I decided to trust no one until the Teamsters' spy was located. It had to be one of three possibilities, and within a few days I was satisfied that I knew who it was. It probably was not illegal—just a rotten arrangement to exist inside an investigating committee.

Even the U. S. mail proved unsafe for transporting the correspondence, testimony and secret reports relating to labor racketeering in the Detroit and Chicago areas.

On December 1, 1953, Representative Clare Hoffman had sent a mail sack containing labor racket material from his home in Allegan, Michigan, to his office in Washington. By the end of two weeks Hoffman was disturbed because the material had not arrived.

When some envelopes that had been in the mail bag drifted into his office a week later, Hoffman angrily charged that his mail had been "pilfered." He demanded an explanation from the Post Office Department.

A Post Office Department investigation showed the mail sack had been misrouted to the Detroit, Michigan, post office. Detroit reported that some unidentified person apparently had thought the bag contained newspapers and had emptied it onto the floor. Several days later it was forwarded to Hoffman in Washington.

"That isn't a satisfactory explanation as far as I'm concerned," Hoffman told me. "The mail sack was clearly marked, and I have the statement of the postmaster of Allegan, Michigan, to support this.

"Even if the bag was accidentally broken open and dumped on the floor, it should have been immediately apparent that it wasn't newspapers. Each of the brown envelopes on the inside was clearly marked with my name, and it would seem to me that they should have gotten here long before this."

He said the delay had been long enough so the material could have been photostated before being forwarded.

Many obstacles arose that December, but there was some progress against Teamsters corruption that passed with little notice. Chairman McConnell of the House Labor Committee became convinced that there was a real problem in protecting union members' funds from piracy. The "borrowing" from union funds to start a night club provided a simple case to use in explaining the problem to President Eisenhower. The dealings between Hoffa and the Dorfmans became the classic example of the enormous power wielded by union officials who controlled these multi-million-dollar insurance deals.

Dr. Leo Perlman, executive vice president of the Union Casualty insurance company, had cultivated such labor bosses as Hoffa and Bert Brennan and Red Dorfman, head of the Waste Material Handlers Local 20467 in Chicago, and Frank Darling, head of Local 1031 of the Brotherhood of Electrical Workers in Chicago.

Union Casualty's direct premium payments jumped from $1,460,000 in 1948 to an astounding $8,900,000 four years later, according to the House subcommittee reports. Nearly 77 per cent of the 1952 premiums came from three big union insurance coups—health and welfare insurance covering more than half of the 25,000 to 37,000 workers in Darling's Local 1031 in Chicago; the health and welfare insurance of Hoffa's Central State Conference of Teamsters and some affiliated groups, and the health and welfare insurance of the Michigan Conference of Teamsters, of which Hoffa was president.

Perlman, a 56-year-old immigrant, collected more than $400,000 in profit from 1948 through 1951 through Union Casualty and Life and the United Public Services Corp., a general insurance agency.

In 1949, the Union Insurance Agency of Illinois came into being in Chicago as an agent for Union Casualty and Life. Allen Dorfman, 30, and his mother, Rose Dorfman, were immediately successful. Between 1949 and June, 1953, the Union Insurance Agency of Illinois received over a million dollars in commissions, expenses, and allowance from Union Casualty and Life and United Public Services Corp.[4]

---

[4] "Investigation of Welfare Funds and Racketeering," report of special subcommittee, pages 5-9.

The insurance executives entertained Hoffa lavishly and often, and several mutual business ventures proved profitable to both. Hoffa had insisted that he received no money for swinging the insurance to the Dorfmans, but he also insisted on his right to make a normal profit by going into joint business deals with them. He couldn't see any possible conflict of interest. The labor advisers to President Eisenhower could.

McConnell and Smith went to the White House to explain the problem of protecting union health and welfare funds. On January 11, 1954, President Eisenhower followed their suggestion by asking Congress to take steps to guard these funds against mismanagement by labor bosses. The President, in his message to Congress, said:

"It is my recommendation Congress initiate a thorough study of welfare and pension funds covered by collective bargaining agreements, with a view of enacting such legislation as will protect and conserve these funds for the millions of working men and women who are the beneficiaries."

I was hopeful that, since the Republicans controlled Congress, this little push from the White House might result in a broad labor racket investigation.

VIII

Minneapolis Hearing—the Fifth Amendment

Between mid-December and early January, 1954, Dave Beck forgot his pledge to oust those borrowing "$10 or $10,000 from union funds." He was unavailable for interviews on Teamsters scandals. The statements were issued by his press man, Eddie Cheyfitz.

"As far as we can see, no illegal acts have been committed by either (Gene) Williams or Hoffa," Cheyfitz said. "If there were any illegal acts Beck would act immediately."

Cheyfitz explained that, as Beck saw it, there was merely a question whether it had been ethical for business agent Williams to arrange the $10,000 "advance" through the pension funds of the Transfer and Warehouse Employees Teamsters Local in Minneapolis, and to "borrow" $1,800 in cash from a union safe.

This wasn't the final word, but Beck would discuss the matter with the Teamsters executive board, Cheyfitz said. Beck was also preparing a definition of "ethics" for Teamsters officials, but he wanted to discuss it with the international board before issuing a reprimand or criticizing anybody. Dave was always very proper about such things, Cheyfitz assured me.

The public picture presented of Beck was that of a man of stern principles regarding his own ethics and honesty, but with the breadth to be humane in judging the frailties of lesser men. It was hard to swallow if you'd ever talked to Beck.

In Seattle, a 61-year-old federal tax agent noticed the news stories referred to Beck as a millionaire.

Claude Watson started working on Beck's tax returns in January, 1954. This small, wiry tax agent found indications that Beck was filing false tax returns. He asked to see Beck's records. At first, Watson thought Beck might have made an honest mistake; he became more suspicious when the request for the records was not granted.

Seattle's "number one citizen" refused to see the Internal Revenue agent alone, and the little tax investigator found himself arrayed against Beck, Samuel Bassett, who was an attorney for the Teamsters as well as for Beck personally,[1] and Ludwig Lobe, Beck's accountant.

Beck would answer no questions. Neither Beck nor Lobe offered to produce records. Bassett gave the only responses, and Watson found it a very unsatisfactory way to get facts. Beck was acting strangely for an honest millionaire who had been praised at a huge testimonial dinner in Seattle in December, 1952, as the "greatest" labor leader in the country.

Beck's net worth was $46,195 in 1938. He'd acquired his first $25,000 by suing a Seattle newspaper which had been critical of him and of Teamsters goon squads. By December 31, 1942, he had boosted his net worth to $63,233.

Tax investigator Watson decided upon examination of Beck's tax returns that Beck hadn't reported enough income or paid enough taxes between 1943 and 1954 to account for increasing his net worth from $63,000 to $1,000,000. If Beck was the millionaire his press clippings said he was, something was wrong and Watson decided more investigation was needed.[2]

The House Government Operations Committee on January 20, 1954, blocked Representative Hoffman's plan to conduct Teamsters labor racket hearings. By a vote of 19 to 1, the committee members handed the labor investigation to a subcommittee headed by Representative George Bender, an Ohio Republican.

Selection of genial George Bender as chairman of a labor

---

[1]McClellan committee, Report No. 1417, page 60.

[2]Transcript of trial, U. S. v. Dave Beck, United States District Court for the Western District of Washington.

racket investigation seemed incredible to me, and I wasn't the only one who was amazed. George was a clown. His political strength lay in his work as a chore boy for constituents, and his back-slapping friendliness. Representative Hoffman was furious.

"They want a friend of labor to run the committee," the irascible old Congressman snapped. "It looks like a whitewash to me."

Hoffman was so suspicious that he wouldn't let Bender see his files on Teamsters corruption "until I see that he means business."

George Bender, a beefy man noted mostly for song-leading at conventions, had the usual happy smile on his face when I called at his office a few hours after he was given the labor racket job. He was a pleasant political wheelhorse, and he had barely shaken my hand when he bellowed that he would "track down all leads on labor racketeering from Congressmen, labor leaders, businessmen or other citizens."

I interrupted his campaign oratory: "George, Clare Hoffman and others tell me this is going to be nothing but a whitewash."

Bender jumped to his feet in rage. "George Bender has never whitewashed anything in his life, and he isn't going to start now."

"I understand you have some Teamsters supporters," I said.

"Sure, I have all kinds of people who support me, but no one has any strings on me," he replied. "I don't know any racketeers, and I wouldn't know a racketeer if I met one."

I commented that he had seemed rather lukewarm toward an investigation of the juke-box rackets in Detroit when he had been on the subcommittee in 1953.

Bender objected: "I asked a good many questions that were mighty pointed, and put those fellows on the spot."

I replied that I hoped he would pardon my skepticism until the Minneapolis hearings were underway.

"I was quite a crusader a few years back," Bender said. "I know you fellows think I joke a lot, but I can conduct an investigation.

"I'm going to get a good staff, and I'm going to do a good job. The gentleman from Michigan (Hoffman) is burned up all the time. To hear him tell it, there are 19 crooks on the committee and he's the only honest man. If I don't do a good job, you tell me. And if you know any good investigators, let me have their names."

"I happen to know a couple of top investigators who are available now," I came back quietly. "They are former F.B.I. men, and they really know the business."

"Give me their names," Bender said. I named Downey Rice and Frank Plant.

"They've already investigated in Minneapolis for Tobey, so your hearings will be practically made," I told him.

Surprisingly, he hired Rice, Plant, Stan Fisher and George Martin. It began to look as though Bender meant business. Then Sam McConnell, the Pennsylvania Republican, started a jurisdictional feud. He said his Labor Committee was going to investigate rackets affecting union pension and welfare funds, and he objected to the Government Operations subcommittee's invading his territory.

Meanwhile, Hoffman sniped at Bender, and warned he was going to watch every move the subcommittee made.

"I've been kicked out of the driver's seat and onto the tailgate, but if the conveyance slows down I'll get out and give it a push," Hoffman threatened in a House speech.

Bender asked for a $100,000 appropriation, but from late January until March 29, 1954, the appropriation and jurisdiction were the subject of controversy. When it was finally unsnarled, Bender received only $55,000.

Even as witnesses were being subpoenaed in Minneapolis, the Democrats on Bender's subcommittee were working to block the investigation. Delay in clearing Bender's appropriation had already damaged the Minneapolis hearings. The power to subpoena witnesses and records became available to Rice and Plant at such a late date it lost much of its effectiveness. By the time subpoenas were issued, important witnesses had fled, and records had disappeared or were unavailable.

Jerry Connelly seemed to have vanished. He was a key figure in the shakedowns, blackmail picketing, dictatorial practices and misuse of funds. Rice and Plant were furious.

The U. S. Marshal in Illinois couldn't find Eugene C. (Jimmy) James, the secretary-treasurer of the International

Laundry Workers union. James was wanted for questioning with regard to a $5,625 check from Minneapolis Laundry Workers Local 183 to Teamsters boss Sid Brennan. Rice had learned that this check, signed by E. C. James, was used by Brennan on March 19, 1952, to make up part of a $17,000 payment on an alleged federal income tax deficiency.

James had been in Des Moines in March, 1954, to try to grab personal control of Des Moines Laundry Workers Local 104. Only a few months earlier, James had claimed a heart condition and escaped testifying in Detroit in November, 1953. He was a mighty active heart patient by March, throwing his weight around in Des Moines, talking tough, and threatening to take over Local 104.

I pushed the James investigation with Rice and Plant. I pointed out he had never been questioned about his activities in Florida during the violent period in 1951. He had evaded Hoffman's investigators. Rice and Plant agreed James was a key figure. He illustrated the linkage between some of the corrupt elements in the Teamsters and the Laundry Workers union. Jerry Connelly demonstrated how a transient labor hoodlum could bounce from Dorfman's Waste Handlers union to the Laundry Workers union, to the Building Service Employees union, and over into the Teamsters.

What were the factors that made this possible? Were other unions so fearful of the Teamsters that they would make room for such characters as Connelly? Was there an actual nationwide network of mobsters who could influence and manipulate the Teamsters union and those small unions that seemed to have become satellites of the Teamsters? These were questions that needed to be answered.

The courtroom on the third floor of the Federal Courthouse in Minneapolis was packed when the hearings opened at 10 a.m. April 9, 1954. Almost immediately there was a move to kill or restrict the hearings.

Tony Schullo, the round-bellied and somewhat bald secretary of Teamsters Local 638, was called as the first union witness. There already had been testimony by two employers that they had made cash payoffs to him. One employer testified he paid

Schullo $150 a month and usually slipped him the cash while seated in a parked car.[3]

A battery of lawyers objected to any questioning of Schullo on grounds that the committee didn't have jurisdiction. The Democrats supported this line of argument.

"I would like to make a point of order that the committee does lack jurisdiction," Representative Frank Karsten (Dem., Mo.) said. He was backed by Representatives William Dawson (Dem., Ill.) and Robert Mollohan (Dem., W. Va.).

I knew that Chairman Bender would rule against Karsten, but I was worried about the committee vote. Bender, Representative Frank C. Osmers, Jr. (Rep., N. J.), and Representative Jeffrey P. Hillelson (Dem., Mo.) would vote to uphold the committee's right to question Schullo and other union leaders.

Representative Hoffman was the question mark. He was irked because Bender had been given the chairmanship, and he had refused to say whether he would support Bender on a vote. I hoped he wouldn't be spiteful, and I told him it was important that the hearing continue.

Hoffman took the step nobody could have anticipated. He simply abstained from voting and then explained to Bender that, in so doing, he had upheld Bender's decision, since a tie meant that the chairman's ruling was sustained. The hearing continued.

Time was limited, so Rice moved swiftly through the list of witnesses. He paid little attention to the constant sniping by two of the Democratic Congressmen who were opposed to the hearings.

Tony Schullo took the Fifth Amendment, refusing to testify on grounds that he might incriminate himself. He refused to talk about his arrest on January 8, 1944, in the company of safecracker Rocky Lupino, when Lupino was picked up on a federal charge of selling whisky to Elks and Moose lodges in Iowa.[4]

Schullo took the Fifth Amendent again when he was asked

---

[3]"Investigation of Racketeering in the Minneapolis, Minn., Area," hearings before subcommittee of the Committee on Government Operations, House of Representatives, 83d Congress, 2d session, April 9 and 10, 1954, pages 1 to 36.

[4]"Investigation of Racketeering in the Minneapolis, Minn., Area," hearings before the subcommittee of the Committee on Government Operations, House of Representatives, 83d Congress, 2d session, April 9 and 10, 1954, page 64.

about his relations with Lew (Luigi Fratto) Farrell, former
Des Moines beer distributor and gambling figure.

"Did you ever have any transactions with anyone respecting
an attempt to obtain a parole for (burglar) Mitchell Schwartz?"
Rice asked.

"I respectfully refuse to answer," Schullo said.

"The facts or the allegation which we have on good authority is that Schullo told a lawyer in this town that $800 was paid
to Sidney Brennan in an effort to fix a parole for Mitchell
Schwartz," Rice said.

"I respectfully refuse to answer," Schullo intoned.[5]

Louis Block, the "acting president" of Connelly's Teamsters
Local 548, testified about the mysterious and highly unusual
way Connelly ran a union local. Block was as disturbed as the
committee about Connelly's disappearance, because Connelly
had taken the union's money and Block hadn't been paid for
three weeks.

Block explained that Connelly had never held an election
in the union, but merely appointed Block as "acting president."

Connelly made him sign checks "in blank" on the union
funds, and spent the money without consulting him, Block testified. When Block tried to find out how the money was being
spent, Connelly said it was none of his business. When Block
asked for an election in Local 548, Connelly warned him that if
he tried to get an election he would be kicked out of the union.[6]

Sid Brennan and Gene·Williams took the Fifth Amendment
on a long series of questions dealing with their personal finances
and union activity.

Williams said he might incriminate himself if he testified
about $89,000, part of which he received as "loans" from various
employers and the rest indirectly through such underworld
sources as Isadore (Kid Cann) Blumenfeld. Committee counsel
Arthur Toll identified Blumenfeld as having received a $16,500
payoff to settle a Teamsters strike at a bakery in Minneapolis.

A letter from John Lisowski, president of the Teamsters

[5]"Investigation of Racketeering in the Minneapolis, Minn., Area," hearings, page 69.

[6]"Investigation of Racketeering in the Minneapolis, Minn., Area," hearings, page 97.

local at Virginia, Minnesota, was put in the record by Rice. The letter stated that Sid Brennan had told Lisowski that if union members on the Iron Range didn't stay in line "they would load up a couple of carloads, take baseball bats and go up on the Range and bat their ears off of them."[7]

Brennan took the Fifth Amendment.

Rice produced an Internal Revenue Service report that stated Brennan had made considerable money buying and selling automobiles during 1946 and 1947 when cars were hard to get, and had failed to report the profit on his federal tax return.

"Most of Brennan's automobile purchases were made from or through operators of fleets of trucks who were in no position to resist his demands that they sell him cars which they could purchase through their fleet contracts," Internal Revenue agents stated.[8]

The report said that, in addition to the tax angle, there was a possible black market violation.

"In most instances Brennan was able to sell or trade these cars a short time after purchase at a substantial profit," the report said.

Brennan took the Fifth Amendment.

Jack (Skimbo) Sabes, operator of American Food and Produce Company, testified he made $3,000 "loans" to Brennan and Williams in the spring of 1949 so they could buy Cadillacs. Sabes had been having trouble on his Teamsters contract at the time.[9]

The Teamsters officials took the Fifth Amendment on these transactions.

Brennan took the Fifth Amendment on questions relating to his financial transaction with Red Truck Line, operated by his friend, James E. McNelis.[10]

Rice produced the records showing that Brennan received

[7]"Investigation of Racketeering in the Minneapolis, Minn., Area," hearings, page 253.

[8]"Investigation of Racketeering in the Minneapolis, Minn., Area," hearings, page 241.

[9]"Investigation of Racketeering in the Minneapolis, Minn., Area," hearings, pages 167-172.

[10]"Investigation of Racketeering in the Minneapolis, Minn., Area," hearings, page 249.

$750 from Nate Shefferman's Labor Relations Associates in Chicago in June 1952. He asked why an employer's representative would be paying such a sum to a Teamsters official.[11]

Rice produced the $5,000 check made out to Brennan against the funds of the Laundry Workers Local 183, and signed by Jimmy James. Why was James giving Laundry union funds to Brennan, who used them to pay a federal income tax deficiency?[12]

Again Brennan claimed that to answer might incriminate him.

Chairman Bender allowed Rice a free rein, but was incapable of giving him forceful backing. There was tension, and sharp and sarcastic words were aimed at Rice by Karsten and Mollohan. Occasionally Rice bristled, but he held his temper.

Karsten and Mollohan charged Rice was disrespectful to them. Rice would not back down, so the pressure was put on to force his resignation. Rice was a casualty of those hearings. The attacks of Karsten and Mollohan crippled his usefulness, and finally, a few weeks later, forced him to resign. Plant quit, too.

It was painful to see two excellent investigators forced out because of their aggressive work against labor racketeers, while political hacks who played footsie with labor still had jobs on Capitol Hill.

Rice and Plant were not run-of-the-mill men. In two days of hearings they uncovered enough to allow United States District Attorney George MacKinnon to call a special federal grand jury to investigate labor rackets.

MacKinnon took the hearing transcript, plus leads from Rice and Plant, and went to work. Eventually he was able to convict Brennan, Williams, Connelly and Jack Jorgenson, who was president of Teamsters Joint Council 32 and a political wheel.

MacKinnon, a former Congressman, was a member of the House Labor Committee at the time the Taft-Hartley law was passed. He acted under these provisions of the Taft-Hartley law:

---

[11]"Investigation of Racketeering in the Minneapolis, Minn., Area," hearings, page 235.

[12]"Investigation of Racketeering in the Minneapolis, Minn., Area," hearings, page 235.

"It shall be unlawful for any employer to pay or deliver, or agree to pay or deliver, any money or other thing of value to any representative of any of his employees who are employed in an industry affecting commerce.

"It shall be unlawful for any representative of any employees who are employed in an industry affecting commerce to receive or accept, or agree to receive or accept, from the employer of such employees any money or other thing of value."

The Bender subcommittee hearings in Minneapolis put a spotlight on Shefferman and that questionable $750 payment to Brennan. A finger had also been pointed in the direction of the Laundry Workers International union and Jimmy James. In neither case did the record indicate the tremendous scope of their operations.

I wrote a letter to Bender, thanking him for exposing the Minneapolis Teamsters. I admitted that I had not been very optimistic when I called on him in January.

Gideon Seymour told me he hoped the hearings would force Dave Beck to oust Brennan, Williams and Connelly.

Gid had recovered in part from the December heart attack, and had returned to his *Minneapolis Star* and *Tribune* office during the hearings, as enthusiastic as a school boy. This was a vital crusade against labor rackets, and Gid was proud of the part he played in starting it.

He arranged for expanding the newspaper to run more than 50,000 words of an edited transcript of the hearings. He was up early the Sunday following the hearings and met me at the office to go over an editorial lambasting the Teamsters.

He invited me to his home that Sunday evening, and insisted I stay after dinner to talk. He wanted to talk labor rackets, and to reminisce about his years as a reporter and his work in Des Moines, Chicago, New York, London and Buenos Aires. There had been nothing in his career that had fascinated him more than the labor racket drama that was beginning to unfold. Gid had a moderately liberal viewpoint, but now he was worried about labor's power.

The government could not shut down the operations of the *Minneapolis Star* and *Tribune,* but a few arbitrary Teamsters officials could. The same was true of almost every business.

Gid said that when such power was lodged in the hands of corrupt men it was perilous for the nation.

Part of the time, Gid talked enthusiastically about plans for the future of the labor investigations—what I should do, and how he thought we should handle it. At other times, he talked of the past with the care for detail of a man who wants certain facts straightened out for the record. A few weeks later he died of a heart attack.

IX

Double Trouble for Beck: Taxes and Hoffa

"Beck is a crook, but nobody has been able to prove it." Ed Guthman stated it emphatically.

Guthman, who won a Pulitzer prize in 1950 as a reporter for the *Seattle Times,* had seen Beck grow from a local union bully in Seattle to the point where he was applauded as a great citizen. But although Guthman was as fascinated as I by the Teamsters, he had reluctantly concluded that Beck had too many political connections that would prevent him from getting what he deserved.

I met Guthman at a reunion of Nieman Fellows at Harvard University in June, 1954. Our mutual interest in Beck and the Teamsters drew us together. In February, *The Wall Street Journal* had done its characteristically thorough job of running down most of Beck's business holdings that appeared on the public record. The *Journal* had pointed up other facts which indicated a strong possibility of a "conflict of interest" in some of these transactions, but dealt with these in an extremely cautious manner. Guthman was able to fill me in on the background of a few business figures in Seattle, and explain why their links with Beck did not represent the best arms-length dealings between management and labor. The associations he described were certainly unethical, but we agreed they were probably not illegal.

Guthman told me how Teamsters goon squads had rampaged in the Seattle area in years past, but he said Beck had never been tied to the illegal activity in such a way that criminal action was possible. He classed Beck as "a physical coward," and explained that the real union organizing was done by Frank Brewster, while Beck stayed in an office to keep his fat face out of range of possible blows.

Brewster, who followed Beck as chairman of the Western Conference of Teamsters, was a pleasant, two-fisted, professional Teamster. He was a handsome and muscular man, with gray hair, blue eyes and an air of physical power, Guthman told me.

Frank Brewster had engaged in brawls, he ran a string of race horses, and he wasn't too careful about the way he used union funds.[1] Brewster led a gay life on the night club circuit. He had been married and divorced three times. He had served two terms on the Washington State Racing Commission. He had no desire to follow in Beck's steps as exalted ruler of the Elks, or as president of the board of regents of the University of Washington. Brewster got along with businessmen, but he did not glory in hobnobbing with businessmen and industrialists as Beck did.

I filled Guthman in on the activities of Brennan, Connelly, Williams, and Jimmy Hoffa. Most of the stories about Teamsters scandals were treated as local news. They rarely were printed outside the specific area where a labor leader had jurisdiction. It just hadn't been apparent to many editors that what they were seeing was not simply a local story, but clear evidence of a national scandal.

Guthman and I agreed to a pattern of mutual cooperation which was to pay big dividends later. We were wrong on one point. We believed Beck's dishonesty had been confined to earlier years, and that he had probably been scrupulously honest since becoming wealthy.

Even as Guthman and I discussed Beck, the Teamsters boss was facing a big problem. He had refused to talk to the tax investigator in March. Following his refusal to talk to federal tax agents Beck became frightened and tried to untangle the skeins of his financial maneuvers. He had to treat his unre-

---

[1]McClellan committee, Interim Report, No. 1417, pages 58, 59 and 60.

ported income as "loans" from the Teamsters or risk a federal income tax evasion indictment.

By June, he concluded he owed the Teamsters a whale of a lot of money and must pay it back to avoid federal tax troubles. He didn't know how much he had taken from the Teamsters, but his accountants made a rapid calculation that $200,000 should wipe the slate clean. Where could he get a quick $200,000?

Beck pressured businessmen who had borrowed from the Teamsters. In late 1953, he had arranged to loan $1.5 million from the Teamsters treasury to help Roy Fruehauf of Detroit in a fight to retain control of Fruehauf Trailer Company. Fruehauf said he couldn't spare the cash in the middle of a proxy fight, but arranged for Beck to borrow $200,000 from a North Carolina trucking firm, the Brown Equipment Company. It was only a temporary solution, but Beck grabbed at the chance to get the money back to the Teamsters treasury.[2]

He was not sure his support of the Republican administration was adequate to risk a federal tax rap.

Meanwhile, there were few signs that any of the three subcommittees with authority to investigate labor rackets would burrow deeply into the Teamsters mess.

Chairman McConnell of the House Labor subcommittee was keeping his small staff tied down to some dull statistical studies of union pension and welfare plans.

Bender's strife-torn subcommittee was making a few passes at the Ohio Teamsters, but I didn't expect much, now that Downey Rice and Frank Plant were gone. Without them Bender was mostly bellow and bluff. Newspaper pressure for action might produce a few hearings in the Cleveland area because Bender was the Republican candidate for the U. S. Senate. Chairman Bender could gain publicity by going into Cleveland for a few days of hearings on Louis N. (Babe) Triscaro, a convicted robber who was president of the Excavating and Building Materials Teamsters Local 436 there.[3]

When Plant left the Bender subcommittee he immediately joined the staff of a Senate Labor subcommittee headed by

---

[2]McClellan committee, Interim Report, No. 1417, pages 85 and 86.

[3]"Investigation of Racketeering in the Cleveland, Ohio, Area," report of the special anti-racketeering subcommittee, 1955, page 17.

Senator Irving M. Ives, the liberal New York Republican. Plant was chief investigator, and another ex-F.B.I. agent, William Leece, was chief counsel.

Leece and Plant made a strong team, and though Senator Ives was giving them a free rein, it looked as though they were starting too late to get into hearings before 1955.

"Don't forget Jimmy James," I said to Plant when I dropped over to the Ives subcommittee offices in the H.O.L.C. Building on Indiana Avenue.

"Can't you forget about Jimmy James?" Plant said with a smile. "Don't you think these committees have something to do besides run down characters that happened to go through Des Moines or Minneapolis?"

I told him that as far as I was concerned Des Moines and Minneapolis had priority, but that Jimmy James would also be a good story for Chicago, Detroit and Miami.

"Well, don't worry about it," Plant said. "A lot of work is being done on Mr. James, and he's bigger than you would have suspected."

Leece and Plant were working with an able staff: William H. Coburn, Robert Dunne, Blake Turner, Fred Suss, Duncan MacIntyre, Arthur Kuhl, Louis Solomon and Joseph Zisman.

The multi-million-dollar health and welfare fund of the Laundry Workers International union was a major project. They were also combing the affairs of Angelo Inciso, president of Chicago Local 286 of the U.A.W.-A.F.L., and Edward J. Gallagher, president of Painters, Cleaners & Caulkers union Local 52 in Chicago.[4]

Leece had made only a casual check on the Teamsters for some statistical reports, but this first contact he had had with them infuriated him. He called at the International Teamsters headquarters for help on some routine studies, and got the cold shoulder from Einar Mohn, Beck's executive assistant.

"He wasn't even civil," Leece told me. "I wonder what they are hiding over there."

The Ives subcommittee, however, had its area staked out in

---

[4] "Welfare and Pension Plans Investigation," Interim Report, 1955, of subcommittee on welfare and pension funds of the Senate Committee on Labor and Public Welfare, pages 24 and 43.

other unions. It paid little attention to the Teamsters. The assumption was that any investigating of the Brotherhood that needed to be done would be handled by Bender or McConnell.

In August, 1954, there were signs that even Chairman McConnell might finally get around to a real investigation. McConnell hired Carmine Bellino, former head of the accounting division of the F.B.I. Bellino was teamed with chief counsel Edward McCabe of the House Labor Committee. The staff was small, but Bellino and McCabe were enthusiastic.

They got their teeth into scandals in the operations of the Sheet Metal Workers International Association. The murder of Jim Hartley, a business agent in Las Vegas, had dramatized the struggle for control of this union's health and welfare funds in the western area that included California, Nevada and Arizona.

Even the club-carrying goon squad of Sheet Metal Workers Local 108 in Los Angeles didn't keep investigator Thomas Mulherin from invading the headquarters, with police help, to serve a subpoena and grab records.

Bellino and McCabe pinned down the story of how a Washington attorney, Arthur A. Peisner, made payments of $45,000 to two officials of the International Hod Carriers, Building and Common Laborers Union. There was testimony the money went to two relatives of Joseph V. Moreschi, president of the union, for using their influence in getting union insurance for a firm operated by Peisner. The money was paid to Faust Moreschi, 35-year-old son of Joseph Moreschi, and Leo Nazdin, who was president of the Laborers district council in Washington.

Testimony from Archie Moore, a former official of Local 368 of the Brotherhood of Painters, Decorators and Paperhangers of America, concerned payoffs from painting contractors. Moore, then 41, testified he shared $6,880 in payoffs with Robert Lowery, secretary-treasurer of District Council 51 of the Painters union.

Moore testified he kept records of the payoffs as part of a plan to prove Lowery was dishonest. When he was sure he had enough evidence, Moore said, he told about the payoffs at a union meeting. The only result was that he was kicked out of the union and Lowery remained in power.

None of these hearings had national impact, but the testimony disclosed that the pattern in the Teamsters union could be found in the Sheet Metal Workers, the Painters, and the Hod Carriers.

The fact that little was being done to clean up these problems demonstrated there was inherent weakness or dishonesty in the top offices of these unions.

In late September, 1954, Bellino uncovered the first bits of evidence that there were scandals buried in Dave Beck's own eleven-state Western Conference of Teamsters.

Beck and Frank Brewster were largely responsible for placing the welfare insurance for the Western Conference of Teamsters. The records showed that the insurance, with premiums in excess of six million dollars a year, went to the Union Group Insurance Company, operated by George C. Newell, a Seattle friend of Beck and Brewster.

To pin down the facts, it was necessary to subpoena Beck, Brewster, or Newell, or all three.

Newell claimed a heart condition made it impossible for him to testify. In the four-day hearing that started September 22, neither Brewster nor Beck was called, and the possibility of getting into this big insurance operation was lost.

Even though Chairman McConnell failed to subpoena Beck and Brewster, Bellino and Mulherin were able to show evidence of what another committee called a "conflict of interest."[5]

Brewster, the flashy, big-spending habitué of race tracks, was in the horse-racing business with insurance man Newell. Indications were that Brewster put little into the enterprise, but took out a good deal more than Newell. If Newell wasn't making payments to Brewster, then he was an amazingly charitable man.

Instead of criticizing the Teamsters and immediately digging into the Western Conference affairs, Chairman McConnell said there were some unanswered questions he hoped to get to later. Instead of castigating the Teamsters, he praised the fine operation of the welfare program.

---

[5]McClellan committee, Report No. 1417, page 40.

At the same time that McConnell was conducting hearings in Los Angeles, Dave Beck and A.F.L. President George Meany were having their first clashes over the way organized labor should react to evidence of improper use of union funds.

The national A.F.L. convention was in progress, also in Los Angeles, and Meany rose on September 27, 1954, to express his concern about evidence of misuse of union health and welfare and pension funds.

"This is sacred money that belongs to our members," the rough-voiced and bald A.F.L. president declared. He said he believed union labor should back a program of new laws to guard the whopping two billion dollars that had accumulated in the welfare funds.

In a stern voice he told the delegates that he believed organized labor should cooperate with any duly constituted investigating body that was trying to do a good job.

Beck was flushed with anger as he stood up to object. In a fiery speech, the pompous little Teamsters boss declared he would take no action against any official of the mighty Teamsters union until the man had actually been tried in court and convicted.

For thirty minutes, Beck boomed out his criticism of Congressional committees, and urged the A.F.L. to "defend the men and women of labor until they have their day in court."

Few, if any, in the great convention hall knew that Dave Beck was pleading for himself. Beck didn't talk about his tax troubles or his other dishonesty. He had been able to fool most of the people most of the time. What the public didn't know, didn't hurt him, Beck reasoned.

It was appearances that counted with Beck. That was one lesson the former poor boy from Seattle had learned since he climbed off a laundry wagon to get into the union organizing business.

Even his closest associates had no real knowledge of the broad scope of Beck's misappropriation of union funds and misuse of union power. Shefferman knew about some of the transactions, but that was a small part of the big financial game Beck was playing. One lawyer knew a little, an accountant had another piece of the puzzle, and a real estate man or banker might have other pieces. Only Beck knew the full extent of his villainy.

Dave Beck was compromising with corruption. That was apparent to me in the fall of 1954, even though Beck continued to maintain a façade of respectability.

He had done nothing to stop the ruthless operations of Hoffa. No steps had been taken to oust Brennan, Williams, or Connelly in Minneapolis. Ring was still the boss Teamster in Kansas City. I assumed that Beck was merely defending his lack of action in these cases because he didn't have the courage, or the political power, to move on Hoffa.

A federal grand jury in Minneapolis had indicted Connelly on September 18 on a charge of "mishandling" $4,021.25 paid to him for union health and welfare purposes. Also indicted were two unions—Teamsters Local 548 and the defunct Building Employees Local 194—that Connelly had operated briefly.[6]

The report of the grand jury indicated there would be some further indictments involving Brennan and other Teamsters. Beck felt that he needed Brennan, particularly since Hoffa was throwing his weight around in the South and even in New York.

As far as Beck was concerned, he would just as soon have fired Connelly. But Connelly was a friend of Hoffa, who had already warned Beck not to meddle with him or his personal friends in the Central Conference of Teamsters.

Hoffa was defending the crooked Teamsters in Minneapolis, Chicago, St. Louis, Kansas City, and Detroit. There wasn't a thing that Beck could do about it, and he knew that some newspaper reporters were hinting in their stories that Hoffa had as much to do with running the International Brotherhood of Teamsters as did Beck. Beck knew it was true, but it hurt his pride to have it said in spite of all the money he had spent on public relations.

In mid-October, John Herling, syndicated labor columnist, wrote flatly that Dave Beck was merely "the front" and that Hoffa was the real boss of the Teamsters.

---

[6]*Minneapolis Star*, September 18, 1954, page 1. See also McClellan committee, Report No. 1417, pages 239-240.

"It is an unmitigated and willful lie," Beck stormed to reporters, who knew Herling was right.

"Hoffa hasn't anything to do with running the Teamsters union other than in his capacity of tenth vice-president in charge of the Midwest," Beck said.

There was a smile of amusement on Jimmy Hoffa's face as he talked with reporters at the Statler Hotel in Washington and denied he pulled the strings that make Dave Beck jump.

The prepared statement distributed to the press said there was no friction between Hoffa and Beck, and that Hoffa was merely one of many vice presidents.

The public relations statement charged that stories of Hoffa's dominance consisted of "rumors planted by employers in an attempt to weaken the New York truck strike."

"This diversionary movement by these selfish and short-sighted employers has failed because more than 8,000 of the 12,000 truck drivers in New York City have already signed, and employers are standing in line to approve contracts," the statement read.

The statement said the rumors of Hoffa's domination centered around the appointment of John J. O'Rourke, chairman of the Teamsters bargaining committee in New York. It had been reported that O'Rourke was a "Hoffa man" and that the appointment had been forced on Beck.

"If you are only another vice-president, why have you been in New York working on the strike, and why are you putting out the Teamsters line on this?" I asked.

"I just want to keep up on how things are going all over the country," Hoffa said with a wink. "I'm one hundred per cent behind Beck. If there was an election tomorrow, I would be the first to jump up to the mike and nominate him."

Reporters pointed out that his eagerness to nominate Beck would not necessarily be an indication that he wasn't running Beck, and might even be interpreted as meaning he was still willing to let Beck wear the title.

Hoffa smiled. He disregarded the caution from Beck's press secretary to "stick to the prepared statement" and quipped:

"For the record, you can say that I'm just a vice-president."

There was no doubt in the minds of the reporters that

Jimmy Hoffa didn't really care what Beck thought. He was willing to mouth the words Beck's press agent had prepared, but Hoffa was as big as Beck, and certainly wasn't afraid of him.

It was also clear that Hoffa had been able to work through John O'Rourke, labor racketeer Johnny Dioguardi, and a variety of underworld contacts to establish a position of firm conttol over some segments of the Teamsters in the New York City area.

The investigations in Detroit in 1953 hadn't frightened Hoffa in the slightest. He was pouring out union money for attorneys to defend crooked Teamsters in Michigan, and he was prepared to continue their union salaries even if they were convicted and sent to jail for selling out union members.[7]

It was hard for me to understand how Hoffa could continue at the same reckless pace more than a year after so many of his activities had been exposed by the House Labor subcommittee in June and November, 1953. It was hard to understand how public officials from the Detroit area, among them judges and prosecutors, could continue to accept big political contributions from such a man.

Jimmy's boyish smile was disarming, but anyone in political life in Michigan should have been aware of the Hoffa pattern. Detroit papers had headlined the bombings and other terror-tactics connected with the convictions of Hoffa, Owen Bert Brennan, boss of Detroit Teamsters Local 337, and some of their lieutenants in 1942 and 1946.

Court records of Wayne County, Michigan, showed testimony in 1945 by Herbert Crimp, then a vice-president of Teamsters Local 247. Crimp had given evidence that displeased Hoffa, and as he left the hearing room, Hoffa shouldered up to him in the hall of the Wayne County courthouse.

"You . . . ., I'll have you killed," Hoffa snapped. "What's the idea? Do you want to make your own testimony?"

There were witnesses to the event, but it was with reluctance that Crimp and other witnesses testified of the threat by Hoffa. Crimp said that after Hoffa threatened him, the little Teamsters boss had pulled him aside and said: "Oh skip it. We're all under tension and get hot."

The fact that Hoffa would make a serious threat only

---

[7]McClellan committee, Interim Report, No. 1417, pages 227, 238 and 239.

because he was angry was not enough assurance for Michigan authorities or Crimp. The Michigan state police were alerted on September 27, 1945, to provide protection for Crimp, his wife, and his two children. Two days later, the grand jury asked that 12 Detroit detectives be assigned to guard witnesses in the labor racket investigation.

I knew Jimmy's background, and I knew that Crimp's case was only one of many in which witnesses were threatened or coerced. It was frightening for me to think of what Hoffa's control of all truck transportation would mean.

I knew that any Michigan politician who did business with Hoffa in the fall of 1954 was either actively corrupt, or too naive for the responsibility of public office.

X

Tax Tangle and Teamsters' Tentacles

While Dave Beck struggled to straighten out his federal tax problem, Jimmy Hoffa took command. He used his underworld friends and the corrupt tentacles of the mighty Teamsters union to join forces with the corrupt and the corruptible in business and in other unions. The Laundry Workers International Union, the International Longshoremen's Association, the United Automobile Workers-A.F.L., and some sections of the Building Service Employees Union appeared as little more than satellites of the Teamsters.

In January, 1955, Dave Beck's accountants completed 700 hours of work on the Teamsters financial records, and they had bad news. Beck would have to repay at least another $50,000 to make good his story that he had merely been "borrowing" from union funds.

Beck wiped a pudgy, freckled hand across his brow and back over his bald head. He was worried. He tried to act like the confident and prosperous ruler of a labor kingdom, but it was difficult.

The $200,000 he had borrowed a few months earlier was due, and the trucking firm executives were pressing for payment. He hadn't expected them to be so insistent. Altogether, he needed $250,000 in cash. He might be able to sell some of his assets and raise $100,000 or so, but that other $150,000 was going to be hard to find.

Other developments complicated Beck's financial problems. George Meany was crusading against the theft and misuse of union funds and welfare funds, and had maneuvered the A.F.L. executive council into supporting him on certain minimum ethical standards.

Beck was beginning to hate Meany. Talk of ousting officials who took union funds could be embarrassing. And Beck didn't like Hoffa any better, although there wasn't much choice except to put up with him. Hoffa and his gangster friends were cavorting so recklessly in New York that the New York Anti-Crime Committee was demanding action.

Spruille Braden, chairman of the Anti-Crime Committee, charged in a February 8, 1955, report:

"In a recent city-wide trucking strike in New York, the accepted spokesman of the trucking union in this community was replaced by order of James R. Hoffa. . . . Hoffa put in as spokesman a man who has been a life-long associate of the worst gangsters in this city. . . . He (Hoffa) is a friend and associate of several major figures in the ranks of gangsterdom. His activities, though well publicized, had not as yet developed in Dave Beck any visible will to take vigorous and forthright action."

On February 18, a federal grand jury in Minneapolis indicted Sid Brennan, Jerry Connelly, Gene Williams, and Jack Jorgenson on charges of taking $5,000 from an employer in violation of the Taft-Hartley law.

Beck was so tied up with his own problems by mid-March that he ceased to care so much about appearances. When Connelly entered a plea of guilty to another federal charge of illegally taking $4,021 from some Twin City employers, Beck stalled. He had said he wouldn't convict a man before the courts did, but now he was in the position of refusing to act even after Connelly had pleaded guilty.

To those of us who were unaware of Beck's desperate financial problems, a few indictments were small consolation. The Democrats had taken control of Congress, and there had been no follow-through on Teamsters investigations.

It was a Congress that would react only to public pressure,

102584 EMORY AND HENRY LIBRARY

and the nation's press had not told the full story. The fragments that had been told were passed off as isolated instances. Public sympathy was still on the side of labor. The scandals were considered insignificant; the indications of widespread thievery of union funds were ignored. Well-meaning liberals denied the fact that big labor was more powerful, and consequently could be more corrupt, than big business.

The Republican performance had been spotty. The few who showed any courage were crippled by a Republican leadership that was weak-kneed and gutless. The Democrats were worse. They hadn't bothered to initiate any real labor racket investigations.

One investigation started in 1954 did continue. The Senate Labor subcommittee headed by Senator Ives, of New York, was allowed to continue functioning under a Democratic chairman, Senator Paul Douglas of Illinois.

Senator Douglas, a former University of Chicago economics professor, was addicted to panel discussions by the so-called "experts" in the field. That was the way he opened his hearings in February, 1955, and I was fearful he would become bogged down in dull discussions of theory.

The tall, shaggy-haired Illinois Senator had been critical of investigating excesses, and it was with some misgivings that he finally started to look into scandals in the Laundry Workers International Union, Local 286 of the U.A.W.-A.F.L. and Local 52 of the Painters, Cleaners and Caulkers Union. Added to Douglas's inherent distaste for a racket inquiry was the fact that all three of the major investigations involved union officials who operated from the Chicago area.

Ed Gallagher, president of Local 52, ran the fanciest vanishing union welfare fund the members of the Douglas subcommittee had seen. A 7½-cent-per-hour levy on employers yielded the Painters, Cleaners and Caulkers welfare fund $215,752 in four years. At the end of the period, the fund had shriveled to $7,339. There was hardly a scrap of documentary evidence to show that union members had received any benefits from it.[1]

Gallagher cashed checks drawn against the fund in spots

---

[1]Douglas, "Welfare and Pension Plans Investigation," Interim Report, 84th Congress, 1st session, 1955, pages 43-51.

ranging from a Chicago bar and grill to a Florida motel. The endorsements on the checks seemed to indicate transactions far from the realm of hospitals and clinics. There was a $1,166 repair bill for Gallagher's new Cadillac; a $347.07 check to an airline for tickets to Miami; a $1,700 payment on a Chrysler for another union official.[2]

Gallagher said that one $500 check, cashed by a furrier, was a ten-week disability payment to a union member who used it to buy something for a "sweetheart" or "whatever you might call it."

The Chicago labor leader admitted he didn't have much evidence of what happened to the $200,000, but he insisted he paid out the cash in "welfares" to members for sickness, births, funerals, and in some cases to get the beneficiaries out of jail.

Even Gallagher's lawyer, Nathan Cohen, conceded that the Senators might term Gallagher's method: "How Not to Operate a Welfare Fund."

Senator Gordon Allott, a Colorado Republican, was shocked at the picture of Gallagher, sitting in an office, his hands full of cash, making arbitrary decisions as to who would get welfare payments, and how much.

"And there is no appeal to any person from your decision as to how funds shall be spent?" Senator Allott asked.

"No, sir," said Gallagher.

Chairman Douglas and members of the committee were unimpressed by Gallagher's protestations of virtue. They concluded "that a great portion of the welfare fund, and for that matter the other fund created by deductions from employees' wages, went to the benefit of Gallagher."[3]

Inquiries into the welfare funds of the Laundry Workers International Union disclosed an even bigger scandal. Sam J. Byers, president of the union, missed the hearings. He claimed he was ill, and presented a doctor's certificate.

Jimmy James, the handsome, well-tailored secretary-treasurer of the union, was there to be questioned about more than

[2]Douglas, "Welfare and Pension Plans Investigation," Interim Report, page 44.

[3]Douglas, "Welfare and Pension Plans Investigation," Interim Report, page 51.

$900,000 that had disappeared in four years from money collected to buy insurance for laundry workers.[4]

Chief counsel William Leece unwound the intricate system of financial juggling by which much of the money passed through the hands of Louis B. Saperstein, a Newark, N. J., insurance broker, and wound up in a bank account controlled by James.

In the fifteen years since he sold out his Detroit pool hall and became a labor organizer, James, a six-foot, 200-pounder, had bulled his way to the top of the 65,000-member Laundry Workers Union. In 1940, he started as a $40-a-week organizer for that union, without benefit of experience with a washing machine or a hot iron. He wasn't that kind of laundry worker.

Five years after the dawn of his career as a labor pro, James was drawing salaries from three unions. His Laundry Workers pay was $175 a week. He got $225 a week salary and $75 weekly expenses from the juke-box local he organized with Hoffa's help in Detroit. The Foundry Workers International, which he served as a vice president, paid him $50 a week for attending meetings.

James had claimed that a heart condition made it impossible for him to testify when the House Labor subcommittee in Detroit wanted to ask him about his association with Hoffa. He couldn't be found to be subpoenaed when the Bender subcommittee wanted to question him about his dealings with Sidney Brennan and Jerry Connelly, the Minneapolis Teamsters.

James had a Cadillac, a ten-room ranch house on a thirty-five-acre estate near Wheaton, Illinois, six horses in the corral, and a beautiful wardrobe with matching accessories. He attended a week-long session of the Douglas subcommittee, and wore a different ensemble every day.

But he was a picture of misery as he sat fidgeting in the front row of the old Supreme Court chamber in the Capitol, where the hearing was in progress.

I had been writing about Jimmy James for more than a year and knew all of his background that had ever appeared in public records, but I had never met him.

He was pleasant enough when I sat down beside him to

---

[4]Douglas, "Welfare and Pension Plans Investigation," Interim Report, page 25.

ask some routine questions about the evidence that was pouring into the record against him.

"I don't want to talk about it, fella," James said. "If I got anything to say, I'll say it when they get me over in that chair."

"I thought you might want to explain some of these things now," I said. "It will be at least a couple of days before you get a chance to tell your story."

"I'll wait," James said. "You reporters can't do much more to me than you've done already. Say, what was your name?"

I had been expecting that question, because I had intentionally garbled my name in introducing myself, but now I had to tell him.

"Mollenhoff, with Cowles Publications," I said.

James pushed back and exploded:

"You're the son of a bitch who has been beating me over the head with those stories in Des Moines and Minneapolis. What do ya do that for?"

"I'm a reporter," I answered.

"That doesn't mean ya gotta make it your business to give a guy a bad time," James said. "There are a lot of reporters, and most of them don't dig up all that dirty stuff about people."

"Weren't the stories accurate?" I asked.

"Where did you ever find all that stuff?" This time James' manner had a touch of admiration. "I didn't know anyone knew that much about me. I'd even forgotten some of it myself."

"I just rummaged around in a lot of old records and picked it up from affidavits and court cases," I explained.

"You had one thing wrong," James said. "I didn't have anything to do with that attempted murder down in Florida."

"The affidavits said you were paying the money to Dave Kay and Sol Isaacs (the men convicted of attempted murder), and I could only go by what is in the record under oath," I explained.

"That was something I didn't know about," James said, trying to con me.

"You were paying them, weren't you?" I asked. "You were down there at the time, and you did get out of the state when the investigation of the attempted murder started."

"I don't have to answer your questions." James became surly. "I'm not going to talk."

"Maybe the committee will ask you about it," I said.

"You can get my answers then," he snapped.

Chairman Douglas rejected my suggestion that James be questioned about things other than the welfare funds. He was unmoved by my argument that it was important to show the backgrounds, criminal records, and criminal associates of those who had gained control of the million-dollar health and welfare funds.

Senator Allott was more cooperative. He wanted all the facts I had, and he checked what he could with the subcommittee staff before James was questioned.

James took the Fifth Amendment two hundred and twenty-nine times at that hearing. The questions involved the money his juke-box local paid to Hoffa's wife, the financing of the attempted murder in Florida, and the $900,000 that was missing from the Laundry Workers' welfare funds.

"Is there any question that we can possibly ask you here, the answer to which will not incriminate you?" asked Senator Ives.

"I respectfully refuse to answer the question on the ground that the answer may tend to incriminate me," James answered.

I had been hopeful that the questions about Hoffa might lead the Douglas subcommittee into the Teamsters union. It didn't turn out that way.

In the meantime, while this sideline investigation was going on, Dave Beck had come up with a novel solution to his financial problem. With an assist from Nate Shefferman, Beck had arranged for the Teamsters executive board to buy his Seattle mansion from him for $163,215. This was the same home that he had built with money lifted out of the Teamsters union treasury. The sale included the provision that Beck could live in the house rent-free for life.[5]

Although the $163,215 check took care of his immediate financial problems, that persistent tax agent, Claude Watson, was pressing hard. The tax investigation now included both

---

[5]McClellan committee, Interim Report, No. 1417, page 68.

Beck and Brewster, and agents were demanding to see the Teamsters' books.

The union refused to turn them over to Watson. Two Seattle banks also refused to produce records demanded by the Internal Revenue Service. It looked as though court action would be necessary to get cooperation from those who had financial records involving Dave Beck.

It was a tough, hard fight for the tax agents. They knew they had to proceed with caution because Beck was a powerful man in Seattle, and in Washington, D. C. Even if the case was solid there could be some high officials in the Internal Revenue Service or Justice Department who would want to drop it. Some could be motivated by politics, but there could be as many who would simply be afraid to prosecute a big labor boss.

When word leaked out that his taxes were being investigated, Beck bluffed. He admitted there was an investigation, but pictured it as a small "technical" problem that any wealthy man of high finance might have. He beamed confidence in public.

Hoffa had become totally arrogant by mid-1955. Although some of his Teamsters pals in the Detroit and Pontiac, Michigan, area had been convicted, he had been able to save two of his favorites—William Bufalino[6] and Frank Fitzsimmons.[7] They were acquitted. Those who were convicted had their lawyers' fees paid out of union funds, and their salaries as union officials continued while they served jail terms on charges of selling out the union membership.

There had been a split between Sid Brennan and Jerry Connelly in Minneapolis. Brennan, with backing from Beck, ousted Connelly from his post as a business agent for Teamsters Local 548 in Minneapolis. Then, despite the fact that the whole Minneapolis Teamsters organization backed Brennan, Hoffa arranged to put the convicted labor racketeer back into office. Also, Hoffa blocked efforts of A.F.L. president George Meany to clean house in the International Brotherhood of Longshoremen (I.B.L.) in Detroit.

The reform-minded I. B. L. (set up to take over the juris-

---

[6]McClellan committee, Report No. 621, pages 89-93.

[7]McClellan committee, Report No. 1417, page 244.

diction of the racket-ridden International Longshoremen's Association) fired Zigmont (Ziggy) Snyder for corruption in the fall of 1955.

Ziggy Snyder, a convicted armed robber, took his members into Hoffa's own Teamsters Local 299. Ziggy became a business agent, working directly under Hoffa, and Teamsters goon squads went to the docks to protect Ziggy's corrupt union and its "sweetheart" contracts from encroachment by the I.B.L.[8]

Hoffa kept Ziggy on the union payroll until the McClellan committee, three years later, told the public about the sweat shop wages in the non-union businesses Snyder ran while functioning as one of Hoffa's business agents.

I had a lot of things to talk to Hoffa about when I called him at the Statler Hotel the night of November 5, 1955. He was busy at the time, but said he would be glad to see me the next morning at 8:30 in the lobby of the Mayflower.

Teamsters business agents and officers crowded the Mayflower lobby as I waited near the Connecticut Avenue entrance. Jimmy was fifteen minutes late. When he whipped in the door, the effect on Teamsters officials was electrifying. Everyone wanted to talk with the crown prince, and he loved it. He shook hands with them, called most of them by their first names, and thumped some of them on the shoulder with the good-natured roughness of truck drivers.

"Hi ya, poison pen," Jimmy greeted me. He didn't say it critically. It was said more in amusement that I could be naive enough to think my newspaper and magazine stories could stop Hoffa in Detroit.

When we were seated at a small table in the hotel coffee shop, Hoffa advised with a smile:

"Why don't you give it up? Nothing will come of it. We're the Teamsters."

Dave Beck had bet his reputation and career on his belief that labor's political power could kill any investigation of his union. Little Jimmy Hoffa didn't mind saying flatly that the Teamsters were bigger than the government.

I told Hoffa I wanted to talk with him about Jerry Con-

---

[8]McClellan committee, Interim Report No. 1417, pages 250 and 251.

nelly and find out why he was keeping him in office long after Connelly admitted misusing funds.

"I've looked over this case of Connelly's, and I don't think it is any more than a technical violation of the Taft-Hartley law," Hoffa said. "He collected some money on a pension plan, subject to some federal approval, and when the approval didn't come through he just used it as union money."

Connelly had used the money as he used other union funds, for the entertainment and enrichment of Jerry Connelly. It would have done no good to bring this up with Hoffa, so I didn't.

Hoffa revealed that he had personally advised Connelly to plead guilty.

"I advised him to cop a plea on that charge and get it over with," Hoffa explained. "I told him there was no need to make a production out of it in court and keep it in the papers for weeks. I figured it would give him a little trouble to start with, but I told him if he'd sweat it out it would soon be forgotten."

Hoffa declared that he certainly wouldn't want to start firing Teamsters officials for technical violations of the Taft-Hartley law.

"In the first place we don't consider it a good law," Hoffa said. "I'd say that ninety-nine per cent of the local labor leaders violate it, and most of them don't even know they are in violation."

"What about the membership opposition to Connelly going back on the payroll of Local 548?" I asked.

"I don't believe it," Hoffa answered. "It is just a couple of guys out there that don't want Connelly back in. Brennan is one of them, and it is strictly a personal matter."

Hoffa said he had been in Minneapolis, and had talked to some union members who had assured him they did want Connelly. He said he had known Connelly about twenty years, but denied that he had been responsible for moving Connelly into Minneapolis, first with the Building Service Employees and later with the Teamsters.

"That was a Sid Brennan move," Hoffa said. "Sid talked to me about it, and I told him that Connelly's mess down in

Florida might give them a bad time. Sid said he didn't think anyone would pay any attention to it."

Hoffa said he had advised Connelly "to run in Florida" when he was being sought on a charge of attempted murder.

"We advised him to get out fast," Hoffa said. "Jerry didn't shoot that guy in Florida. He was just unlucky, and got connected with a couple of screwballs who did the shooting."

"But won't reinstatement of Connelly damage the labor movement?" I asked.

"I have the philosophy that you never let a fellow down just because he is in a little trouble," Hoffa answered. "Connelly is one of our people. I try to take care of them."

"Where would I be today if people hadn't stuck with me?" Hoffa asked, not expecting an answer. "Jerry's case is like my own case. It was a technical violation, but it gives me a record. You gotta fight these things. You gotta sweat it out. You can't be running forever. If I had run out when I got indicted, where would I be today? I stick and I fight and the boys haven't let me down."

"Wouldn't it be better for the Minneapolis Teamsters if you moved Connelly to some other area, if you think it is necessary to keep him?" I asked.

"Jerry isn't as young as he used to be," Hoffa replied. "He had to run out of Florida. He can't keep on running forever. Sometime you gotta stand and fight. If he doesn't stay in Minneapolis, he'll have to move, and it isn't so easy to start again."

"But aren't you concerned about the public opinion of the Teamsters and the labor movement?" I asked. "Aren't you hurting labor when you keep a convicted labor leader like Connelly in a position of importance?"

"Who gives a damn what the public thinks as long as the union members think it's okay," Hoffa said. "The boys in Minneapolis are going to go along with us. I know, I've talked to a lot of them."

I said I was going to keep pointing up the Connelly case at every opportunity, and that I thought he and Beck should be taking some drastic action to get their house in order.

"Now looka here, Clark," Hoffa said. "They don't pay newspaper reporters enough for you to be giving me the bad time that you've been giving me. Everyone has his price. What's yours?"

He said it coolly and clearly, looking me straight in the eye. I was uncomfortable for a moment. I wondered if he thought I had been critical of the Teamsters to set up a payoff, or if this was just the normal method of "Hoffa, the direct actionist" that I had heard so much about.

My embarrassment gave way to amusement at the guts of this guy's throwing such a proposition at me. I hadn't said or done a thing to indicate anything but firm opposition to Teamsters corruption.

"You don't have enough money, Jimmy," I answered with a laugh. It seemed best to treat it as a joke. "Let's get on with the interview."

Hoffa grinned, shrugged with the "well-I-tried-anyway" attitude, and we resumed our discussion of Connelly, other union crooks, the power of unions, and Teamsters jurisdiction.

That was the month that Hoffa joined hands with a group of New York gangsters to set up seven phony Teamsters locals in New York. It was a move to grab control of Teamsters Joint Council 16, which had jurisdiction over the trucking industry in the New York City metropolitan area. The move was designed to create enough votes in the new local to install John O'Rourke, a Hoffa favorite, as chairman of Joint Council 16.

Hoffa's pal, Johnny Dioguardi, a convicted labor extortionist, was a key figure in the strategy. Also involved in the Hoffa-O'Rourke move was Anthony (Tony Ducks) Corallo, a labor racketeer with a narcotics conviction and a penitentiary term on his record.[9]

Dioguardi and Corallo had been officials of the U.A.W.-A.F.L., and had operated through as corrupt a group of organizers and officials as existed outside of Detroit and Chicago. There were convicted bootleggers like Joe Curcio, convicted thieves like George Atkins, convicted black market operators like Harry Reiss, convicted burglars like Harry (Little Gangy) Davidoff, convicted bookmakers and gamblers like Dominick Santa Maria, Arthur Santa Maria, and Sam Goldstein, and a large number of extortionists and thugs, including Charles

---

[9] McClellan committee, Report No. 1417, pages 162-173.

(Charley Duke) Kaminetsky, who served a term in Sing Sing for being an accessory to murder.[10]

While Hoffa was dealing with the Dioguardi and Corallo group in New York, the Douglas subcommittee exposed a Teamsters tie-up in Chicago with another U.A.W.-A.F.L. official, Angelo Inciso, president of Local 286.

Inciso, a convicted burglar and bootlegger, arrived at the hearing room with two armed body guards, who checked their guns at the Capitol door.

The union business as a racket was dangerous, but it was lucrative. From $350,000 to $400,000 poured into Inciso's union pool each year, and the 42-year-old labor baron used it as if it were his own. He went on a $3,400 tour of Europe, junketed to South America, Jamaica, Mexico, and Puerto Rico. He flitted back and forth to California, and stopped en route in a $45-a-day hotel suite in Las Vegas.[11]

Inciso hadn't kept very good records, but he said he believed he gave one $1,200 "gent's diamond ring" and another $1,100 "gent's diamond ring" to Edward Fenner, an official of an independent Teamsters union. The union had also paid $360 for a diamond studded money clip which Inciso said was given to John T. (Sandy) O'Brien, secretary-treasurer of Chicago Teamsters Local 710.

Why was Inciso dipping into U.A.W.-A.F.L. funds to buy such expensive gifts for Teamsters officials?

"When you are on strike, it is wonderful to have friends who will . . . help you . . . and the Teamsters . . . have done me many such favors," said Inciso.

In 1955, Sandy O'Brien was certainly the man to know if you wanted Teamsters help in Chicago. The 61-year-old labor boss was a vice president of the International Teamsters, as well as boss of Teamsters Local 710. He was a close friend of Jimmy Hoffa, and Joseph P. (Joey) Glimco, the Capone-connected boss of taxi drivers Local 777.[12]

But Sandy O'Brien wasn't in need of gifts from other well-

[10]McClellan committee, Report No. 1417, pages 170-173.

[11]Douglas, "Welfare and Pension Plans Investigation," Final Report, 1956, pages 207-215.

[12]McClellan committee, Report No. 1139, pages 567-607.

heeled labor leaders, even if his listed union salary was only $11,700 a year. Sandy and the other officers had taken care of themselves with a commission arrangement on all dues paid by the 11,000 to 14,000 members of the union. The "commissions" that Sandy took were so great that he had increased his salary to more than $60,000 a year, plus a huge expense account, and he had plans to boost it to over $94,000 a year by 1958.[13]

Regardless of what Inciso thought, Sandy O'Brien was hardly the guy who would sell out for such a trinket as a $360 diamond studded money clip.

Bull-voiced Anthony Doria, international secretary-treasurer of the U.A.W.-A.F.L., told the Douglas subcommittee he found nothing wrong with Inciso's free-spending policies, or his gifts to Teamsters. At the very time Doria was dealing with Hoffa, Dioguardi had joined other corrupt elements in the underworld drive to control truck transportation in New York.[14]

At the same time he was dealing with the New York underworld for control of the New York Teamsters, Hoffa was defying the A.F.L. and planning an alliance with the outlawed International Longshoremen's Association.

On November 27, 1955, the Teamsters signed an agreement with the racket-controlled I.L.A. in arrogant disregard for the A.F.L. and its president, Meany. Hoffa also agreed to a $490,000 loan to the I.L.A. at the very time the A.F.L. was trying to promote an honest longshoremen's union to kill the I.L.A.

When the A.F.L. and C.I.O. merged in December, 1955, it was immediately apparent that there would be some controversy over what to do about corruption. Walter Reuther and James Carey of the C.I.O. talked loudly about the need for cleaning up the labor movement.

Meany, who became president of the merged A.F.L.-C.I.O., looked like a compromiser who would talk, but do nothing. Sam Byers and Jimmy James attended the merger convention as the top officials of the Laundry Workers Union, despite the Douglas subcommittee report accusing James of "embezzling" about $1 million from the union welfare funds. Meany had claimed that

---

[13]McClellan committee, Report No. 1139, pages 561-563.

[14]McClellan committee, Interim Report No. 1417, page 193.

since each union was autonomous, all the A.F.L. could do was recommend a house cleaning.

In early 1955, I had hoped for a voluntary clean sweep by Meany. My hopes dimmed a little in the late spring, when Meany was nasty and belligerent in response to my questions about the Teamsters and the Laundry Workers. I excused this, to a certain extent, because he was having problems of his own in negotiating the A.F.L.-C.I.O. merger.

In December, it appeared that Meany was going to leave the Teamsters cleanup to Beck and Hoffa, and rely on Sam Byers and Jimmy James to bring honesty to the Laundry Workers.

It looked as if there would be no Congressional prod for Big Labor in 1956. Senator Ives and Senator Allott wanted the Douglas subcommittee continued, with broad jurisdiction to investigate the Teamsters and other unions, but they were in the Republican minority and had no effective voice in the decision. Senator Douglas opposed the idea, and he was preparing to disband his subcommittee. I was depressed, and wondered just how much evidence it would take to force Congress to make the full-scale inquiry that was needed.

XI

Bombs, Bullets and Blinding by Acid

There were times in those years from 1953 to late 1956 when it seemed to me no progress was being made against labor rackets. Most newspapers paid little attention to labor racketeering as a national menace. It was treated as a local story, even when it involved Jimmy Hoffa or an international officer of the Laundry Workers Unior such as Jimmy James. A few other reporters took jibes at me, and said it appeared that I was becoming a "reactionary."

"I just don't like the brutality and the thieving from union members' funds," I explained, without too much success.

It would have been a totally frustrating time except for the sympathetic group of editors on the *Des Moines Register*— Kenneth MacDonald, Frank Eyerly, Ray Wright, and Charles Reynolds. When the story was moving, they gave it excellent display as well as editorial support. Patience was essential for me in avoiding a sense of complete futility.

Congressional investigations hadn't frightened Jimmy Hoffa. He and many of his subordinates seemed more contemptuous than ever of the law and of law enforcement officials. Bombings, shootings and beatings continued in Tennessee as the labor hoodlums bore down on employers and honest union members who opposed them. Teamsters union money was used for a $20,000 payoff to a judge to fix a criminal case.[1] Teamsters mil-

---

[1] McClellan committee, Report No. 1417, pages 360-367.

lions were available throughout the Middle West for political contributions to assure the cooperation of mayors, sheriffs, prosecutors, judges, parole boards, liquor commissions, and governors. There was considerable evidence to support Hoffa's view that "everyone has his price." It appeared that most public officials could be bought, or at least frightened into submitting to Teamsters pressure.[2]

Teamsters money didn't always corrupt, but it certainly had a tendency to neutralize the law enforcement officials and courts.

Two convictions for shaking down employers didn't stop Jerry Connelly of Minneapolis.[3] Early in February, Connelly sat in a Miami hotel and gave orders to a squad of Teamsters dynamiters who bombed the car and home of two union men who opposed his organizing activity.

Accompanying Connelly on the Florida trip was Benjamin Dranow, an officer of John W. Thomas and Company, a Minneapolis department store. "It . . . appeared that Dranow and Connelly were sharing adjoining rooms in the Waves Hotel in Miami, Florida, at the time of the bombings. . . . The hotel bills for Dranow and Connelly (who was using the name of Cohen) were paid for by the Thomas Department Store on the premise that Dranow was entertaining a possible investor in the store," said a later report by the McClellan committee.[4]

A few months later Dranow was able to arrange two large loans from the Teamsters—one for $200,000 and another for one million dollars—with the help of Connelly's pal Jimmy Hoffa. The store was in critical financial condition at the time. These loans allowed Dranow to take control of the large Minneapolis department store, and then embezzle more than $100,000 before being caught and prosecuted.

That same month Hoffa boldly made a public announcement of his plans to loan $400,000 in Teamsters funds to the outlawed I.L.A. The deal was to include a mutual assistance pact with that gangster-dominated union in defiance of the A.F.L.-C.I.O.[5]

The Southern Conference of Teamsters dipped down in the

[2]McClellan committee, Report No. 1417, pages 244 and 245.
[3]McClellan committee, Report No. 1139, page 360.
[4]McClellan committee, Report No. 1417, page 241.
[5]McClellan committee, Report No. 1417, page 210.

treasury to loan $18,500 to Glenn W. Smith, the top Teamster in Tennessee. Smith later testified the money was used as part of a $20,000 payoff to Judge Raulston Schoolfield to fix a criminal charge, the McClellan committee stated.[6] Smith, a convicted burglar and robber, continued high in Hoffa's favor.

Smith's subordinates were brazen about their disregard of police and prosecutors. They had reason for it: Police and prosecutors seldom followed through aggressively in cases in which the huge trucking union was involved. Teamsters goon squads ranged across a five-state area, shooting at trucks or uncooperative truck drivers, bombing trucks and buildings, slashing tires, and pouring sugar in truck gasoline tanks to foul the engine. There were more than one hunded fifty acts of violence within the span of a few years.

In Oregon, a Portland beer distributor said the Teamsters were willing to put $10,000 into the campaign of Robert D. Holmes, the Democratic candidate for governor. In return, he said, the Teamsters wanted one of their officials appointed to the state liquor commission.[7]

The Teamsters wanted to keep liquor from certain eastern distilleries out of Oregon until the distillers yielded to union demands.

Howard Morgan, state chairman of the Oregon Democratic Party, rejected the offer as "ridiculous," but this didn't stop Oregon Teamsters' efforts to influence political decisions.

In Portland, a Teamsters-gangster alliance was trying to use political power and the picket line to control gambling, illegal liquor joints, and prostitution.[8]

Frank Brewster ranged up and down the 11-state Western Conference of Teamsters, tossing big bundles of cash into political campaigns for state and local officials.

Undisturbed that a House subcommittee had uncovered examples of Western Conference financial mismanagement in 1954, Brewster continued to dip into the union treasury for his own high living. Union funds paid his personal bills. Union

---

[6]McClellan committee, Report No. 1417, pages 360-366. See also Report No. 1139, page 710.

[7]McClellan committee, Report No. 1417, pages 23-25.

[8]McClellan committee, Report No. 1417, pages 30-33.

funds paid for transportation of his race horses, his jockey, and his horse trainer. Brewster was sure it would go on forever and made no effort to repay the thousands of dollars he had taken.[9]

Labor union violence flourished on the East Coast. On Wednesday, March 7, 1956, there was a gangland attack on Theodore (Teddy) Nalikowski, a 47-year-old businessman agent for Teamsters Local 478 in Newark. He was shot twice as he got into his car at Broadway and Murray Streets in Newark.

Three days later a gunman attempted to murder Louis B. Saperstein, the Newark insurance man who had testified before a New York grand jury on his admittedly dishonest dealings with union officials. Earlier, state officials in New Jersey had barred Saperstein from the insurance business because of his crooked dealings with the International Laundry Workers Union and the International Distillery Workers Union. Saperstein and a woman friend were seated in his car on a Newark street when a gunman fired four shots into him and fled with three companions in a car.

A few weeks earlier Saperstein had told a New York grand jury about the racket connections that brought him two million dollars in union welfare insurance commissions. Little Augie Pisano, a prohibition-era underworld figure and associate of Al Capone, had demanded and received big payoffs on the insurance, Saperstein said. He added that George Scalise, a convicted labor racketeer, and Sol Cilento, a trustee and officer of the Distillery Workers Union, also were paid off.[10] There had been cash payoffs of more than $500,000, and gifts of Cadillacs, furs and trips to Europe.

Less than a month after the attempt to assassinate Saperstein there was a fiendish attack on Victor Riesel, a labor columnist who specialized in exposing the labor racketeers. Late in the evening of April 5, a hired thug stepped out of a crowd in midtown Manhattan and threw acid in Riesel's face, blinding him.[11]

This vicious attack shocked the nation and caused a flurry of investigations by New York District Attorney Frank Hogan

[9]McClellan committee, Report No. 1417, pages 41-58.

[10]McClellan committee, Report No. 621, pages 267 and 268.

[11]McClellan committee, Report No. 1417, page 163.

and United States District Attorney Paul Williams, who had jurisdiction in that area.

Immediately after the attempted slaying of Saperstein, I talked with enforcement officials in Newark and New York. Hogan's office was trying to do a thorough job of tracking down the labor racketeers. Al Scotti, Hogan's assistant, had evidence in his files to prove that there was a wide network of gangster control of unions.

Under New York law Hogan and Scotti had obtained judicial authority to tap telephones, and they had transcripts of conversations showing the activities and the power of certain underworld figures in the labor movement.

Some of these transcripts had been made a part of an appeal record in a case involving Saperstein, Cilento, Scalise and Pisano. Scotti gave me a copy. I was fascinated by the conversations and wrote a series of stories based on this public document, which the New York press had never once mentioned.

I shared the transcripts with Dick Preston of the Scripps-Howard Washington bureau, because I wanted his help on an Ohio Teamsters angle with which he was familiar.

Dick and I hoped the operations of Scalise and Pisano, and the blinding of Vic Riesel, would have sufficient impact to convince Senator Douglas that he should continue and expand the investigation. We talked to Douglas, and had other reporters talk to him, urging him to investigate the Teamsters. Alice Johnson, the Washington reporter for the *Seattle Times,* talked with him and asked editors on her paper to write letters urging the Teamsters inquiry. Douglas rejected our suggestions and let the subcommittee die in mid-April, 1956.

Dave Beck continued to talk of cleaning up corruption in the Teamsters union, but it was mostly public relations posing. Beck and Hoffa bowed to the pressure of Meany and the newly merged A.F.L.-C.I.O. to kill the $400,000 loan to the discredited International Longshoremen's Association.

It was a very slight concession. Hoffa was riding high, and he was cocky. On March 23, 1956, the Hoffa slate had swept into full control of the A.F.L. in Wayne County, Michigan. The A.F.L. and C.I.O. had not yet merged on the lower level at that stage.

In New York, on April 3, Hoffa's candidate, John J. O'Rourke, seized control of Teamsters Joint Council 16, in spite of a federal court order prohibiting him from ousting the incumbent, Martin T. Lacy.[12]

On April 11, Jimmy Hoffa, who quit school at 14, went to Harvard University to give a lecture on transportation problems. I assumed Professor Sumner Slichter, one of the nation's top economists, had invited Hoffa to display an unusual exhibit, but I did not feel at all certain that the academic world was competent to cope with Hoffa. Jimmy is a glib salesman, and those who would listen to him had not had my opportunity to make the Hoffa empire a subject of continued study.

On April 20 there was a huge James R. Hoffa testimonial dinner at the State Fair Coliseum in Detroit. The $100-a-plate event was to recognize the rise of Jimmy to national prominence, though he was still not well known except by labor reporters, politicians, labor leaders, economists and truckers.

The main address was by Dave Beck. Wild cheering from the convicted robbers, burglars and extortionists helped leading industrialists and political leaders pay tribute to pal Jimmy. Some officials of the United Automobile Workers-C.I.O. were there, but U.A.W.-C.I.O. president Walter Reuther did not attend.

Acting Mayor Louis G. Miriani went through the superfluous gesture of giving Hoffa the key to the city of Detroit, and the two thousand eight hundred guests cheered. A check for $265,625, collected as a testimonial to Hoffa, was presented to the little Teamsters boss. Although estimates of his indebtedness ranged from $70,000 to $100,000 at the time according to his own testimony, Hoffa made the grand gesture and presented the check to Simcha Pratt, Israel's consul general, for construction of a children's home in Israel.

Harold Gibbons, suave St. Louis Teamsters boss, and the public relations men were trying to create a new image of Hoffa. The picture of a brawling associate of the underworld would not do for what they had in mind. The new Hoffa was presented as a humanitarian, broad-minded student of world transportation problems, a man of deep insight into international politics.

---

[12]McClellan committee, Report No. 621, page 2.

Jimmy's wide grin and the physique of a healthy farm boy made him an attractive and saleable product. But it was the same old Jimmy Hoffa who was running the Teamsters union when the testimonial dinner was over. There was no change in his cynical attitude toward conflicts of interest.

In May, Hoffa used his union connections to borrow $125,000 for purchase of Fruehauf Trailer Company stock in his own name. Part of the money was pulled out of the union treasury.[13]

He took advantage of his position in other ways, too.

Business agents of the Teamsters union worked on construction of a home owned by Hoffa and his chief Teamsters lieutenant, Owen Bert Brennan, in northern Michigan.

Hoffa and Owen Brennan used $150,000 in Teamsters funds to buy the Chicago estate of Paul (The Waiter) Ricca, a notorious Capone mobster, to use as a training school for union business agents.[14]

In June, Hoffa arranged the transfer of $300,000 in Teamsters funds from a Detroit Bank to the Florida National Bank at Orlando, which then loaned money for development of Sun Valley, Inc.,[15] in which Hoffa had an interest. This was a Florida land promotion scheme. A few months later, he transferred another $200,000 to persuade the reluctant bankers to loan another $200,000 on the land scheme.

Hoffa and Owen Bert Brennan had an option to buy a 45 per cent interest in Sun Valley, Inc., at the original cost.[16] It meant they risked nothing and could deal themselves in by exercising the option at any point the land development scheme became a sure money maker. The management of the project was put in the hands of Henry Lower, a former Detroit Teamsters business agent who became "Colonel Lower," a land expert. Union money backed the borrowing Sun Valley did, and Hoffa's friends in the Teamsters pushed the project with union members.

On May 10, 1956, Hoffa went through the motions of pretending he was cleaning up the Teamsters in Minneapolis with

---

[13]McClellan committee, Report No. 1417, page 229.
[14]McClellan committee, Report No. 1417, page 236.
[15]McClellan committee, Report No. 1139, pages 630 and 631.
[16]McClellan committee, Report No. 1417, page 225.

the public announcement that he was reading Jerry Connelly out of the Teamsters because of his convictions for extortion and dynamiting. Behind the scenes, Hoffa was still supporting Connelly and arranged to spend $54,381.55 for lawyers for Connelly and other Minneapolis Teamsters who had been convicted of selling out their members.[17]

But in the cases of most of his Central Conference of Teamsters, Hoffa didn't even go through the pretense of a house cleaning. In St. Louis, Harold Gibbons, the secretary-treasurer of the Central Conference of Teamsters, hired a convicted burglar as an organizer. Branch W. Wainwright had been out of the penitentiary only a short time when Gibbons hired him as an organizer for the Missouri-Kansas Conference of Teamsters. Gibbons later appointed Wainwright a business agent for Teamsters Local 245 in Springfield.[18]

Gibbons, the self-styled "intellectual Teamster," explained that it was his interest in "rehabilitation" of criminals that caused him to hire Wainwright and a half-dozen other police characters for union work in Missouri.

Barney Baker, twice-convicted thug, was rampaging from Chicago to Omaha, to Kansas City, Minneapolis and Des Moines on wild-spending forays paid for by the dues of rank-and-file Teamsters.

In Illinois, Joseph P. "Joey" Glimco, pal of Capone mobsters, had been acquitted on a charge of extorting money from employers in the poultry product business in the Fulton Street Market. He was tightening his grip on businesses in the area, and operated Teamsters Local 777 with an iron fist. Cash "kickbacks" from the other officers of the union totaled more than $500 a week. Glimco had become a Hoffa favorite.[19]

Genial John T. "Sandy" O'Brien, the secretary-treasurer of Chicago Teamsters Local 710, had no aspiration to anything greater than his present title as a vice president of the International Brotherhood of Teamsters. He was already milking Local 710 of more money than the $50,000-a-year salary Beck received as International President.

---

[17]McClellan committee, Report No. 1417, pages 239-241.
[18]McClellan committee, Report No. 1139, pages 704 and 705.
[19]McClellan committee, Report No. 1139, pages 514-569.

Sandy's listed salary was only $11,700 in 1956, but his "commissions" on union dues totaled more than $61,000 in that year. He also arranged for himself a Christmas bonus of $1,000 and a vacation bonus of $300, making his total take $74,000.[20]

Frank Charles Schmitt, president of Local 710, and Michael Joseph Healy, vice president, had also been dealt into this lucrative commission and bonus arrangement. Schmitt's share was $57,597.98 in 1956, and Healy received $36,913.12. These figures didn't include what they took out of the union on big expense accounts.[21]

In Indiana, Eugene San Soucie, boss of the Indiana Conference of Teamsters, hired an ex-convict as business representative for the Indiana Conference. The fact that Gus Zapas had more than forty arrests and a prison record didn't bother San Soucie, because he had had his own trouble with police in St. Louis before leaving there a few years earlier to take over Teamsters Local 135 in Indianapolis.[22]

Big Bill Presser continued to boss the Ohio Conference of Teamsters with the help of his little pal, Babe Triscaro, convicted armed robber and president of Teamsters Local 436.[23] In Youngstown, Ohio, the Teamsters local with jurisdiction over juke boxes and coin machines was bossed by Joseph Blumetti, a convicted white slaver.[24]

It pained me to see the success of the Gibbons-directed public relations drive to picture Hoffa as a new man with a broad international view and the outlook of the humanitarian.

Newspapers and the public are often suckers for the organized manipulators and exploiters of society. A few hundred dollars' donation to a hospital, a church, a United Givers campaign, the Boy Scouts or a school is about all that is needed to deceive the public. The newspaper stories do not mention the gift-maker's police record. If they did, it would cause complaints that this was persecution for past offenses.

But let a reform-minded prosecuting attorney raise his voice in indignation in the court, or be seen once in public after too many beers, and he is likely to be denounced as a hypocrite.

---

[20]McClellan committee, Report No. 1139, page 569.
[21]McClellan committee, Report No. 1139, pages 561-563.
[22]McClellan committee, Report No. 621, pages 29, 31, 34 and 159.
[23]McClellan committee, Report No. 1139, page 636.
[24]McClellan committee, Report No. 1139, pages 713-715.

XII

Bobby Kennedy Meets the Teamsters

In early 1956, Robert F. Kennedy made his first visit to the plush five-million-dollar International Teamsters Headquarters in the nation's capital. It was not a trip that could have been regarded as significant at the time. The 30-year-old lawyer knew virtually nothing about trade unions, and he was only a boyish-appearing tourist as he walked through the lavish comfort of Dave Beck's castle. He made the tour at the request of Beck's public relations man, Eddie Cheyfitz, and it was largely a gesture for political good will.

In his role as counsel for the Senate Permanent Investigating Subcommittee, Bob Kennedy would not have merited much attention from the bouncy and talkative Cheyfitz. However, Bob Kennedy was rich and came from a politically prominent family, and his big brother, Senator John F. Kennedy, was a member of the Senate Committee on Labor and Public Welfare. Cheyfitz made it his business to build rapport with members of the Senate and House labor committees.

Cheyfitz had suggested to Bob that he should learn something about unions, and particularly the Teamsters. He took Bob to lunch in the sparkling new marble and glass headquarters, gave him a sales talk on the political punch of the big transportation union, and introduced him to old John English, the veteran secretary-treasurer of the International Teamsters.

Dave Beck wasn't around, but Bob did meet Ann Watkins, Beck's attractive and efficient secretary, and Einar Mohn, Beck's executive assistant.

Senator Kennedy's best-selling *Profiles in Courage* was then achieving its first popularity and Cheyfitz said Beck would like an autographed copy. Bob promised to see that his brother provided a copy with a special inscription for Dave Beck. As soon as he returned to the Senate Office Building, Bob left word at Senator Kennedy's office that a copy should be autographed and delivered to Beck at the earliest possible moment. Bob Kennedy wanted Teamsters president Beck to think well of his brother.

A few months earlier, I had talked with Bob Kennedy about a Teamsters investigation. Somehow, it hadn't made much impression. I had tried to convince him that a labor racket investigation would provide him great opportunity, and also that he had a responsibility to do the job. Bob had other things on his mind at that time, including an investigation of frauds in the purchase of military clothing. He was only mildly interested in conversation about labor rackets. He said the permanent investigating subcommittee had about all the work it could do, and suggested that a labor racket investigation should be done by the Senate Labor Committee.

I explained my theory that such an investigation clearly came under the jurisdiction of the Government Operations Committee, or its permanent investigating subcommittee, since the operations of two agencies—the Internal Revenue Service and the Labor Department—were involved.

"The Internal Revenue Service just isn't fulfilling its responsibility," I said. "Financial records are being destroyed and the Internal Revenue Service isn't doing anything about it. It is resulting in the loss of millions of dollars in revenue."

I pointed out specifically that Hoffa had admitted under oath in 1953 that he destroyed the union's financial records every year. I explained the laxity of the Labor Department in failing to police the financial reports required under the Taft-Hartley law. False reports could be filed with virtually no danger of prosecution.

Bob Kennedy indicated he might be interested in some aspects

of the labor racket investigation at a later time and steered me
to his assistant counsel, Paul Kamerick.

In a memorandum for the files Kamerick noted the general
nature of the cases I outlined, the legal theory for jurisdiction,
and the names of some of the key officials. Although I badgered
Bob Kennedy relentlessly, I usually did it in a half-joking
manner. Occasionally, I taunted him by questioning his courage
to take on such an investigation. At other times I prophesied
such an investigation could do for him what the Kefauver crime
investigation did for Rudolph Halley.

Actually, I did not promote the investigation in earnest
until I was certain the Douglas subcommittee would fold. On
May 15, 1956, Kennedy told me that Chairman McClellan had
subpoenaed John Dioguardi, the convicted extortionist, along
with Albert Anastasia of Murder, Inc., and ten other racketeers
for questioning in connection with the clothing procurement
scandals.

When Dioguardi, Anastasia and their racketeering friends
appeared at a closed session of the McClellan subcommittee,
they refused to talk on grounds they might incriminate themselves. It was young Bob Kennedy's first contact with underworld
society. He was intrigued by these cold, surly men, seemingly so
sinister and quiet. But there was not enough evidence linking
them to the clothing procurement scandals to justify open
hearings.

As I tried to stimulate Bob Kennedy's interest in the labor
racket inquiry, his mood blew hot and cold. I didn't know what
to make of it. When he neared the end of the clothing procurement hearings, I assumed he was just another young lawyer who
didn't want to take on the job of fighting the labor racketeers.
I didn't blame him completely, for there were few prosecutors
with the interest and the courage to investigate labor rackets. It
was a thankless task in many ways. Undiscriminating newspaper
cartoonists, editors and the uninformed voters were apt to accept
the premise that those who prosecuted labor leaders were anti-
labor.

It was hard to expect a public figure to put his head on the
chopping block to fight corruption if he couldn't depend on
reasonable intelligence by the press in reporting and interpreting

what he was trying to do. Intelligence and integrity in reporting would win for the investigator the necessary support from the public.

By that summer of 1956, I was beginning to doubt there was anyone in political life with the ability, the balance, the courage, the honesty and the energy needed to fight the Teamsters. I knew it would take a tough hide to withstand the criticism, and persistence and durability to stay with it until the people of the nation started to understand the full danger of a criminal syndicate in labor.

For many reasons Bob Kennedy would not have been my first choice as counsel at that stage, but he seemed the only possibility. He was young. It was true that he had practically no knowledge in the labor area, but I knew he was bright and aggressive. In some respects his lack of knowledge of the power and cunning of the Teamsters was advantageous to my cause as I discussed it with him.

I was in the McClellan committee office shortly after noon, August 1, 1956, when Maxine Buffalohide finished typing a report for the permanent investigating subcommittee. She asked Bob if she could take the rest of the afternoon off.

"It looks as though I'll have to find some new project to keep you busy," Kennedy said, half-joking.

"This looks like a good time to take on something tough, like the investigation of the Teamsters," I injected. "This is a big investigation, and it is just waiting for someone with guts enough to do it."

"If it's such a big investigation, why haven't the labor committees been doing something about it?" Kennedy asked.

"Nearly everyone is afraid of the Teamsters," I said. "They've been able to frighten off half a dozen committees that have done a little work on Teamsters corruption."

"Why is it that you think the Government Operations Committee should do it?"

"Because the Labor Department and the Internal Revenue Service aren't doing an effective job of policing union funds," I said, re-emphasizing a point I had been trying to make. "If you start to make an investigation of the way they handle these things, you'll be right in the middle of a major scandal in union finances."

"How do you know this?" Kennedy said.

"Because the committees that have been in this field have exposed the pattern in enough cases, and there is every indication that the pattern would be the same throughout the Teamsters union and some other unions," I answered.

"If this is such a big story, why wasn't there more in the newspapers about the other committees?" Kennedy asked.

I told him that the hearings had not been handled properly to have the full public impact they could have had. I repeated my belief that under a strong chairman in the Senate they could be "bigger than the Kefauver crime investigations."

"The social and economic significance of a labor investigation will have a tremendous impact on business, industry and the whole labor movement," I told him.

"Come on down to my office, and let's talk about it," Kennedy said. He called assistant counsel Paul Tierney and investigator Robert E. Dunne into his office to take notes.

Kennedy and Tierney wanted to know more about my legal theory that the Government Operations Committee had jurisdiction. I told them that Hoffa had testified in November, 1953, that he used union funds—tax-exempt funds—for political contributions. An inquiry should be made of the Internal Revenue Service as to why nothing was done about this, I said. I pointed out that Hoffa, every year, had arranged for the locals in his Teamsters Joint Council to destroy their financial records, a violation of the regulations of the Internal Revenue Service.

A second inquiry should be made at the Labor Department as to what kind of financial reports were being filed by Hoffa's union—and a large number of others.

I also suggested that the committee might have jurisdiction over some labor rackets through the Federal Trade Commission. On July 26, I had received a letter from Ed Guthman, of the *Seattle Times,* about a juke-box monopoly the Teamsters were allegedly trying to enforce in Portland, Oregon.

Two reporters for the *Portland Oregonian*—William Lambert and Wally Turner—had written an exceptionally fine series of stories a few months earlier. Those stories exposed a conspiracy to control juke-box placement, gambling, illegal liquor joints, and even prostitution.[1]

Turner and Lambert had recordings of conversations involving the Teamsters and several underworld figures from Seattle who were connected with the deal.

Guthman's letter was my first knowledge that he had been working with Turner and Lambert on the Seattle angles. Guthman had come across information that Arthur Kaplan, then an assistant attorney general in Oregon, had made a rather detailed report to the Department of Justice concerning Teamsters union involvement with rackets in the whole area of coin-operated machines—juke boxes, pinball machines and slot machines.[2]

I explained to Bob Kennedy how the Teamsters union used its power of the picket line to stop delivery of such items as beer, bread and meat to night clubs, taverns or restaurants unless they used union-approved juke boxes. There had been testimony about this strategy in Detroit and Cleveland, and a similar situation existed in Chicago and Portland.

Guthman wanted me to gain access to Kaplan's juke-box report. It seemed to me it would be much better if a Congressional committee obtained the report. A few days later I delivered Guthman's letter to Kennedy, after having carefully torn off the last paragraphs to keep Guthman's name and Kaplan's out of it at that stage. (Kaplan later became an assistant counsel for the McClellan Labor Racket Committee, and handled the nationwide juke-box investigation.)

Kennedy still blew hot and cold on the investigation during those first weeks in August. He was bothered by the fact that the investigation looked so good, and he kept wondering why it hadn't been done by others.

Carmine Bellino, the investigator-accountant who had worked on the McConnell House committee, had been working with Kennedy on the clothing procurement investigation.

"Keep after him," Carmine urged. "He's just about sold, but he needs encouragement."

I suggested that Kennedy talk with Downey Rice, Frank Plant, Bill Leece, Paul Cotter, Ed McCabe, Lester Condon, and

---

[1]McClellan committee, Report No. 1417, page 7.

[2]McClellan committee, Report No. 1139, pages 741 and 742.

William McKenna—the lawyers and investigators who had conducted some of the earlier investigations.

Finally, Kennedy asked Senator McClellan for authority to begin, and late in August McClellan told his staff members they were embarking on one of the biggest investigations ever undertaken by a Senate committee. Mrs. Alice Dearborn set up a card file for labor rackets in a little four-inch-deep recipe box. I smiled at it, and told her she should get a full drawer. None of us imagined then that the investigation would stretch on for three years, or that the index cards alone would fill three huge cabinets containing fifty file drawers.

The Great Investigation suddenly started rolling on September 12. Attorney Frank Martocci, acting for a reform group in Teamsters Local 445 in Yonkers, N. Y., made a telephone call to Bob Kennedy. The reform group had possession of union financial records, under a court order, and wanted the Senate investigators to see them before crooked Teamsters maneuvered back into power.

It was late afternoon, but Kennedy assigned Bellino and Tierney to the case. I met them rushing out at about 5 o'clock. By 9 p.m. they had dug deeply enough in the books of Local 445 to run across the name "Johnny D." They were intrigued by the possibility that this might be Johnny Dioguardi, the convicted extortionist.

This was Bob Kennedy's first look into union books, and he was amazed at the financial mess.

In the fall of 1956, Teamsters bosses were flying high. Even as the McClellan-Kennedy team started the investigation, I had feared that it would never really come off. Obviously, the Government Operations subcommittee had limited jurisdiction. Chairman McClellan was a cautious, conservative Democrat with a pronounced distaste for unnecessary political brawls.

In the five years since he had graduated from the University of Virginia, Bob Kennedy had had no trial experience. He had been chief counsel for the Government Operations subcommittee when it toppled Air Force Secretary Harold Talbott and the Interstate Commerce Commission chairman, Hugh Cross. Kennedy had shown that he knew how to dramatize hearings during the clothing procurement investigation, but he also had shown signs of unsteadiness. He sometimes lost his temper, and occasionally a little-boy impetuousness marred his performance. Members of the press were inclined to give a major part of the credit for those successful investigations to Carmine Bellino, Jerome Adlerman, Alphonse Calabrese, and other older, more experienced members of the staff.

To the press, "Bobby" was just the little brother of Senator John Kennedy, the Massachusetts Democrat who had barely lost his party's Vice Presidential nomination to Senator Kefauver. Others regarded him as the socialite millionaire son of Joseph Kennedy, who was best known as a conservative Democrat and former United States Ambassador to England. It was general knowledge that Bob Kennedy had been given one million dollars at the age of twenty-one, and had married the equally wealthy Ethel Skakel. He did not have to work for a living. He was likeable, but he was not a politician. He had a tendency to use acid sarcasm, and he was inclined to be irritable or rudely blunt when he was crossed.

Kennedy and McClellan had to overcome public sympathy for union labor. The scandals in labor were considered insignificant. Indications of thievery of union funds were ignored. Much of the public viewed labor leaders as a class dedicated to unselfish defense of the workingman against the oppression of management. Well-meaning liberals denied the fact that Big Labor was more powerful, and consequently could be more corrupt than Big Business, as I have previously suggested.

No wonder Beck and Hoffa were confident and arrogant. In one way or another they had been able to obstruct and emasculate a long list of Congressional committees. They believed they could crush or coerce any chief counsel or committee chairman who had the audacity to investigate the Teamsters.

There were many reasons to doubt whether Bob Kennedy could be any more successful than those who had gone before him.

XIII

The Dizzy Descent of Dave Beck

In 1956 labor leaders, who within the year that followed were indicted on criminal charges, had entree to the White House. Maurice Hutcheson, president of the 800,000-member Carpenters union, and his promoter pal, Maxwell Raddock, had a personal audience with President Eisenhower. Labor Secretary James P. Mitchell considered this meeting a mistake even as it was taking place. Much to Mitchell's disgust, Raddock managed to get in some praise of Jimmy Hoffa as "a great little labor leader."

Mitchell interrupted Raddock's bubbling flow of praise for Hoffa as quickly as he could, and told President Eisenhower there were many who would not agree with Raddock's views on Hoffa. Mitchell told me later that he tried to be diplomatic about shutting it off, but that he was angry at Raddock and at Hutcheson for bringing him. When arrangements were made for that meeting, Mitchell had not known that Raddock would accompany Hutcheson.

President Eisenhower accepted Hutcheson's invitation to speak at the seventy-fifth anniversary dinner of the International Brotherhood of Carpenters and Joiners of America in October, and he fulfilled the engagement at the Sheraton-Park Hotel in Washington. It was an election year, and Hutcheson was in the Republican camp.

I knew Mitchell regarded Hoffa as a menace and a blot on the labor movement. He had told me so. Mitchell did not like Beck, either, and didn't trust him. But, at that time, he was unaware of Beck's specific crimes.

Even on President Eisenhower's crowded pre-election schedule for October 15, 1956, there was room for a conference with Dave Beck. Dave Beck was not only general president of the Teamsters union, he was chairman of an independent advisory committee for the trucking industry. Photographers were called in and Beck and the President of the United States shook hands for a picture. Respectfully standing aside were three men who had come to the White House with Beck: Roy Fruehauf, president of the nation's biggest truck-trailer manufacturing company; B. M. Seymour, president of the nation's biggest trucking company, and Arthur D. Condon, law partner of Beck's good friend, Senator James Duff, a Pennsylvania Republican.

When Beck left the White House a few moments later and gave his political endorsement to President Eisenhower, it was a big news story. Most of the leaders of labor were supporting Adlai Stevenson, the Democratic candidate. Beck had straightened out much of his financial mess, and he was hopeful that a little political influence might keep him out of serious federal tax trouble.

Beck's visit to the White House dramatized the prestige and power the Teamsters union still had while the investigation was being launched by the McClellan-Kennedy team. It explained the arrogance of the Teamsters, their attitude that they were fully as big as the United States government.

Then Bob Kennedy took a month off to campaign with Adlai Stevenson. The Teamsters investigation operated in low gear until after the election. But on November 14 the action was speeded up. Committee attorneys Adlerman and Tierney went to Chicago for a labor racket survey. Kennedy and Bellino flew to Los Angeles, on the trail of several leads on suspicious activities involving Anthony Doria, the secretary-treasurer of the Allied Industrial Workers Union, and officials of a Teamsters local with jurisdiction over the Los Angeles garbage collecting industry.

Tierney and Adlerman, on November 21, learned from an

informant that Nathan Shefferman seemed to have some peculiar power as a peacemaker in labor troubles involving the Teamsters. There was also the record of the Bender subcommittee showing that Shefferman, the labor relations consultant, had paid that $750 fee to Sidney L. Brennan, the Minneapolis Teamsters boss.[1] The two attorneys were in the neighborhood of Shefferman's office, and decided to try to see him.

It was raining when they stepped into a pay telephone booth near 75 E. Wacker Drive. Adlerman called while Tierney listened. Shefferman said he didn't want to see them.

Adlerman was insistent, and Shefferman made it a flat refusal:

"Even if you come up here, I won't see you. That's final."

The leads that had taken Adlerman and Tierney to Chicago were not very strong, and there were other chores to do. Tierney returned to work on the "paper locals" set up by Hoffa and Beck in New York. Adlerman returned to Washington, D.C., to do legal research for Bob Kennedy in preparation for another trip to the West Coast.

During those first weeks of the investigation Kennedy did not suspect Beck of taking union funds. The information of improprieties pointed to Hoffa, Brewster, and Sid Brennan. Brennan already had been convicted on one charge of accepting money from employers.

Kennedy was even a little more naive than one would expect when he dialed Sterling 3-0525 on November 26, 1956, to talk with Einar Mohn, Beck's 58-year-old executive assistant.

He told Mohn he would like to have the cooperation of the International Teamsters in an investigation of Hoffa, Brewster and Sid Brennan. He got a brushoff from Mohn before he had even explained fully the purpose of the call. Mohn became belligerent and uncommunicative.

Slim, boyish "Bobby" Kennedy seemed even younger than he was. The Teamsters did not take him seriously. They con-

---

[1] "Investigation of Racketeering in the Minneapolis, Minn., Area," 83rd Congress, 2d session, hearings before a subcommittee of the Committee on Government Operations, House of Representatives, April 9 and 10, 1954, pages 234 and 235.

cluded that this was a boy trying to do a man's job. They didn't resent it at first. They were just amused.

"Mohn was downright nasty," Kennedy told me. "He certainly didn't give the impression that he wanted to help clean up any corruption."

Kennedy was suspicious of Beck and Mohn the next day when he and his assistant counsel, Adlerman, flew to the West Coast to look into the Portland situation. Before he left, Kennedy asked me to wire reporter Ed Guthman in Seattle and tell him Kennedy wanted to see him. Kennedy also talked to Wally Turner and William Lambert of the *Portland Oregonian* on that trip.

On November 28, while Kennedy was in Portland, I received a call from George Lodge, then press secretary for Labor Secretary Mitchell. "Could you come over? The Secretary would like to visit with you."

I said I would be right over.

Mitchell told me the administration was gravely concerned over the labor rackets problem and wanted to do something about it. He quoted President Eisenhower as telling George Meany: "If there is any help the government can give you in cleaning up the racketeers, we will do it."

Slouched in a green chair in his inner office, Mitchell took down his hair. "Hoffa is a racketeer and a dictator, and he has his hands around the trucking industry of this nation," the Secretary said. "Many responsible labor leaders are concerned about this, and they have given me some tips on racketeering. They want it cleaned up."

Mitchell confided that he had had some discussions with Warren Olney III, then assistant attorney general in charge of the criminal division of the Justice Department. Justice was going to try to act, but there were many things in the operations of some unions that were highly unethical but just weren't a violation of the law. These things needed to be exposed, Mitchell said.

The Labor Secretary said the political situation made it difficult for him to pass information directly to the McClellan committee, and that he would be glad to give me leads to run down or pass to McClellan, as I saw fit.

Targets he suggested for full-scale investigation included Max Raddock, who a few weeks earlier had been at the White House to praise Hoffa. Meany had blacklisted Raddock's publication, the *Trade Union Courier,* as being little more than a shakedown for funds for labor protection.[2]

"Raddock is a close friend of Hoffa," Mitchell reminded me.

Other targets he suggested were Abner (Longie) Zwillman, the New Jersey liquor runner and racketeer, and Phil Weiss, a friend of Hoffa and a number of other big labor leaders, who ran a labor relations firm.[3]

Mitchell, who was from New Jersey, said Zwillman had mysterious connections with the Teamsters union and was operating a coin-machine business and several other enterprises. He said Weiss was selling industrial oil and good labor relations to the construction trades in New York, Detroit and Chicago under highly suspicious circumstances.[4]

I told him I would pass the leads to Bob Kennedy or one of his investigators. Since Kennedy was gone, I called the committee and dictated a memorandum to Ruth Price, secretary to the committee's chief accountant-investigator, Bellino.

Even then as 1956 drew to a close, almost four years after those first rumbles in St. Paul, the political pressures had started to work on Senator McClellan. I was in his office in the first week in December when he received a telephone call from Minneapolis. As I listened to the first comment by McClellan, I knew what was being tried.

"Yes, I remember serving with you in the House, Congressman Ryan," McClellan said.

Friendly at first, McClellan's tone had cooled by the time he spoke again. "Yes, Congressman Ryan, we have a Mr. O'Donnell out in Minneapolis, but I am not familiar with the Brennan investigation."

I knew then that Elmer Ryan was trying to use his acquaintanceship as a former Democratic congressman to obtain favored treatment for Brennan. McClellan smiled at me, and held out

[2]McClellan committee, Report No. 621, pages 591 and 592.
[3]McClellan committee, Report No. 1139, pages 557 and 575.
[4]McClellan committee, Report No. 621, page 573.

the receiver so I could hear a part of Ryan's plea. It wasn't a direct request for a deal. It was the weaseling half-suggestions of a political lawyer.

"Brennan's made a few little mistakes," was Ryan's pitch. "We'd be glad to cooperate to help your staff get the goods on Hoffa. Hoffa is the real crook."

McClellan said he would be glad to tell the staff, and he would appreciate any assistance that Brennan could give staff members. His voice had become totally impersonal, and he was operating at arms distance.

This was the first of dozens of efforts to soften or sidetrack the labor racket inquiry by talking to Chairman McClellan. They all ran into the same stone wall. Some were veiled hints of political support. Some were mere requests for a favor out of friendship. When the investigations were at their heights there were many bold threats of political reprisal.

While Teamsters were making efforts to pull political strings in Washington, D. C., Bob Kennedy was making fast progress on the West Coast. After two days in Portland, Kennedy and Adlerman took a night plane to Seattle, visited with Guthman and set up headquarters at the Olympic Hotel. It rained the three days they were there. They saw neither Mount Rainier, nor Dave Beck. But they did run across an informer—a man well acquainted with Beck and Frank Brewster.

The informer rolled out details of unrestrained spending by Brewster, who was racing those thoroughbred horses on his salary from the Teamsters. Many of the racing costs were paid out of union funds, the informant said.

Then he startled Kennedy with revelations about Beck himself. Beck was milking thousands of dollars from union funds, and had close financial ties with a number of persons who employed Teamsters union members, the informant said. He also mentioned that the union's influence and money aided various business concerns, whose officers and stockholders included Beck's wife, his son, relatives, and friends.

In addition, Teamsters money had been used to pay part of the cost of building Beck's home at 16749 Lake Shore Boulevard, on the north end of Lake Washington.

On December 6, after five more days in Portland, Ken-

nedy returned to Seattle, this time with chief accountant Bellino, leaving Adlerman and Al Calabrese to set up an office in
Portland. Kennedy called the informant again, and was steered
to a second informant, who was equally helpful with details of
Beck's misuse of union funds.

Beck wasn't available for questioning, and neither was
Brewster. It was impossible to check a report that John Lindsay,
a Seattle contractor, had built Beck's house with material purchased by the Teamsters union.[5] Lindsay was said to be out
of the city.

Kennedy and Bellino left Seattle and went to Los Angeles
to look into some other phases of the inquiry, but they put
out lines to try to locate Brewster. On December 14, they learned
he was to arrive in Seattle the next day. They immediately flew
there, and at 9 a.m., Saturday, December 15, walked into the
office of the Western Conference of Teamsters at 551 John Street.

Brewster was surprised as he was served two subpoenas.
They called for him to be in the nation's capital December 28,
with the financial records of the eleven-state Western Conference
of Teamsters which he headed, and also the records of Teamsters
Joint Council 28, Building Association, in Seattle. A third subpoena was served on Nugent LaPoma, secretary-treasurer of the
local, to produce the records of Seattle Teamsters Local 174—
the huge organization that had been home base for both Beck
and Brewster.[6]

On general questions about the Teamsters, Brewster talked
freely, adopting the attitude that he was willing to instruct the
boy investigator. Then Kennedy's questioning moved to whether
Brewster used Teamsters money to finance his race horses and
pay personal expenses. The tough veteran of union battles flew
into a rage. How could Kennedy ask such questions?

"I might be impressed if we didn't already have proof you've
lied to us about several things," Kennedy snapped back.

Kennedy was not as harmless as he looked, Brewster discovered. He talked little after that, but he was unintentionally
helpful about Beck's relationship with Nathan Shefferman, the

---

[5]McClellan committee, Report No. 1417, pages 57, 58, 61, and 63.

[6]Senate Government Operations subcommittee, hearings, January 16, 1957,
pages 38 and 47.

operator of that Chicago labor relations firm. Shefferman had never been on the union payroll, and he had performed no services for the Western Conference or any other Teamsters affiliate within the Conference's jurisdiction, Brewster said.

Kennedy asked for the Teamsters financial records so Bellino could examine them, but Brewster said he would have to talk it over with his attorney, Sam Bassett.

The answer came about 6 p.m. The union books would not be available.

Kennedy and Bellino made one more unsuccessful attempt to find John Lindsay, the construction man who had built Beck's Seattle mansion. Then they boarded a night plane for Minneapolis. They were sure they had a good case against Beck, but they were learning how hard it was to buck Teamsters opposition.

On Sunday, December 16, Kennedy, Bellino, and assistant committee counsel Don O'Donnell interviewed Sidney Brennan in Minneapolis. Brennan claimed that Jerry Connelly had been planted on him by Hoffa, and that Hoffa was "the real crook" in the Teamsters union.

Kennedy and Bellino arrived in Chicago December 17 and made arrangements to see Shefferman the next day. The 69-year-old labor relations man lost his brass after Kennedy and Bellino had talked with him for a short time.

"I'm too old to go to jail for covering up for Dave Beck," the white-haired man said as he peered over his heavy-rimmed glasses. He was willing to talk. He admitted paying thousands of dollars in bills for Beck, Beck's family and Beck's friends. Before it was completed the list included $650 for Beck's television set, $14 each for Beck's ties, $43 apiece for Beck's Sulka shirts.[7] The total was at least $94,000.

Beck paid him back, Shefferman said. He didn't know where the money came from. Yes, there were books. His son, Shelton Shefferman, had the books and would be back in two days.

Kennedy was picking up confidence and interest as he went along. Now he was aroused. From Chicago he telephoned the Seattle construction contractor Lindsay.

Lindsay was scared. Yes, he admitted, some of the construc-

---

[7]McClellan committee, Report No. 1417, page 63.

tion costs on Beck's home were paid out of union funds.[8] He would say no more. He said he had some tax problems, and he wanted to talk with his attorney before he answered any more questions.

The same day, Kennedy and Bellino called on International Teamsters vice-president William Lee of Chicago. It was unproductive. He was pleasant but guarded.

"I gained the impression he followed the code of those who don't talk about their fellow union officers to representatives of government agencies," Kennedy told me. "He was not very helpful."

Shelton Shefferman was back in Chicago on December 20, and he agreed to deliver his father's financial books. It was shortly before noon when Bellino, Kennedy, and Carl Schultz of the General Accounting Office, went to the National Boulevard Bank and the Harris Trust and Savings Bank in Chicago to get them. After a brief review of the books in the bank vault, Bellino smiled: "This is what we want, Bob."

Kennedy, Bellino, and Schultz left the bank with their arms loaded. Shefferman's records indicated that at least some of the money Beck had repaid to Shefferman had come from the union treasury.

Bellino found a deposit slip showing that Shefferman had deposited a check for $8,826.98 from a Los Angeles bank. The check was drawn against the special public relations account of the Western Conference of Teamsters. Bearing in mind Brewster's statement that Shefferman never had done any work for the Western Conference, Kennedy assigned Bellino the job of making a detailed analysis of the rest of the records. Then the investigators went home for Christmas.

McClellan granted Brewster's request that his appearance in Washington be postponed until January. There was much work to be done before Kennedy and Bellino could document the wholesale corruption and misappropriation they had uncovered.

When Bob Kennedy returned to Washington, D. C., on December 27, he was elated.

"I think we've got Dave Beck," he told me.

---

[8]McClellan committee, Report No. 1417, page 63.

I said I was surprised to hear that the self-styled millionaire labor leader was stealing union money.

"Is it big, and are you sure?" I asked. "It is big," Kennedy said. "I can't talk to you about it now. I'm pretty sure it is solid. We'll know in a few days."

Carmine Bellino was even more optimistic. He said he could see no logical explanation for Beck's activity, and that if the committee subpoenaed Beck he was sure the Teamsters boss was finished. Carmine wouldn't give me details on what he had found, but he referred me to a federal court case in which Internal Revenue agents were balked in efforts to get Beck's books. That record indicated to me that if Beck wasn't finished, his halo was in danger of being knocked off.

XIV

McClellan Faces Defiance and Sabotage

Bob Kennedy had not talked to Dave Beck, but on December 27, 1956, he put documentary evidence before Senator McClellan indicating that Beck, boss of the biggest union in America, was involved in large-scale corruption. Kennedy also told McClellan of the unwillingness of Teamsters officials to cooperate and to produce records. In some cases it looked like a conspiracy to thwart the work of the subcommittee, Kennedy said.

McClellan listened—stony-faced, tight-lipped and angry. Beck's Teamsters were openly defying the authority of Congress. John McClellan would not let the challenge go unanswered.

On Bob Kennedy's recommendation, the chairman made out a subpoena for Beck's appearance. He said he would use all of the power that went with his position to get the records of the Western Conference of Teamsters, and of Seattle Teamsters Local 174, Beck's hometown union.

Kennedy called Teamsters national headquarters in an effort to find Beck. He was informed, "Mr. Beck would rather not be subpoenaed." Beck would be willing to sit down and talk on a voluntary basis, but he did not want a committee subpoena to interfere with a trip to Europe that he had planned for the first week in January.

Kennedy and Bellino had been moving fast, so Beck and

the Teamsters lawyers tried to use their political connections with other Senators to head off the investigation. It did not work. McClellan was backing young Bob Kennedy all the way.

On January 3, 1957, while Beck was indicating that he would cooperate, a committee of Teamsters attorneys met at the Palmer House in Chicago to discuss ways of blocking McClellan and Kennedy.

Among those present at the meeting was J. Albert Woll, who was general counsel for the Teamsters and also for the A.F.L.-C.I.O. The lawyers decided to attack the McClellan committee's jurisdiction to investigate labor matters. They also decided to advise Teamsters that taking the Fifth Amendment before Congressional committees would not make them subject to union punishment.[1] If no one would produce records or talk about union finances, the lawyers reasoned, the McClellan-Kennedy team could be stymied.

Kennedy telephoned J. Albert Woll on January 4. "Where is Mr. Beck?" Kennedy asked. Woll said he didn't know. Kennedy replied that he knew Beck was scheduled to fly from Seattle to New York, and that if he didn't want a subpoena, he should make himself available the next night. Woll promised that Beck would meet with Kennedy in New York the next night.

That same afternoon, Kennedy and Bellino had some luck on another aspect of the case. They called at the office of attorney Alfons Landa, a director of the Fruehauf Trailer Company, who had arranged the $1.5 million loan from the Teamsters a few years earlier. Beck had insisted publicly that it was a "cold-blooded business loan," and declared he had received no benefits from Fruehauf and would accept none.

Kennedy asked Landa for the files on the loan, and they were produced. In questioning Landa, Kennedy and Bellino learned that Fruehauf and Landa had helped Beck borrow $200,000 as a personal loan in the summer of 1954—about six months after the loan to Fruehauf. The pattern of Beck's operations was beginning to piece together quickly.[2]

---

[1] Senate Government Operations subcommittee, hearings, January 18, 1957, pages 180-181.

[2] McClellan committee, Report No. 1417, pages 66, 68 and 69.

Shortly after 9 p.m. January 5, Kennedy had his first meeting with Beck. Attorney Woll met him in the lobby of the Waldorf-Astoria Hotel in New York and took him to Beck's suite. Present with Beck was Simon Wampold, a Seattle attorney who was on the Teamsters payroll as a legal adviser and who also was involved in business ventures with Beck.[3]

Kennedy carried a letter from Chairman McClellan. If Beck could give a satisfactory explanation of his dealings with Nathan Shefferman, and a reasonable story about using union money to pay some construction costs on his house, Kennedy was authorized to leave without delivering the letter.

For most of the ninety minutes they were in the labor ruler's suite Kennedy and Bellino were treated to one of Beck's explosive tirades against Congressional investigations. He shouted out his pet theories about the Constitution. He declared that young lawyers like Kennedy didn't realize how difficult it was to clean out "the Communists and racketeers." He said he would "crucify any s.o.b. caught muscling or racketeering." But on the crucial questions by Kennedy concerning dealings with Shefferman, Beck would not talk. He said he could not discuss them unless his personal attorney was present. Two Teamsters lawyers were in the room at the time.

"It was one lie after another," Bob Kennedy told me later. "We had enough documentary information to know he was not telling the truth."

Kennedy handed Beck the letter from McClellan. Beck put on his reading glasses. He read the note informing him that McClellan planned hearings in mid-January, 1957, at which time evidence would be introduced that indicated Beck had "misused" thousands of dollars of Teamsters funds. It was requested that he be present to hear the charges, and to answer them if he saw fit.

The bald head and pink cheeks of the Teamsters boss turned deep red with rage. It had been a long time since anyone had had the effrontery to slap him with a charge of personal dishonesty.

---

[3]McClellan committee, Report No. 1417, page 87. See also the Bellino report on the Beck interview in the exhibits of the Hoffa trial in the United States District Court for the District of Columbia.

"You'll hear about this," he warned as Kennedy and Bellino left. Beck still had influence and friends in high places. They had always helped him in the past.

Beck was not under subpoena when he boarded a plane in New York the afternoon of January 6 to fly to London for a meeting of the International Transport Workers Federation. Chairman McClellan told me Beck called him before leaving, promising to be present at the hearings in mid-January.

Again various obstacles came up to plague the McClellan-Kennedy team. Two Seattle banks, depositories for the multi-million-dollar International Teamsters treasury, refused to produce records for McClellan's investigations. In Seattle, a mysterious burglary took place at the office of the Western Conference of Teamsters, and the financial records sought by the committee were reportedly ransacked.

Einar Mohn, Beck's executive assistant, quietly wired the Teamsters International vice presidents, notifying them that Teamsters attorneys agreed that the McClellan committee had no authority to inquire into labor matters. The wire said they could take the Fifth Amendment without fear of disciplinary action. Mohn said he was acting for Dave Beck.[4]

In Washington, a jurisdictional dispute arose which made it seem likely that the McClellan-Kennedy team would be stopped before it held its first hearing. McClellan had decided that he needed a special authorization from the Senate if his Government Operations subcommittee was going to do the full job required. He drew a resolution asking for additional authority and a special appropriation of $350,000. Senator Irving Ives, the New York Republican, had also introduced a resolution asking for a special subcommittee of the Senate Labor Committee to tackle the same job. Ives had first broached his resolution in 1956.

These rival resolutions created the conflict the Teamsters and certain other unions wanted. Even honest labor viewed McClellan with some suspicion because of his conservative political philosophy. The A.F.L.-C.I.O. lobbyists worked constantly with the members and staff of the Senate Labor Committee, and they preferred to deal with that committee. McClellan, however,

---

[4]Senate Government Operations subcommittee, hearing, January 18, 1957, pages 180-181.

was impervious to political pressure, and he went ahead with his first witnesses.

Boldly, Frank Brewster followed the strategy of the Teamsters lawyers. He refused to answer any questions, on grounds that the Government Operations Committee had no jurisdiction. His lawyers argued that the Labor Committee should handle such an investigation and the Ives resolution proved it.

During the next few days the same pattern of defiance was followed by Einar Mohn, Nugent LaPoma of Seattle Local 174, and Harry Reiss, an official of one of the Teamsters "paper locals" in New York City.

Beck went further: he simply failed to show up at the hearings. But by now Bob Kennedy had inserted enough material into the public record to give strong indications that Brewster and Beck were misusing funds. McClellan indicated he would initiate contempt action against Brewster, Mohn, LaPoma, and Reiss. Kennedy had seized a copy of Mohn's telegram outlining the conspiracy of silence. The Teamsters' actions were a flat contradiction of A.F.L.-C.I.O. policy. The A.F.L.-C.I.O. had stated that a union official's refusal to answer questions about union finances could be grounds for removing him from union office.

McClellan told his fellow Senators about Mohn's telegram, and declared that the authority of the government was being challenged. That did it.

The problem of jurisdiction was settled quickly by agreement between Ives and McClellan. Together they worked out a special eight-member, bipartisan Select Senate Committee on Improper Activities in the Labor or Management Field. Ives was to be the ranking Republican and vice chairman under McClellan. This effectively destroyed one Teamsters gambit: they had raised the cry that if Senate control shifted to the Republicans, the Government Operations Committee would fall into the hands of Senator Joseph R. McCarthy, the controversial Wisconsin Republican.

On January 22, A.F.L.-C.I.O. President Meany sent a letter to Labor Secretary James Mitchell. It contained two names from which the Eisenhower Administration could choose a representative to the International Labor Organization meeting in

Hamburg, Germany. Beck had offered his own name in response to Meany's request for someone from the Teamsters union. George M. Harrison, president of the Brotherhood of Railway Clerks, had sent the name of Harold D. Ullrich of Boston, a regional official of the Railway Clerks Union. It looked as if Dave Beck, a crooked labor official who was defying Congress, was going to represent the United States at an international conference.

Beck returned from Europe for an A.F.L.-C.I.O. meeting in Miami, then took off again across the Atlantic. At Teamsters headquarters everyone acted as though he had already been designated the U. S. representative at the Hamburg meeting. The McClellan committee still hadn't subpoenaed him.

Late in the afternoon of January 30, 1957, the Senate unanimously approved the special McClellan committee and its $350,000 appropriation. For the first time, a specially authorized committee with plenty of money, a skilled investigative staff (initially twenty investigators and twenty-five accountants), and a tough chairman was on the trail of Dave Beck, Jimmy Hoffa, and other labor racket figures.

It was to be an eight-member committee, with an even number of Democrats and Republicans selected from the Government Operations and Labor committees of the Senate. Democrat McClellan would be chairman and Republican Ives vice chairman, since they had put in the resolutions calling for the investigation. Senator McCarthy, Wisconsin Republican, and Senator Karl Mundt of South Dakota jumped at the chance to use their seniority to get seats on this select committee. Arizona's Barry Goldwater, a Republican with a special interest in labor, was happy for the opportunity.

Decisions were not made so quickly on the Democratic side. Two high-ranking members of the Government Operations committee—Senators Stuart Symington of Missouri and Henry M. Jackson of Washington—declined the honor. Dave Beck was a political power in Jackson's home state of Washington. Symington was a man with Presidential ambitions who had a political friendship with Harold Gibbons of St. Louis, one of Hoffa's top aides in the Central Conference of Teamsters.

When Jackson and Symington waived their rights, the

Government Operations seat fell to Senator Sam Ervin of North Carolina.

Senator John Kennedy was warned that taking part in the labor racket investigation could mean disaster to his Presidential ambitions. Several gave him that advice, including Majority Leader Lyndon Johnson. Johnson said it was madness for Jack Kennedy to think he could take part in the investigation, head a labor subcommittee writing the reform law, and still be a serious contender in 1960.

Initially, I was unsure of what Senator Kennedy would do in the face of the A.F.L.-C.I.O. pressure and his political ambitions. When I first talked to him about the jurisdictional controversy he seemed undecided.

"The Labor Committee seems to have the best claim on jurisdiction," he said, "but Bobby has worked terribly hard on this investigation, he believes it is important, and he wants to do it."

Although the arguments for Labor Committee jurisdiction had been persuasive, the fact that Bob Kennedy wanted to do the investigation proved fully as important to Jack Kennedy.

Senator Kennedy disregarded all of the well-meant advice and told brother Bob it was time for full speed ahead against the labor racketeers.

The fourth Democrat was Senator Pat McNamara, a genial former labor leader from Detroit, who was the most liberal member of the committee. He was expected to keep his hand in the questioning to make certain organized labor's view was presented on a committee that had a strong conservative complexion.

Friends of the Teamsters were at work, even before the committee members had been selected. Edward Cheyfitz, public relations man and lawyer, had a falling out with Dave Beck and had quit or was fired. He became a bosom companion of Jimmy Hoffa. Cheyfitz suggested that Bob Kennedy should meet Hoffa, and when Kennedy agreed, Cheyfitz invited both men to dinner at his home. Kennedy had only grazed the edges of Hoffa's operations, but he was curious about the tough little Teamster. The dinner was set for February 19, 1957.

The experience of other labor racket investigators made

Kennedy wary of spies, but the problem had not yet been brought home to him as dramatically as it would be later.

Six days before that scheduled dinner with Bob Kennedy, Hoffa conferred in his Detroit Teamsters headquarters with Hyman I. Fischbach, a Washington lawyer, and John Cye Cheasty, a New York lawyer whom Fischbach had brought in. The mysterious trip from Washington to Detroit, complete with fictitious names and a night meeting at Hoffa's office, was climaxed when Hoffa reached into a drawer, handed $1,000 in cash to Cheasty, and agreed to a retainer of $2,000 a month for nine months.[5]

The next day, Cheasty telephoned Kennedy's office and told the young counsel he wanted to see him.

"I have some information that will make your hair stand on end," Cheasty said. When he and Kennedy got together the following day, Cheasty said he had been offered $18,000 by Hoffa to get a job on the McClellan committee and spy on the investigators. He said Hoffa had given him $1,000 in cash, and he dumped $700 of it on Kennedy's desk.

Kennedy hurried Cheasty down to McClellan's office. McClellan listened to the story, then called the F.B.I. Arrangements would be made to set a trap for Hoffa if Cheasty was willing to be the bait. Although suffering from a heart condition, Cheasty said he would play along if that was what McClellan and F.B.I. Director J. Edgar Hoover wanted.[6]

While waiting to see whether Hoffa would fall into the trap, McClellan and Kennedy shifted their attention back to Beck. Evidence indicated he had misused $300,000 to $400,000 of union funds. On February 16, McClellan dictated a letter to him in Europe: " . . . It is expected that your testimony will be desired by the committee. As you know, information has already been developed reflecting upon your personal finances as related to union activities. . . . "

Bob Kennedy kept me fairly well posted on the Beck case, but he said nothing about the Hoffa angle until February 19, when he said he wanted a list of some of Hoffa's racketeering

[5]Transcript, U. S. v. Hoffa and Fischbach, in the United States District Court for the District of Columbia, Criminal No. 294-57, page 466.

[6]Transcript, U. S. v. Hoffa and Fischbach, Cr. No. 294-57.

lieutenants. I provided him with a list, but I had no idea of the mysterious events that were taking place. Actually, Bellino and Kennedy's secretary, Angela Novello, were the only members of the staff who were aware of the Cheasty operation.

At 6 p.m. that night, arrangements were made for Cheasty to meet Hoffa on the corner of Seventeenth and I Streets, N.W., and pass some information to him. Two F.B.I. agents drove Cheasty to Seventeenth Street and Pennsylvania Avenue, and one of them shadowed him and watched from across the street when the meeting took place.

Kennedy had already received a report of the successful surveillance of the Hoffa-Cheasty meeting when he left the office at 7:15 p.m. that night on an uneasy mission—dinner at the Cheyfitz home with Jimmy Hoffa.

The young lawyer was slightly nervous as he approached Cheyfitz's split-level white brick home. He wasn't sure about the wisdom of meeting with Hoffa, but he was curious about the man. He wondered whether he should have told McClellan and the F.B.I. about the engagement.

As Kennedy and Hoffa shook hands and sized each other up for the first time, Kennedy remarked that from what he'd heard of Hoffa he probably should have worn "a bullet-proof vest." Hoffa grinned.

Hoffa didn't drink. Cheyfitz offered Kennedy a drink, but he declined, so Cheyfitz also went without. After a few quips, the conversation turned to high-level discussions of the abuses of power by the Teamsters and by business. Both Kennedy and Hoffa were guarded. It was downright dull at points.

After a roast beef dinner, Cheyfitz tried to liven things up. "If you don't ask a few of the embarrassing questions, then I will," he said. He went on with questions about Hoffa's associations with the underworld and the "paper locals" in New York. Kennedy was getting into the discussion when there was a pre-arranged call from his wife at 9:45 p.m.

"Your wife wants to talk to you," Mrs. Cheyfits told him. Hoffa said: "Better hurry up, Bobby. She probably called to see if you're still alive."

At the telephone, within hearing distance of Hoffa and Cheyfitz, Kennedy answered:

"I'm still alive, dear. If you hear a big explosion, I probably won't be."

Kennedy left a few moments later. He already had decided that Hoffa was not the little superman he was supposed to be.

"I'd heard he was a likeable fellow, but that he was tough," Kennedy told me a few days later. "He talked so much about how tough he was that I had difficulty believing he really was tough."

On February 29, 1957, two days before the first hearings of the select committee, I wrote in a feature story:

"The mop-haired and boyish-appearing little brother of Senator John Kennedy (Dem., Mass.) is on the move."

It was a highly flattering article that ran more than two columns in length. It was a forecast of fame for the unknown little brother, and included a general background sketch of Bob Kennedy and the investigation.

I was surprised to find that Bob Kennedy was a little displeased with it. I had referred to his status as "a millionaire," his father's many millions, and the "political prominence of the family."

"Why do you reporters have to bring politics, family and my money into it?" Kennedy snapped. "Those things aren't important." He wanted to stand on his own feet.

"The money is more important than you realize now," I replied. "I've seen the pressure these Teamsters can bring against an investigation. You are going to need all the money and political friends you have before this is over."

Kennedy asked if I meant he might be bought if he wasn't wealthy. I said I didn't mean he could be bought, but that the security and financial independence of the chief counsel could be an important factor when the going became rough. I wasn't sure I convinced him then, but before the first year was completed he knew precisely what my fears had been.

On February 26, McClellan and Bob Kennedy launched the first public hearings of the special committee. They called in a gaudy array of pimps, prostitutes, politicians and pinball operators. Indeed, there were critics who said that McClellan and Kennedy were staging a sex show, and that it had nothing to do with the authorized investigation.

In the initial hearings Big Jim Elkins, former Portland gambling king, was the key witness.[7] McClellan was cautious. He emphasized that it was never safe to stake the reputation of the committee on the veracity of one witness. Elkins was examined and cross-examined before he was called for public testimony. His story was checked in every possible way. Corroboration of the story was produced by the bushel, including recordings of conversations involving the Teamsters and gangsters who were taking over control of Portland vice. Even then, McClellan and Kennedy used Elkins' testimony cautiously and kept him within the bounds of what had firm corroboration. It was a pattern they were to follow consistently.

Criticism of the committee evaporated as it became clear that the Western Conference was thoroughly rotten. Teamsters political power had been used in an attempt to take over organized vice. Frank Brewster had signed checks to pay the expenses of Seattle racketeers who controlled Portland gambling, prostitution, and liquor operations. Teamsters power and pickets enforced mobster deals.[8]

The political activity of the West Coast Teamsters was an insidious thing. Tax-exempt Teamsters union money was dumped into gubernatorial campaigns. It influenced the appointment of Teamsters and their friends to a wide range of high offices. Clyde Crosby, the Oregon Teamsters boss, admitted he was responsible for paying telephone bills and other expenses for a couple of Seattle mobsters who were in Portland working to elect William M. Langley as district attorney of Multnomah County, Oregon.[9]

Brewster admitted a broad pattern of political giving on the West Coast.[10] He said that $4,000 was dropped into the McFarland-for-governor campaign in Arizona in 1954. He said he put at least $5,000 of tax-free Teamsters funds into a campaign fund for California Governor Goodwin J. Knight. Knight said he knew nothing about the contribution, but he did appoint one of Brewster's friends as port director in San Francisco.

---

[7]McClellan committee, Report No. 1417, pages 7-12.

[8]McClellan committee, Report No. 1417, pages 9-15.

[9]McClellan committee, Report No. 1417, pages 37-39.

[10]McClellan committee, Report No. 1417, pages 54 and 55.

The smell of stinking politics on the West Coast wafted back to Washington, D. C., and on March 4, McClellan received a call from Labor Secretary James P. Mitchell, who wanted to discuss the subject.

McClellan laid details of the Beck case on the Secretary's table, but would make no recommendations as to whether the administration should let Beck represent the United States at the International Labor Organization meeting.

"That is a decision for the administration," McClellan said.

Within an hour after the meeting, Mitchell decided to reject Beck's nomination. He called George Meany and told him so.

For weeks Beck had been saying he was not evading Mc-Clellan, but was merely staying in Europe to get ready for the I.L.O. conference in March. Now Mitchell wired Beck that he would not be named a delegate, so the conference would not interfere with his returning to any business he might have with McClellan.

At Teamsters headquarters, Beck's aides were enraged. Vice-president Mohn told friends he had talked with Mitchell and had been "assured" that Beck would be the I.L.O. representative, or that he at least would be given a chance to save face by rejecting the appointment.

Like Beck, Mohn had guessed wrong about how much influence he had.

XV

Hoffa, Cheasty and the F.B.I.

On March 12, 1957, Hoffa's telephone in Detroit rang, and a voice asked for "Diane."

"Eddie Smith is calling," said the voice, and Hoffa's secretary gave a number at which Hoffa could be reached. The caller was John Cye Cheasty, who had informed the McClellan committee that he and Hoffa had agreed that he would use the code name "Eddie Smith" when making contacts. F.B.I. agents were listening to Cheasty's end of the conversation.

When Cheasty reached Hoffa, they arranged to meet at Dupont Circle in Washington. There, while F.B.I. cameras took pictures of the transaction, Cheasty gave Hoffa a committee memorandum concerning Beck's dealings with Nathan Shefferman. Hoffa allegedly slipped Cheasty $2,000 in cash. Cheasty later testified that after reading the memorandum, Hoffa exclaimed, "If that's what they have on Beck, it looks like his goose is cooked."

Arrangements were made for Cheasty to deliver more papers to Hoffa the next night. The F.B.I. agents had about as much as they thought they needed, but to clinch the case they wanted to catch Hoffa in possession of a confidential file of the McClellan committee.[1]

The public hearings went on as usual the next day, March

[1] Transcript, U. S. v. Hoffa and Fischbach, Cr. No. 294-57.

13. The focal point of attention was on the tall, lean figure of Clyde Cardinal Crosby, boss of the Teamsters in Oregon. The handsome, dark-haired union boss was a cool witness and a colorful figure. His brown eyes and unsmiling face had a fascination for the women reporters, and he had a cat-like quality when his slim-muscled figure glided across the huge kleig-lighted hearing room in the Senate Office Building.

Clyde Crosby testified he had been married five times. He admitted he had been arrested in September, 1938, convicted on a burglary charge, and under the name of "Bob Harper" had served a fifteen-month prison term in Arizona. It was as a convicted burglar that he entered the Teamsters organization, and still had the old conviction hanging around his neck when he was named an organizer for the International Teamsters by Dave Beck.[2]

The "Bob Harper" conviction had remained hidden, and Crosby became active in politics in Portland. He won office as a city commissioner, then widened his swath as a force in Multnomah County and state politics. The political contributions and the economic prestige of the Teamsters even created a favorable climate for Crosby in Arizona—scene of his burglary conviction at the age of twenty-three.

In August, 1956, he had successfully prevailed upon a judge in Prescott, Arizona, to enter an order expunging his conviction from the record, Crosby testified.

Crosby's rise as a power in politics and in the Teamsters was an interesting one, but an even more fascinating drama was going on out of the range of the public and the press.

At the noon recess, I walked with Bob Kennedy from the hearing room to his office. We talked of the morning hearings and the afternoon schedule, but Kennedy seemed preoccupied.

A short, smiling man with thinning grey hair greeted Kennedy in the office. They chatted briefly, and Kennedy with a mischievous glint in his eye introduced the man to me as John Cye Cheasty.

"Cheasty is one of the lawyers on the committee," Kennedy said, a little smile playing on his lips. "I think you should interview him, and do a story on him."

---

[2]McClellan committee hearings, Part 2, pages 674 and 675.

Cheasty was about the only staff member that I didn't know, and I assumed there must some angle that made him particularly important. Kennedy dashed away without explaining.

I assumed Cheasty was from Iowa or Minnesota, and would make a local story. He told me he was from Brooklyn. He said he was a retired Coast Guard officer, and had been in private investigative work. He had been working in the McClellan committee's New York office.

If there was a story for me in Cheasty, I couldn't see it. I gave it up as a bad job, and decided I could ask Kennedy what the angle was later. Cheasty was a pleasant enough fellow, but I figured my note-taking had been just so much wasted energy.

Shortly after the afternoon session started, Chairman McClellan and Bob Kennedy mysteriously excused themselves and left the hearing room. Vice Chairman Ives took charge, and to my surprise Cheasty questioned the witness, who at that moment was committee investigator Al Calabrese.

I did not know why Kennedy and McClellan left, but after a few minutes I concluded that Cheasty either didn't know the material or was a poor questioner. It was fortunate that Calabrese knew the Portland case well enough to testify without much prompting. I learned later that Cheasty had no advance knowledge he was to question any witnesses, and was totally unfamiliar with the Oregon investigation. Kennedy had tossed him into the chair because he was the only assistant counsel present at the time. Kennedy and McClellan left to plan events which that night overshadowed the public hearings.

At 11 p.m. March 13, 1957, the F.B.I. arrested Hoffa as he entered the elevator of the Dupont Plaza Hotel. He had confidential committee papers in his possession, and the F.B.I. charged him with an attempted bribe of Cheasty, committee employee and double agent.

Ethel Kennedy, Bob's wife, called me at home shortly after the arrest, and I rushed to the court house. Bob and Ethel were there for the triumphant moment. Jimmy was glum as he paced about the room, waiting arraignment.

"Well, Jimmy, so you finally slipped, and slipped good," I said as I met him. "I was beginning to wonder if anyone would ever catch up with you."

Hoffa was in no mood for the jokes or needles we usually tossed at each other. There was no smile, only cold hatred registered on his face at that moment. There was also a touch of fear, which was not usually a part of his makeup. The F.B.I. arrest, and a charge in federal court in Washington, were things he had not had to cope with before now. This was not Wayne County, Michigan, where he knew the ropes.

Strangely, Kennedy and Hoffa struck up a good-natured conversation, keeping it far off the subject at hand. It ended in an almost friendly debate about which of them could do the greatest number of pushups, but neither of them actually did any.

I was elated over the story, but I felt a little sorry for Jimmy Hoffa, now that I believed he was finished. Jimmy was the personification of the worst in labor, and his methods had a corrupting influence on government. He was totally insensitive to the normal ethical standards on conflicts of interest, and thought nothing of borrowing thousands of dollars from employers, union business agents or others who dealt with the union. He associated with gangsters in defiance of society.

Still, there was a touch of the heroic in this little fellow who seemed willing to fight the world. Hoffa had started with nothing and had fought his way to dominance of the massive union, of employers and of government officials.

Driven by poverty and fear, then by ambition, he had accepted the theory that every man has his price. Jimmy believed it, and his experience indicated he was almost right. Too many of the so-called pillars of society and government would sell out or chicken out in a tight squeeze. Those who would not sell out would usually reject the offer but say nothing about it.

The incident with John Cye Cheasty did not mean that Hoffa's theory was wrong. It merely meant the percentage finally caught up with Jimmy, and he had come face to face with an honest man who would take action against him. Jimmy was a hard worker, and he could be a charming little fellow. He could have been a tremendous force for good if his ethical standards had not been mixed up at some early stage. Now it was too late.

At the hearing the next morning, McClellan commented: "This action by Mr. Hoffa is clearly indicative of the steps the

gangster elements are taking and will continue to undertake to
hinder, hamper, obstruct, and destroy this committee. . . . We
will try to meet them, and accept their challenge, and deal with
them accordingly."

When Bob Kennedy was subsequently asked by reporters
about the indictment of Hoffa, the young attorney said he
considered it airtight. "If Hoffa isn't convicted, I'll jump off the
Capitol," Kennedy quipped. He thought it was off-the-record,
but it got into print. It was indiscreet, and Teamsters attorney
Edward Bennett Williams was to throw it in Kennedy's face for
weeks.

In the big Senate caucus room Bob Kennedy turned his
attention to finishing off Dave Beck. Beck had returned on
March 10, three days before Hoffa's arrest, and a week later
appeared before a panel of newsmen on the C.B.S. show, "Face
the Nation." Beck brazenly told the national television audience
he had "borrowed" $300,000 to $400,000, interest free, from the
Teamsters treasury. So what?

The Senate caucus room was jammed when Dave Beck went
before the McClellan committee. He bragged that he could "blow
the top off the Capitol" if he really wanted to talk about how he
had spread Teamsters' money around among politicians. But
he did not want to talk about his finances. Under oath he admitted he was Dave Beck, and from there on took the Fifth
Amendment sixty-five times.

Between questions he bellowed and shouted, pounded the
tables and commented at length on the Beck version of the
Constitution of the United States. He chanted over and over
that he was taking the Fifth Amendment only because his attorney, former Senator James Duff, a Pennsylvania Republican,
had told him to. Actually, Duff didn't appear with him; Duff
had just been retired from the Senate and did not feel it would
be proper to come back before his colleagues. But Beck used his
name until it became ridiculous. Duff finally withdrew from the
case in disgust.

Although Beck didn't talk, almost everyone else did—
especially Nathan Shefferman. Shefferman said Beck helped him
sell a new filing system to Teamsters union locals. Shefferman's

net profit on the deal was $61,000, of which Beck received $24,000.[3]

Shefferman said Beck ordered the furniture for both the old Teamsters headquarters in Washington, and the new palace at 25 Louisiana Avenue. Mrs. Beck's cousin, Norman Gessert, shared profits with Shefferman's Union Merchandising Company on that sale.

Beck helped Shefferman convince Teamsters locals to buy toy trucks, of all things, at prices ranging from $15 to $30 each. Each local was given a quota of at least five toy trucks with union labels, and Beck pushed the deal with telegrams. The two Shefferman firms involved netted $80,000 in profits, part of which went to Beck's son, Dave Junior.[4]

On March 27, Dave Beck took the witness chair for the second time. He still was not talking. Senator McClellan charged that Beck had misappropriated at least $320,000 in Teamsters union funds. Beck took the Fifth Amendment, and McClellan excused him while investigators continued to patch together the full story of what was being referred to as "Beck's Beckadillos."

Out in Yakima, Washington, members of Teamsters Local 524 hung an effigy of Dave Beck, set fire to it with cigarette lighters, and cheered. It was ironic because Beck had risen to national prominence in Yakima in 1941, when he declared war on the Yakima Valley apple industry. At that time, urged on by Beck, midwestern Teamsters agreed to treat Yakima Valley apples as "hot cargo" and refused to unload the fruit from railroad sidings.

Apples rotted. The Yakima Valley growers took one look at the nationwide economic squeeze and decided to get in line. The incident brought Beck before a Congressional committee, then, but he bluffed his way through.

On April 2, 1957, Bob Kennedy received a call from Fred Perkins, the veteran labor reporter for the Scripps-Howard newspaper chain. Perkins had information that Shefferman had tried to arrange a $71,000 rakeoff on the Teamsters' purchase of land for Washington headquarters. Shefferman, with Beck's approval, had tried to get representatives of the American

---

[3]McClellan committee, Report No. 1417, page 65.

[4]McClellan committee, Report No. 1417, page 65.

Legion to sell the Louisiana Avenue location to an intermediate corporation which would boost the price and sell it to the Teamsters.[5]

Investigator Duffy subpoenaed Teamsters records and talked to witnesses. The Shefferman plans for the $71,000 rakeoff fell through, but Shefferman had obtained a $12,000 commission from the Teamsters on the false claim that he had reduced the price. Further checking showed an $8,000 kickback to Beck.

On April 6, Kennedy, Bellino and investigator Pierre Salinger called on Nate and Shelton Shefferman at the offices of Labor Relations Associates in Chicago. Kennedy wanted to find out more about that $750 check Shefferman's firm had given to Minneapolis Teamsters boss Sid Brennan.

"What man did you have on that job?" Kennedy asked.

Shelton Shefferman volunteered that a look at the daily reports would show, and Kennedy asked to see them. It was the first indication that the firm kept daily reports, and a brief look showed these were a gold mine of information.

Within a few hours, Kennedy had investigators running in every direction. Salinger followed up in Toledo and Clyde, Ohio, and Webster City, Iowa, and he also made trips to Kentucky and Mississippi. Investigator Walter Sheridan took over in Marion, Ohio, and later followed leads into Boston. Investigator Irwin (Count) Langenbacher was put on the trail of George Kamenow, in Detroit and Flint, Michigan. The investigation of the classic labor consultant case was well on the way.

On April 7, Kennedy and Bellino arrived in Seattle for three more days of field work. Cooperation came easier now that Beck was on the way down. Kennedy called on Fred P. Loomis, the financial adviser who had Beck as a client from 1947 to 1955. Loomis told Kennedy he had resigned in protest against Beck's ethics, and produced the letter of resignation.

The letter gave Bob Kennedy an important insight into Beck's methods. His various deals, enterprises and manipulations, both large-scale and petty, were handled with the help of many people, none of whom knew very much about what the others were doing. None, therefore, could tell the story.

The next day Kennedy called on Irving Levine, operator

---

[5]McClellan committee, Report No. 1417, pages 64 and 65.

of two Seattle beverage distributing agencies—K & L Beverages and K & L Distributing Company.

Beck had told Levine that he could deliver to him the distributorship for Budweiser beer in the Seattle area—if Dave Junior, then twenty-five, was allowed to buy into the firm. It looked like a good deal to Levine. Beck had a talk with J. J. Carroll, vice president and sales manager of the Anheuser-Busch brewery division and the Budweiser brewery division. The Budweiser distributorship—soon to become the biggest "Bud" territory in America—was delivered smoothly.

The attitude of Anheuser-Busch people toward Beck was spelled out in memos exchanged in the St. Louis office. Beck was described as "His Majesty, the Wheel."[6] It was a fact that 50 per cent of the Anheuser-Busch employees were members of the Teamsters union, and "cooperation" with Beck seemed advisable.

Eventually, Beck demanded that his son be elevated to the presidency of K & L Beverage Company. Levine told Kennedy he objected until the Teamsters refused to unload one of his trucks. His Majesty, the Wheel, remarked that this proved Levine did not know how to handle labor relations with Beck's Teamsters Local 174. Levine capitulated, and Dave Junior became president of the company.

Ultimately, Levine went to Anheuser-Busch for help. Anheuser-Busch authorized a $112,500 line of credit so Levine could buy out the Beck interest in K & L. It meant that Levine had to give the Becks a whopping profit, but that was better than trying to operate in a partnership with them, or having the trucks stop.[7]

On April 9, Kennedy and Bellino reviewed the reports of Stewart Krieger, an auditor for the Teamsters. Krieger had admitted that he was on the Teamsters payroll for eighteen months while he spent practically all of his time keeping books on the beer distributing business operated by Dave Beck Junior. The union also financed a six weeks' trip for Krieger to survey the finances of Beck's beer outlets in Alaska.

On April 10, Kennedy and Bellino questioned Don Hedlund, a mortgage investment broker for the Teamsters. Hedlund

---

[6]McClellan committee, Report No. 1417, page 73.

[7]McClellan committee, Report No. 1417, pages 71-74.

said Beck had channeled more than $9 million in International Brotherhood of Teamsters funds into mortgage purchases through the National Mortgage Company—a Seattle concern in which Joseph McEvoy, Beck's nephew, had bought a one-third interest with money he got from Beck.[8]

Hedlund said he also had entered into a mortgage deal with Beck involving "The Ray Leheney Memorial Fund." Beck was trustee of this $80,000 fund, collected through the Teamsters union for Leheney's widow. Beck and Hedlund made a joint personal profit of $11,500 on mortgages sold to the fund.

Bob Kennedy was astounded. Dave Beck, trustee of funds for a friend's widow, had made a profit out of a sale to the trust![9]

Kennedy returned to Washington, D. C., to launch hearings on April 16 on a nasty labor situation in Scranton, Pennsylvania.

There had been anonymous threats on the life of investigator LaVern Duffy, who was operating in the Scranton, Pennsylvania, area; but the investigation didn't stop. Duffy developed a devastating documentation of bombings, misuse of union funds, and fixing of union elections. Paul Bradshaw, an admitted member of a Teamsters bombing squad in Scranton, had made a recording of conversations with other Teamsters thugs and turned it over to J. Harold Brislin, a Scranton newspaper reporter.[10] (Brislin was awarded a Pulitzer Prize in 1959 as a result of later work on labor rackets.)

Duffy worked with Brislin to develop the story of union terror and Teamsters influence on local law enforcement officials. Again there was the disgusting spectacle of the top Teamster in Pennsylvania, Harry Tevis, attending a testimonial dinner for a group of convicted terrorists from the Teamsters and other unions.[11]

The McClellan committee hearing showed a deplorable condition in Scranton. Acts of harassment, intimidation and destruction of property against individual home owners and businessmen were sanctioned, directed and often participated in by officers of the Teamsters and the Building Trades Council.

---

[8]McClellan committee, Report No. 1417, pages 75-80.
[9]McClellan committee, Report No. 1417, pages 80 and 81.
[10]McClellan committee, Report No. 1417, page 95.
[11]McClellan committee, Report No. 1417, page 105.

"There was a betrayal of the responsibility and trust of high union office by John Durkin, secretary-treasurer of Teamsters Local 229 and a vice-president of the Pennsylvania Federation of Labor. Durkin, who was among four Scranton labor leaders convicted of conspiracy to dynamite a home then under construction by a non-union contractor, was also linked to a 'war of nerves' against a Scranton bakery which culminated in its stink bombing."

"There was a similar betrayal of responsibility . . . by Joseph Bartell, president of the Building Trades Council of Scranton. . . . Bartell, along with Durkin, was convicted of conspiracy in the . . . dynamiting of a local home . . . ; in addition, he was found guilty of conspiracy in a case in which a wall in another home under construction was pushed over."[12]

"Although Scranton law enforcement authorities eventually prosecuted these criminal acts, they were generally slow to seize their responsibilities. The stink bombing of the bakery resulted in no prosecution whatever. The contractor of the home where the wall was pushed over testified that he was never contacted by city police at all, and by state police only after the incident of the dynamiting of a second home, some six months later."[13]

"A distinct conflict of interest existed in City Solicitor James McNulty's simultaneous function as legal representative for the building trades."

"Dubious ethics were reflected in statements by two international union officers at a testimonial fund-raising dinner for Durkin and Bartell, after their conviction for conspiracy in the dynamiting case . . . William Kendrick, international vice president of the laborers union, found it fitting to assert that the . . . men had been 'framed.' On the same festive occasion, Harry Tevis, a Teamsters international vice president, flatly declared that the international did not feel the four were guilty and that it would take no disciplinary action against them."[14]

With the Scranton hearing out of the way, there was time for more work on Dave Beck. On April 23, I took a night plane to Seattle, to do some research for *Look* magazine on an article

[12]McClellan committee, Report No. 1417, page 104.
[13]McClellan committee, Report No. 1417, page 105.
[14]McClellan committee, Report No. 1417, page 105.

about Beck, and to familiarize myself with the setting. The next day, Ed Guthman and I went to lunch with Charles Carroll, the King County prosecutor. Carroll, a pleasant and ruggedly independent lawyer, was a favorite with Guthman. Political strings were being pulled by some of the Beck political stooges, but Carroll was already convinced that he had Beck sewed up on a larceny charge.

Carroll explained certain features of the law in Washington State that practically pulled the investigative teeth of prosecutors. In the absence of a grand jury, the county prosecutor had no subpoena power, Carroll explained. The law, in Washington, had no provision for the periodic impaneling of a grand jury, as there was in most other states, Carroll said. It took a rather unusual set of circumstances to get the courts to set up a special grand jury.

The McClellan committee had established one of those unusual circumstances, and a special grand jury was being established on the day I was visiting with him. Carroll was sure he was going to have all the tools he needed to jail Beck, despite some Beck favoritism that lingered in the person of at least one judge. The statute of limitations barred action on many of Beck's crimes, but there were some that Carroll was certain were actionable.

For three days I rummaged through the old records in the King County courthouse, piecing together the financial rise of Dave Beck from the time he bought his first little house upon returning from the Navy after World War I, until he became a man of wealth.

Ed Guthman drove me past the Teamsters headquarters at Sixth Avenue and Denny Way. We passed many Beck real estate projects, and the half-dozen businesses in which the Beck family had gained a foothold as a result of his power as Teamsters boss. We took a long drive north along Lake Washington to the Beck compound. This was the site of Beck's lavish mansion, and of the homes Beck constructed for the little group of favorites of the "Teamsters Court."

Seattle is a beautiful city in the spring, and there was that day a spring-like atmosphere among the newspaper people and businessmen and politicians who had endured a long period of cold fear of the union tyrant. They were confident that Beck was finished, that he had lost his influence on local and state politics.

On Saturday, April 27, I returned to Washington to appear on the "Meet the Press" television panel that was to question Bob Kennedy on Sunday afternoon.

Ethel Kennedy was her usual vivacious self when we met at the television studio: "Gee, Clark, I'm glad to see you on the panel."

Ethel commented on how tough reporters are on some of the guests and that it was good that "Bobby has at least one friend."

"I think Bob can take care of himself," I said. "If he can't then this is a good time to learn."

Bob Kennedy was nervous, and I chided him about finally learning how Dave Beck felt. He didn't want to make any slip that would hurt the McClellan committee's work, and I said I didn't think he'd have any trouble if he remembered his role as counsel and avoided being pushed into sitting in judgment on labor.

Then, during the show, I landed on him hard with one question after another, probing for his opinion on matters before the committee. The persistence of the questions and the tone made him slash back at me in irritation. He was surprised, and I am sure would have reached out and slugged me had we been close enough. But he retained his composure and refused to be pushed into indiscreet answers.

Bob accepted it as part of the game; but Ethel commented: "Clark Mollenhoff, I should scratch your eyes out."

I told her tough questioning had to be expected from all reporters, and that it was Bob's responsibility to handle them. "Bob handled himself very well, and I'm sure made a good impression," I told her. "He was honest, and he handled the tough questions without any bobbles."

Ethel's tremendous loyalty prevented her from accepting my explanation until Bob had assured her that I was merely doing my job. His assurance was all she needed, and we were friends again.

On May 1, Beck returned another $100,000 to the Teamsters treasury in a final effort to square accounts. In less than three years he had put back $370,000, contending it had only been borrowed. The restitution was too late. A grand jury was already at work in Tacoma, Washington. On May 3, the grand jury returned an indictment charging Beck with evading $56,000 in taxes for 1950. It was a charge that could send him to jail.

Five days later Beck arrived at the Capitol for his third round with the McClellan committee. He knew they were going to take him apart. One of his attorneys, Edward Bennett Williams, told him to listen to the questions and answer them. But Beck was nervous. His pink cheeks had turned red, his voice had lost its snap, and his football-shaped body had lost its bounce. He took refuge behind the Fifth Amendment.

When he told us afterward that he was certain he would be re-elected general president of the Teamsters in the fall, he did not sound as if he believed his own words.

On May 16, he was recalled for his final appearance, after a full week in which testimony and documents had answered his demand "to be faced by my accusers." Some witnesses testified freely and completely. But even at that late date others were hesitant; they still had lingering fears of offending the man who might somehow continue to run the powerful Teamsters.

By the time Beck took his place in the witness chair in the huge, high-ceilinged Caucus Room, Chairman McClellan had compiled a list of 52 examples of Beck's misuse of Teamsters power and Teamsters money. The misappropriated funds totaled at least $300,000. Beck took the Fifth Amendment more than 60 times before he was excused, with caustic comments, by McClellan.[15]

Even at the end, Beck occasionally bellowed authoritatively. He strutted from the hearing room beside his attorney, Williams, with the same confidence of bearing he had when he entered it in March.

"Sure, I'm going to run for office," he told reporters. He whistled a little as he waited for the elevator, and he whistled as he walked across the Capitol Plaza to the huge Teamsters temple he had built conveniently nearby so he could keep an eye on Congress.

Already the wolves in his own organization were after him,

---

[15]McClellan committee, Report No. 1417, page 61.

and on May 26, 1957, Dave Beck announced he would not seek re-election as general president of the Teamsters. On June 7, A.F.L.-C.I.O. president George Meany suggested that the Teamsters should oust Beck, even before his term ended in September. Beck complained that an unseemly scramble had developed to grab his job. The charge of conspiracy to bribe was still pending against Jimmy Hoffa, but there were others angling for the top position.

In seven short months, from that peak moment in the White House with the President of the United States, Beck had landed at the bottom. If he could beat that income tax rap, he seemed to believe, he might still manage to retain the rent-free, ranch-type mansion, with its all-weather swimming pool and artificial waterfall. He was still worth about half of a million dollars, if the defense lawyers didn't eat up too much of it. Also, there was that $50,000 a year lifetime union pension he had arranged for himself.

But he had lost one thing he wanted more than anything else: respectability.

XVI

Union Problems and Power Politics

Thousands of letters and hundreds of leads swamped the McClellan committee in more confusion than organization in May, 1957. Bob Kennedy was busy conducting hearings almost every day, and even on a schedule from 8 a.m. until midnight he could not keep abreast of everything. He assigned Jerome Adlerman and Paul Kamerick as coordinators, but then pulled them off to do field work demanded by some members of the committee. I was fearful the whole investigation would break down or be bungled because one hand certainly did not know what the other was doing.

Amid this confusion, Kennedy hired Kenneth O'Donnell, a young Massachusetts man who had been football captain at Harvard in the late 1940's. O'Donnell had no prior experience in investigation, and he was not a lawyer. His only notable asset was association with Kennedy on a college football squad. I questioned the selection, as did many others. I learned later that Kennedy had his own doubts and was concerned about whether McClellan or the Republican Senators might raise some objection.

O'Donnell surprised many of us. He became one of the most valuable staff members. He did not know investigative techniques, but he learned them. He read every report and knew what every investigator was doing. He had a phenomenal memory for names and details in the complex pattern of criminal activity from San Antonio to Duluth, and from San Diego to Buffalo. His motivation probably was too political; but when Kennedy was tied down with hearing preparation, it was Kenny O'Donnell who had the ability and the authority to get things done.

Those thousands of letters causing administration problems for the McClellan committee were also causing other problems for A.F.L.-C.I.O. They contained leads on scandals in other unions.

By the end of May troubles were flaming around A.F.L.-C.I.O. president George Meany. He had managed to force Dave Beck out of the A.F.L.-C.I.O. Executive Council for taking the Fifth Amendment on questions dealing with the misuse of $300,000 to $400,000 in union funds.[1] But no one knew better than Meany that this was not solving the big problem of Teamsters corruption. Should the A.F.L.-C.I.O. expel the mighty Teamsters union—the union that put the real bite in organizing drives? Could the A.F.L.-C.I.O. work with old John English, secretary-treasurer of the Teamsters, to reform the huge drivers union? If the Teamsters union was ousted, should the A.F.L.-C.I.O. set up a rival, honest union to organize truck drivers?

Complicating the problem was evidence that several other unions had corrupt leadership. How aggressively could Meany act against such corruption without blasting apart the recently merged A.F.L.-C.I.O.? Obviously pressure from these unions would have to be taken into account in deciding what to do about the Teamsters.

It was possible, in the late spring of 1957, to point to nearly a dozen unions in which there would be trouble. The Laundry Workers International Union was in bad shape. Jimmy James, the secretary-treasurer, had embezzled nearly one million dollars and Meany knew he couldn't look to Sam Byers, the international president of the L.W.I.U., to fire James. Byers had served a prison term for extortion in the 1930's, before he changed his name from John Jilson and got into union work.

There was a mess in the U.A.W.-A.F.L. (later to become known as the Allied Industrial Workers), where Anthony Doria, the loud-mouthed secretary-treasurer, dominated the picture.

---

[1]McClellan committee, Report No. 1417, pages 60-63 and 83.

Doria associated with racketeers and handled the union's money as if it were his own. Angelo Inciso was another problem child in that union.

More or less similar difficulties, at the local or national level, could be found in the Building Service Employees International Union, the United Brotherhood of Carpenters and Joiners of America, the International Union of Operating Engineers, the International Hod Carriers, Building and Common Laborers Union of America, the Hotel and Restaurant Employees and Bartenders International Union, the International Jewelry Workers Union, the Amalgamated Meat Cutters and Butcher Workmen of North America, the Sheet Metal Workers International Association, the Bakery and Confectionery Workers International Union, and the United Textile Workers of America.

Although the majority of labor unions were reasonably clean, corruption was sufficiently widespread to make it hard for the A.F.L.-C.I.O. to discipline the ones which were not. And the McClellan committee was already at work on cases that could involve the top leadership of four large unions—the Carpenters, with 800,000 members; the Operating Engineers, with 280,000; the Bakery Workers Union, with 160,000; and the United Textile Workers, with 50,000.

Road scandals in Indiana had resulted in fraud allegations against Carpenters union president Maurice A. Hutcheson, second vice-president O. William Blaier, and others.[2] The scandal-scarred Operating Engineers Union was already under investigation for misuse of funds, improper financial dealings with employers, and dictatorial practices.

Scandals in the Bakery Workers Union and the Textile Workers union were beginning to be exposed by the McClellan committee. It was a forecast of the problems for Meany in other unions.

---

[2]In 1960, Hutcheson was convicted on charges of conspiracy and bribery growing out of Indiana's highway scandals. On October 2, 1963, the Indiana Supreme Court reversed the conviction and held the conviction had been based on insufficient evidence. Hutcheson was convicted on a federal charge of contempt of Congress for refusing to answer questions for the McClellan labor racket committee that dealt with the Indiana highway scandals. He was sentenced to a six-month jail term and a $500 fine, but the court put him on probation for two years and wiped out the six-month jail term.

The first activities of the McClellan committee gave courage to Curtis Sims, the secretary-treasurer of the Bakery and Confectionery Workers International Union of America. In March, 1957, he filed charges against that union's president, James G. Cross, and its vice-president, George Stuart, for misuse of union funds. He also told the McClellan committee that Cross was using union money to support a known prostitute, and that Cross had engaged in the brutal beating of a leader of an opposition faction at the union convention in San Francisco in October, 1956.

Investigators George M. Kopecky, LaVern Duffy, and accountant James F. Mundie seized records that showed union funds were "plundered" after Cross became international president in 1953.

The McClellan committee found that "Cross sold a group of his members down the river by secretly conniving to extend a substandard contract . . . with a man to whom he was then personally indebted $40,000 to buy a Palm Beach home, to whom he had been personally indebted $57,600 to buy a Washington home, and from whose brother he had earlier secured a $16,000 mortgage to buy a Chicago home.[3]

"In 1956, Cross falsified an affidavit of compliance to the N.L.R.B. by indicating that his compensation and allowances totalled $17,500 annually, when, in fact, he received almost $40,000 in expenses alone that year.

"The committee cannot accept as proper union expenses a $130 item for a hotel room engaged solely for poker games of Cross' executive board during a 10-day meeting in New York; it cannot accept as credible a $2,980 expenditure by Cross for a six-day stay in Miami when he collected $1,079 for driving from Washington to his home in Palm Beach during this same period.[4]

"Cross cast ignominy on his union membership by hiring as an 'organizer' a woman with a police record for grand theft, (and) for residing in a house of ill fame.

"Miss (Kay) Lower's association with Cross cost the Bakers Union upwards of $10,000 . . . (including) an indeterminate

---

[3]McClellan committee, Report No. 1417, page 128.

[4]McClellan committee, Report No. 1417, page 129.

amount in hotel bills on journeys in which she often appeared in Cross' company.

"Cross sanctioned the use of violence including the beating of the 14-year-old son of a bakery owner during a Los Angeles strike. Cross himself was charged by two witnesses with having taken part in slugging of union critics at the time of the union convention in San Francisco.[5]

"George Stuart mulcted Chicago Bakers locals of $40,000. One of his most brazen manipulations involved a $13,000 appropriation for a 'joint organizational drive' with (Detroit) Teamster Joint Council 43, which, as intermediary, then purchased two Cadillacs at $6,500 apiece for Stuart and Cross.[6]

"Thefts by Stuart were possible under two Chicago trusteeships (Local 300 and Local 100) of the most arbitrary and capricious stripe. . . . In the case of Local 100's trusteeship, Stuart peremptorily imposed it without any hearing. . . . Gilbert Mann, the ousted local president, testified that his first notification of the matter came when he found Stuart at his desk brandishing a gun.

"The collection of some $85,000 in funds for a testimonial dinner for International Vice President Max Kralstein . . . went forward under circumstances most charitably described as dubious. Much of the money was gleaned from New York bakery owners, a number of whom testified that they either had experienced or feared labor trouble. . . . The fund raisers were by and large union business agents who serviced the shops whose owners they solicited.[7]

"Herman Cooper, counsel for the bakers union acted improperly and unethically by failing in his duty to represent the interest of the union itself, protecting rather the specific interests of Cross. . . .

"The committee was deeply shocked by Cooper's admission that he had personally prepared a predated document suspending one of the challengers, Secretary-Treasurer Curtis Sims, even before Sims' charges against the Cross regime had been aired before the union's executive board. The committee finds this is

---

[5]McClellan committee, Report No. 1417, page 129.

[6]McClellan committee, Report No. 1417, page 130.

[7]McClellan committee, Report No. 1417, page 130.

a shameful breach of the honorable traditions of the American legal profession."[8]

By fancy fund juggling, top officials of the United Textile Workers of America were able to conceal from George Meany their misuse of more than $100,000 in union funds. President Anthony Valente and secretary-treasurer Lloyd Klenert smugly assumed they had covered their tracks, until chief counsel Robert Kennedy assigned investigators Al Calabrese and Ralph Mills, both former F.B.I. men, and Morton E. Henig to the case.

They moved in quickly with subpoenas.

It was a small union—50,000 members with annual income of only about $1 million—but "the funds appropriated by its two top-ranking officers totaled $178,000, or about 18 per cent of the union's entire intake in any one year."[9]

"Valente and Klenert fraudulently diverted ($95,000) union funds to the purchase of new homes for themselves," the Mc-Clellan committee reported.

The committee found that "$17,500 subsequently withdrawn from the union by Valente and Klenert for 'organizational expenses' went for large purchases for their new homes, including down payments for air conditioning and a $2,786.50 piano for Klenert."[10]

The Textile Workers' executive council "exhibited a morality of the same low level as Valente's and Klenert's by slavishly accepting their version of their financial manipulations and white-washing them in a report request by the AFL," the McClellan committee said.

"Joseph Jacobs, the counsel for the UTWA, behaved in a manner unbecoming a member of the legal profession. Jacobs derived benefits from his union connection simultaneously as owner of a firm which leased cars to the UTWA. He was also a member of the UTWA subcommittee which supposedly 'investigated' the Valente-Klenert speculations and gave the two men a clean bill of health."[11]

The McClellan committee also reported that the union's

---

[8]McClellan committee, Report No. 1417, page 131.
[9]McClellan committee, Report No. 1417, page 159.
[10]McClellan committee, Report No. 1417, page 160.
[11]McClellan committee, Report No. 1417, page 161.

lawyer "was instrumental in having the union pay part of an assessment levied by the Internal Revenue Service on Valente and Klenert for faulty income tax returns.

"The (UTWA executive) council passed a resolution approving the annual destruction of all union records, except those of 'historical nature' at a time when Valente and Klenert were under income tax investigation. It also raised the salaries of the two men."[12]

Valente got "the lion's share" of the $66,000 in union funds that he and Klenert misused for personal expenditures. The personal items included $566.50 for a color TV set; $222 for a woman's black suit; $20 for a handknit sweater; $49.50 for a golfer's lamp; $11,411 for theater tickets ($2,564 of it spent for tickets to the stage musical show "My Fair Lady").[13]

These shenanigans in the newly united "House of Labor" were making life hard for George Meany. But the McClellan committee was having troubles of its own. Beck and Hoffa had taken a pasting, and the Teamsters were not in a mood to take it sitting down. They started a whispering campaign in the late spring to undermine the committee, and specifically to try to discredit Bob Kennedy and John McClellan. Teamsters propagandists, playing on the Republican dislike of Walter Reuther and his United Automobile Workers-C.I.O., portrayed McClellan and Kennedy as being involved in a political conspiracy with Reuther.

The Teamsters peddled the story that McClellan and Kennedy were plotting to discredit Beck and Hoffa so Reuther could take control of the 1.4 million members of the Teamsters. In return, Reuther was said to be ready to throw his political support behind John Kennedy for the Democratic Presidential nomination in 1960. The fact was that neither McClellan nor Bob Kennedy had met Reuther, and both of them were conservatives with no leanings towards Reuther's ultra-liberal viewpoint.

Some of Hoffa's closest friends in the trucking industry met with other truck-line owners and told them Reuther was trying to take over the Teamsters union. Certain frightened employers were urged to tell newspaper editors, business friends

---

[12]McClellan committee, Report No. 1417, page 161.
[13]McClellan committee, Report No. 1417, page 161.

and political leaders about this alleged Reuther-inspired conspiracy to destroy Beck and Hoffa.

The story was peddled to me by one of my informants in the trucking industry. It came to me again from a Washington lawyer who represented trucking interests. An editor on one of the Minneapolis newspapers called me to ask what there was to this report he had heard in business circles as "the real story" behind the Teamsters investigation. And I heard it again from two Republican members of the McClellan committee.

"There are investigators working on some aspects of the U.A.W.-C.I.O. operations," I told the editor. "Such a plot would be inconsistent with McClellan's view of Reuther. Remember that McClellan is a conservative from the South. Unless Bob Kennedy is fooling me, he has no intention of covering up any of Reuther's activity."

"But if the Teamsters are destroyed, can't Walter Reuther grab trucking for his union?" I was asked.

I said it would be totally unrealistic to believe that George Meany or anyone else on the A.F.L.-C.I.O. executive board would agree to toss Reuther even 50,000 more members, let alone the 1.4 million Teamsters.

Some Republicans on the McClellan committee accepted this Teamsters' story at face value. Privately, these Republicans started complaining that McClellan and Kennedy were out to get Beck and Hoffa, then let Reuther take over. Reporters familiar with the A.F.L.-C.I.O. were unsuccessful in convincing them that they were the victims of Teamsters propaganda. The rumor caromed around Capitol Hill until it broke into print in a national news magazine.

Senator John Kennedy and Bob were enraged. Chairman McClellan called a meeting at 2 p.m. on July 18 for a showdown with Republicans on complaints about Bob Kennedy. Republican Senator Irving Ives of New York disassociated himself from the accusation that the Kennedys were using the committee for partisan politics. He stood with McClellan all the way.

Senator Kennedy read a sentence from a story in *Newsweek* magazine that said, "The counsel, Robert Kennedy, has ignored continual demands for an investigation of Reuther, GOP members say privately."

In polite terms, John Kennedy challenged the other Republicans to put up or shut up. He said if they had any complaints, now was the time to make them.

"I was wondering about . . . whether it was believed that there had been a deliberate slowdown and whether this was an attempt by the counsel, with my support, to prevent an investigation," said Senator Kennedy, putting it to them bluntly.

"I have insisted on a complete investigation of the political activities of the UAW and the CIO and I have been assured by the staff that that will take place," said Senator Goldwater. "So, as far as this Republican member is concerned, I am happy as a squirrel in a little cage."

"I appreciate that, Senator," John Kennedy commented, and added, "I just wanted to try to determine . . . that it is not the opinion of the members that there is some, what they call 'Reuther protection game' going on."[14]

Senator Goldwater indicated he believed the stories were just a result of excessive exercise of "freedom of the press," and gave his own philosophy: "I just treat newspaper articles and magazine stories in the light of the fact that these boys out here have to make a living and what they write is up to them."

Stern-faced committee chairman McClellan turned to Senator Karl Mundt, the South Dakota Republican who had also indicated a strong interest in an investigation of Reuther.

Senator Mundt denied any part in causing political troubles in the committee. He assured McClellan: "I am as happy as a South Dakota pheasant in a South Dakota cornfield."[15]

Republican Senator Carl Curtis of Nebraska chimed in: "I want the record to show that I have complete confidence in our chairman and our staff and I believe that this committee will continue to cooperate and do a good job."

Chairman McClellan relieved Senator Kennedy of a complaint that Republican members weren't being told what was going on.

"I take the responsibility although I do not alibi for it,"

[14]McClellan committee, hearings of July 18, 1957, on "Committee Policy," page 3.

[15]McClellan committee, hearings of July 18, 1957, on "Committee Policy," pages 3 and 4.

McClellan said. "The Chair, himself, and I try to be pretty diligent about it, cannot possibly keep current with even daily conferences with the chief counsel, and sometimes with other members of the staff."

McClellan concluded the meeting with this defense of Kennedy and the staff: "They are not perfect and neither is this committee. With our imperfections, but with the purpose of achieving a goal that is worthy of the dignity and stature of the United States Senate, and of results that will serve the welfare of this country, we shall now adjourn this love feast and proceed with the business at hand."[16]

---

[16]McClellan committee, hearings of July 18, 1957, on "Committee Policy," pages 6 and 9.

XVII

A Labor Lawyer's Sex Setup

.In those first months of the McClellan committee hearings in 1957, one incident in Chicago dramatized how far a few local union attorneys would go in corrupting government officials. It was unusual in its scope, and in the clear use of sex to control key political figures by the underworld-union alliance. But, it was not unique, for throughout the investigations there ran a pattern of big money, wild spending and union-financed debauchery with a purpose. In some areas it was used discreetly, or only to coerce a public official on a specific case.

In Chicago, it had become a standard operation for a smooth little union mouthpiece who represented one Teamsters joint council, a number of locals of the Teamsters and several other unions. His title: general counsel for the Illinois Federation of Labor.

The night of Sunday, June 2, 1957, the body of Daniel D. Carmell hurtled from a fifteenth floor apartment at 1640 E. Fiftieth Street in Chicago and smashed onto the freshly sodded grass plot below. Carmell was dead when police arrived, and so was the criminal trial which could have shaken the Chicago political world as it deserved to be shaken. Word of the death was flashed on news programs a few minutes after police identified the dead man as one of the most prominent labor lawyers in Illinois who had also been a power in Chicago politics.

Carmell's death sent a feeling of relief through a group of nervous, sleepless union and political figures who had been waiting for the 58-year-old labor lawyer to go on trial the next morning. At 9 a.m. on June 3, 1957, Carmell was scheduled to appear in federal court on a charge of violating the White Slave Act by transporting a 19-year-old Davenport, Iowa, girl into Illinois for purposes of prostitution.

Had the charges been filed in a state court, there might have been a way of killing it, or at least of limiting the testimony to the narrowest possible scope on technical grounds. Some federal judges in the Chicago area would have been inclined to give a break to Dan Carmell or to some of his political friends who might have been implicated in the case. It was Carmell's bad luck that the case was assigned to Federal Judge Julius Hoffman, a jurist with a reputation for being tough-minded and impartial in running his court, and immune to the subtle and not-so-subtle political pressures that often surround such a case.

The criminal case on which Carmell was indicted was no ordinary White Slave Act case, for Carmell was no ordinary pimp or procurer. The tough, free-spending Chicago lawyer not only was counsel for the Illinois Federation of Labor, but also was counsel for the Chicago Federation of Labor and attorney for several local unions. With a liberal supply of cash, he entertained important city, county, state and federal officials. Dan had wrapped up key officials in Chicago and Illinois with lavish union-financed entertainment. With a high good humor and back-slapping geniality, he picked up their dinner and drink tabs at such expensive restaurants as The Chez Paree, The Swiss Chalet and The Pump Room.

Dan could tip with a flourish of a $100 bill, give $50 to an orchestra leader to play a favorite song. Directly or indirectly, the money came out of dues paid by union members.

When the more conventional public entertainment was concluded for the evening, Dan would whisk his friends off to private parties, complete with oriental films, two lesbians, and a huge Negro man who performed interesting acrobatics. There were young girls available for those more interested in participation than in spectator sports. The girls were not assigned but were under instructions to let the politicians do their own selecting, and they were ordered not to accept money from Dan's guests.

"I'll pay the bills," he told the girls. He reprimanded one girl who had accepted money. Dan didn't want his guests to view his hospitality as commercial. He wanted to give them the satisfaction of believing they had made a personal conquest.

Those who accepted Carmell's hospitality were forever in his debt, for Dan Carmell didn't just guess what went on behind the bedroom doors in the penthouse and the apartments he used for his parties. He watched, strolling from bedroom to bedroom. A politician who had gone through even one such night with Dan Carmell looking on would find it difficult to shut any door in the face of the lawyer or the labor groups he represented.

Carmell's downfall began in October, 1955, at the Illinois Federation of Labor convention in Rock Island, when he asked an attractive 18-year-old Iowa girl to join a party he was giving for some of the men attending the convention. Later, some other girls joined them.

At first it was understood that each girl would receive $100 for merely sitting at the table with the union leaders, union lawyers and their political friends. But by the end of the fourth day a pretty young brunette named Dee had spent the night in Carmell's hotel room. She had received more than $900 in cash for partying. It was more money than she'd ever had before.

To Dan Carmell it was just another convention fling, and he made no pretense that the girl meant anything to him personally. Nevertheless, he always had an eye open for new faces and figures to serve as bait in his Chicago sex trap. He left his Chicago telephone number, and told Dee and friends of hers that he would pay their expenses and set them up in a high-class prostitution operation if they ever decided they wanted to move to the big city.

The $900 was gone in February, 1956, and the Iowa girls were having trouble making ends meet. One called Carmell to see if his offer was still open. It was.

He lived up to his promises about the money, but the pace was killing. There were morning sessions and afternoon sessions, dinners in the evening and then the lengthy private parties. It was exciting for the young girls to meet the political big shots of Illinois under such circumstances. One grey-haired man was introduced as "the Senator," but the girls weren't sure what his name was or whether he was a state senator or a United States Senator. These girls had been around a little, but after the first drunken stupor had worn off the extent of debauchery was sickening. They had never heard of most of the things they submitted to at the Carmell parties. In less than three weeks they packed and went home.

The Davenport boy friend of one of the girls ran across indications that the Chicago trip had been more than temporary employment with a Chicago lawyer. He told the Federal Bureau of Investigation his suspicions concerning Carmell's operations.

By early September, 1956, Roy L. Stephenson, the United States district attorney in southern Iowa, was ready to take the white slave case to a federal grand jury. Stephenson and his assistant, John C. Stevens, had the case in the final stages before Carmell and his political cronies knew what was happening in Iowa. Word leaked out only after a subpoena had forced the appearance of the Chicago madam who managed Carmell's stable of girls.

In Illinois, Carmell had the connections to fix such legal problems quietly. In southern Iowa he had no such facilities, and his only chance was to frighten all his political friends into coming to his aid. Carmell didn't try to conceal his problem from his political pals. His closest associates passed the word among themselves that they were all in this together.

"If Dan goes down, we can all go down with him," was the message in its simplest form.

To Democrats and Republicans alike it carried the implications that they would have to pull all political strings or risk personal disgrace and smashed careers.

For ten months Carmell's political friends trembled. No one knew whether he would be implicated. It was difficult to remember details of the dates when the parties had taken place or the names or looks of all the girls present. Every effort was made to save Carmell—to quash the indictment or to move the trial to Chicago where a judge might be found who would restrict the testimony and give Carmell a break.

One high Illinois political figure called district attorney Stephenson to ask whether another political associate would be implicated.

"He isn't implicated with Carmell in anything in our jurisdiction," was all Stephenson would reply.

The corrupt labor-political machine of Chicago wanted no part of a trial in Iowa. Stephenson was a tough prosecutor who had proven his ability as a brilliant trial lawyer. He had a reputation for being incorruptible.

Federal Judge Henry Graven, who presided over the case in Iowa, was stern and impartial. He was totally unconcerned over the political upheaval the Carmell trial might create in Illinois.

To add to Carmell's problem, he would be tried in an area where it was likely that some strait-laced Iowa farm women would be among the jurors. It was hardly the forum in which he could expect any break on a charge involving total debauchery.

The defense strategy had one goal: Move the case to Chicago.

Judge Graven rejected the motion for a change of venue and set the case for trial in Iowa. The bill of particulars filed by the federal district attorney on November 21, 1956, made it clear why Carmell and his friends were panicky. It charged that Carmell had transported one of the girls to Chicago with the following understanding, among other things:

"That (name of the girl) would engage in excessive sex indulgence with the defendant and other men; would engage in unnatural sex acts, acts of sex perversion with the defendant and with other persons, male and female, all for the entertainment of the defendant and his friends."

It was a case that would have made the notorious cafe society procurer, Mickey Jelke, seem a prude. Carmell's attorneys challenged Judge Graven's decision and asked for a review. They couldn't afford to pass up any maneuver that might move the trial to Chicago.

Carmell's appeal seemed hopeless. It ran head on into a published ruling by the U. S. Eighth Circuit Court of Appeals in which that court stated:

"We think that, in the interest of an expeditious, efficient and orderly administration of justice, controversies about venue (the site of trial) should be finally settled and determined at the District Court level."

The Eighth Circuit Court could hardly have been more definite in stating that it was judicial policy to avoid interfering with the District Court decision.

Consequently, the question of change of venue was to be left to the federal district judge. Judge Graven had refused to let the case be moved out of Iowa, and Stephenson was optimistic.

Carmell pleaded that many prominent people, including six Illinois state court judges, had said they wanted to give testimony as to his good character. Letters from six judges were included in the petition, along with their assertions that they did not feel they could leave their courts in Chicago to appear for Carmell in Iowa.

On February 25, 1957, the Eighth Circuit Court of Appeals reversed its policy and gave Carmell what he wanted. The case was ordered sent to Chicago for trial in the area where he was most familiar with the political jungle.

District attorney Stephenson was furious about losing the jurisdictional tug-of-war.

"Dan Carmell was the toughest political figure I ever tackled," Stephenson said.

Stephenson turned the files over to Robert Tieken, the United States district attorney in the Chicago area. Tieken had been cooperating with Stephenson for months, and the delay occasioned by the appeal had given him time to run down even more leads on the Carmell sex trap operations, involving girls imported from California.

Tieken would be as severe as Stephenson in prosecuting, but Carmell hoped for assignment of a politically friendly federal judge. Thus, the indictment might be quashed, or at least a major part of the evidence that had been amassed against him might be suppressed.

Hope turned to despair when the trial was assigned to Federal Judge Julius J. Hoffman, a firm and impartial man who could not be approached by Carmell's henchmen. Despite all the legal maneuvers, Carmell was going to go to trial before a judge with a reputation for unflinching integrity.

On Sunday, June 2, 1956, Carmell was despondent. He

brooded all day and into Sunday night about the trial that was
to begin the next morning. He told his wife, Mildred, he dreaded
the ordeal of going to trial before Judge Hoffman.

In the late evening, Carmell went into the bathroom of
their apartment. When he failed to return, Mrs. Carmell opened
the door and rushed to the open window. Fifteen stories below
she saw the crushed body of her husband on the newly sodded lawn.

Committee investigator Alphonse Calabrese had been in
contact with Carmell in the weeks before the Chicago attorney
jumped to his death. The initial contact with the suave little
Chicago lawyer had not involved Carmell's personal activities.
It concerned an investigation of the financial affairs of a local
of the Bakery and Confectionery Workers of America which he
represented.

Carmell was a genial mouthpiece as he talked with Calabrese, and he went out of his way to be helpful and gain the
good will of the committee investigator. Calabrese had been on
the case for some time before it was called to his attention that
the union attorney was under indictment on a white slave
charge.

There were many conflicting appointments clouding the
future for Carmell when death intervened. In addition to his
own criminal trial, he was scheduled to appear before the
McClellan committee that same week as attorney for some officials of the Bakery and Confectionery Workers Union.

Robert Kennedy had been so intent on Dave Beck and
other union officials that he was unaware of Carmell's corrupt
operations as a labor union attorney until I talked to him
about it.

"I think you should have hearings on the Carmell case," I
told the committee counsel. "His activity represents the most
dramatic example of how a few union attorneys have used the
money and position available to them to destroy the integrity
of local government officials."

"He's dead," Kennedy said. "I don't like to use the investigators on the activities of dead men if we can help it. There
is plenty of work to be done on the affairs of those who are still
operating."

He suggested that I bring it up later, and in the meantime I wrote a memorandum on the case to Kenneth O'Donnell, Kennedy's administrative assistant. I knew from conversations with Stephenson, the federal district attorney in southern Iowa, that the white slave indictment had only scratched the surface of the fantastic story of labor law as practiced by Dan Carmell.

XVIII

Hoffa's Mouthpiece Maneuvers

"If Hoffa isn't convicted, I'll jump off the Capitol," committee counsel Robert Kennedy said at a press conference in March, 1957, shortly after Jimmy Hoffa's arrest by the F.B.I.

There was cockiness in Kennedy's comments, but the young lawyers had reason for a little cockiness. In a few weeks he had done things that none of us believed could have been done in so short a time. Portland's sordid political-Teamsters alliance had been exposed, and Dave Beck's pompous proclamation of honesty had been exploded. Now it appeared that Hoffa was on his way to prison.

Bob Kennedy's comment on Hoffa's trial hadn't been intended for quotation, but due to a misinterpretation of the press conference ground rules Don O'Connor printed it in *The Detroit Times,* then other newspapers used it. But even with Hoffa's attorneys frantically exploiting every slip, Bob Kennedy's indiscreet comment was of no great concern. It was believed that this was as solid a case as could be built.

Kennedy treated the subject of Hoffa as if the rowdy Detroit Teamsters boss had been disposed of as a union power. He said the Hoffa arrest made him less uneasy about eliminating and exposing Beck. He viewed Hoffa as "a worse influence than Dave Beck," and had been fearful that destruction of Beck might

James R. Hoffa

Senator John L. McClellan, Clark Mollenhoff

Clark Mollenhoff, Attorney General Robert F. Ken

Clark Mollenhoff, Senator Karl E. Mundt

Frank Matula

Edward Cheyfitz, Dave Beck

Robert B. (Barney) Baker
(The Des Moines Register and Tribune)

Eugene C. (Jimmy) James
(The Des Moines Register and Tribune)

Joey Glimco

Edward Bennett Williams, James R. Ho

John Roosevelt, John English, James R.

hn Cassidy, William French

Daniels, Edward G. Partin, Sargent Pitcher

*President Kennedy with the U.S. Advisory Commission on Information in 1963
— Mollenhoff was a member of the commission*

deliver the Teamsters organization to the ruthless little pal of the underworld.

A.F.L.-C.I.O. president George Meany declared that F.B.I. agents had removed one of the worst influences in labor when they arrested Hoffa on the bribery-conspiracy charge.

Hoffa was through. That was the general attitude in the press and in the government. Some of the stories were a little flip about what a "rube" Hoffa had been in falling into the F.B.I. trap. Even Hoffa's lawyers were pessimistic.

F.B.I. Director J. Edgar Hoover and twenty-eight of his special agents had taken part in the planning from February 15, 1957—the day Cye Cheasty told committee chairman John Mc-Clellan and Bob Kennedy that Hoffa had offered him $18,000 to "spy" on the labor racket committee. Cheasty had cooperated fully in the plans leading to Hoffa's arrest.

Agents of the F.B.I. listened when Cheasty talked with Hoffa on the telephone. They could corroborate his testimony as to the numbers he called, and they had heard his end of the conversation. On February 19, 1957, when Cheasty passed confidential McClellan committee files to Hoffa on the corner of Seventeenth and I Streets, N. W., in Washington, F.B.I. agent Carl J. Martin was watching from across the street. Dozens of F.B.I. agents had swarmed around Dupont Circle at 6 p.m. on March 12, when Cheasty slipped Hoffa another file. They could swear that Cheasty had given Hoffa a confidential file because they had examined it earlier, and had kept him under constant surveillance. F.B.I. agent Paul E. Morrison drove the taxi that took Cheasty from the Dodge Hotel to Dupont Circle, where Hoffa entered the cab. Morrison had even heard some of the conversation between Hoffa and Cheasty.

Cameras operated by F.B.I. agents had photographed the meeting of Hoffa and Cheasty. The photographs showed Cheasty handing the file to Hoffa, and Hoffa slipping $2,000 in cash into Cheasty's hand.

There could be no doubt that Cheasty had received the money from Hoffa. An F.B.I. agent drove the cab Cheasty flagged to return to the Dodge Hotel, where other F.B.I. agents removed forty $50 bills from his pocket.[1]

---

[1] Transcript, U. S. v. Hoffa and Fischbach, Cr. No. 294-57.

Special agents arrested Hoffa as he entered the Dupont Plaza Hotel elevator shortly after 11 p.m. the next night.

This looked like an air-tight trial case. It wasn't necessary to depend on some pimp or burglar for the main thread of testimony. The chief witness, Cheasty, was a lawyer-investigator who had testified in dozens of trials. He was a careful investigator, and he had kept the slips of paper, airline tickets and other material to corroborate his meeting on February 13, 1957, with Hyman I. Fischbach in Washington, and the subsequent trip with Fischbach to Detroit, where he talked to Hoffa.

"It is just a matter of putting the case in the record, and of avoiding reversible error," said Assistant U. S. Attorney Ed Troxell.

Troxell, the first assistant to U. S. Attorney Oliver Gasch, appeared for the government at the arraignment of Hoffa the night of March 13. He was in charge of the case from that time on. The Justice Department had assigned a special assistant, but it was Troxell's case. He kept it that way throughout the trial.

The narrow-faced, sandy-haired lawyer with the thick-lensed glasses was not an impressive figure in the court room. He didn't have the personality or versatility to make a great trial lawyer, but he seemed adequate in the light of the tight case prepared by the F.B.I.

On Hoffa's side of the courtroom, Edward Bennett Williams, at 36, was one of the best publicized lawyers in the nation. A part of that reputation was based on court victories, but a few successful appeals to the U. S. Supreme Court had given him more stature than merely that of mouthpiece for such underworld figures as racket king Frank Costello.

Ed Williams was just another bright young lawyer in 1952 when he went into a law association with one of the shrewdest public relations men in Washington, Edward T. Cheyfitz. In a few years he had parlayed a few big-name clients, a few victories, and connections in a civil liberties group into a big reputation.

Cheyfitz had many talents and many connections. He was a professional ex-Communist, and prided himself on being an informer for the F.B.I. He had a degree in mathematics from the University of Michigan in 1934, and had made a pilgrimage to Moscow. He said he headed a diecasters division in the Communist-dominated Mine, Mill and Smelter Workers Union of the C.I.O. before breaking with the Communist Party in 1940.

Cheyfitz, although several years older than Williams, was a student in classes in criminal law and evidence taught by Williams at Georgetown University between 1948 and 1952. The wily Cheyfitz was quick to see the Williams potentiality. Ed Williams was a press agent's dream. He was a tall, curly-haired, and articulate charmer. The baby face lacked ruggedness, but it was a mobile enough countenance to register convincing warmth, sincerity or anger. Williams was the type the women jurrors would love.

"A great trial lawyer," Cheyfitz proclaimed in 1953 and 1954, spreading the word to his newspaper friends that Edward Bennett Williams was going to be one of the great names in law.

Williams had his first real whirl in the national spotlight in 1954 as the tail on the kite of Senator Joseph R. McCarthy, the controversial Wisconsin Republican. When censure charges were filed against Senator McCarthy by his Senate peers, Williams agreed to serve as his lawyer.

The McCarthy censure case could hardly be called a victory for Ed Williams except as it spread his name and picture from coast to coast. The Senate voted condemnation of McCarthy's actions, but the loss was not necessarily chargeable to Williams. McCarthy had bulled through a series of Senate hearings aimed at Communists in a way that did not help his case with his colleagues. In fact, it was a tribute to the ability of Williams that his own reputation suffered no damage in the explosive affair.

In 1955, Ed Cheyfitz promoted Williams as defense attorney in the criminal case involving four Minneapolis Teamsters officials charged with illegally accepting money from an employer. The theatrical dynamism of the big city lawyer left the Minnesota jurors unimpressed. Williams saw his clients convicted on charges of selling their trust as union officials. The Teamsters union paid him a fee of $26,953, according to Congressional committee records.[2] He blamed the loss on the inflamed atmosphere caused by hundreds of stories on labor

[2]McClellan committee, hearings, Part 14, pages 5383-5384.

racketeering that had appeared in the *Minneapolis Star* and *Tribune*.

"You'd filled those people up there so full of labor racket stories that it would be impossible for any labor leader to get a fair trial," Williams complained to me at the time.

"We've written so much about labor rackets that it is impossible for defense lawyers to fool the jurors," I replied.

In March, 1957, it was Cheyfitz who called Williams to spring Hoffa on bail the night he was arrested on the bribery-conspiracy charge. It was Cheyfitz who continued to boost the image of Williams in Teamsters circles despite the loss of the Minneapolis cases, arguing that no one could do as good a job as his office partner.

Cheyfitz commented to me in that period that Williams couldn't lose in defending Hoffa on the bribery-conspiracy case.

"If Hoffa is convicted, it is what everyone expects," Cheyfitz told me. "If Hoffa is acquitted, then Williams is a hero. It will put him in a class with (Clarence) Darrow and Jerry Geisler."

The legal maneuvers by Edward Bennett Williams in May and June of 1957 seemed to be designed to delay and hope for a break.

Except for the indictment, Hoffa was the logical successor to Dave Beck as general president of the International Brotherhood of Teamsters.

Cheyfitz told me there was still a strategy which might put Hoffa in control of the International Brotherhood of Teamsters.

"If Hoffa can avoid a conviction before the September convention, he can be elected president and control his successor," Cheyfitz explained.

In the event of a later conviction it would be possible for Hoffa to turn the Teamsters over to Harold Gibbons, of St. Louis, until Hoffa had served his time, Cheyfitz said. Gibbons, a tall, suave former Socialist, was regarded as the "intellectual Teamster." He was a favorite with both Cheyfitz and Williams.

On May 11, 1957, Williams asked for a six months' postponement of the Hoffa trial. Federal Judge Burnita S. Matthews gave him three weeks.

Hoffa received a big break on June 3, 1957, when the U. S.

Supreme Court upset the Clinton E. Jencks conviction. Jencks, a labor union official, had been indicted for filing a false non-Communist affidavit with the National Labor Relations Board. At his trial he had filed a motion requesting an inspection of reports made to the F. B. I. by government witnesses. The trial court rejected Jencks' plea in line with past decisions, and Jencks was convicted. It had been the practice for the trial judge to examine such government documents to determine their relevancy and materiality without opening them up to examination by the defense attorneys.

This time, the Supreme Court overturned the conviction, with five Justices concurring. The Court stated that the defendant and the defense attorney were entitled to make a personal examination of government reports.

The Jencks case was tragic for normal prosecution strategy. The F. B. I. and federal prosecutors liked to hold back some aspect of a case to use as surprise rebuttal evidence if the defendant took the witness chair and played too loose a game with the provable facts. The Justice Department was frantic about the Jencks decision. It was regarded by many as a license for defense lawyers to rummage through F. B. I. files.

Williams moved quickly. He filed petitions demanding access to all memoranda, notes and reports made by Cye Cheasty or any F. B. I. agent in developing the bribery-conspiracy charge against Hoffa.

Although the Jencks decision was a break for Hoffa, Williams continued to flay the prosecution and the F. B. I. with every argument and every device in his legal bag of tricks.

Judge Matthews had respect for the cleverness Williams displayed in exploiting anything that seemed to be potentially reversible error. There were no clear guide lines for interpreting the Supreme Court decision in the Jencks case, so she leaned over backward in an effort to avoid error. The prosecution was ordered to let Hoffa's attorneys see all memoranda, reports and notes written by all anticipated government witnesses. This, of course, meant there would be no surprise testimony. Jimmy Hoffa was given a full, long look into the government's hand, and knew exactly what information the prosecutor had and didn't have.

Although the Jencks decision disclosed nearly all the evidence, Assistant U. S. Attorney Ed Troxell was still full of confidence as the trial started.

"Anyone could try this case," Troxell told me. "When a case is prepared the way the Bureau (the F. B. I.) has prepared this one, it is just a matter of putting it in the record."

I had never seen a prosecutor who was so confident, but then I had never seen a prosecutor who had photographs of the alleged crime. Troxell expected the conviction to be automatic. He was certain that Williams would not permit Hoffa to take the witness stand in his own defense. Ed Troxell was already savoring the victory he expected over Edward Bennett Williams.

I asked both Cheyfitz and Williams whether Hoffa would testify in his own defense. They wouldn't say flatly what the strategy would be, but the implications seemed clear to me when Cheyfitz said: "We've done some research on defendants in federal court who have failed to testify in their own defense. Almost all of them were convicted."

If the statistics meant anything, they meant that Jimmy Hoffa would try to talk his way out of this one and the prosecution should start getting prepared for such a strategy. I told Troxell my views, but he did not agree.

XIX
_____

Jockeying to Beat the F.B.I.

"We figure the best chance we have is to get reversible error in the record," Cheyfitz explained to me. "When the prosecution has pictures of the alleged crime, it is pretty unrealistic to bank on acquittal by the jury."

There was one quick maneuver after another involving technical questions. On June 19, Williams claimed he had information that evidence against Hoffa was obtained by illegal wire tapping. He demanded that Attorney General Herbert Brownell be subpoenaed to testify as to whether the F.B.I. had been authorized to use a wire trap. Williams claimed his information came from a Detroit man named Lawrence Burns, but that he had been unable to find Burns to have him testify.[1]

Troxell was irritated. He told Judge Matthews the government used no wire taps or other interception devices in any phase of development of the Hoffa case.

Judge Matthews ruled that since Williams had no evidence to support his claim that a wire tap had been used, and the government denied it, she would reject his plea.

Williams told reporters he was certain the government had used illegal tapping devices, and he was going to keep probing.

He kept on probing even as attorneys went through the process of selecting a jury for the joint trial of Teamsters boss

[1]Transcript, U. S. v. Hoffa and Fischbach, Cr. No. 294-57, page 6.

James R. Hoffa and Miami attorney Hyman I. Fischbach on bribery-conspiracy charges.

The jury selection process was only half completed when Williams and Daniel Maher, attorney for Fischbach, made a last effort to stall the Hoffa-Fischbach trial until October. In an effort to out-flank Judge Matthews, they petitioned the U. S. Circuit Court of Appeals.

Newspaper and television publicity following Hoffa's arrest made it impossible to get a jury that would not be prejudiced, they argued. They also asserted that they needed a delay because Williams had been unable to make an adquate preparation, having been tied up with the trial of racketeer Frank Costello in the Southern District Court of New York.

The three-man Circuit Court panel rejected the defense effort to delay the trial. On Monday, June 24, 1957, Troxell made his opening statement to the jury. Williams and Dan Maher waived their right to make an opening statement. This avoided committing Hoffa or Fischbach to any story until all government witnesses had been heard.

From the beginning, Williams' trial tactics revolved around an attack on Cye Cheasty, the key government witness. Every conceivable effort was made to destroy him in the eyes of the jury.

Cheasty had barely been called by Troxell when Williams tried to bar all of his testimony. Hoffa's attorney pleaded that a lawyer-client relationship existed between Hoffa and Cheasty from the night Hoffa talked with Cheasty in Detroit. Williams declared it would be highly improper for the court to allow Cheasty to testify, for this would be a breach of legal ethics.

Troxell argued that Hoffa had hired Cheasty for the illegal purpose of putting a "spy" on the McClellan committee, and there had never been any lawyer-client relationship. Judge Matthews rejected the defense contention and ruled that Cheasty could testify.

Williams objected strenuously and dramatized his efforts with great flourishes of his arms and pacing before the bench. He expressed grave concern for what was happening to American justice.

"If Williams gives her enough tough ones to field, she's

going to fumble one of them," Cheyfitz said confidently.

In the first days of testimony by Cheasty, things looked bad for Hoffa. On June 25, Cheasty testified Hoffa told him that, including Cheasty as a spy, he had a "triple cover" on the activities of the McClellan labor racket investigators. Cheasty testified that Hoffa told him the other spies were "a girl on Capitol Hill," and a man on the staff of Republican Senator Joseph R. McCarthy.

Hoffa was grim-faced as he listened to Cheasty testify to their meeting, the passage of money and secret files, the telephone calls, and the fictitious names used to cover their tracks. But in the halls of the court building, Jimmy had plenty of bounce and braggadocio.

On June 26, Frank Brewster, chairman of the Western Conference of Teamsters, was found guilty on all thirty-one counts of an indictment for contempt of Congress for his initial refusal to answer questions before the Senate Government Operations subcommittee.[2] The trial was in the same courthouse, and a cloud of pessimism settled over the Hoffa camp. Public opinion was certainly against the Teamsters. That was the day Cheasty testified how the F.B.I. had covered all 10 of his telephone calls to Hoffa and Fischbach.

Jimmy was irritable when I talked with him in the corridor at recess.

"The trouble with you, Clark, is you're anti-labor," Hoffa snapped.

"I'm not anti-labor," I defended myself. "I'm against the way union funds are being tossed around, and I'm against the kind of ethics some of you Teamsters practice."

"What's wrong with my ethics?" Hoffa shot back.

I recalled the "conflicts of interest" in the profits he received from a truck leasing firm, Test Fleet Corporation, and his loose use of union funds. I reminded him I had told him more than a year earlier that he should get rid of all business holdings that touched on the trucking industry, and fire some of the ex-convicts on his union payroll.

"If you'd paid attention to what I told you about ethics

---

[2]The conviction of Frank Brewster for contempt was reversed by the United States Court of Appeals for the District of Columbia.

then, you wouldn't be in the jam you're in today," I told him.

"With your kind of ethics you'd run a union in the ground in sixty days," Hoffa sneered. "I'll give you a local—Local 90 out in Des Moines—and see if you don't run it in the ground. I know unions, and you can't run 'em with the kind of ethics you talk about."

I reminded him that A.F.L.-C.I.O. president Meany certainly wasn't anti-union, but he was critical of Hoffa's ethics.

"Who in hell is George Meany to talk about ethics?" Hoffa growled. "Isn't he the guy who visited Joey Fay in prison? You won't write anything about Meany, and there is plenty."

"If you know anything, let's have it," I said. Hoffa said he would think about it.

On June 27, the government produced a series of twelve pictures taken by the F.B.I. of the meeting between Hoffa and Cheasty at 6:05 p.m. March 12, 1957, on the west side of Dupont Circle. The F.B.I. did not explain how the photographs had been taken on the busy Circle at dusk, but the pictures were so clear that it was easy to identify Hoffa and Cheasty and the passage of documents.

Hoffa glared menacingly at Cheasty during the testimony, but in the hall he said: "Just wait. We haven't had our turn at bat yet."

The little Teamsters boss also commented that he would "take care of Cheasty later."

Cheasty and his family had been under an F.B.I. guard, and for the duration of the trial Cheasty was not available for interviews. At the noon recess we passed in the hall. He grabbed my hand.

"It is good to see you out there," Cheasty said. "It is good to see a friendly face, and not just that bunch of thugs that tails around after Hoffa. It was good to see Ethel Kennedy (Bob's wife) was here. Would you pass my regards to her?"

In the District of Columbia, where more than one-half of the population is Negro, there is a strong likelihood that on any jury selected in federal court at least half of the panel will be Negro. In Hoffa's trial, eight of the jurors were Negroes. There were those in the Hoffa camp who felt that it would be easy to use this to Hoffa's advantage.

Robert B. (Barney) Baker, the twice-convicted Teamsters hoodlum from the New York waterfront, had been an organizer for a Teamsters local in Washington, D. C. It was a local that included many Negroes. Baker had also been a big wheel in civil rights activity in the District of Columbia and in 1952 had been a key figure in a Democratic presidential primary in which New York Governor Averell Harriman had defeated Senator Estes Kefauver of Tennessee.

Baker, a 380-pound confidence man, had been organizing for Hoffa's Central States Teamsters in St. Louis, Detroit, Chicago, and Omaha. When the Hoffa trial started, it brought Barney hurrying back to Washington to cultivate his old friends in the Negro section of the city.

Teamsters contacts were made with former heavyweight boxing champion Joe Louis, and Baker arranged his accommodations in Washington for the final stages of the trial.[3]

From the outset, it was clear that the Hoffa forces were going to play the race issue. It was injected into the court proceedings June 28, when Williams hurled a question at John Cye Cheasty, accusing the government's key witness of investigating the National Association for the Advancement of Colored People (N.A.A.C.P.) in Florida.

Cheasty had testified for three and one-half days, and the cross-examination by Williams was just well under way when the racial issue was injected. Williams first tossed a barrage of questions aimed at shaking the detailed story Cheasty had told on direct examination, and at raising doubts about his motives.

Then the defense attorney asked Cheasty if he had taken any drugs during the period of time he was testifying, and Cheasty answered he had taken nitroglycerine for a heart condition.

"Have you taken any form of narcotics?" the defense lawyer continued to press the theme, and Troxell flared angrily:

"I object, your honor, this is an infraction which is disgraceful."[4]

Williams quickly followed this by asking if Cheasty had not used fictitious names when acting as an investigator. Cheasty

---

[3]McClellan committee hearings, Part 13, pages 5086-5090.

[4]From trial transcript, June 28, 1957, pages 938-939.

said he had used fictitious names on some occasions, but could not say on how many occasions.

"When you were employed by the city of Tallahassee to investigate the National Association for the Advancement of Colored People, you used a fictitious identity didn't you?" Williams fired the question quickly.

Reporters were stunned at the suddenness with which Williams had rammed the race issue into the trial.

"I object to that," Troxell shouted, leaping from his seat too late to block the Williams thrust.

Cheasty remained calm. He retorted that he had not used a fictitious name in Florida. He said he had not investigated the N.A.A.C.P., and added that he would be glad to tell Williams all about it.

Williams tried to shut off Cheasty's answer, but Judge Matthews ruled that since Williams had opened the subject, Cheasty was entitled to explain.

Before Cheasty's explanation could be gotten into the record, Williams had repeated his charge that Cheasty was investigating the N.A.A.C.P. "to break up the bus boycott."

"You are testifying, Mr. Williams," Cheasty complained of the comments by Williams in front of the jury.

When Williams was finally shut off, Cheasty testified:

"In Tallahassee I didn't use a fictitious identity. I went down there as John Cye Cheasty, a New York lawyer. I showed my credentials to the chief of police under that setup there."

And Cheasty testified in direct contradiction to the self-serving comment by Williams that Cheasty had gone there "to break up the bus boycott."

"I recommended that they cut the color line on the busses down there; and they let people come in and sit as they wanted on a first-come-first-served basis," Cheasty explained.

Williams blustered about the race issue being brought into the case. It was prejudicial to Hoffa to have in the record such explanations as Cheasty had just given, Williams argued. Judge Matthews showed no sympathy. She declared that if the race issue had been improperly injected into the trial it was because Williams had done it, and he was in a poor position to complain.

"I was amazed when Mr. Williams went into that in the first

place, but after he did it seemed to me, after he mentioned it, then it was a matter that should be allowed," Judge Matthews explained her ruling.[5]

Williams dropped the bus boycott and got back to his general attack on Cheasty. Apparently, it was to be a nagging and ragging process to wear down the mental alertness and the physical strength of the 49-year-old heart patient.

The government had forty witnesses—most of them F. B. I. agents—but the "crucial witness" was Cheasty, who kept himself alive with daily doses from the bottle of nitroglycerine he carried in his left trousers pocket.

One reason the F. B. I. and Justice Department were anxious for an early trial was the precarious state of Cheasty's health. He was the key witness, and loss of Cheasty's testimony would jeopardize the case. Bob Kennedy and I were fearful the ordeal of cross-examination could kill Cheasty and wreck the case. I asked myself why Cheasty, ill as he was, would risk his life by playing the dangerous game of serving as a double agent in setting a trap for Hoffa and Fischbach.

"It takes a lot of courage for a man to do what Cheasty did," I told Ed Cheyfitz. "I think he is an honest man, and he's being unjustly abused by the cross-examination."

"I don't know what it is, but there is something wrong with the guy," Cheyfitz answered. "There is some other angle to it, and Williams is going to keep him on (the stand) until he finds out what it is."

Cheyfitz said the strategy was to make the jury doubt Cheasty's honesty, and that he thought Williams had what he needed to raise this doubt. Hoffa had insisted he had given Cheasty $2,000 at their first meeting in Detroit on February 13 instead of the $1,000 reported by Cheasty.

"The jury is going to wonder what happened to that other $1,000," Cheyfitz said.

"You don't believe that Hoffa gave Cheasty $2,000 do you?" I asked.

"I don't know what to believe," Cheyfitz answered. "That is Hoffa's story, and we will make the most of it."

The cross-examination of Cheasty by Williams was long

---

[5] Transcript of the trial, July 1, 1957, page 1022.

and detailed, worrying every conceivable weakness or seemingly vulnerable point. Williams emphasized that Cheasty had lived a life of deception for a month and had lied to Hoffa and Fischbach. Cheasty stood up remarkably well under the endurance test from Williams, but there were a few weaknesses. Cheasty couldn't account for all of the $300 he had spent out of the $1,000 he received from Hoffa the night they met in Detroit.

The money, Cheasty said, went for airplane tickets, meals, and other expenses in carrying out the conspiracy. But he also admitted that he had given his wife $20 of it to buy some shoes for his children.

Williams jumped on this as showing a streak of dishonesty in Cheasty's makeup—and in his whole story. Williams also indicated that Hoffa would testify that $2,000 had been given Cheasty in the first meeting and that Cheasty had conveniently forgotten $1,000 of it.

While Williams was busy in court, some of Hoffa's friends and Teamsters associates were busy with other activities of questionable legality. Most of this activity was directed at injecting even more of the explosive-laden segregation issue into the minds of the jurors.

On July 6, 1957, the *Afro-American,* a newspaper, published a highly inflammatory pro-Hoffa issue that was circulated to Negro homes in Washington, D. C. The name of a "Frank Crowling," of Detroit, was signed to advertising in the *Afro-American* as director of the Detroit Citizens Civic Committee.[6]

Under a heading, "The Facts Behind the Hoffa Trial," the paper criticized Judge Matthews and Senator McClellan as tools of big business from the Old South. Hoffa and Edward Bennett Williams were praised as champions of civil rights and Negro equality.

The paper printed a huge picture of Williams and Hoffa with Mrs. Martha Malone Jefferson, an attractive Negro lawyer from Los Angeles. Mrs. Jefferson was identified as having joined Williams in the defense of Hoffa. She had been around the

_____

[6]McClellan committee hearings, Part 13, pages 5086-5087 and Part 37, page 14095. The "Frank Crowling" was identified as John L. Cowling, an employee of the treasurer's office in Wayne County, Michigan, and a man who had received political contributions from Hoffa and from the Teamsters.

court for several days. On a few occasions she had gone to the front of the courtroom and talked with Williams or Hoffa in the presence of the jury, but she had not taken part in presenting the case.

A column and several articles in the paper took the same line as the advertising. They said Cheasty had investigated "Negroes only" in the Tallahassee bus dispute, and that he had also investigated "Negro school teachers" and "the N.A.A.C.P." The statements were without authority, and flatly contradicted what Cheasty had testified to in the trial.

The columnist colored his criticism of Judge Matthews by saying she "hails from the magnolia state of Mississippi, the same commonwealth which thrust Sir James C. Eastland (a United States Senator) upon the Democratic party."

Williams was called "the White Knight" and the "Sir Galahad" of civil rights, and Hoffa was described as the "hardest hitting champion" of the Teamsters union, which has "167,000 colored truck drivers."

Nothing could have been more prejudicial to the government's case than to have a copy of that July 6, 1957, issue fall into the hands of even one of the eight Negro members of the jury. It contained references to a long list of persons identified as champions of Negro rights, and stated that it was the opinion of these people that Hoffa "had been framed."

The circulation of the *Afro-American* newspaper in Washington came to the attention of Judge Matthews on Monday, July 8. The judge saw press reports that the newspaper was delivered to the jurors in the Hoffa case. Without public explanation of her reason, she ordered that the jury should be isolated from the general public for the duration of the trial. She wanted to avoid having any inflammatory material being read by the jurors.

The members of the jury were instructed to call home and make arrangements to remain at the courthouse in the custody of the U. S. marshals and matrons until the trial was concluded. All newspapers were to be clipped before being delivered to the jurors.

Williams and Dan Maher, Fischbach's counsel, objected to the isolation of the jury. Judge Matthews disregarded the protest, and said she was taking the step on her own volition. She obviously wanted to avoid jury tampering.

Williams voiced his objection to locking up the jury in the presence of the jurors, and Judge Matthews made a special effort to avoid the impression that either the government or the defendants had caused their inconvenience.

"Members of the jury," Judge Matthews said, "as you were going out you will recall that Mr. Williams arose and stated that he desired the record to show that it was over his objection that the jury was being kept in the court house at night. You are told that the court is requiring this on its own volition. No one has requested of the court that you be so detained."[7]

Williams told reporters he had no knowledge of the *Afro-American* newspaper incident until after the paper was circulated. He said he strongly disapproved of such prejudicial material being circulated, but couldn't be held accountable for what was printed in every newspaper.

He said he had posed for a picture with Hoffa and Mrs. Jefferson, the Negro attorney, but declared he did not know the use to be made of the picture by the *Afro-American*. Williams also said that Mrs. Jefferson was not associated with him in the case, and that he had not identified her as his assistant for the photographer or for the *Afro-American* reporters or editors.

Cheyfitz said he regretted the *Afro-American* incident. He assured me no one from the Williams-Cheyfitz law office would have anything to do with such unethical tactics.

But Cheyfitz said the decision by Judge Matthews to lock up the jury "was probably a lucky break for Hoffa and for Williams."

"I told Williams it was a lucky break for us," Cheyfitz explained. "Jimmy has a strange bunch of friends, and you can never tell what some of his friends might try to do to get him off. They'll think they can operate the same way they do up in Detroit. We (Cheyfitz and Williams) want to win this fairly or not at all."

---

[7]From the transcript of United States v. James R. Hoffa and Hyman I. Fischbach, United States District Court for the District of Columbia, Criminal No. 294-57, page 1625.

The *Afro-American* episode had hardly settled when another knotty problem was tossed into the trial. On Wednesday, July 10, 1957, Fischbach arrived in court without his attorney, Dan Maher. He said Maher had suffered a heart attack, and that he could not proceed without Maher's services. At the same time, Fischbach said he would not be prepared to make any motion in his own defense until he had talked with Maher.

Ed Troxell, the assistant United States district attorney, was skeptical. He asked that Judge Matthews appoint a government doctor to examine Maher since Fischbach could give the court no precise information about his attorney's illness, or how long it would be before Maher could return to the trial. Later, Troxell informed the court that Dr. Bernard Walsh, a government-appointed heart specialist, had examined Maher.

The electrocardiograph showed there had been no heart attack and no damage to Maher's heart, Troxell told the court. The examination did show that Maher had a heart condition, and there were indications of physical exhaustion that would make it advisable for him to remain in bed for several days.

Williams suggested a temporary delay until it could be determined clearly whether Maher could continue. At the same time, Fischbach was arguing that he could not get another attorney and proceed with the trial. He said he had depended upon Maher's advice, and it would take weeks for another attorney to learn enough about the case to represent him properly.

Judge Matthews was obviously, and understandably, distraught. She had been forced to isolate the jury because of the activities of some friends of Hoffa. Now she was being urged to recess the trial for at least several days and possibly several weeks. To do so would mean leaving the jurors locked up like prisoners. That was impossible; but on the other hand, Fischbach couldn't be forced to proceed without a lawyer.

There was an optimistic attitude in the Hoffa camp, where it was felt that any court action except a mistrial and a delay might put reversible error in the record. Hoffa was still angling for a delay that would get him past the Teamsters convention in late September and early October.

Judge Matthews solved her problem by severing the Fischbach case from Hoffa's and deciding to move ahead with Hoffa's trial separately. Williams bounced forward to contend that the severing of the Fischbach case was prejudicial to Hoffa and constituted error. This was the same Williams who had been seeking to sever the cases a few days earlier. Now he was contending that Jimmy Hoffa was going to suffer a grave injustice because severance would mean Fischbach's testimony would not be available and Hoffa would lose "more than 50 per cent of his defense."

"Maher's illness put her (the judge) in a box," Cheyfitz later said with glee. "It doesn't make any difference which way she goes, the judge can be in trouble on this one."

"This ruling is our insurance policy," Williams said in the court corridor. "We'll win this one on appeal if the jury goes against us."

The complexion of the testimony was still strongly against Hoffa. Chairman John McClellan was called by the government to tell how Cheasty was hired after relating to Bob Kennedy and himself that Hoffa had paid him $1,000 the night of February 13, 1957, to get a job on the committee and spy on its activity. McClellan was a strong witness, clear on his facts, and experienced in the trial of both criminal and civil cases. Williams was wise enough to avoid trying to break McClellan down with cross-examination.

When Kennedy was called as a witness, it was a different story. Kennedy lacked courtroom experience, and Williams tried to take advantage of this fact with a needling cross-examination. Kennedy had a momentary unsteadiness, but then became amazingly firm.

Williams tried to get him to concede that there was no real danger to the McClellan committee operations in allowing the so-called "confidential" files to be examined by persons other than the staff. Kennedy snapped back that Hoffa plotted "to destroy" the committee with "spies." He said the fear was not imaginary, but very real.

The attempts of labor racketeers to plant spies "was rather a major problem with us," Kennedy said. He related that Cheasty had told him that Hoffa "had someone on Senator McCarthy's staff and already had a girl on our staff."

Williams did not try to cross-examine the F.B.I. agents on

the facts, but he probed to find if there was a federal wiretap in the case. Most of his attack centered on F.B.I. agent Anthony J. Maloney, who made the tactical error of saying that he would have known if there had been any wiretaps, and that there were none. It was too broad an answer, and Williams pounced on him and asked if he could swear there were no wiretaps on the Detroit end of calls between Cheasty and Hoffa.

Troxell vaulted out of his chair to object. He declared that of course Maloney couldn't testify as to any wiretaps put on in Detroit by Hoffa or others.

Williams fired several questions as to whether it was common practice for the F.B.I. to wiretap, and whether Maloney knew it was illegal to intercept telephone conversations with a wiretap.

Judge Matthews finally ordered Williams to relate his questions to the case and not to stray to general questions about what was or was not a practice of the F.B.I.

Williams complained that Judge Matthews had told him he could bring out any evidence of wires being tapped, and now she was barring him from doing it.

Exasperated by Williams' constant criticism, she said sharply: "You are not foreclosed from this avenue. If you have any evidence of wiretapping in this case, you are at liberty to use it."

"Do you have any evidence there was wiretapping in this case?" I asked him at recess.

"The F.B.I. has tapped a lot of telephone wires," Williams said. He was sure they had engaged in it in this case.

"Do you have any evidence of it?" I asked again.

Williams said he had only indications that it might have been done, and that he was being barred from exploring this avenue for his client.

XX

Joe Louis—a Heavyweight for Hoffa

On Monday, July 15, 1957, the government ended its case, and Williams made a motion for acquittal on grounds that Hoffa had been lured into the crime by Cheasty. He argued that it was "entrapment" of the little Teamsters boss. Judge Matthews ruled against him.

The defense took the initiative with testimony from Teamsters business agents and a lawyer who was a partner of Fischbach. Most of them were Hoffa's subordinates.

Hoffa, who had been grim-faced and menacing when Cheasty was testifying, exuded boyish charm when he took his place in the witness chair to testify in his own defense. It was a surprise to Troxell, who had told me only a day earlier that he didn't think Hoffa would dare take the stand. I had disagreed with Troxell, but still I was a bit surprised. Jimmy had a background that made him appear to be a sitting duck for a tough cross-examination.

The questions Williams put to Hoffa were intended to paint a sympathetic picture of a poor boy who dropped out of school at fourteen, worked long hours, fought for better wages for the working people, and emerged as a vice president of the International Brotherhood of Teamsters.

Hoffa admitted those facts in the indictment which were solidly documented and corroborated. He disputed Cheasty's version when it was not possible to substantiate fully by the testimony of F.B.I. agents, or by documents, that this version was correct.

Hoffa passed off his two criminal convictions as "technical" violations of the law, and his long arrest record as the result of the malice of anti-union police.

I had known that Jimmy was glib, but I hadn't realized how glib. He testified he didn't know that Cheasty was employed by the McClellan labor racket committee. He had merely hired him to do some legal work in connection with the investigation. Jimmy said he hadn't noticed that the papers delivered to him by Cheasty were the confidential files of the committee.

In fact, Jimmy told the jury, he just couldn't think of any reason why the committee would want to investigate his union.

I was amazed when I heard the testimony. This was the same Jimmy Hoffa who had Barney Baker, the twice-convicted New York hoodlum, working as an organizer in the Central Conference of Teamsters. This was the Jimmy Hoffa who had hired convicted armed robbers Herman Kierdorf and Frank Kierdorf as union officials in Flint, Michigan, and in Detroit. This was the same Jimmy Hoffa who was backing a convicted racketeer, Gerald P. Connelly, in Minneapolis, and who numbered Johnny Dioguardi, the new York extortionist and crook, among his close friends.

The story he told the jury about his union financial records was strictly phony. Jimmy had been before a House subcommittee, and he had admitted that in his Joint Council 43 the records were destroyed every year. When it was called to his attention that this was a violation of Internal Revenue Service regulations, Jimmy had defiantly told the subcommittee that his lawyers had told him he could get away with doing it, so he was.

In my opinion, Jimmy went too far. He had opened the door for a severe cross-examination of his connections with racketeers and of the finances of unions under his control. Troxell hadn't been brilliant in putting in the government case, but he had been adequate. I was certain Troxell would rip Jimmy's story apart in the cross-examination.

Another problem arose that day that concerned me as much as Jimmy's glibness. Joe Louis, the former boxing champion, appeared in court and mingled with the Hoffa crowd. The well-known Negro boxer was the object of considerable attention from the jurors, who spotted him in his seat in the small court-room.

Labor racketeer Barney Baker had made arrangements for Louis in Washington, and there was speculation that the Brown Bomber from Detroit was going to testify as a character witness for Hoffa.

"What are you here for, Joe?" I asked at the afternoon recess as we stood in the corridor.

"I'm just here to see what they are doing to my old friend, Jimmy Hoffa," the former heavyweight champion responded in much the same heavy-lipped style he had answered questions for sports announcers in earlier years. But he didn't fumble the way he used to. In essentially the same words, he answered other reporters who were equally curious about why he had appeared at the Hoffa trial.

"We've got Joe down here to punch you in the nose," Williams joked with me. Hoffa added that if Louis would land a hard right on my jaw it certainly would please him. Joe just smiled.

Louis drifted off into the courtroom, and other spectators started in to find seats. Williams also went into the court. Hoffa and I remained in the hall, chatting in a friendly fashion about things not connected with the trial. We had avoided touchy subjects since several days earlier.

Suddenly, Jimmy stopped our conversation and said he had to get into the courtroom. I was directly behind him as he entered the door, and I noticed that the jurors were already entering the jury box. I expected Hoffa to walk quickly to the front of the court and take his place in the witness chair. Instead, he walked slowly down the aisle to where Joe Louis was seated in the aisle seat on the right. What was going to happen was apparent, so I watched carefully from a point of vantage that gave me a view of Hoffa as well as the jury.

Hoffa stopped beside Louis's seat, clapped a hand on the big Negro fighter's shoulder, and said he was certainly glad to see him there. Louis reached up and put his hand on Hoffa's arm, and the two engaged in conversation. Most of the animation came from Hoffa.

It was a strange scene, and a strange greeting, between two men I had seen talking together in the court corridor only a few minutes earlier. But the Hoffa-Louis exchange wasn't missed by some of the jurors. It was a scene that would have been difficult for them to miss under the circumstances. One who didn't notice at first was elbowed by a neighbor, calling his attention to that touching scene between big Joe Louis and his little pal, Jimmy Hoffa, defendant.

When the case was adjourned for the day, I talked to Troxell to see if he was prepared to cross-examine Hoffa. I believed that all of Jimmy's big show, on the witness stand and off, could be nullified by searching cross-examination. Troxell told me he had not known that Hoffa had testified before a Congressional committee about the destruction of financial records in unions under his jurisdiction. Troxell wasn't familiar with the details of how Hoffa's wife had received money from Teamsters locals, nor did he know how a truck-leasing firm had been set up for Mrs. Hoffa by a firm which hired Teamsters. All this information seemed pertinent to me to explain why Hoffa would want to sabotage McClellan and Kennedy.

I was worried by then, and I hurried up to the Senate Office Building to talk with Bob Kennedy, who was working on hearings on the Textile Workers Union. I told him I thought the case could be lost if Troxell didn't do an effective cross-examination, because Hoffa had been a persuasive witness for himself.

"I'm beginning to believe you'd better get ready to jump off the Capitol," I told Kennedy.

Kennedy was furious over the Joe Louis matter and the ethics involved in this and other incidents that had taken place on the fringe of the trial. He was upset over the fact that even I thought an acquittal was possible. He knew I thought the case was strong. Kennedy gained some consolation from a talk with Courtney Evans, the F.B.I. official who was working with the McClellan committee.

"Courtney says the government has a lot more information to bring out, and that Cheasty may be recalled by Troxell as a rebuttal witness," Kennedy said.

That made me feel a little better, but just to make sure that Ed Troxell was briefed on some of Hoffa's early history, I dropped off a series of stories I had written concerning Hoffa at Troxell's office that night.

I tried not to be critical of the prosecution because I knew Troxell had a tough job. But I tried to emphasize to him that he couldn't know too much about Hoffa, and that he shouldn't underestimate Hoffa's ability.

Troxell still seemed confident. The case was soild, and anyone with intelligence should be able to see that Cheasty had been corroborated on all major points, Troxell said.

"Hoffa's story doesn't even make sense," Troxell said.

I agreed with his opinion of the story Hoffa had told from the witness chair, but I said I was not sure the jurors understood the weaknesses in Hoffa's story. I told him that some of the reporters who had followed the case were confused, and that most of them were much more intelligent about these matters than members of an average jury.

The cross-examination was a pitiful mismatch. Troxell sparred with Hoffa for only thirty-two minutes, failing to dig into the details of his criminal convictions, the sad condition of Teamsters financial records, or the racketeers who associated with Hoffa in the union. He had made few, if any, inroads on the story told by Hoffa when he suddenly dropped his cross-examination. I was shocked, and I felt sick.

The rebuttal consisted of testimony by two F.B.I. agents on important but undramatic technical points that wouldn't register as important with the average juror unless they were driven home.

Troxell's first summation to the jury was not dramatic, but it made me more optimistic. He had worked hard on it, and his presentation made me hope he might have repaired some of the damage done by the weak cross-examination.

The prosecutor told the jurors that Hoffa's contention that Cheasty was hired as a lawyer was unbelievable.

"Cheasty (on February 19) called Metropolitan 8-6565 (in Washington, D.C.) and talked to Hoffa," Troxell said.

"Now that number, as showed by the evidence yesterday, is the telephone number of Mr. Cheyfitz and Mr. Williams. I want you to clearly understand that I am not suggesting in any way, shape or form that Mr. Williams is involved in this conspiracy. I don't want you to even think that. I am suggesting to you at this time that Mr. Hoffa was surrounded by counsel; that Mr. Hoffa at that time did not have to hire a man like Cheasty to be met on street corners for the purpose of getting legal advice when he had lawyers at hand, and . . . had a bunch of regular Teamsters lawyers meeting on February 22, in Chicago, concerning what to do about this investigation."

"He (Cheasty) wasn't being employed by Hoffa as a lawyer," Troxell said. "He was hired to . . . be a spy to destroy a committee of Congress."

The two hours and thirty-five minutes Williams took in his summation was a sharp contrast to Troxell's colorless but methodical performance. The strong-voiced defense attorney smiled, coaxed, grew angry and almost cried as he marched back and forth before the jury. He accused Troxell of making a "scurrilous, sly, unfounded innuendo" against him in the comments on the telephone call to Williams's law office.

"I hope with all my heart, I pray that I never will lust for victory so much," Williams said.

Williams spent most of his time castigating Cheasty as "a deceiver" and as an admitted "falsifier" who had lived a lie to draw Hoffa into a trap.

"An honest man would have said 'No, Fischbach, I don't want any part of the dirty business, and you shouldn't either. I am leaving. Where's my hat'." That was how Cheasty should have reacted to the original deal made by Fischbach if he was an honest man, Williams told the jurors.

He noted that Cheasty carried a rosary in his pocket and turned that fact around to the discredit of the key state witness.

"What kind of a man is it who, while carrying a symbol of truth, honesty, beauty, a symbol of faith some of us hold dear—the rosary—can deceive and falsify at the same time?" Williams said.

The defense attorney's views of some of the evidence was getting across to some of the jurors. They were a confused group looking for someone to lead them and to tell them what all this conflicting evidence meant. Williams was willing to tell them that poor little Jimmy Hoffa, the working man's friend, was the victim of a dastardly conspiracy.

"What you do will have the greatest impact on his (Hoffa's) life . . . of anything that has ever gone before or that will ever take place in all his future," Williams said with intensity.

"Jimmy Hoffa has fought many battles for labor. . . . He has fought with a mind and heart without fear, and he has never betrayed a trust. . . . I ask you to send him back to the good fight."

Williams was white and shaken when he finished, but the jury had been moved. Troxell needed punch in his final argument. He didn't have it. The thorough work behind his first statement had given him a kind of effectiveness, but now he seemed to lack organization.

Troxell commented that Hoffa's account of the meetings with Cye Cheasty was improbable. He praised Cheasty as a man of integrity, truthfulness, and patriotism. The prosecutor seemed to forget his lines. He returned to the counsel table to shuffle through papers.

There was no drama in Troxell's final plea. There was no authority. At times, he hardly seemed an advocate for conviction.

"Did Hoffa, when he was sitting on the stand, appear to be a truth-telling individual?" Troxell asked the jury. "If he appears to be, believe him, and acquit him. If you think he was not a truth-telling individual, and if you think Cheasty was telling the truth, believe Cheasty and convict Hoffa. But it is up to you to decide whether or not Cheasty is telling the truth. If you think he is, I think you can find the defendant Hoffa guilty, if you find him guilty beyond a reasonable doubt.

"But on the other hand, if you think Hoffa is telling the truth, that is up to you to decide, and I think you will decide that question properly," he told the jurors.

At 10:30 a.m. Friday, July 19, Judge Matthews completed her instructions to the jury. I was pessimistic, but I still had hope. Maybe the jurors in this case were intelligent enough to see through the mass of confusion created by the defense. There was nothing that could be done about it now.

The courtroom was almost cleared of spectators, and Ed

Williams was standing by himself, to one side of the room, when I approached him.

"What do you think it will be?" I asked of him because I was genuinely interested in his opinion, and not with any intention of carrying on the needling we usually gave each other.

"I'll be satisfied with a hung jury," he said.

"This is something we can agree on," I replied. "I'll settle for a hung jury, because I'm fearful of an acquittal."

Williams said he had little hope for an acquittal for Hoffa.

"I thought Troxell would be grilling Jimmy for two days," Williams said. "I was reluctant to put him on, but I felt we had to take the chance."

"The chance paid off," I said. "I didn't believe Jimmy, but I'm afraid you sold a bill of goods to that jury."

"When the prosecution has taken pictures, it is pretty hard to overcome it," Williams said. "Sometimes you think you have a juror in your corner, but you can never be sure."

I told Williams I had been disappointed at the injection into this trial of the race issue.

Williams said he had not intended to introduce that issue, but had used it merely to explore Cheasty's credibility on the question of whether he had used a fictitious name in Florida. Williams said he had based his questions on information he believed was reliable.

"I was trying to refresh his memory," Williams insisted.

Williams declared everyone is entitled to a defense, and that a defense attorney owes his client the obligation to raise every question and to take every step that is legal and ethical.

I said I didn't believe the destruction of Cheasty was justified by any facts I had heard, in or out of the court.

"Are you going to represent Hoffa in the wire-tap trial in New York?" I said.

"I've about had it," Williams replied. "I didn't know what I was getting into with Hoffa and his friends. You get into a case like this, and it is hard to get out before it is over."

He said he had nothing to do with the incident of the courtroom visit by Joe Louis or the *Afro-American* newspaper stories. Some people, he admitted, would be hard to convince on this point.

"It isn't worth it," Williams said. "I can get plenty of other clients, and there won't be that bunch of Teamsters lawyers second guessing every move."

I felt sorry for Ed Williams as I left the Federal court building while the jury was still deliberating. He seemed to have had his fill of Teamsters, and of attorneys who worked for them. I was glad he had decided to sever relations with them. I disliked seeing his talent wasted defending the underworld and the Hoffa crowd.

A few minutes later, I stopped by the McClellan committee office to bring Bob Kennedy up to date on the trial. He was still burning with fury over the treatment Williams had given Cheasty a few days earlier. I told him I had just visited with Williams, and that I felt Williams was disgusted with the Hoffa crowd and would have no more to do with them.

There had been a reasonably good relationship between Kennedy and Williams until the Hoffa trial started. Kennedy had at first been disappointed at the way Williams conducted Hoffa's defense, and later he had been angry. Now, he said he hoped that Williams was really through with Hoffa and the Teamsters.

"It is a waste of a lot of fine talent for a damned unworthy cause," I said. "I don't blame any lawyer for defending any criminal in one given case, but it is dangerous to get too close to them."

I told Bob I feared there would be an acquittal in the Hoffa case, but that there could be a hung jury. I also told him Williams said he would settle for a hung jury.

Investigator Al Calabrese caught me outside of Kennedy's office and, half in jest and half in seriousness, said I shouldn't bring Kennedy the bad reports on the Hoffa hearings.

"Bob's been so upset about the way the Hoffa case is going that I just can't get him to sit down and really concentrate on the Textile Workers," Calabrese said.

I told Al that it probably would be all over in a few hours.

I accompanied Kennedy to the McClellan committee hearing room in the Senate Office Building, where I decided to listen to some of the testimony on the Textile Workers Union while awaiting notice that the Hoffa jury had reached a verdict. We didn't expect a verdict for at least a couple of hours, and the courthouse was a one-minute cab ride from the Capitol.

A slip of yellow paper was passed to Bob Kennedy as he interrogated a witness on the Textile Union scandals late that afternoon. He stopped suddenly, gasped and looked deathly sick. I knew what had happened when I saw his face.

"Hoffa was acquitted," was written on the paper. It took only a few seconds for the whispered word to be passed down to the press table. We had expected some warning that the jury was coming back to Judge Matthews' courtroom. We had wanted to be there. I rushed to the federal court building.

The impossible had happened, and the friends of Jimmy Hoffa had turned the court into a noisy carnival. Barney Baker moved his 380-pound bulk in front of me and slapped a hand on my shoulder.

"Jimmy's a real champ. Jimmy was right on this one, and I hope some of you newspaper boys will give him a break and write something nice about him."

Barney Baker, twice-convicted thug, thought this was something nice to write about.

"God bless the judge and jury," shouted one of the spectators.

"Jimmy is a real guy," chimed in Louis N. "Babe" Triscaro, the Cleveland Teamsters boss with a robbery conviction in his past. "Jimmy is a winner."

At the front of the courtroom, Jimmy was repeating his views of the case. "This proves once again that if you are honest and tell the truth, you have nothing to fear."

Hoffa had a pat on the back for Ed Williams, saying, "Thanks a million."

Then he turned to reporters and praised "all my attorneys," but particularly Williams, for a "masterful job of presenting the facts, not fiction, in this case."

Williams called reporters' attention to Kennedy's comment that he would "jump off the Capitol dome if Hoffa is acquitted." He added, "I'm going to send Bobby Kennedy a parachute."

The acquittal made it certain that Williams would be one of the most sought after defense lawyers in the nation. Now he was enjoying the congratulations and back slapping as he walked off with a noisy, jubilant mob that included Hoffa, other Teamsters lawyers, and a group of those Teamsters business agents closest to Jimmy.

"Jimmy, you are a lucky bastard," I said as he passed.

"I just live right," Jimmy answered with a wink.

U.S. District Attorney Oliver Gasch tried to make it easier for Cheasty: "I think Cheasty is an honorable man and a very courageous man, and I very much admire him and what he did."

Senator Irving M. Ives, the New York Republican, bluntly said he considered Hoffa's acquittal to be "a miscarriage of justice."

"Mr. Hoffa's troubles have far from ended," Senator Ives said. "He has not yet appeared before the Senate Select (labor racket) Committee, and I anticipate he will."

"Joe Louis makes a pretty good defense attorney," commented Senator Barry Goldwater, the Arizona Republican, who was also displeased with the verdict.

As Hoffa left the courthouse, the bouncy and happy Teamsters boss encountered two members of the jury that had freed him.

"Boys," he told the bewildered jurors as he shook their hands, "if you ever want to drive a truck, see me."

The beaming Hoffa posed for pictures with his arms around his wife, his son Jimmy, 16, and his daughter Barbara Ann, 19.

All of us who had lived with the trial asked him, "Are you a candidate for the presidency of the Teamsters?"

Hoffa replied that he was calling a meeting of about 500 Teamsters representatives at the Shoreland Hotel in Chicago within six days. "Then we'll determine my future plans in the Teamsters."

On the third floor of the federal court building, Assistant U. S. Attorney General Ed Troxell walked into his office with his head down to discuss the bad news with Cye Cheasty and the F.B.I. agents who had worked the case.

"I feel like I have been kicked in the stomach," Cheasty told me.

From the third-floor window in the front of the courthouse, we watched Hoffa, Williams and the Teamsters business agents posing for pictures and carrying on merrily.

When Cheasty had gone, Troxell commented: "Cheasty is an honest guy with a lot of courage. He is the fellow I feel sorry for. There is a guy with a bad heart, who risked his life and his reputation to do what every good citizen should do.

"He undertook a dangerous job for a month, and he has had a tough nine days on the witness stand. I hope his disappointment doesn't affect his health adversely," the prosecutor added.

I felt sorry for Troxell, too. He had tried, but the jury had released Jimmy Hoffa to gobble up the Teamsters union and everything else he could grasp in his greedy little hands.

It was a hell of a colorful story, but I got no satisfaction out of writing it—or contemplating what it might mean to the transportation industry and the nation.

XXI

Hoffa Goes Down, but Not Out

The day after James Riddle Hoffa's acquittal was a Saturday, but McClellan's committee wasted no time brooding over the verdict. Bob Kennedy called and asked if I could come to his home. Carmine Bellino, Ken O'Donnell, LaVern Duffy, Pierre Salinger, and others from the committee were going to be there to prepare for a thorough investigation of Hoffa.

Since Hoffa's arrest in March, Kennedy had not pursued him. He assumed Hoffa was finished and there was no point in beating a dead horse. Only one staff member, Irwin (Count) Langenbacher, had been assigned to Detroit in recent weeks, where he had been looking into some aspects of the union-busting tactics of Nathan Shefferman's labor relations firm, headquartered in Chicago. The Count's targets included Frank Kierdorf and Jack Thompson, two ex-convicts who, with Hoffa's help, became officials of Teamsters Local 332 in Flint.

At Kennedy's request I reviewed Hoffa's business deals, his misuse of union power, and the names of the convicted gamblers, armed robbers, thieves, narcotics peddlers, and white slavers who infested his Teamsters empire.

Kennedy said he felt it necessary to conduct hearings and get the full Hoffa story to the public before the Teamsters convention in late September, 1957.

It would be tragic if he is elected president of an organization as powerful as the Teamsters," Kennedy said.

Kennedy instructed Bellino to go to Detroit to take charge of the accounting side of the case. Other investigators were to join him as they became available.

Langenbacher went to Pontiac, Michigan, where he was steered to a man who knew Hoffa's operation from the inside— Robert P. Scott, former secretary-treasurer of Pontiac Local 614 and a former lobbyist for Hoffa at the Michigan Legislature.

Scott had fallen out with the Hoffa group and had quit the Teamsters. He was a former barber, so he managed to get himself appointed to the Michigan Board of Barber Examiners. He told Langenbacher an amazing story of what it had meant to be Jimmy Hoffa's political arm in the period from 1945 to 1952.[1]

Scott told Langenbacher that he was originally appointed to a Teamsters office by Hoffa, and that when he finally was elected it was "rigged" by the Hoffa forces.

Scott related that he had traveled the state, making political connections and spending Teamsters money to try to increase Hoffa's influence with state and local officials in Michigan.

But Scott's story of Hoffa's activity in other areas was even more fascinating. Scott said that when a grand jury was investigating Teamsters officials, Hoffa had used him to relay secret reports on evidence given against the Teamsters in the grand jury. He said Hoffa had told him about having a witness chased out of the state for giving testimony linking Hoffa to an effort to fix a liquor license case.

Scott said that on Hoffa's instructions he hid William Hoffa, Jimmy's convict brother, from the police. Jimmy had ordered that William should be kept on the Teamsters union payroll while hiding, and the union paid the bills for his hotel hideout, Scott disclosed.

The former Teamsters lobbyist said he had expected to be assigned regular lobbying chores, but he was amazed when Hoffa and Owen Bert Brennan tried to use their political influence to persuade a Michigan sheriff to let some of Hoffa's friends open

---

[1]McClellan committee, Report No. 1417, pages 244 and 245. See also Scott's testimony.

a gambling joint. On another occasion, he said, Hoffa asked him to try to arrange a parole for an underworld figure.

Union money and business agents were used to do remodeling work on Hoffa's summer home at Lake Orion, Michigan, Scott added.[2]

It was hard to believe that anyone could be involved in so many devious activities at one time. Dozens of other incidents popped up as Carmine Bellino and a big Senate committee investigation crew descended on Detroit.

The Detroit Teamsters officials were arrogant. They seemed unconcerned about the McClellan committee. They were confident that Jimmy Hoffa was bigger than the committee. The acquittal had put Hoffa on top, and the ordinary thugs, narcotics peddlers, dynamiters, arsonists, and assorted criminal satellites wanted to keep him there. Tough little Jimmy Hoffa had licked that rich kid, Bob Kennedy, and outwitted the F.B.I.

Witnesses had been frightened. Friendly judges seemed available. Hoffa's hoodlum friends felt there was really nothing to fear from McClellan and Kennedy so long as there was union money to buy good mouthpieces, and the union officials had the guts to do whatever was necessary to beat each rap.

Hoffa traveled from coast to coast setting up an apparatus he hoped would make him general president of the International Brotherhood of Teamsters. He was contemptuous of Kennedy, McClellan and the F.B.I. They had had what they thought was a tight case, and they hadn't been able to make it stick.

When committee accountant Bellino pressed Hoffa for union books and financial records, the Detroit Teamsters ruler narrowed his eyes and said menacingly to the accountant: "I've looked into you, Bellino. You've got seven kids, and you're going to have to earn a living for a long time."

Kennedy was informed there were threats on barber Robert Scott's life after he had talked to committee investigators. Scott had been warned by anonymous telephone callers that he should not testify against Hoffa if he wished to live. There were characters in the Hoffa organization who would go that far to protect pal Jimmy.

---

[2]McClellan committee, Report No. 1417, pages 244-245. Also, see testimony of Scott and other witnesses.

McClellan and Kennedy did not move directly against Hoffa when the new hearings opened. First, they ripped into scandals in the Allied Industrial Workers Union (formerly the U.A.W.-A.F.L.), involving the financial dealings of bull-voiced Anthony Doria, international secretary-treasurer of the Allied Industrial Workers, and his dealings with labor racketeer Johnny Dioguardi.

Dioguardi and Tony (Ducks) Corallo, a convicted narcotics law violator, obtained charters in the U.A.W.-A.F.L., and some of these were later used to set up seven "paper" Teamsters locals in New York—locals with phantom officers, few members and little legitimate function. They were created to enable some of Hoffa's cohorts—among them John O'Rourke and John Mc-Namara—to grab control of New York Teamsters Joint Council 16.[3]

It made no difference where the spotlight played. Hoffa always showed up in the background. The Hoffa henchmen included Dioguardi, Corallo, McNamara, and John O'Rourke, the top Hoffa man in New York. O'Rourke took refuge behind the Fifth Amendment on all questions involving union finances.

Dioguardi and Corallo had brought into organized labor forty men who had convictions for crimes that included extortion, burglary, accessory to murder, robbery, bookmaking, possession of stolen mail, bootlegging, larceny, dope peddling, and bribery, the Senate committee later reported. Some of them had sold out the union members they were supposed to represent by signing contracts that gave the workers only the bare national minimum wage of one dollar an hour. Puerto Ricans particularly were exploited on a grand scale.[4]

To Dioguardi, trade unions were just another racket. He had operated a nonunion dress shop in Pennsylvania; when he sold the shop he took an $11,000 bribe to use his connections to assure that it would stay nonunion. Dioguardi's labor consultant firm in New York City, Equitable Research Associates, was "devoted to keeping employers nonunion through the medium of payoffs," the McClellan committee found.[5]

---

[3]McClellan committee, Report No. 621, page 2, and Report No. 1417, page 221.

[4]McClellan committee, Report No. 1417, page 218.

[5]McClellan committee, Report No. 1417, pages 163-219.

It was a story I had covered years before, but it was still shocking to hear how gangsters were used to win control of Joint Council 16, which dominated trucking in New York.

"Such racketeers as John Dioguardi and Anthony Corallo present a dangerous enough problem, but when they have the backing of top officers of the nation's largest union, particularly James R. Hoffa . . . the situation becomes one for national alarm," the committee said.[6]

Hoffa was his usual fluent and cocky self when he appeared before the Senate committee on August 20. After one week in front of the television cameras, Bob Kennedy had him reeling. Repeatedly he forced Hoffa into corners with evidence that included details on telephone taps, facts which had been legally obtained by New York City District Attorney Frank Hogan.

"To the best of my recollection, I cannot recall, and this does not refresh my memory as to this conversation," Hoffa testified, repeating that evasion time and again after listening to telephone recordings of his conversations with Johnny Dioguardi. Jimmy claimed he couldn't remember whether he had put Minafones, electronic recording devices, on Teamsters business agents to spy on a grand jury. He claimed he had no recollection of other matters that would be equally difficult to forget.[7] Senator Irving Ives of New York declared that Hoffa had "the best forgettery" he had ever seen.

Chairman McClellan and other committee members concluded that Hoffa was finished, finally caught. Bob Kennedy and the investigators had barely scratched the surface, but they had already implicated Jimmy in a pattern of activities even more sordid than Dave Beck's. In a 48-point summary McClellan outlined the worst examples of Hoffa's misuse of union power and money.

Hoffa's confusion lasted only until he was out of the witness chair. He rallied forces to control delegates to the International Teamsters convention. He pledged to fight the A.F.L.-C.I.O. should it carry out an earlier threat to expel the Teamsters if he was elected general president.

Godfrey Schmidt, a New York attorney, filed a suit in

[6]McClellan committee, Report No. 1417, page 221.
[7]McClellan committee, Report No. 1417, pages 211-215.

Federal District Court in Washington, D.C., on behalf of twelve rank-and-file Teamsters from the New York area. It charged the Hoffa forces were "rigging" the Teamsters convention.

Federal Judge F. Dickinson Letts issued an injunction to prohibit the Teamsters from holding their convention. Teamsters attorney Martin O'Donoghue appealed to the Circuit Court, and that court reversed Judge Letts. The Court ruled that if there was actual evidence that the election was rigged, such evidence should be brought before the Teamsters convention, and, if the convention acted improperly, the evidence then should be brought to court after the election. The rank-and-file group contended this was an unsatisfactory solution in the light of evidence the convention was being rigged and controlled by Beck and Hoffa. They asked review of the Circuit Court ruling by the Supreme Court of the United States in a last desperate move to stop the Hoffa steamroller.

Kennedy and Bellino worked feverishly to button up as much Hoffa information as possible before the last two weeks of September. Robert Scott was one of the key witnesses and what the committee found was devastating:

Hoffa had "borrowed" thousands of dollars from Jack (Babe) Bushkin, a Detroit labor relations adviser; J. L. Keeshin, a Chicago truck line operator, and Henry Lower, promoter of a Florida real estate project in which Hoffa had an interest.[8]

Hoffa's so-called "borrowing" from Lower (with no interest) came shortly after Hoffa helped arrange for Lower to borrow $75,000 at four per cent interest from a Detroit bank where Hoffa kept the Teamsters' money.

Hoffa's home Local 299 and Local 337, also in Detroit, loaned $75,000 to the Marberry Construction Co., owned by Herbert Grosberg, the Teamsters' accountant, and George Fitzgerald, the Teamsters' attorney. This was at about the same time Hoffa obtained an $11,500 loan from Grosberg.

Hoffa helped Samuel (Shorty) Feldman, a convicted Philadelphia safe-cracker, robber and burglar, get a charter in the Hotel and Restaurant Workers Union. Later Feldman became a business agent for Philadelphia Teamsters Local 929.

Hoffa was a close friend and supporter of Joseph (Joey)

---

[8]McClellan committee, Report No. 1417, pages 223 and 224.

Glimco, identified by the committee as an associate of Capone mobsters in the Chicago area. Hoffa allowed Glimco to operate as trustee of Chicago Teamsters Taxi Local 777.[9]

Hoffa had hired Herman Kierdorf, a convicted armed robber, as a business agent for the Detroit Joint Council shortly after Kierdorf was released from the penitentiary. A few months later, he hired Frank Kierdorf, another convicted armed robber, as a business agent in the Flint Teamsters Local.[10]

The outline of a nationwide network of underworld connections was emerging. Chairman McClellan charged that in Pontiac, Michigan, and in Joplin, Missouri, Hoffa used the union trusteeship device to prevent reform groups from taking control and to keep corrupt local union officials in power.

Members of the McClellan committee hoped that the exposure would hurt Hoffa's chances, but the integration explosion at Little Rock, Arkansas, took over the front pages of the newspapers and killed much of the impact of the September hearings. There wasn't enough space left to print the details of the shocking testimony about how Hoffa had tried to corrupt police, sheriffs, prosecutors and judges to take care of his underworld friends.

Kennedy was sick about the way the Little Rock story buried much of the Hoffa story. In addition, the Little Rock racial strife created a public relations problem for the Senate committee. McClellan took the traditional position of Southern Democrats. He publicly opposed the United States Supreme Court decision to force integration in schools of the South.

Teamsters seized on McClellan's civil rights position in an effort to discredit the McClellan labor racket investigation. They were successful to a minor degree, for there were cartoons and editorials panning McClellan. From that point on, the civil rights issue was a constant irritant to Bob Kennedy. He was painfully aware of the need for nationwide public support in tackling the seemingly amoral power of some labor and management officials.

Appearances on television panel shows could have given Senator McClellan an opportunity to educate the public on Teamsters corruption, and the significance of racketeering in

[9]McClellan committee, Report No. 1417, pages 235-254.
[10]McClellan committee, Report No. 1417, page 223.

this gigantic, economically pivotal union. Instead, the Arkansas Democrat was invariably faced with questions on Little Rock and segregation. His frank answers were probably good politics in Arkansas, but they were often turned to take some of the force out of his comments on the Teamsters.

Hoffa sneered at the McClellan committee. He laughed at the edict of the A.F.L.-C.I.O. to the Teamsters to "get rid of Hoffa."

When convention time arrived, the well-heeled and tough-talking Hoffa crowd dominated the scene at the Eden Roc Hotel in Miami Beach. They out-shouted their brother Teamsters in the Miami Beach Auditorium. I went to a party staged for Tom Haggerty, the Chicago Milk Drivers Union official who was regarded as the leading candidate against Hoffa. We joined in singing with the Haggerty crowd: "H—A double—G—E—R—T—Y spells Haggerty."

I hoped that Tom Haggerty would win, or at least make a substantial showing. I wanted some evidence of effective opposition, but there was no ring of truth to Haggerty's boasts of delegate strength. He was whistling in the dark, and hoping that he wasn't irritating the Hoffa forces too much.

As I started to leave the Eden Roc I spotted Hoffa on the mezzanine floor. He waved.

"Hi, Poison Pen," Jimmy called out, grinning. He didn't look like a dejected candidate as he stood there with some of his key supporters, including Ray Cohen, secretary-treasurer of Philadelphia Local 107.

"Just a minute, and I'll be with you," Hoffa told me.

"What's it look like, Jimmy?" I said, when he finally came over to where I was standing. "Could the (Tom) Hickey, Haggerty and (William) Lee forces join hands and stop you?"

"I've got it sewed up now," Hoffa said. "Those fellows are wind bags. The three of them won't have any more than 20 per cent of the votes.

"I know where I stand with every delegate, and Lee and Haggerty are counting a lot of votes they don't have," Hoffa continued. "Those they have they are counting twice."

Hoffa said he had so many votes that the credentials committee was going to throw out some of his delegates without any objection being raised.

"I've got a five-to-one majority, and we've got votes to burn," Hoffa said.

He outlined for me his slate of vice-presidents, and he added that he was planning to get rid of Frank Brewster of Seattle and Sidney Brennan of Minneapolis. He wasn't going to purge these men because of Brennan's Taft-Hartley conviction or Brewster's admissions that he used Teamsters money for his race horses and high living, Hoffa advised me. He was taking action because they were the opposition, and he was going to wipe them out to make room for some of his team.

Hoffa's team was to include John O'Rourke, who six weeks earlier had taken the Fifth Amendment on questions dealing with union finances.

"I've got one guy you'll approve of," Hoffa said, grinning again. "I'm putting Gordon Conklin from St. Paul on my ticket in place of Sid Brennan. I understand you kinda liked Conklin."

I told Hoffa that I liked Conklin and had always found him to be truthful in what he told me.

Conklin had been helpful to me in January, 1953, when I had first gone to Minneapolis. He had helped me round up Teamsters to obtain information about Sid Brennan's activity. He had told me he had Hoffa's approval.

"I'd feel better about this election if there were more like Gordon Conklin on your ticket," I told Hoffa.

Hoffa smiled. He was confident and he was not irked at a few jibes at his slate. He was sure there was nothing the McClellan committee, the federal courts, or the newspapers could do to stop his election now.

He wanted to pull a "Babe Ruth." He was going to hit several home runs, and he wanted the pleasure of telling me ahead of time which home run would land in which bleacher and which would go out of the park.

It pleased him to wink at me from the stage of the Miami Beach Auditorium, or to give me the "I-told-you-so" smile as he bounced into the wings of the stage.

When I saw Gordon Conklin the next day, I called him aside.

"I understand you are going to be a vice-president on Hoffa's slate," I said.

"I can't say anything about it," Conklin said.

"It's okay," I said. "Jimmy told me about it last night. Are you going to go along with that Hoffa gang?"

"It doesn't look like there is much choice," Conklin said.

"Haven't you been reading the papers?" I asked. "Don't you know what the McClellan committee has put on the line about Jimmy?"

"I don't like it, Clark," Conklin said apologetically. "I don't see what I can do. Jimmy has always treated me okay. He backed me when I had my back to the wall in the fight to keep Brennan's boys from taking over St. Paul. You gotta support the guys that supported you. Even if I wanted to object, I can't see where it would do any good. Jimmy has the organization, and he has the votes. I could end up on the outside—and with nothing gained."

It depressed me to think of the futility of fighting Hoffa. Conklin didn't relish the prospect of going back to Minnesota and facing the scorn of some of his friends for having voted for Hoffa. His attitude was typical of other convention delegates and officials. They didn't approve of Hoffa. They simply wanted to survive and keep on drawing their union pay checks. It was easier for them to swallow their pride than to pull in their belts and get along without that salary.

Dave Beck was presiding, pretending to be a figure of importance when everyone knew he was cringing before Hoffa in hopes of hanging on to that $163,000 Teamster-purchased home and the $50,000-a-year lifetime pension.

Beck held the center of the stage as general president—in name only. The applause was regulated by hand signals from stocky Jimmy Hoffa, who stood at the side and controlled crowd responses like a puppeteer. It was not that all the delegates were so enthusiastic about Hoffa. They merely wanted to appear enthusiastic to the well-organized Hoffa demonstrators.

Old John English had been George Meany's hope for a clean-up of the Teamsters, but the veteran secretary-treasurer of the international union had no disposition to fight Hoffa. He was a candidate for re-election, and he had a lifetime pension to think about.

"I love this little fellow," he told the convention in Florida.

So it was that English, who less than six months earlier had been named to the A.F.L.-C.I.O. executive board to replace Beck, gave his endorsement to the man the A.F.L.-C.I.O. had condemned.

In a meeting of the Central Conference of Teamsters, Hoffa showed even more impressive strength. No one voiced opposition as he whipped through a resolution that endorsed expenditure of $170,000 in union funds for expenses and attorneys for a group of extortionists and dynamiters.

Ironically, one of the delegates in the Central Conference meeting was a Minnesota man who had been the victim of a dynamiting planned by labor racketeer Jerry Connelly whom Hoffa had defended.

Beck promised that the convention would be handled in "strict fairness" and impartiality. Then, as presiding officer, he urged the delegates to support Hoffa. With no indication that he was himself involved, Beck said that "some" Teamsters officials might have "committed errors," but he warned:

"I would like to see the man stand up—he who is without sin—and cast the first stone."

No one stood up.

The decision on the rank-and-file Teamsters' suit to stop the election at this convention was announced by the Supreme Court of the United States on October 1.

It was Dave Beck who read to the convention the telegram stating that Chief Justice Earl Warren had turned down the rank-and-file effort to delay the election.

Hoffa led the cheers of the 1,900 delegates. He treated Warren's ruling as a personal victory in his drive for the Teamsters presidency. He bounded to the front of the stage in the huge auditorium, smiled broadly, and lifted Beck's arm in a victory salute.

"Get it going, Jimmy," was the shout from the crowd. "Let's get this election over with."

On October 3 Hoffa forces howled down the efforts of an Oakland Teamster to get a full discussion of the charges of corruption against Hoffa, Beck, Brennan, and Brewster.

On October 4, Hoffa declared open warfare on George Meany without even waiting for the balloting on the Teamsters presidency. He announced a campaign to rally strength within the A.F-L.-C.I.O. to block any effort to expel the Teamsters.

That same day Beck announced to the convention that he would step out as general president on October 15 instead of waiting until December 1. This was designed to give the Hoffa clique immediate command of the campaign to persuade other unions to revolt against Meany's ouster edict.

Thomas (Honest John) Hickey, international vice-president from the New York area, was dejected when he told me he figured Hoffa would get all but about 300 or 400 of the votes on the first roll call.

"The delegates in this convention have asked to be kicked out of the A.F.-L.-C.I.O., and none of them can say that they didn't know it when they voted," Hickey told me.

I had first met Tom Hickey in New York three years earlier, when I dropped into his office to discuss his fight against Hoffa's invasion of New York. As we visited in his union office, over-looking the waterfront, he had seemed a stern and tough man. He still had hopes of beating the gangster-backed groups when I interviewed him for Dumont Television during the McClellan hearings in August, 1957. Now, he was weary from the fight and looked like a tired old man.

When the election finally was held on October 4, it was an anticlimax. Hoffa polled 1,208 votes; William A. Lee, 313; and Thomas J. Haggerty, 140.

It was a big day for Hoffa's supporters. They hoisted Hoffa to their shoulders, stomped around the hall, and cheered.

Election partying hadn't ceased when two plane loads of Hoffa henchmen decided to treat themselves to a Caribbean trip with union money. They had elected their man Hoffa by running roughshod over the Teamsters constitution, and they had spent thousands of dollars putting him across. This was no time to be careful with the dues money of the union members, for they knew Jimmy wasn't going to object to a little loose spending. He couldn't.

Two days after the convention, Hoffa received a telegram of congratulations from Maurice Hutcheson, the Carpenters union president who was also a vice-president of the A.F.-L.-C.I.O. Hutcheson said he thought the Teamsters had cleaned up enough to justify keeping them in the A.F.L.-C.I.O.

Another opinion came from Senator McClellan. He declared that scandalous activity and dictatorial practices had set the stage for Hoffa's election.

A "preliminary examination," said McClellan, showed that some records of the convention credentials committee were missing and the available ones were inadequate.

"We found several instances where Dave Beck instructed the credentials committee to disregard the Teamsters constitution," McClellan said.

Although Hoffa was elected by a large margin, McClellan said that investigations disclosed union membership was disregarded in so many cases that the bulk of the delegates should have been disqualified. McClellan made the evidence of the rigged election available to the rank-and-file group dissidents and this time U.S. District Court Judge F. Dickinson Letts was asked to prevent Hoffa's taking office.

On October 14, one day before Hoffa was to take over, Judge Letts signed a temporary order barring him from office for ten days. The order also directed the Teamsters union to appear in federal court October 21 and "show cause" why the Miami Beach election should not be held void as a violation of the Teamsters constitution. Martin O'Donoghue, attorney for the Teamsters, said he intended to appeal to the Circuit Court, but he dropped that plan, and the case went to hearings.

On October 24, the A.F.L.-C.I.O. executive council suspended the Teamsters, and said the union would be expelled if Hoffa continued as an officer. The vote was twenty-five to four, Hoffa's support coming from John English, Maurice Hutcheson, the Letter Carriers Union president, William Dougherty and Herman Winter, president emeritus of the Bakery Workers Union.

A few minutes before Meany read the A.F.L.-C.I.O. announcement, Hoffa strode out of the hearing room and through the lobby of the A.F.L.-C.I.O. headquarters. He and the half-dozen Teamsters vice-presidents accompanying him were angry.

"There will be no statement," Hoffa said grimly. "That's it."

His effort to frighten the A.F.L.-C.I.O. into compromise with corruption had failed.

XXII

Hoffa's Helpers in the Garbage Rackets

Jimmy Hoffa had enough problems to break the nerve of the average man. There was a federal perjury indictment hanging over him in New York, along with a charge of illegally arranging to have the telephones in his Detroit headquarters tapped. Committee investigators were digging into Teamsters scandals in Tennessee, and they were dredging the affairs of the Philadelphia Teamsters. Hoffa's name was always involved.

Even the investigation of Nathan Shefferman, Beck's suave labor consultant friend, had turned up indications that the Shefferman firm could make deals with officials in the Michigan Conference of Teamsters, Hoffa's personal bailiwick.[1]

The garbage workers' scandals in New York City involved Bernard Adelstein, a Hoffa supporter, and garbage workers' scandals in Los Angeles involved another Hoffa man, Frank Matula, Jr.[2]

Hoffa was also plagued by the proceedings before Federal Judge Letts in Washington. Godfrey Schmidt, a New York lawyer, was scouring the country to find Hoffa enemies who would testify about irregularities in the selection of delegates to the recent Teamsters convention.

Hoffa was to be in Federal court in New York City Friday,

---

[1]McClellan committee, Report No. 621, page 706.
[2]McClellan committee, Report No. 1417, pages 325-330.

October 25, in connection with the perjury and wire-tap charges that were soon coming up for trial.

When I arrived in the New York courtroom, Hoffa was already there, with the usual entourage of attorneys and Teamsters. It was only a routine procedure involving preliminary motions, but you never could tell when something worth a story would take place if Hoffa was present.

He was unusually glum. I wondered if the strain wasn't beginning to bother him. It was easy to see why he might be shaken. The indictments against him in New York included some factors that made his defense more difficult than in the bribery-conspiracy case in which he had been acquitted three months earlier.

There would be closer government scrutiny of the jury. Also, the prosecution had wire-tap recordings of some of Hoffa's conversations that would be difficult for glib Jimmy to explain.

The courts had held that it was illegal for Federal investigators to use wire-taps to obtain evidence, but it was permissible for Federal officials to use wire-taps that were legally obtained by state law enforcement officials.

New York District Attorney Frank Hogan had many recordings of telephone conversations between Hoffa and Johnny Dioguardi and other labor racket figures. The McClellan committee had effectively used some of the tapes to refresh Hoffa's recollection in August. That was the one time I had seen arrogant little Jimmy turned into a helpless witness.

Bob Kennedy had other recordings of Hoffa's conversations, but he told me he had not used "the best ones."

"We are saving them for a surprise for Hoffa if he testifies in his own defense in New York," Kennedy said. U.S. Attorney Paul Williams planned to use those recordings in the perjury trial.

Judge William Herlands set the trial for November 4.

"What are you doing here?" Hoffa asked me as we left the courtroom.

"I came up to see how you were getting along, Jimmy," I replied. "You're my favorite subject."

"You oughta give me half your salary," Hoffa said. "I don't know what you'd put in your papers if you didn't write about me."

"If you spend much more time in court, you'll be qualified for a law degree," I said.

"I know a lot more about some of those things now than the lawyers do," Hoffa answered. I was sure he was right.

"How do you think you are coming out in this trial?" I asked.

Hoffa indicated he was fairly sure he would win, but he didn't sound as if he were convinced. He talked about the "unfairness" of the government's use of wire-taps of his conversations to convict him. He claimed that tactic was a violation of his rights. He hoped there would be a United States Supreme Court ruling in the Salvatore Benanti case that would prohibit Federal attorneys from using the wire-taps.

The Benanti case involved a Federal bootlegging conviction based on evidence obtained as a result of wire-tapping by state officials. The conviction had been upheld by the Second Circuit Court.

I asked him if he was having any success in his campaign to undermine George Meany and his ruling that the Teamsters had to get rid of Hoffa as president or get out of the A.F.L.-C.I.O.

On this subject Hoffa was genuinely optimistic. He said he didn't see how the A.F.L.-C.I.O. could go through with the expulsion of the Teamsters without smashing the recently merged organization.

He said the Carpenters union and the Operating Engineers would not go along with ouster of the Teamsters because they were already targets of Senator McClellan's investigators.

Hoffa said he had talked with James Cross, president of the Bakery Workers Union, and that he had local Teamsters officials talking to leaders of other unions to develop opposition to Meany's order.

"George Meany says he isn't going to back down under any circumstances," I said.

"Meany's got a lot of guts talking like that," Hoffa said. "He hasn't been too careful about conflicts of interest. And isn't that the same George Meany who visited Joey Fay in prison? He is no crusader. He is letting himself be pushed into this by Walter Reuther."

Hoffa hated Meany, and he hated Reuther. He had confidence in the Teamsters union as an instrument for coaxing or clubbing other unions into agreement.

"The A.F.L.-C.I.O. needs the Teamsters worse than the Teamsters need the A.F.L.-C.I.O.," he said. "You've been around, and you know it."

I didn't like to admit it, but I was afraid that he was right. It was going to take a lot of courage for Meany to expel the Teamsters.

Later, I went to the office of United States Attorney Paul Williams. He seemed to believe that the perjury case against Hoffa was strong, but he was worried about the appeal in the Benanti bootlegging case. If the United States Supreme Court upset the Benanti conviction because of evidence obtained through the wire-tapping of a state agency, then the perjury case on Hoffa would be destroyed. If the conviction was sustained, he said, the perjury case would be a better bet for the prosecution than the wire-tap indictment.

I mentioned the first Hoffa trial and told Williams I hoped he wasn't overconfident. He assured me he was not. I knew nothing of his ability in court, but he was working hard in preparing for trial. I had visited with Williams periodically since he had been named a Federal attorney, and he had always been aggressively interested in Hoffa and the underworld group connected with Teamsters operations in New York.

I was feeling optimistic about the outcome of this Hoffa prosecution when I returned to Washington, D.C. that night to resume covering the hearings on the labor relations activities of Nathan Shefferman. If the Benanti conviction were upheld by the Supreme Court, I felt that Hoffa would be finished.

The Shefferman hearings were important to Bob Kennedy and Senator McClellan because they put the spotlight on union-busting practices by large business firms.

There had been criticism of the McClellan committee for stressing the corruption of labor while giving little attention to illegal or unethical activities by management. I did not feel that the complaint was justified. Evidence developed from February through October in 1957 had disclosed the improper activities of dozens of large business concerns. Some had gone out of their way to bribe union officials. Others had submitted to labor's threats. Chairman McClellan and Senator John Kennedy of the committee had been publicly critical of businessmen who had improper financial dealings with labor leaders.

However, the Teamsters union, as well as the A.F.L.-C.I.O. and some editorial writers, ignored that record and criticized John McClellan as if he had been covering up for business. The attacks had not been damaging, but McClellan and Bob Kennedy wanted to point up management corruption in such a dramatic way that it would muffle this criticism.

Nate Shefferman was the ideal subject. He had approximately 400 clients, including Sears, Roebuck & Co., the Mennen Company, and dozens of the largest department stores. In the seven-year period from January 1, 1949, to December 31, 1955, his Labor Relations Associates, Inc., had grossed $2,481,798. His major offices were in New York, Detroit and Chicago, but he operated from coast to coast.[3]

Even before the hearings started on October 22, Shefferman was known as the man who bought everything from three-dollar bow ties to television sets for Dave Beck and Beck's friends and relatives.

"A source of a great deal of Shefferman's power was his close association with Dave Beck," the McClellan committee found.[4]

"Shefferman . . . was able to sell employers his friendship with Beck and was able to rely on Beck's Teamsters for effective assistance in efforts to defeat organizing drives.

"While Shefferman exuded soothing platitudes in speeches at union conventions . . . his large staff of agents, many operating under aliases, mounted vicious anti-union drives in all parts of the country."

The McClellan committee discovered that Sears, Roebuck & Co. used Shefferman extensively "to beat down union drives, particularly by the Retail Clerks International Association."

"On the recommendation of Sears officials, Labor Relations Associates was used for the same purpose by Sears, Roebuck suppliers and subsidiaries," the committee said.

[3]McClellan committee, Report No. 1417, pages 255 and 300.
[4]McClellan committee, Report No. 1417, page 298.

One of the most "flagrant cases," according to the committee, was Shefferman's activity in a campaign against Sears employees in Boston who wanted to join a union.

"They spawned a phony company union and expended funds for its continued life," the committee report said. "They paid off the leaders of the spurious group and discriminated against those who favored the legitimate organization. Finally they dumped their own (company union) group in favor of a no-union movement which they also invented and financed. For operating these activities and for successfully preventing a legitimate unionization of this store, Sears, Roebuck paid Shefferman some $78,000."[5]

The committee also said that "companies such as the Morton Frozen Food Co. of Webster City, Iowa; the Whirlpool Corporation plants at both Marion and Clyde, Ohio; the Allstate Insurance Co. (of Sears, Roebuck) in its Michigan offices, and the Englander Co. in Chicago had set up improper, if not illegal, so-called spontaneous, anti-union committees made up of the employees of their company."

It is illegal for a company to finance a union, but operating through the Shefferman concern, many of them established "Vote No" committees and other theoretically spontaneous organizations of employees who opposed unions.

Shefferman also developed a procedure for using survey questionnaires to find out whether employees were likely to vote for a union—and which ones among the workers might become leaders in a legitimate union movement. The latter, according to the Shefferman pattern, were to be fired.

James T. Neilsen, alias James Neal, alias James Edwards, was the head of the Shefferman operations in Boston and the McClellan committee said his activity appeared to be in direct violation of the Taft-Hartley Act.[6]

His hotel bill averaged $100 a day while he was meeting with, and entertaining, members of the Sears, Roebuck company union in Boston. In all, Neilsen-Neal-Edwards spent $6,780 on entertainment during his successful campaign to prevent unionization of that Sears store.

---

[5]McClellan committee, Report No. 1417, page 298.
[6]McClellan committee, Report No. 1417, pages 297-300.

He testified that he had been a friend of Harold Gibbons, a St. Louis Teamster, for years and had entertained him at Sears' expense. Bob Kennedy said Neilsen had made twenty-five or thirty telephone calls to Gibbons and had charged as much as $139 on one occasion for entertainment for him.

George Kamenow, who headquartered in Detroit, was one of the biggest spenders in Shefferman's organization. The committee focused its attention on his efforts in the Flint, Michigan, area, where he had succeeded in getting the Teamsters union to call off its drive to organize several small business concerns.

"The committee cannot condemn too strongly the activities of George Kamenow of Detroit, who, in apparent collusion with Teamsters officials in Flint settled the labor problems of a number of small . . . businessmen."[7]

Frank Kierdorf and Jack Thompson, two ex-convict Teamsters officials, had been lavishly entertained by Kamenow, who told businessmen that he had taken them on fishing trips to Canada and to the Rose Bowl football game.

"The pattern of activity in Flint presents to the committee a clear picture of extortion," the McClellan Probe Report said. "A number of these businessmen testified that the Teamsters union in Flint would demand recognition or would place pickets in front of their establishments. For the payment of certain amounts of money Kamenow would undertake to solve the problem. In every case the committee heard, these payments to Kamenow brought about a cessation of union activity and withdrawal of picket lines."

Kierdorf and Thompson hid behind the Fifth Amendment on the grounds they might incriminate themselves. So did George Kamenow.

By the time Nate Shefferman and his son, Shelton, were called to testify on November 5, 1957, their labor relations business was a wreck. Nate, who had been a garrulous witness in March, was now a beaten old man.

Stanford Clinton, attorney for the Sheffermans, told Chairman McClellan the Sheffermans had been indicted with Dave Beck in Tacoma. The charge was that they had "combined and conspired" to help Beck evade federal income taxes. Clinton said

---

[7]McClellan committee, Report No. 1417, page 299.

the older Shefferman's health was "impaired" and that his business was "in ruins."[8]

McClellan refused to grant a delay in the Sheffermans' appearance before his committee. They took the Fifth Amendment on the grounds that they might incriminate themselves, and McClellan accepted that opportunity to lambast the business firms that had utilized the Sheffermans' services in making allegedly dishonest deals with labor leaders.

A few days later, on November 12, the National Labor Relations Board ruled that "hot cargo" contracts between the Teamsters union and truck lines were contrary to good public policy and therefore invalid. The N.L.R.B. found that the union's refusal to load cargo which had been handled by a firm involved in labor difficulty violated the law against secondary boycotts.

That same day, the McClellan committee opened hearings on Teamsters scandals in the garbage collecting industry in Los Angeles and New York. It was referred to more politely as "the carting industry," but this didn't change the odor of the product —nor the unions' activity. Again, it was Hoffa supporters who were involved—Frank Matula, Jr., of Local 396 in Los Angeles and Bernard Adelstein of Teamsters Local 813 in New York.[9]

Through collusive agreements between the unions and private carting companies, certain underworld groups had gained a near-monopoly in the multi-million-dollar garbage collecting business, the committee learned. Conservative estimates set the carting business volume at fifty million dollars a year in New York and twenty million in Los Angeles.

"In the . . . case of New York, the field has been invaded and ruled by hoodlums of every stripe, many of them members

---

[8]On August 28, 1957, Dave Beck was indicted by a Federal grand jury in Tacoma, Washington, and seven counts of tax evasion charging he concealed $254,000 income in the 1951 to 1953 period, and had evaded $185,000 in taxes. Jointly indicted with Beck for conspiracy to help him evade taxes were Dave Beck, Jr., Nathan Shefferman, Shelton Shefferman, Norman Gessert and Fred Verschueren, Sr., a Teamsters Union accountant. The Supreme Court upset the conviction of Beck on the tax evasion counts, but upheld his conviction on charges he filed false union tax returns. The Justice Department on March 14, 1963, dismissed the conspiracy charges against Beck and the other five defendants. United States Attorney Jack S. Obenour said the charges were dropped because Beck was then serving a five-year prison term for filing false tax returns for the Teamsters Union.

[9]McClellan committee, Report No. 1417, pages 326 and 328.

of the infamous international brotherhood of Mafia and the holders of criminal records awesome in their length and variety," the McClellan committee reported.[10]

Racketeering had caused garbage hauling costs in some cases to be quadrupled (from two dollars to eight dollars a week) within the space of a few weeks. The committee blamed the gangsters, charging that they ran those businesses with the help of Teamsters officials who had a "blatant public-be-damned philosophy."[11]

Vincent (Jimmy) Squillante, described by federal narcotics authorities as a major source of illegal narcotics, shifted from docks and policy rackets into the carting business, the committee said.

In the sham role of labor relations expert, Squillante moved in on the carting business and ended up as executive director of the New York Cartmen's Association.

"Ruling with the absolute power of a czar, he stripped garbage-collecting firms of any voice in their own economic destinies, imposed a business dogma totally alien to free competition, and enriched himself and his relatives and court favorites to an extent that can never be fully calculated," the committee report declared.[12] (Squillante boasted that he was the godson of the late Albert Anastasia, lord high executioner of Brooklyn-based Murder, Inc.)

Louis Iannacine, convicted of a union shakedown in the fruit and vegetable industry, was an officer and stockholder with Squillante's brother, Nunzio, in the General Sanitation Company, a firm used as "a whip" to keep others in the cartmen's association in line.

"Bernard Adelstein of Teamsters Local 813, the dominant union in New York carting, betrayed every principle of trade unionism by serving as an abject tool in all of Squillante's empire-building activities," the committee said.

"Adelstein was able to put his union at Squillante's complete disposal in enforcing monopolies, punishing trade association

[10]McClellan committee, Report No. 1417, pages 300 and 301.
[11]McClellan committee, Report No. 1417, page 325.
[12]McClellan committee, Report No. 1417, page 327.

critics of Squillante, and winking at Squillante-favored non-union firms.

"He (Adelstein) failed to enforce union wage rates for workers at the Sunrise Sanitation Service . . . in which (Carmine) Tramunti and his underworld boss, Anthony (Tony Ducks) Corallo, had an interest."[13]

Adelstein, Vincent Squillante and Nunzio Squillante later were convicted on charges of extortion through the carting industry. They were sentenced to prison in New York.

Captain James E. Hamilton of the Los Angeles Police Department told the committee that Frank Matula used the Teamsters picket line in Los Angeles as an enforcement arm for the cartmen's association. Matula was convicted of perjury for denying the charge before a California state legislative committee.

This use of an employers' association and a Teamsters union to create a monopoly was versatile. I had first become aware of it in the juke box field in Michigan and Ohio. While studying Hoffa's background, I discovered that his first conviction for federal law violation involved the use of a similar device to enforce a monopoly in the wastepaper industry in Michigan and several surrounding states. There was no limit to the evil that could flow from such a practice if it were allowed to go unchecked.

During that period, Dave Beck held what was his last big press conference in Washington, D.C. He was still posing as the man who ran the Teamsters, but now it was obvious to everyone that it was a sham. He was still general president, but only because Federal Judge Letts had barred Hoffa from office pending a hearing on the charge that Hoffa had "rigged" the convention in Florida. The Hoffa forces had actually taken charge of the International Brotherhood of Teamsters.

The Congressional hearings, the Federal indictments, and the pressure of maintaining reasonable relations with Hoffa had aged Beck. He still bellowed, but there was no assurance in his voice. His rambling declaration that there was no substantial racketeering in the Teamsters union was now ludicrous.

At that last press conference Beck announced that Edward

---

[13]McClellan committee, Report No. 1417, page 329.

Bennett Williams had been hired as general counsel for the Teamsters.

I was surprised. Williams had given me and others the impression he was through with the Teamsters, and that was the story his patron in the law, Ed Cheyfitz, had told me only a few weeks earlier. Cheyfitz had said that he and Williams had sadly concluded there was little hope for a cleanup under Hoffa. Cheyfitz said then that the only reason he and Williams had stayed with Hoffa so long was their belief that they might reform him and do something fine for a big union.

I didn't know why Williams had decided to get so close to the Teamsters as to actually be their legal adviser. I was afraid he would live to regret the decision for there were many more worthwhile things to which he could have devoted his talents.

XXIII

Teamsters' Defiance and Expulsion

There was almost unbelievable defiance of the McClellan committee by some Teamsters officials, and by officials of some other Michigan unions who were friendly to the Hoffa group.

Only a month after ex-barber Robert Scott testified against Hoffa, he found himself subject to harrassment and a move to eject him from membership in Local 552 of the Barbers Union. To be kicked out of the union could have cost him his job as a member of the Michigan Barber Commission. He finally obtained a court order to prevent the Barbers Union from taking action to expel him.[1]

During those same weeks, in late October and early November, 1957, Teamsters business agent Herman Kierdorf was putting pressure on certain firms in Detroit to give their laundry business to a concern which the McClellan committee described as having underworld connections.[2]

Old Herman Kierdorf, the convicted bank robber, hadn't been slowed in the least by his questioning before the committee in September. Hoffa was still keeping the old robber on as business representative for Detroit Teamsters Joint Council 43, and he was continuing his old tricks, with variations. He had implicit

---

[1]McClellan committee, hearings, Part 36, pages 13685-13691.
[2]McClellan committee, Report No. 621, page 675.

faith in Hoffa's resourcefulness and the power of the Teamsters to keep him out of jail.

Fortunately, there were some areas where there was aggressive action by law enforcement officials. On November 14, 1957, Sergeant Edgar D. Crosswell of the New York State Bureau of Criminal Investigation led a raid on the palatial home of Joseph Mario Barbara, Sr., of Apalachin, New York. When the police appeared, the guests abandoned their shiny new Cadillacs, disregarded the damage to their fancy clothing, and fled through the woods and fields.

When police rounded them up as they came out on the highways, miles from the Barbara estate, it was alleged that they had been attending a gangster convention. Some of the top names in the Mafia were among the 58 arrested, and there was a sprinkling of labor leaders, labor relations consultants, vending machine operators, old-time bootleggers, and convicted robbers who were now parading behind legitimate business fronts.[3]

The McClellan committee at that time was conducting hearings on Mafia connections with the labor-underworld control of the carting business in New York. McClellan investigators also were piecing together the nationwide pattern of underworld infiltration of the juke-box and vending-machine business.

There was one theory that the underworld convention was called to discuss ways of blocking the McClellan investigators— or quieting the witnesses.

Bob Kennedy was already checking on some members of that Apalachin group. He took immediate steps to bring others under scrutiny. The labor racket investigators were delving into the vending-machine business, and knew something of Gerardo Vito (Jerry) Catena, who was associated with Abner (Longie) Zwillman in a vending-machine empire.

Another "delegate" to the gangland convention, Russell Bufalino, 54, of Kingston, Pennsylvania, was of interest to Kennedy for several reasons. He was a close associate of several labor racket figures, including Johnny Dioguardi, and received payments as "an expediter" for several nonunion dress manufacturers. Bufalino was an uncle of William Bufalino, president

---

[3]McClellan committee, Report No. 1139, pages 487-489.

of Teamsters Local 985 which had juke-box jurisdiction in Detroit.[4]

The McClellan committee found there were many interesting figures in attendance at Apalachin. Carmine Lombardozzi, 44, of Brooklyn, operated as a labor relations consultant and had demonstrated that he had a certain strange power over the underworld while promoting a juke-box combine in the New York City area. Frank Zito, a convicted bootlegger of Springfield, Illinois, was operating a vending-machine business.[5]

Vito Genovese was one of the top gangsters in the country. He had been on the fringe of many labor rackets, and he was identified as a key figure in an international narcotics ring.

James Vincent La Duca of Lewiston, New York, was secretary-treasurer of Local 66 of the Hotel and Restaurant Employees Union in Buffalo. Frank Thomas Majuri of Elizabeth, New Jersey, was vice president of Local 364 of the Hod Carriers and Common Laborers Union. Rosario Mancuso of Utica, New York, was president of Local 186 of the laborers union.

John Scalish, 45-year-old Clevelander, operated a large vending-machine business in that Ohio city. He had served two terms in the Ohio penitentiary for robbery.[6]

There were enough persons with labor and coin-machine connections at that Apalachin crime convention to give Bob Kennedy plenty of material to work on, and he lost no time in getting at it. The labor racket significance became much clearer as time went on.

I talked to Edward Bennett Williams, who asserted that his employment as counsel for the Teamsters Union didn't mean that he was also the lawyer for those persons who were on trial in criminal cases. Williams was to represent the Teamsters in the suit brought by rank-and-file union members in Judge Letts' court in Washington. Attorney Martin O'Donoghue had dropped out. Williams said he had little hope for a favorable ruling from Judge Letts. He said he would rely on appeals to win for Hoffa.

The opening of hearings before Judge Letts on December 2, 1957, meant that the Teamsters were on the defensive in four

---

[4]McClellan committee, Report No. 1139, page 504.

[5]McClellan committee, Report No. 1139, pages 737 and 749.

[6]McClellan committee, Report No. 1139, pages 501-504.

arenas: Beck was being tried for grand larceny in Seattle, Hoffa was on trial on a wire-tapping charge in New York, the McClellan committee was questioning Hoffa's friends in the Tennessee Teamsters, and the A.F.L.-C.I.O. was sitting in judgment on the proposed expulsion of the Teamsters. It was hard to determine which of the many performances it was most important to watch.

I decided to divide my time between the McClellan investigation and the hearings before Judge Letts, and squeeze in a trip to New York City to see how Hoffa was getting along.

On December 4, A.F.L.-C.I.O. President Meany tried to split Hoffa from the other Teamsters. He announced that he would drop the move to expel the Teamsters if Hoffa would quit as international president and the Teamsters would accept an A.F.L.-C.I.O. overseer to supervise a house cleaning.

"We'll see," was all Hoffa would say.

Harold Gibbons said he couldn't see any advantage in the Teamsters' accepting such an offer. Meany had dodged the question of whether Hoffa would have to give up control of the Central Conference of Teamsters.

The Teamsters played power politics when the A.F.L.-C.I.O. convention took up the expulsion matter on December 6, 1957. Einar Mohn was the lead-off spokesman for the mighty drivers' union, and he painted a picture of Chairman McClellan as being a part of the anti-union forces seeking to cripple all labor.

"For any individual or body to reach the conclusion that the Teamsters are 'dominated, controlled or substantially influenced in the conduct of their affairs by corrupt influences' is erroneous and fails to show an understanding of our make-up," Mohn told the convention.[7]

Mohn recalled for his listeners: "It has become traditional and customary for labor unions in practically all industries to call upon the Teamsters local unions for assistance when they have disputes. and in organizing campaigns.

"Nothing can change the strategic importance of the Teamsters, and nothing can change the dependence that the local unions affiliated with the other organizations that are in the

---

[7]Proceedings of the A.F.L.-C.I.O. constitutional convention, 1957, Vol. I, page 69.

Federation will continue to have on Teamsters locals throughout the country," Mohn warned.

Alex Rose, president of the United Hatters, Cap and Millinery Workers Union, served as chairman of the Committee on Appeals. He answered Mohn. He declared that the A.F.L.-C.I.O. was not condemning the Teamsters union, but was condemning a system that works "to the benefit of Dave Beck and Jimmy Hoffa."[8]

"The arrogance, the defiance of the Teamsters convention has created a climate for all the antitrust legislation that we fear," Rose declared.

"Defiance can be very courageous if it is against oppression," Rose told the convention. "But against whom was this defiance demonstrated at the Teamsters convention? It was defiance against the Ethical Practices Committee and the (A.F.L.-C.I.O.) Executive Council. . . . It was defiance against the head of our organization, President George Meany, who by his courage and straightforwardness saved the good name of labor. It was defiance against public opinion. . . . This was not defiance as an act of courage. This was defiance as an act of vulgarity and irresponsibility."

Elderly John English had been Meany's hope for a housecleaning in the Teamsters union, but now he pictured the A.F.L.-C.I.O. as trying to expel the Teamsters "for two or three fellows who have gone wrong."

"We are on the chopping block now, but who is going to follow us?" said English, and it was a realistic question that he posed. "Be judged by what you do here today, and don't come weeping on our shoulders. We'll be able to take it. I wonder, will you be able to take it the way we are going to take it?"[9]

He reminded the convention that the Teamsters paid $750,000 a year into the A.F.L.-C.I.O. He begged for "one year to clean up our house."

"Beck is gone, Brewster is gone and Brennan is gone," English said. "There is only one man—Jimmy Hoffa. And Jimmy Hoffa has done more for our international union than

[8]Proceedings of the A.F.L.-C.I.O. constitutional convention, 1957, Vol. I, pages 72 and 73.

[9]Proceedings of the A.F.L.-C.I.O. constitutional convention, 1957, Vol. I, page 87.

anybody connected with it, including myself. How in the hell can we kick him out? Does he deserve that? He is fighting to get clear himself, and if he can't be cleared, then that is up to us.

"Teamsters never forget their friends," he warned. "As far as our enemies are concerned, they can all go straight to hell. . . . You can throw us out today but, brothers, the boys on the platform are waiting to give it to some more of you."

When the vote was tallied it showed the leadership representing 10,458,598 members of the A.F.L.-C.I.O. voted for ouster, with 2,266,497 opposing the ouster report.

Conspicuous among those voting against expulsion of the Teamsters were three large unions under investigation by the McClellan committee—the Carpenters, the Hod Carriers, and the Sheet Metal Workers.[10]

On the morning of December 9, I spoke before the American Press Institute, and then rushed down to Federal court to cover the Hoffa trial. The United States Supreme Court meeting that noon had handed down a decision in the appeal of the Benanti bootlegging case.[11] The opinion was precisely what Jimmy Hoffa wanted. It prohibited the use of wire taps in Federal court cases. It meant that United States Attorney Paul Williams would not be able to use the most conclusive evidence he had against Hoffa. Keeping the wire taps out of the McClellan hearing in August had done no good, and Hoffa no longer had to worry about his own words being played back to him in court.

I had never seen a more joyful group than the Teamsters crew that streamed into Federal court that afternoon. Hoffa, Bill Bufalino, Dave Previant, and George Fitzgerald were actually merry.

"I told you how it would come out," Hoffa said to me with a grin.

"You're a lucky little bastard," I said.

"I just live right," Jimmy replied.

Paul Williams was disappointed and told me he was afraid he would have to drop the perjury indictment against Hoffa.

---

[10]Proceedings of the A.F.L.-C.I.O. constitutional convention, 1957, Vol. I, page 105.

[11]Opinion of the Supreme Court of the United States, Salvatore Benanti, petitioner v. United States of America, December 9, 1957.

"Without the wire taps of Hoffa's conversations, the government just doesn't have much of a case," he said.

At that moment he was more concerned about the wiretapping trial. He had the case before a judge he considered to be stern, fair-minded and not subject to Teamsters pressure or influence. He felt he had a reasonably good jury, but there were indications that some of his government witnesses were trying to back away from the stories they had told the Federal grand jury.

It was plain hell to go through these Teamsters trials, worrying constantly about whether some hoodlum elements were trying to fix the judge, coerce the witnesses or buy the jurors. Paul Williams was irked at one principal witness and said he was going to use every effort to put that man in prison for perjury, if he didn't stand up to his grand jury testimony.

Despite the Supreme Court decision on the Benanti appeal, it seemed as though the roof was falling in on the labor racketeers during those first two weeks in December.

Johnny Dioguardi and John McNamara were indicted on a charge of extortion.[12] The A.F.L.-C.I.O. expelled Hoffa's pal, Paul Dorfman, head of the Chicago Waste Handlers Union, for misconduct of union affairs and for "compromising personal ties" with the insurance firm that handled Teamsters insurance.[13]

The same day on which these setbacks struck, the United Textile Workers Union, which had been under suspension, was restored to membership in the A.F.L.-C.I.O. following the ouster of its two top officers, Anthony Valente and Lloyd Klenert.

On December 13, a Chicago grand jury indicted Jimmy James on a charge of evading $562,982 in personal income taxes for the four-year period from 1951 through 1954. He was accused of reporting only $67,611 of a total income of $808,896 acquired while playing fast and loose with the health and welfare funds of the Laundry Workers International Union.

Although Meany had forced the expulsion of James and the union's former president, Samuel J. Byers, there were indi-

---

[12]Dioguardi and McNamara were convicted, but the convictions were upset by the appeals court.

[13]Proceedings of the A.F.L.-C.I.O. constitutional convention, 1957, Vol. II, pages 560 and 582.

cations that James still dominated the laundry workers' organization from the outside.

The A.F.L.-C.I.O. expelled the laundry workers' union because of this domination by James. Also expelled was the bakery workers' union because its president, James G. Cross, continued a dishonest and dictatorial reign. The distillery workers' union was continued on probation after agreeing to supervision by the A.F.L.-C.I.O. Ethical Practices Committee.[14]

Meanwhile, on the West Coast, local law enforcement had branded Dave Beck as a common thief.

On December 14, a jury of five housewives and seven men in Washington State convicted Beck of stealing $1,900 in union funds by pocketing money received for the sale of a union-owned Cadillac. Dave Beck, Jr., had been convicted on November 23 on charges of grand larceny for keeping the $4,650 he had received when he sold two union Cadillacs.

The Beck convictions showed local officials could punish some labor crooks if they would aggressively enforce the law. Ed Guthman called long distance from Seattle to tell me about Beck's conviction. He was bubbling with enthusiasm over the triumph of justice over evil. Prosecutor Charley Carroll had followed through as he told us he would in April, and I told Ed to pass on my congratulations.

"There's still a lot to be done, but Dave Beck is through in Seattle," Guthman said with sureness now, and added, "I never thought it would happen."

---

[14]Proceedings of the A.F.L.-C.I.O. constitutional convention, 1957, Vol. II, pages 423-468 and 506-542.

XXIV

Teamsters' Terrorists in Tennessee

The hearings on labor scandals in many areas of the nation had shown strong evidence of corrupt or careless local law enforcement, and there had been indications that even the courts had been influenced by Teamsters politics or money. It took the hearings on Teamsters activities in Tennessee to detail the picture of how a venal union can contaminate government.

Again it was Hoffa men who were exposed when the McClellan-Kennedy team turned its attention to the misuse of union funds and the violence in Tennessee. The Teamsters and the barbers' union were jointly responsible for some of the bombings, shootings, beatings and other violence there.

The hearings disclosed, among other things, a $20,000 payoff with Teamsters funds to a state judge for fixing a criminal charge against Glenn W. Smith, the top Teamster in Tennessee; H. L. Boling, secretary-treasurer of Chattanooga Teamsters Local 515, and others.[1]

I had been interested in the Tennessee story for months. I had met John Seigenthaler, a reporter for the *Nashville Tennessean*, when I went to the American Press Institute at Columbia University to speak on investigative reporting. Seigenthaler told

[1]McClellan committee, Report No. 1417, pages 360-370.

me about Teamsters corruption in his state, and I suggested he get in touch with the McClellan committee.

Bob Kennedy was busy and paid little attention to Seigenthaler's story at first, but Seigenthaler was persistent. Finally, Kennedy assigned two of his best investigators to Tennessee.

Investigators LaVern Duffy and James McShane broke cases of violence that local officials had been too lazy or too political to touch. With some strong assists from Seigenthaler, Duffy and McShane started checking into circumstances indicating that there had been a Teamsters payoff to Judge Raulston Schoolfield.

Judge Schoolfield controlled the grand jury in Chattanooga, and he was the judge involved in fixing the Smith-Boling Teamsters racketeering case, according to findings of the McClellan committee.[2]

The word was passed to Duffy and McShane that Judge Schoolfield didn't like what they were doing, and that they might be thrown in jail if they remained in the county. They called on Judge Schoolfield to determine if this was true.

He told them he felt they were exceeding their authority by prying into local governmental matters, and that he would be forced to take steps against them if this continued. Duffy and McShane ignored the threat and continued investigating, after informing Chief Counsel Bob Kennedy of their problem.

They found that Glenn W. Smith, the president of Teamsters Local 515 in Chattanooga, was a convicted robber and burglar. Despite his record, the Hoffa organization allowed him to reign as president of Teamsters Joint Council 87, with jurisdiction over all Teamsters in Tennessee and part of Kentucky.

Glenn Smith . . . was identified with a number of dynamitings, arsons and other violence, not only in Chattanooga but in Knoxville, in Jackson, Mississippi, and in Florida, at the time he served as international organizer there," the McClellan committee said.

W. J. Reynolds, president of Teamsters Local 621 in Knoxville, was labeled ". . . as one who had been active in the dynamiting of the car of a nonunion employee of a company being

---

[2]McClellan committee, Report No. 1417, pages 360-366.

struck by Local 621, and in the highway ambush and shooting of two trucks."[3]

In cases where these leading officials among Tennessee Teamsters did not personally participate in violence, they endorsed and supervised the activities of a roving goon squad operating in a five-state region, the committee found.

"The squad most frequently operated out of Nashville Local 327. . . . Prominent squad leaders were three Nashville Teamsters officials just below the top stratum: W. A. (Hard-of-Hearing) Smith, Perry Canaday and Ralph (Red) Vaughn, all business agents of Local 327. Added to dynamiting and arson, the fiendish accomplishments of this brutish operation included the pouring of syrup into the power mechanisms of trucks, window-smashings, shootings and sluggings.

"Law enforcement agencies in Tennessee accorded Teamsters criminals this scandalous immunity from prosecution because of an underlying and widespread fear of tangling with Teamsters union power.

"Everett Gourley, coroner of Davidson County and its acting sheriff during a period of Teamsters violence in 1956, admitted that the sheriff's office had a policy of noninvolvement in labor disputes; and the present Davidson County sheriff frankly ascribed this policy to a desire for 'self-preservation'."[4]

It was a sickening display of frightened and corrupted officials refusing to follow up complaints of Teamsters violence, even when it involved the shooting of truck drivers or the bombing of trucks. There was evidence of the fixing of criminal charges in those cases that were pressed. In the few cases in which Teamsters officials were jailed, law enforcement officials were found to be making special concessions so that Teamsters bullies wouldn't have to work on road gangs.

Chairman McClellan was furious. He denounced the shoddy law enforcement and the Teamsters hierarchy that allowed convicted robbers and burglars to control local and regional unions.

His committee's record showed that John T. McReynolds, an investigator for the Tennessee Bureau of Criminal Identification, had admitted that he had an abundance of evidence linking

---

[3]McClellan committee, Report No. 1417, pages 366-370.

[4]McClellan committee, Report No. 1417, page 369.

"Hard-of-Hearing" Smith to the shooting up of trucks on the highways—but McReynolds stopped the inquiry simply because Smith refused to talk.

Bob Caldwell, a Knoxville truck driver, had reported that his car was blown up at his home and his pregnant wife thrown out of bed by the explosion. The committee discovered that, although Caldwell had made a statement in writing about the incident to Attorney General Hal Clements the following morning, "Clements had simply 'passed the statement back,' and that he (Caldwell) had heard nothing more about it."[5]

Frank Allen, the manager of a trucking company's branch office in Nashville, testified that in July, 1956, "Hard-of-Hearing" Smith came to his office and beat him so severely he was hospitalized for a week.

Allen filed charges of "assault with intent to kill" against Smith for the unprovoked assault, but later dropped them at the urging of his employer, Joe Katz, president of Terminal Transport Company of Atlanta, Georgia.[6]

Katz related that Gene San Soucie, Indiana Teamsters boss, and Jimmy Hoffa had called on him and asked him to use his influence to get his branch manager to drop the charges. Katz said he went to Nashville and persuaded Allen to do so, in the hope that his company might "possibly get along better with the union."

"Certain top officials of the Teamsters union, particularly James R. Hoffa and (Murray W.) Dusty Miller, were fully aware of their responsibility," Chairman McClellan said.

"They not only took no action against the perpetrators of this violence, but, in the case of the brutal assault on Frank Allen . . . (Hoffa) actually intervened with Allen's employer to get (criminal) charges quashed against . . . Smith."[7]

Glenn Smith, W. A. Smith, Vestal, Candy, Boling, and Red Vaughn all took the Fifth Amendment when questioned about the bombings, payoffs, beatings, and shootings.

Senator McClellan said Tennessee law enforcement appeared to be a jungle, with racketeers, thieves and thugs taking over the

---

[5]McClellan committee, Report No. 1417, pages 368 and 369.

[6]McClellan committee, Report No. 1417, pages 331-335.

[7]McClellan committee, Report No. 1417, pages 334 and 335.

area. There was evidence of the same kind of Teamsters domination of local law enforcement officials and judges in other sections of the land.

While Tennessee terrorism was being exposed in the caucus room of the Senate Office Building, other stories of villainy in the Teamsters union were unfolding a few blocks away in the court of Federal Judge F. Dickinson Letts. Hearings were in progress there on charges that Hoffa plotters had rigged the election of delegates to the convention in Miami and had ignored the union constitution and the desires of ordinary union members.

The rank-and-file group opposed to Hoffa had little money, but it had the support of courageous Teamsters who testified despite threats of physical violence and loss of their union jobs. One after another of these men told stories of union members and officials fighting vainly against the crushing weight of money and political power that Hoffa's followers threw against them.

William Richard Bennett, a Miami truck driver, testified that his life was threatened after he had protested the appointment of one of Hoffa's friends as president of Miami Local 390. Bennett thought he had good reason to object when Murray W. (Dusty) Miller, chairman of the Southern Conference of Teamsters, appointed Ernest C. Belles to head Teamsters Local 390.

Bennett told Judge Letts that Belles had been kicked out of Teamsters Local 375 in Buffalo, New York, after a union panel found him guilty of embezzling $38,000 in union funds. Bennett said he saw no reason why the Miami local should be saddled with a man who had betrayed his trust in another union.[8]

A few days after registering the protest, Bennett testified before Judge Letts. He had been approached on the street by a stranger who told him that if he didn't keep his nose out of union affairs he "would have his head blown off."

James Luken, the 35-year-old president of Joint Council 26 in Cincinnati, Ohio, testified that the Hoffa gang had tried to buy him off. Luken said he appealed directly to Hoffa for the removal of a convicted criminal who had been named an officer of Cincinnati Teamsters Local 122.

Luken said he told Hoffa that Ohio Teamsters boss Bill Presser had appointed Harry Friedman as head of Local 122

---

[8]McClellan committee, Report No. 1139, page 875.

within a few months after Friedman had been released from a federal penitentiary, where he had served a term for interstate theft of an automobile.[9]

Friedman had boasted that he was "a Hoffa man," and Luken asked Hoffa whether the convicted auto thief was bragging, or actually had Hoffa's backing. According to Luken's version, Hoffa said Presser was his man in Ohio, and if Presser wanted Friedman, that was it.

Luken testified that he had resisted the efforts of the Hoffa-Presser group to dominate Cincinnati, and that, as a result, he had been subject to continual sniping for three years. Some of Hoffa's closest friends in the Teamsters suggested that if Luken would bow out of the Teamsters quietly, he could have a new car and $10,000 in severance pay. Later, Luken said, there were indications that the offer would be boosted to $25,000.

The Cincinnati Teamster said he told Hoffa's friends that he wasn't interested in being bought out, and that he would fight Hoffa's efforts to take over in Cincinnati. He added that he had heard of others who had taken "severance pay" rather than face continued harassment.

I knew McClellan committee investigators were turning up evidence that Joey Glimco, friend of the Capone mobsters, had actually bought out the officers of a Teamsters local in Chicago. Some of the local's officers just didn't have the courage or the honesty to withstand the double pressure of threats and bribes.[10]

Jim Luken was one of the few Teamsters officials with the courage and the ability to stand against Hoffa. As a result, Cincinnati was one of the few little islands that Hoffa had not been able to invade successfully.

"I admire your guts," I told Luken when we had lunch together. "I hope you'll stay in there fighting. Hoffa and Presser can't operate the way they do forever without slipping—I hope."

"I hope you're right," Luken said. "Sometimes I wonder whether they can't go on forever. Hoffa has been operating this way for 20 years now, and he seems to get stronger. I'm holding out because I don't think I have any choice, not because I'm sure he'll fall."

---

[9]McClellan committee, Report No. 1139, pages 588-591.
[10]McClellan committee, Report No. 1139, pages 523-527.

After three weeks of testimony, Judge Letts, on December 20, recessed the hearings until January, 1958. As long as the case continued, Dave Beck stayed in office, and Hoffa was barred from taking over the presidency. Beck was a thief, but it would be worse to have Hoffa get control. At least, Beck cared what people thought, and he wouldn't openly deal with the worst underworld elements in the country. Beck wanted respectability; all Jimmy wanted was raw, brutal power.

A lone juror—Earl T. MacHardy—saved Hoffa from conviction on the wiretapping charge in New York. MacHardy, a 49-year-old vice president of Refined Syrups and Sugars, Inc., of Yonkers, New York, held out more than thirty hours against the arguments of the eleven jurors who voted for conviction.

Federal Judge Frederick VanPelt Bryan submitted the case to the jury at 4 p.m. on Wednesday, December 18. At 8:30 p.m. Thursday, the jury foreman, Mrs. Lillian Doren, sent a note to Judge Bryan:

"We have had the case 28 hours and we cannot agree unanimously."

After conferring with attorneys for Hoffa and the government, Judge Bryan called the jury into court and instructed, "It is your duty to decide this case one way or another if you can do so conscientiously."

At 9:45 p.m. the jury was back in the courtroom asking for additional information on the rules of evidence relating to conspiracy.

Two hours later, they were back again. This time, the foreman reported that eleven members were in agreement, but that one member refused to give credence to circumstantial evidence.

With an air of exasperation, Mrs. Doren turned to MacHardy and said: "Go ahead, Mr. MacHardy. Ask the judge."

Judge Byran asked MacHardy if anything was bothering him.

"No, nothing is bothering me," MacHardy replied. Then he asked what circumstantial evidence could be used in determining whether a conspiracy existed.

Judge Bryan gave this example: "If you are in a subway and people enter with wet clothing, you can infer it is raining, but the evidence is circumstantial."

It was midnight when the jurors went back for further deliberation. At 12:30 a.m. they still could not agree, and no solution seemed possible in the light of MacHardy's staunch refusal to vote conviction.

Judge Bryan excused the jurors, and a jubilant Jimmy Hoffa rushed to the telephone to call his wife and report another victory over the government.

United States District Attorney Paul Williams said he would seek a new trial as soon as possible.

Even before this latest Hoffa trial had been concluded, District Attorney Williams notified the F.B.I. of an alleged effort to tamper with one of the prospective members of jury. The juror, a Miss Catherine Barry of New York City, had reported to the court that she received a telephone call from a man identified as Richard Pastor, an employee of Local 1-S of the Retail, Wholesale and Department Store Union.

Pastor was later questioned by a grand jury on this matter. He was also questioned by the McClellan committee. He denied having ever talked to Hoffa and retreated behind the Fifth Amendment when questioned as to why he had approached Miss Barry. He again exploited the Fifth Amendment when asked if he had been a member of the Communist party.[11]

(In the hearing record, Chief Counsel Bob Kennedy commented: "We have had . . . testimony regarding Mr. Hoffa's attitude toward courts, grand juries, prosecutors and judges." Kennedy stated that the committee had information that Pastor had been an active member of the Communist party in New York, at least during the 1940's. Kennedy said that the record also showed that Hoffa had been in contact with an active Communist in the New York branch of Harry Bridges' longshoremen's union. Kennedy explained that Pastor was being questioned to determine whether there were operational connections between certain Communists and the gangsters and hoodlums in some unions.)

With Pastor taking the Fifth Amendment, there was no way of getting to the bottom of his actions. The F.B.I. kept the matter open for study, but it seemed law enforcement just couldn't cope with attempted jury tampering under such circumstances.

---

[11]McClellan committee, hearings, Part 40, pages 15091 and 15255-15259.

XXV

Holidays and a Chat with Hoffa

On December 23, 1957, Bob Kennedy asked me to come to his home for lunch. He was having a Christmas party for the members of the committee's huge staff. It was one of the few times when nearly all of them were assembled, and it was the first time that some had met. For the moment the reunion spirit crowded out concern over problems the McClellan committee had encountered.

There was some light verse about Beck, Hoffa and bakery union president James Cross, and the staff presented a travelling bag to Kennedy as a Christmas present. Up to that time the young millionaire had been lugging around a battered old satchel with a clasp that popped open at unpredictable intervals.

Standing on the steps on the east side of the house, Kennedy thanked the staffers for their long hours of work in the past year and told them there would be an equally hard year ahead if corruption were to be exposed and eradicated from American labor by proper legislation.

He commented on my role in launching the investigation, and asked me to say a few words.

I knew each of them, and the cases on which each worked. I knew they had been working ten to sixteen hours a day, six and seven days a week. I wanted to tell them that it was worth the effort, that it was important, and that they would look back on it as an exciting experience, as well as a vital accomplishment.

"This is one of the biggest investigations in the history of our country," I said. "It might well be the biggest investigation before it is concluded. It has already had resounding impact on the labor movement, and it will have an even broader impact before it is over."

I spoke of the days when it seemed the public had paid too little attention, the pay seemed too little, and work hours seemed too long.

"In these times, it is necessary to keep this in historic perspective, and to appreciate the privilege of being a part of the great events of our time," I reminded them. "You will be proud to tell your grandchildren you had a part in this investigation."

The acquittal of Jimmy Hoffa in Washington, D. C., in July, and the hung jury he enjoyed in New York a week earlier had been crushing blows to all of us. I said that such things could not go on forever.

"Two years ago there were people who told me that Dave Beck would never fall, and that it was impossible to get a thorough investigation of the Teamsters union," I said. "There was much evidence to indicate that Dave Beck was too big for the government to handle, and then McClellan, Bob Kennedy, Carmine (Bellino) and the rest of you went to work."

I expressed the view that Jimmy Hoffa had just about run out of luck, and that I didn't believe anyone could consistently defy society and survive. I admitted I might be naive in believing in the eventual triumph of right over wrong, but that the essential ingredient was hard work on the part of those on the right side.

"Jimmy Hoffa knows the union business, and he works long hours at his schemes," I said, wanting them to admire Hoffa's diligence and not underrate his ability. "Hoffa's methods have been successful because of government officials who have been corrupt, lax, or lazy. Dedicated work can be victorious."

On Christmas night, 1957, I took a plane to Detroit for a closer look at the operations of Hoffa and Walter Reuther. The next day I spent digging in newspaper files and court records, and a little before 9 p.m. I decided to go out to see Hoffa's home at 16154 Robson Street.

There was a light in the living room, and it occurred to me to find out if Jimmy was at home. I usually kept someone advised when I visited men like Hoffa, but this was a spur of the moment decision. The taxi driver was the only available person. I paid him and told him I wanted him to wait for me unless I motioned for him to leave.

"If I go inside, I want you to remember that my name is Clark Mollenhoff, with *Look* magazine and the Des Moines and Minneapolis newspapers," I said with emphasis. "I am visiting the home of Jimmy Hoffa, and if anything happens to me I want you to report it to police. Can you remember that?"

The driver said he would remember it, but as I walked to the door I wondered about my optimism in believing that a Detroit taxi driver would give police any information involving Hoffa.

Jimmy had a puzzled look on his face when he saw who was at the door.

"Well, hello, Trouble. What brings you here at this time of the night?" he said.

"I wanted to talk with you, and I wondered if I could see you for a few minutes," I said.

"I'm not talking about that wire-tap indictment," Hoffa said.

It was only fair to agree not to talk about the Federal wire-tap charge that was pending against him in New York, so I assured him it wouldn't be mentioned.

It was 9 p.m. when I seated myself and Jimmy curled his feet under him in a chair near the ceiling-high Christmas tree. It was after midnight when I left. In those three hours we covered his dislike of United Automobile Workers-C.I.O. leader Walter Reuther, his hatred for Bob Kennedy, and his plans to boost newspaper drivers' salaries to show the publishers they shouldn't be so critical of the Teamsters. I also brought up the names of nearly every major hoodlum in his union—and heard Hoffa's defense of them.

He was anxious to talk about Walter Reuther, and he referred to him caustically as "the leader of Soviet America."

"I don't think Walter Reuther will stand up under an

investigation of his personal finances as well as the Teamsters union," Hoffa said.

"I don't think there is a union in the country that will take the kind of an investigation we got from the McClellan committee and come out of it as clean as the Teamsters union. I don't think Walter Reuther or George Meany, or any of these holier-than-thou boys, can take a real investigation," the Teamsters ruler said.

On one hand, Hoffa accused Bob Kennedy of being "on the side of the employers" and being out to "wreck the labor movement." A few moments later he was accusing Kennedy of being in league with Reuther, and trying to protect the auto workers' chieftain to gain political advantage for Senator Jack Kennedy in 1960.

"They put only three men on that case against Reuther, and they had 50 men on the Michigan Teamsters one time last year," Hoffa said. "You can't investigate the U.A.W. with only three men, and Kennedy knows it. I think it is dishonest of him."

Hoffa said that an informant he had inside the McClellan committee had told him that Bob Kennedy was trying to have secret hearings on Reuther, instead of open hearings.

"He can't kid me," Hoffa said. "I know what goes on at his meetings, and I know what he is doing to protect Reuther."

Hoffa told me he had passed information about Walter Reuther to Republicans on the McClellan committee, and that Matt Smith, an official of a union known as the Mechanics Educational Society, was the best source of information on Reuther's activities. He suggested I see Smith.

There was no doubt in my mind that Hoffa was still pushing hard for a Reuther investigation, and that he hoped it would split or discredit the McClellan committee, thus taking the pressure off the Teamsters.

He complained that while only three investigators were working on the U.A.W.-C.I.O. investigators "are watching every move the Teamsters make."

"We had an election, and a guy named (Walter) Sheridan is calling up the day after the election to carry the ball for some guy that the membership didn't want," Hoffa explained.

"This Sheridan wanted to get the ballots, and we told him

it was none of his damned business how we ran our elections. It is their job to pass legislation, but to keep their nose out of how we run our elections."

He said Sheridan was told the ballots had been destroyed.

"We always destroy the ballots after the election, and that was none of his damned business either. I don't see this committee getting into Reuther's elections. Do you think Walter Reuther would be president of the U.A.W. if it was left up to the membership?" Hoffa paused for emphasis before continuing.

"I know damn' well he wouldn't be. I'd be willing to go on a referendum vote if Reuther and Meany would do it, but I don't have to worry because they won't. I'd be willing to go on that, I'd agree to step out if he beat me—but I know he wouldn't."

Hoffa asserted that there was organized gambling in plants organized by the U.A.W., and that it was being carried on by some of Reuther's union stewards.

"Does Reuther get anything from this?" I asked him.

"I can't say he gets anything from it, but I don't think anyone would believe Reuther didn't know it was going on. He knows what his stewards are doing. They are picking up the bets right out in the open."

"What about all the convicted criminals in your union?" I said.

"I think Reuther has more convicted criminals than we have from a percentage standpoint," Hoffa said. He declined to name persons he had in mind but told me that one of Reuther's vice-presidents had a felony conviction.

I brought up name after name of Hoffa's associates, and he excused each of them for one reason or another.

I asked him about Ohio, where Louis N. (Babe) Triscaro, a convicted armed robber, was president of Teamsters Local 436.

"In Ohio, I've got Triscaro and Blue (Joseph Blumetti, a convicted white slaver from Youngstown)," Hoffa said. "I can't think of anyone else over there that's done time."[1]

"What about Harry Friedman in Cincinnati?" I said. "Didn't he do a federal term for interstate auto theft?"

"Oh, Presser's brother-in-law," Hoffa recalled. "He came

---

[1]McClellan committee, Report No. 621, page 636.

over with us (the Teamsters) from the electrical workers, where he had that juke-box operation in Cincinnati."

"How about (William) Presser himself?" I continued. "Wasn't he convicted on a charge of violating the antitrust laws by creating a monoply in the coin-machine business?"

"Presser's never done a day's time," Hoffa said, defending the boss of the Ohio Conference of Teamsters. "That fine ($1,500) was all on the monopoly, and he was in management when it happened."

I asked him how he could justify making room for Ernest Belles as an official of a Miami Teamsters local when Belles had been ousted from a Buffalo local for alleged embezzlement of $38,000.[2]

"I'm not sure that Belles did anything wrong that we can prove," Hoffa said. "He was kicked out of that Buffalo local, but there never was a final decision by the international officers. The case is up for appeal, and I'm on the committee handling it. I think Ernie can show that he had authority from the executive board for spending all that $38,000 they say he embezzled."

"Would you clear a man on that basis?" I said.

"There was some authority to use it for organizing," Hoffa said. "I don't know whether Ernie kept any of the money. He says he didn't get any of it. He said it went for organizing expense, and if we don't have any other evidence we gotta take his word for it."

Hoffa was agile in thinking of excuses for keeping those who were accused of playing fast and loose with Teamsters money and power.

I shifted my aim. "What about Glenn Smith? He has convictions for robbery and burglary. How can you let him continue as boss of a Teamsters' joint council over all of Tennessee and part of Kentucky?"[3]

"These convictions were a long ways back," Hoffa snapped. "I don't like to use guys with that kind of a record, but Glenn is the kind of a guy we needed down there in Chattanooga. You gotta have somebody who will kick those hillbillies around, and keep them in line. Glenn does it."

---

[2]McClellan committee, Report No. 1417, page 254.

[3]McClellan committee, Report No. 621, page 6.

He said he had pulled Smith out of Tennessee for awhile and used him on a Miami project.

"We put a guy named Wallace in charge in Chattanooga, and things started falling apart. He was too nice a guy, and we started losing members. We brought Smith back up there, and he has things in line again."

Hoffa had flamed up angrily, talking of the "hillbillies" in the Teamsters union in Tennessee who wouldn't stay in line. Although he normally poses as a friend of management, his anger blazed again as he referred to "them lice" who operate truck lines in the South and are antiunion.

I raised the question of W. A. (Hard-of-Hearing) Smith, the business agent for a Teamsters local in Nashville, who, according to the McClellan committee, was a dynamiter, arsonist and central figure on a roving muscle squad.[4]

"Smitty is a little rough, but like I say, those hillbillies in Tennessee need somebody tough to keep them in line." Hoffa bit the words. "Nobody is writing much about the kind of employers we got down there. This is no cream-puff organization, and it can't be when you gotta deal with the kind of employers we got in the South."

He was irritated when I asked about Don Vestal, another who took the Fifth Amendment before the McClellan committee on questions dealing with union finances and also on the question of whether he had been a Communist.[5]

"Vestal got a dirty deal," Hoffa said. "They knew they had him taking the Fifth Amendment, so they sneaked in that Communist question to smear him. Sure, he worked for Harry Bridges. I knew that. I know that Vestal is no Communist, and that was a mighty dirty thing for Kennedy to do, when he asked that question about being a Communist when he didn't have any evidence."[6]

Hoffa was full of rationalizations. He had excuses for associating with Johnny Dioguardi, the twice convicted labor extortionist; Ducks Corallo, the convicted narcotics peddler, and

---

[4]McClellan committee, Report No. 1417, pages 335-345.

[5]McClellan committee, Report No. 1417, page 336.

[6]Don Vestal was a Hoffa supporter in 1957, but later became a leader in a reform movement among the Tennessee Teamsters.

Joseph (Joey) Glimco, the man the McClellan committee said associated with Capone mobsters in Chicago.

"Joey Glimco is the least of our problem in Chicago," Hoffa said. "Sure, Glimco hangs around with all of those old Capone mobsters, but he hasn't any record."

Glimco was identified by the McClellan committee as having been "twice arrested for murder, and a crony of the Capone gang mobsters."[7]

"I know what his associates are, but those are guys that he has been hanging around with for years. They grew up in the same neighborhood. There are a lot of guys with bad records in the Teamsters in Chicago, but most of them are the old guys who have been in the union for 20 or 30 years."

"Are you going to try to clean up Chicago?" I asked.

"I don't know how we can clean it up," he said. "I know that the McClellan committee isn't going to clean it up."

He made such admissions reluctantly. It wasn't that he had any great urge to purify the Teamsters in the wicked city. He just didn't like to show weakness or admit there were things he could not control.

He was contemptuous of the ruling of the National Labor Relations Board and the Interstate Commerce Commission, outlawing the "hot-cargo clause" in the Teamsters contracts.

"I've already sent out word to pay no attention to the I.C.C.," Hoffa said.

"The I.C.C. is just a regulatory agency, and doesn't have any enforcement powers. We are going to continue to insist on the hot-cargo clause as we have in the past, and deal with it as we have in the past."

He said the Teamsters could get along without the hot-cargo clause and many of the other advantages labor had under the law. But, he said, the legislation and rulings that would merely slow the Teamsters would be crippling to other unions.

I asked Hoffa why he didn't get the Teamsters out of the juke-box and coin-machine organizing operations. "Why should the Teamsters be in it? There are racketeers all around the fringes of it, and all it does is bring your union trouble."

Hoffa replied that the Teamsters "have jurisdiction over any-

---

[7]McClellan committee, Report No. 1139, pages 526-527.

thing you can haul on trucks, or anybody who isn't organized."

Instead of getting out of the juke-box area, Hoffa said he had big plans in coin machines, and that they could be an important arm of his union in a few years.

Hoffa spelled out his plans as if there were not the slightest obstacle in front of him.

"Jimmy, why don't you just sit tight for a time and clean up what you've got, instead of going out looking for more people to organize?" I said. "Why in hell do you feel you have to organize everyone whether they want it or not?"

"Every unorganized plant is a threat to union security," Hoffa replied. "If the workers don't want to be organized for their good, then we gotta organize them."

"Jimmy, you have power that is about as great as the power the industrial barons had back at the turn of the century," I said, in preparation for a question.

"I've got more power than they had," he cut in proudly.

"But, Jimmy, do you think it is right for anyone to have that much power?" I chided him. "Doesn't it frighten you to think of that much power in a few hands? Can anyone be trusted with that much power in our economy?"

"It might be bad if it got in the wrong hands," Jimmy said. "I don't abuse it."

It was after midnight when I asked Jimmy to call a cab. He said he would arrange for someone to show me around the Teamsters headquarters on Trumbull Avenue the next morning, Saturday. Hoffa himself had to leave town for contract negotiations, and he apologized because he would not be there to escort me.

With the federal indictment still pending in New York, the rank-and-file suit pending in Washington, and half of the McClellan staff on his trail, Hoffa was carrying on Teamsters negotiations as if he didn't have another care in the world. I had to admire his industry and his guts. Most men would have broken under the strain. But then, most men would have had more trouble with their consciences.

XXVI

Political Troubles

Chairman McClellan and Bob Kennedy got through 1957 with a minimum amount of criticism, but a number of forces were building up to plague them in 1958. It was a political year, and the terms of three members of the committee were to expire.

Senator Barry Goldwater, the conservative Republican, was headed into a tough campaign against Arizona's Governor Ernest McFarland, a former Democratic leader in the Senate. Barry was eager to fulfill his promise to expose and discredit U.A.W.-C.I.O. President Walter Reuther.

Senator Irving Ives, the liberal Republican from New York, was in ill health, but he had not yet said whether he would seek re-election. He had a weather eye out for labor racket information that would embarrass his old political foe, Governor Averell Harriman.

Senator John Kennedy had great popularity in Massachusetts, but this young Democrat was straining for a landslide Senate victory to boost his stock for the Democratic Presidential nomination in 1960.

Union labor's leadership viewed Senator Kennedy's political aspirations as an opportunity to create political feuds that might smash or discredit the McClellan committee. Discrediting the committee was the only way the Teamsters could hope to neutralize the effect that exposure of the union's decaying core had had on the public.

Many in the A.F.L.-C.I.O. also wanted McClellan stopped. They feared the scandals would arouse public feeling against all organized labor and result in legislation to restrict labor's power.

In addition to his membership on the McClellan committee, John Kennedy was chairman of the Senate Labor subcommittee which had responsibility for writing legislation to curb union dictators and their misuse of union power and money. It was a difficult role for a man with Presidential aspirations. There were those in the A.F.L.-C.I.O. who said the elder Kennedy brother would accept their views if he could be convinced that was the only way to make his political dreams come true.

Jimmy Hoffa had many problems at the start of 1958, but he had a simple strategy he seemed to believe would solve all of them. To gain the Teamsters' presidency, he would make a deal with the financially poor rank-and-file members from New York, promising to pay their attorneys and to operate the International Brotherhood of Teamsters under a three-man monitorship appointed by the federal court.

To disrupt the McClellan committee, Hoffa peddled information and unsubstantiated rumors about U.A.W. leader Walter Reuther to Republican members of the committee, telling them the Democrats were trying to cover up for Reuther. Hoffa told me about this.

He believed that time and the power of the Teamsters in labor disputes would eventually defeat George Meany and put the Teamsters back in the A.F.L.-C.I.O. on Hoffa's terms.

The rank-and-file hearings to bar him from the Teamsters' presidency were resumed January 7, 1958. By January 20, Ed Cheyfitz, Ed Williams and Hoffa had negotiated the court-appointed monitorship. Hoffa would be allowed to become provisional president under court supervision. The arrangement included an agreement under which the International Teamsters would pay the costs and attorneys' fees.[1]

---

[1]Cunningham *et al.* v. English *et al.*, Civil Action 2361-57 in the United States District Court for the District of Columbia.

On recommendations of both sides, Judge Letts named a three-man board of monitors—Godfrey Schmidt, the attorney for the rank-and-file; L. N. D. Wells, a Dallas attorney who represented the Hoffa-dominated Southern Conference of Teamsters, and Judge Nathan Cayton, a retired member of the Municipal Court of Appeals for the District of Columbia.

Both sides hailed the agreement as a victory. Schmidt and Pat Kennedy, the spokesman for rank-and-filers, said it would provide tight supervision over Hoffa.

"Schmidt will be waking Hoffa up every morning to see if he's got tonsils," Pat Kennedy quipped, describing the degree of authority the monitors would have.

Ed Cheyfitz told me the monitorship was his idea, and that he and Williams had to sell the plan to Hoffa. Cheyfitz said they regarded the monitorship as providing only advisory powers, but he added quickly that he felt this would be sufficient pressure to get Hoffa to throw out the racketeers.

"Jimmy Hoffa has really learned his lesson, and intends to try to make the Teamsters a clean union," Cheyfitz confided to me. "He's changed a lot. The hearings have been a real shock to him. You'll be interested in one thing he is going to do out in Minneapolis. He's going to get rid of Sid Brennan and Gene Williams."

Cheyfitz always sounded sincere, but I hadn't seen much of the crusader in Hoffa when I visited him at his Detroit home in December. I didn't doubt that Williams and Cheyfitz would like to see Hoffa clean out the crooks, but I did doubt that such clever operators would intentionally promote a settlement that would give the federal court really effective control over him or over the treasury of Teamsters.

The Williams-Cheyfitz view that the monitors were "purely advisory" did not square with what Schmidt and Judge Letts told me.

I visited Judge Letts and asked him about the power of the monitors. He said he regarded the agreement as one in which the whole power of the Federal court could be used if Hoffa failed to go along with the recommendations of the three-member board of monitors. He hoped that recommendations by the monitors would be sufficient. Since Schmidt was the nominee of the rank-and-file, and Wells represented the Hoffa group, Judge Letts said, the board's effectiveness would depend largely on the chairman he had appointed, Judge Cayton from the District of Columbia.

This monitorship over a union was a new device, and I was skeptical about its effectiveness. I was even more skeptical when Godfrey Schmidt told me that Judge Cayton was siding with Wells, the Teamsters-appointed monitor, on most interpretations of the monitors' power. Apparently, Judge Cayton had a traditional labor lawyer's approach to the problem. It looked to me as if Hoffa and his lawyers had out-flanked Schmidt and Judge Letts.

Although Chairman John McClellan had won extension of his special labor rackets committee for one year, and an additional $500,000 appropriation, he had a Republican uprising on his hands. The stories about Reuther that Hoffa had peddled to businessmen, reporters and Republican Senators were beginning to pay off in committee dissension. Senators Goldwater and Mundt were complaining that too much time was being spent on the Teamsters union, and on labor violence and payoffs. Explanations that the Teamsters corrupted and controlled many other unions didn't satisfy them. Goldwater and Mundt wanted hearings on Reuther, and regarded the explanations as merely Democratic excuses.

By the time McClellan and Bob Kennedy started hearings on the multi-million-dollar scandals in the operating engineers union, the Republicans were roaring for hearings on the U.A.W.-C.I.O.. With backing from McClellan, Kennedy paid no attention to the complaints and started hearings on the operating engineers on January 21.

In the following two weeks, the McClellan committee produced evidence linking the operating engineers' president, William E. Maloney, and his top aides to gangster elements in Chicago, New York, New Jersey and Philadelphia. The San Francisco local, with jurisdiction over 24,000 members in California, Nevada, Utah and Hawaii, was involved in admitted election-rigging and gross misuse of union funds.

The 280,000 members of the International Union of Operating Engineers provided the skill in handling the heavy equipment for giant construction projects—bridges, highways, buildings and military bases. In this vital industry investigators found that William E. Maloney had used hoodlums and mobsters to seize control of two Chicago locals, and to keep them under dictatorial control for 29 years. After grabbing control of Chicago Locals 150 and 399, Maloney used the same mobsters and their weapons of terror to take over the international union presidency in 1941.

From 1929 until the hearings in 1958, Maloney allowed no elections, and he stifled frequent membership efforts to escape from his dictatorship. Arthur Imhahn and Andrew Leach, who supervised Local 399 for Maloney, siphoned off at least $17,566 for personal luxury living, the McClellan committee found. Maloney also enriched himself at the expense of union members, entered into collusive deals with employers, and misused hundreds of thousands of dollars in union funds.[2]

"There was an under-the-table relationship between . . . Maloney and Stephen A. Healy, founder and head of the S. A. Healy Co., one of the nation's largest contractors," the committee said.

The committee condemned Healy for "lack of candor . . . and his refuge behind the Fifth Amendment to avoid telling what he did with more than $200,000 in company funds which were listed as nondeductible business expense."

"Mr. Healy's action in making payoffs of $125,000 to Big Mike Carozzo, a Chicago mobster, which the contractor admitted before a New York grand jury, presents grave evidence as to the methods which Healy felt were necessary to insure labor peace," the committee report stated.[3]

The committee said that Maloney had used $35,000 from the union funds to buy a yacht, representing it as a boat to be used in inspecting dredge jobs in the Miami area. The ship's captain testified that to his knowledge the boat had never been used for this purpose but had been used solely for the enjoyment of Maloney, Joseph Delaney and other union officers. (It was significant that Delaney followed Maloney as president in what

[2]McClellan committee, Report No. 1417, pages 371-372, and 437-443.
[3]McClellan committee, Report No. 1417, page 376.

the A.F.L.-C.I.O. accepted as a cleanup of the operating engineers union.)

It took months for investigators Al Calabrese, Jack S. Balaban, and Jim Mundie to piece together the story of ruthless domination of working men through violence, intimidation and other dictatorial practices. Only 46 per cent of the union's 280,000 members were allowed to vote for officers, and even those who voted were robbed of the benefits of union democracy through stuffing of ballot boxes and other election-rigging tactics.[4]

The committee found that William DeKoning, Jr., and his late father, William DeKoning, Sr., ran Local 138 of the operating engineers as "a closed family corporation." Opposition to the DeKonings' operation of that Long Island local was often suppressed by brutality. The case of Peter Batalias was cited as an example of a rank-and-file member who was viciously beaten because he rose at a meeting to question the actions of the local's officers.

When Batalias and Lou Wilkens complained to law enforcement authorities about the beating, William DeKoning, Jr., revoked their membership.[5]

The McClellan committee found San Francisco Local Three had purchased a 40-foot Chris Craft inboard cruiser with union funds. It was used for the entertainment of union business manager, Victor Swanson, his two sons and other union officers.

A defense fund of $75,000 was set up for the announced purpose of fighting right-to-work bills, but committee investigators could substantiate the spending of only $25,000 for this purpose. Union officers gave conflicting stories about the $50,000 in cash that disappeared from the treasury.

The committee found that officers of the operating engineers' Local Three enriched themselves at the expense of union members through dealings in union-purchased land, not unlike some of Dave Beck's schemes.

"The fact that these officers managed to profit to the extent of some $47,000 in buying and selling of this land through

---

[4]McClellan committee, Report No. 1417, page 371.
[5]McClellan committee, Report No. 1417, pages 408-411.

'dummies' represents . . . fraud and embezzlement," the committee concluded.

Chairman McClellan and his committee members found that responsibility for the high-handed manipulation of Local Three had to be shared by manager Victor Swanson, president Patrick Clancy, treasurer P. E. Vanderwark, and secretary Clarence Mathews.[6]

Operating engineers' Local 542 in Philadelphia was looted of nearly three million dollars in the ten-year period just prior to 1946, when it was run by labor racketeer Joseph S. Fay. Fay's conviction for extortion took him out of the picture, but the McClellan committee found that the union members "have since fared little better than they did with the Fay machine."[7]

"The present supervisor of the local, Hunter P. Wharton, recently elected international secretary-treasurer of the I.U.O.E., not only has taken no steps to return the local to its membership but played a key role in the brutal assault on a Local 542 crane operator, T. C. McCarty, Jr.," the McClellan committee found.

McCarty's protest against the union management had resulted in his being beaten by union goons. "Wharton ordered the use of union funds to defend the men who participated in the assault on McCarty, and to pay their fines after they were convicted," the committee revealed.[8]

In addition to Fay's corruption in Local 542, he was found to have been "the recipient of some $238,000 in benefits from Newark Local 825, both while he was serving in the penitentiary and after his parole."

"This money came in the form of payments to his wife for nonexistent office work and a lifetime pension to the convicted extortionist," the committee reported. The union members' money also paid $60,000 in legal fees for Fay, despite the fact he was convicted of extorting $63,000 from contractors on a promise to sell out the rights of the union members.

The committee found that Peter Weber, later the business manager of Local 825, was involved in several "conflicts of interest

---

[6]McClellan committee, Report No. 1417, pages 385-401.

[7]McClellan committee, Report No. 1417, page 440.

[8]McClellan committee, Report No. 1417, pages 427 and 428.

of a serious nature." He was the business partner of a number of contractors with whom he negotiated union contracts.[9]

But the arch criminal of the International Union of Operating Engineers was William E. Maloney, who resigned as international president shortly after the Congressional hearings. The case of William E. Maloney gave impetus to the arguments in favor of federal legislation to limit the dictatorial uses of union trusteeships.

Not even the magnitude of the scandals among the operating engineers could distract Republican Senator Barry Goldwater from what he considered the most important investigation—Walter Reuther and the U.A.W. Bob Kennedy and John Kennedy resented the Republican insinuations that they were a part of a deal to shield Reuther. Senator McClellan was enraged because some Republicans had made comments which indirectly questioned his fairness.

"I am not opposed to an investigation and hearings on Reuther," McClellan told me. "I've given the Republicans their own counsel and several investigators to use as they want to in following down any leads on Reuther. They are bound and determined to prove he's misusing funds, and they haven't come up with anything."

McClellan said he believed there were several areas in which the U.A.W.-C.I.O. and Reuther could be criticized, and that he believed these matters should be subject to hearings.

"There is some improper or illegal use of the secondary boycott, and there has been violence in the Kohler and Perfect Circle strikes in which the top leaders of the U.A.W. must accept criticism and responsibility," Senator McClellan said.

"Too much politics is being injected into this investigation, and I don't like to go ahead under those circumstances, but we have no choice," he told me.

Even before the U.A.W.-C.I.O. hearings opened on February 26, 1958, there were disputes over the order in which witnesses should be called. Bob Kennedy wanted to call Walter Reuther first, to get his explanation of various events before revealing committee evidence. This would leave the way open so that Reuther could be called for further testimony if there

---

[9]McClellan committee, Report No. 1417, page 418.

was any inconsistency between his first story and evidence that developed later, McClellan said.

Republicans objected. They viewed the whole idea of calling Reuther first as some Kennedy-inspired maneuver to make Reuther look clean.

"I know the best way to proceed on these matters, but if they are going to insist on their way, then they will have to take the responsibility," McClellan told me later.

It was with reluctance that McClellan bowed to the demands of the Republican members on the order of witnesses. He was a sad and a bitter man in those days, for he felt he had consistently leaned over backwards to keep partisan politics out of the investigation.

Although he let the Republicans call the shots, he put the responsibility fully on their shoulders when the hearings opened.

"The proceedings that will be followed here are not the proceedings in keeping with the Chair's views as to how this matter should be presented," McClellan stated for the record.

"I have yielded to this procedure out of what I conceive to be deference to a higher duty and responsibility. I believe the work of this committee . . . transcends all other consideration of any person, any individual, any party, anybody's policy, or the political fortunes of any member of this committee."

For more than a month after that, the McClellan committee was embroiled in bitterness. Partisan politics dominated the questioning. Bob Kennedy questioned the witnesses only to bring out the basic facts, then faded into the background as the various Senators quarreled with witnesses and put into the record speeches about their philosophies of unionism and government.

McClellan was quietly smoldering. It pained him to see the investigation degenerating into a political brawl. When he injected himself into the hearings, he scolded both sides with equal vigor. There was Senate criticism of the conduct of the hearings, while editorials and cartoons shouted that the McClellan committee was destroying itself.

"This is the only way," McClellan said to me privately in his office. "We had no choice. We have got to have this hearing now, and I think that if we are careful we can keep it on the track."

The fuss within the committee made the opponents of the investigation brave. A.F.L.-C.I.O. president Meany went before Senator Kennedy's legislative committee with a cutting criticism of the legislation that the Massachusetts Democrat had suggested. Meany said he didn't believe any legislation was needed, because labor could clean its own house.

Senator Kennedy said that the A.F.L.-C.I.O. had a right to criticize, but that labor had not cleaned its house and should be willing to suggest alternatives if it did not like what he proposed.

Al Hayes, chairman of the A.F.L.-C.I.O. Ethical Practices Committee, made a speech in Massachusetts and slapped at Senator John Kennedy and other "so-called friends of labor" who were proposing what he believed was restrictive legislation.

Senator Kennedy snapped back that unless the A.F.L.-C.I.O. came through with some constructive proposals, it might find itself saddled with tougher legislation than it had bargained for.

The toughness in Jack Kennedy showed through in those weeks. He told me he wanted to be reasonable with the A.F.L.-C.I.O., but he wasn't going to be pushed around by Meany, or anyone else.

Those were bad days for the McClellan committee and the cause of labor reform. The Teamsters were jubilant, and Ed Cheyfitz said he thought McClellan's investigation was "about all washed up."

When the McClellan committee issued its report on March 25, 1958, Democratic Senator Pat McNamara of Michigan refused to sign it. He declared that it was biased against organized labor.[10]

The report stated that the first year of investigations had showed that more than ten million dollars in union funds had been misused by the Teamsters, International Union of Operating Engineers, Allied Industrial Workers, Bakery Workers and Textile Workers Unions. It charged Hoffa had "grossly misused some $2,400,000" in union funds for the benefit of himself,

---

[10]McClellan committee, Report No. 1417, page 454.

his cronies and his hoodlum friends.[11] This was in addition
to the hundreds of thousands of dollars that Hoffa, his relatives,
and racketeering associates obtained from sources where it appeared they had "sold out" Teamsters union members, the
report said.[12]

A.F.L.-C.I.O. president Meany called the report "a disgraceful example of the use of sensationalism in an attempt
to smear the trade union movement."

"While the committee has gratuitously insulted the entire
labor movement, it has carefully avoided a similar indictment
of management which has done nothing to eliminate evil from
its ranks," Meany said.

Senator McNamara, a former labor leader, declared the
McClellan committee had outlived its usefulness. He resigned
from the committee, and there was no rush to fill the vacancy.
It is a bad omen when politicians don't seek a place on a
well-known investigating committee. It was finally necessary
for the Democratic leadership to assign Senator Frank Church,
a young Idaho Democrat, to the vacancy.

The U.A.W. hearings turned into such a sea of bitterness
that all members and the staff were glad when they were concluded. Republican members told me they had been misled
as to the nature of material that would be available for the
Reuther hearings. Their informants simply hadn't produced,
and it had left them in a difficult and embarrassing position.
I had a little sympathy for them, for I had been temporarily
misled on some of the same half-truths from the Teamsters.

The Teamsters enjoyed the U.A.W. hearing. It took the
spotlight off them, and they were sorry to see it end. Hoffa's
boys had seen a chance that McClellan and the Kennedys would
be wrecked, and that the searching reconstruction of Hoffa's
finances and his empire would never be completed. The
maneuver had worked out better than Hoffa expected, for even
his enemy George Meany was joining in the attack on McClellan.

Before the U.A.W. hearings ended on April 1, 1958, the
McClellan-Kennedy team had plans to repair the damage and
regain the committee's lost stature. They did so quickly. First,

[11]McClellan committee, Report No. 1417, page 252.
[12]McClellan committee, Report No. 1417, page 451.

they moved into hearings on the Hotel and Restaurant Workers Union and the Teamsters union in Philadelphia. It was, figuratively speaking, a black-and-white case, and all members of the committee had to oppose such outright corruption.

The Philadelphia hearings had opened on April 15, 1958, with testimony regarding the convicted criminals hired by Teamsters Local 107, the misuse of union funds, and the brutal beatings suffered by those who tried to oppose the Raymond Cohen apparatus of misrule.

After more than a full year in the huge kleig-lighted Senate labor rackets committee hearing room, I could still become angry when I heard eye-witness accounts of the vicious suppression of union democracy. And never was a story more heart-rending than that of Vincent Minisci, a former Philadelphia truck driver.

The imprint of a ballpeen hammer in his skull told only a part of the brutality Minisci had suffered for opposing the Raymond Cohen machine in the City of Brotherly Love. In 1954, he was severely beaten by three Teamsters goon enforcers, including Joseph Cendrowski. Cendrowski was a convicted thief and burglar whom Cohen had made chief dispatcher at Philadelphia Teamsters union headquarters.[13]

Minisci reported the vicious assault to the police, but no action was taken.

Unafraid, the tall truck driver and a group of about ten Teamsters started to form a committee in 1956 to seek to dislodge Cohen and force an accounting of union spending. They had heard Cohen used union money to buy a yacht.

Following one of the committee meetings, Minisci went to the truck yard for a 3 a.m. work shift. As he was getting into his truck, three men grabbed him and stretched him across the vehicle's seat. One beat his head and arms with a hammer. Two used pipes to club his legs. He was left broken and bleeding. He had to be hospitalized.

Minisci testified that the Cohen crowd was not satisfied with this but brought pressure on his employer to fire him, then used the power of Local 107 to block his efforts to get a job with another trucking firm.[14]

---

[13]McClellan committee, Report No. 621, pages 380 and 381.

[14]McClellan committee, Report No. 621, page 391.

Unable to get work, Minisci lost his car, went in debt and finally was forced to mortgage his home. His wife received harassing telephone calls, became ill, and more debts piled up. His family wanted to stay in Philadelphia, but in desperation Minisci sold what was left and moved to California. It seemed the only possible way to escape the brutality and economic pressures that had made life unbearable.

"I just tried to exercise my rights, and I finally ended where I am at," he told a sympathetic Senate committee.

Outside the hearing room I was stopped by a man and woman from Baltimore. They had seen me in August, 1957, on the televised hearings on Hoffa and his ties with the New York locals, video reports which were carried along the East Coast.

"Mr. Mollenhoff, how can such things happen in America?" the woman said. "Can't somebody do something about it?"

"The citizens can do something about it, and I believe would do something about it if all the hearings were televised," I said. "It costs too much for the networks to carry these programs, and the public just won't read all the details and learn of the rot that has ruined law enforcement in many areas."

"What can we do?" the man challenged me.

"Vote against any political figures who are proved to be on close terms with the underworld or union racketeers," I said. "If you are ever on a jury, use your head and don't be misled by the phony emotional pleas that lawyers for the organized criminals use."

In the fall of 1957, the committee had questioned Raymond Cohen, secretary-treasurer and business agent, briefly on a few questionable financial dealings in Philadephia Teamsters Local 107. He had been elected on the Hoffa slate as one of the three trustees of the International Brotherhood of Teamsters. Cohen answered a few questions, but when chief counsel Kennedy asked about the source of $17,000 used by Cohen to purchase a yacht, the cold-eyed and unemotional Philadephia union boss joined the crowd and took the Fifth Amendment.[15]

Kennedy produced records showing that on March 30, 1955, a union check for $17,000 cash was drawn by Ben Lapensohn, then a business agent for Local 107. The check was cashed at

---

[15]McClellan committee, Report No. 621, pages 414 and 513-517.

the Broad Street Trust Company in Philadephia. On the same day, Cohen obtained a $17,000 treasurer's check from the Broad Street Trust Company, made out to Earl M. Reed in payment for Cohen's yacht.

Senator McClellan wanted to know if Raymond Cohen hadn't used union funds to purchase a yacht for himself. When Cohen said an answer might incriminate him, McClellan declared this was a sad commentary on the type of men serving as trustees over the $40 million treasury of the International Teamsters.

Efforts to question business agent Ben Lapensohn were still unsuccessful when the Philadelphia hearings opened. Bob Kennedy said Lapensohn had taken his family to Europe in May, 1957, when investigators first started digging into Local 107. Although Lapensohn's family returned to the United States in September, 1957, he went to Montreal, Canada—outside of the subpoena power of the McClellan committee. He had refused to talk to a committee investigator, Kennedy informed the committee members.

"What are your responsibilities as international trustee?" Kennedy said to Cohen.

"To check the financial records of the international," Cohen answered.

"Was it felt that you had a good deal of experience with finances, and that was why you were selected for this job?"

"I cannot say why I was elected to the job," Cohen answered.

"Did you tell them about how you were handling the finances of Local 107?"

"I make monthly financial reports to the international union," Cohen answered, and Kennedy snapped, "Are those accurate?"

"I decline to answer the question on the ground that I am not required to give evidence against myself under the Fifth Amendment," Cohen replied.

The committee heard testimony that the Cohen union had at least $250,000 in checks drawn to cash in a period of less than five years, with no satisfactory explanation of where the money went. The union funds were also used for a $31,000 financial spree at the Florida convention that elected Hoffa, for Florida trips for Cohen and his wife, and to buy suits, undershirts, robes, ties and shirts for Cohen.

"I think you should resign . . . Mr. Cohen," rapped Senator John Kennedy.

"That is a matter of opinion," Cohen replied. "I think a 14,000 membership has a right to say whether I should resign or not."

Senator Carl Curtis, the Nebraska Republican, declared that Cohen's members were "captive" because they had to stay in the union or lose their jobs.

Cohen declared that the members of Local 107 "had their choice to vote as to who they wanted for secretary-treasurer in 1954 by secret ballot."

"You might be reminded, sir, that some of them who didn't vote for you got beat up," Chairman McClellan said. "It looks like it is a little bit captive to me."

A sharp controversy developed between members of the McClellan committee and two Philadephia lawyers who represented Local 107 and Raymond Cohen. Actually, attorneys John R. Carroll and Richard H. Markowitz represented several members and officials of Local 107. As each appeared before the committee the Fifth Amendment was invoked.

Before the hearing started, Bob Kennedy told me that it appeared there was a conspiracy of silence in Local 107 to protect Raymond Cohen. Witnesses who had indicated they might testify refused to talk to committee investigators and Kennedy was deeply disturbed.

"Some of these witnesses have done nothing wrong, and there is nothing we are going to touch that could incriminate them," Kennedy said. "This is an abuse of the Fifth Amendment to cover up for Cohen."

Before the hearings started, investigators Robert Dunne and Leo Nulty had notified defense counsel Carroll that the committee intended to question Cohen and others about alleged misappropriation of union funds. They told Carroll it seemed improper for a lawyer to represent both the union officials charged with misappropriating union funds and the union from which the money was reported to have been taken.[16]

---

[16]McClellan committee, Report No. 621, pages 479 and 485-487.

In defense, John Carroll had obtained an opinion from the Philadelphia Bar Association which constituted approval for him to represent union officials who invoked the Fifth Amendment on questions dealing with misuse of union funds.

McClellan committee members were unanimous in their disapproval of the position Carroll and attorney Richard Markowitz were taking.

Senator Kennedy said the Philadelphia bar unit should re-examine its position. He declared that he didn't believe a union should foot the bill for lawyers for persons who chose the Fifth Amendment as a reply to questions on misuse of union funds.

"This would be similar to having a bank retain an attorney to defend a person charged with embezzling bank funds," Senator Kennedy told me.

"It is, to my mind, a rather queer use for union funds to be put to," commented Senator Sam Ervin, who had served as a judge on the Supreme Court of North Carolina.

Senator Curtis of Nebraska informed Carroll that "I would think by your own admission there is a conflict of interest that would impel you to withdraw."

Chairman McClellan declared the wholesale use of the Fifth Amendment appeared to be "a part of the cloak they are hiding behind."

"On the face of it, particularly with all the circumstances attending this particular investigation, I think it is most reprehensible, and I do not agree with the attorney (Carroll) when he says there is no conflict of interest. . . . There is no moral law nor ethical standard that would tolerate representing such a conflict of interest as obviously appears here."

Upon re-examination, the Philadelphia Bar Association advised Carroll and Markowitz they should not only avoid a situation where a conflict existed, but should also bow out of a representation of a client where it appeared likely that one might arise. John Carroll continued to represent Raymond Cohen but reluctantly dropped his representation of Teamsters Local 107. Markowitz withdrew as counsel for Cohen.[17]

The problem of lawyers being paid by union funds but

---

[17]McClellan committee, Report No. 621, pages 479-480.

representing officials charged with misuse of union funds was one that ran throughout the hearings. The Philadelphia story prompted Bob Kennedy to comment: "Even Dave Beck had the propriety and judgment to go out and get an outside attorney when he appeared before the committee."

The problem of legal ethics also came up with regard to payments made by Local 107 to Thomas D. McBride, after he became attorney general of the state of Pennsylvania. McBride had been a member of the same law firm as Carroll, and had represented Cohen's Local 107 prior to being appointed chief law enforcement officer in Pennsylvania on December 14, 1956. Teamsters records showed that Local 107 presented a $500 "Christmas present" to McBride a few days after he became attorney general.

Records also disclosed that he received checks of $1,250 a month from Local 107 in January, February and March, 1957, after assuming office.[18]

Public comment and the questions raised by these payments resulted in McBride's requesting to go before the committee to explain.

On April 18, 1958, Senator Joseph Clark, the Pennsylvania Democrat, accompanied Tom McBride to the hearing room. He vouched for McBride as "a man of unimpeachable integrity, a leader of the Philadelphia and Pennsylvania bars, a friend whose judgment I treasure and whose friendship and affection I am proud to have.

"I am confident that every word that he says to this committee will be the truth, the whole truth and nothing but the truth," Senator Clark told his colleagues in as glittering an endorsement as any witness ever received.

McBride said he had written the profession guidance section of the Philadelphia Bar Association in December, 1956, to find out if it would be considered proper for him to serve as attorney general and continue to receive a $15,000 a year retainer from Cohen's Local 107.

On January 17, 1957, the Philadelphia bar ruled that the attorney general could not receive a retainer from the Teamsters.

McBride said he cashed the January and February checks

[18]McClellan committee, Report No. 621, pages 479-484.

totaling $1,250 each because he felt this was proper as he had done some work up to February 1, 1957. The March check was cashed by a secretary, but McBride said he made out a personal check to his law firm on this. After March's delivery, McBride said, he did not receive the checks; they were sent to his old law firm.

The Pennsylvania attorney general said he assumed the $500 Christmas check was merely appreciation for work he had done for Cohen's union in the past.

Throughout the Philadelphia hearings McClellan had a unified committee. The coordinated assault on crime and corruption continued through the hearings on Max Block, Louis Block, and the scandals in the butchers' union.

McClellan had his committee functioning smoothly again by the time hearings were staged on Maurice Hutcheson, president of the carpenters' union and a power in national Republican politics. Hutcheson, too, had found security in the Fifth Amendment before the Senate Public Roads subcommittee that had investigated the Indiana road scandals. Hutcheson and several other key officials of the carpenters' union were under Indiana State indictment on criminal charges involving the purchase and sale of property for the Federal highway program.[19]

But Hutcheson did not take the Fifth Amendment on questions the McClellan committee asked concerning his handling of union affairs. That would have been cause for his expulsion from the A.F.L.-C.I.O. executive counsel, if the Dave Beck precedent were followed. Instead, Hutcheson simply refused to answer key questions about alleged misuse of more than $500,000 in union funds.

Chairman McClellan declared that Maxwell Raddock, one of Hutcheson's pals, had "perpetrated a fraud against the union" by misrepresenting what it had cost to produce a book about the life of William Hutcheson, the father of Maurice. McClellan further stated that Maurice Hutcheson, O. William Blaier and Frank Chapman shared the responsibility for this fraud, which cost the membership several hundred thousand dollars.

"The testimony further indicates that certain high officials

---

[19]Maurice Hutcheson and several other top officials of the carpenters' union were later convicted, but the Indiana Supreme Court upset the conviction.

of both the Teamsters and the carpenters' union, two of the largest unions in the country, with the help and assistance of Mr. Raddock were involved in a conspiracy to subvert justice in the state of Indiana," McClellan said.

Maurice Hutcheson refused to answer when asked if Max Raddock had been paid union funds to assist in preventing a criminal indictment of Hutcheson in Indiana. The carpenters' union president also refused to say whether he had made any arrangement with Jimmy Hoffa, under which Hoffa would perform certain tasks for Hutcheson in return for Hutcheson's support in the A.F.L.-C.I.O.[20]

---

[20]McClellan committee, Report No. 621, pages 560-64 and 592.

XXVII

Barney Baker—Romance and Rough Stuff

The 300-pound figure of Robert B. (Barney) Baker rolled into national prominence in the summer of 1958, but he was far from being a new figure to me. It was in late 1954 and early 1955 that I first started hearing of the fabulous six-foot four-inch, 380-pound fat man who had become an organizer for Hoffa in the Middle West.

Baker was a fellow who couldn't go unnoticed. His police record included two prison terms in New York for throwing stink bombs in theaters in union drives. Big Barney was identified as one of a group of waterfront thugs who had slugged a waterfront reformer, then threatened to put the reformer in a concrete suit and throw him in the river.[1]

New York waterfront hearings had identified Baker as "the collector" for a mob that in the mid-1940's included John (Cockeyed) Dunne and Andrew (Squint) Sheridan, a couple of killers.

When Sheridan and Dunne were electrocuted for the murder of Anthony Hintz, an honest hiring boss, Barney got out of New York—fast. He drifted to Florida and Las Vegas, and his companions included such mobsters as Bugsy Siegel and Meyer Lansky.

In the late 1940's, Barney settled down in Washington,

---

[1]McClellan committee, Report No. 621, pages 70-74.

D. C., and eventually became president of Teamsters Local 730 which included many Negro truck drivers and warehouse workers.

By 1952, the smooth-talking labor goon had worked his way into the inner circles of the Democratic party in Washington. He was a remembered figure in the victory that New York Governor Averell Harriman posted over Senator Estes Kefauver, the crime-busting Tennessee Democrat, in the Presidential primary in Washington in 1952. Baker specialized in lining up Negro voters for Harriman. He was a big talker on civil rights.

Some undefined internal union dispute in Washington caused Barney to migrate to St. Louis in late 1952 to help St. Louis Teamsters boss Harold Gibbons.

By December, 1955, Barney Baker had been accepted as a trusted organizer for Hoffa's Central Conference of Teamsters. He was a pal to Hoffa. He was a political bed-fellow of Harold Gibbons and a working companion of Richard Kavner, an organizing power in the Central States Teamsters' machine.

In December, 1955, I was in Omaha, Nebraska, and talked to officials of two Nebraska trucking firms about the violence that plagued their operations. Officials of the Coffey Transfer Company and the Clark Bros. Transfer Company, both of Omaha, were frantic. They said their major problems started when Baker came in to organize them. Tires on their trucks were slashed. Sugar was poured in the gasoline tanks to gum the motors. Wires were yanked out of truck motors. Drivers were threatened. Equipment was dynamited.[2]

Local law enforcement had been helpless. Officials were desperate for aid in exposing the mess, but there was no Congressional investigating committee to which they could turn. Since most of the crimes were of a local nature, the F.B.I. couldn't help. The truck-line owners were protecting their property in the best way they could. Padlocks were used to lock the hoods of the trucks. Gas tanks were padlocked shut. These measures didn't stop tire slashing and broken windows. Guards had to be placed over the locked equipment to stop this.

Baker was directing organizing from a suite in the Blackstone Hotel, where in a few short weeks his spending and eating habits had become legendary. It was Teamsters money that Barney

---

[2]McClellan committee, Report No. 621, pages 33-36.

poured out on big tips, and he paid fifteen to thirty dollars each for the gargantuan meals. A gracious employer who was under Teamsters jurisdiction even put a Cadillac at "Mr. Baker's" disposal for part of his time in Omaha.

I wanted to find out if Baker was taking any steps to make Teamsters sympathizers stop the terror tactics. Also, I was curious to meet this huge pistol-packing waterfront hoodlum who had become such a favorite with Hoffa.

"Mr. Baker is out of the city," was the message I got at the Blackstone. Missing Baker only stimulated my interest, and I took every opportunity to piece together his past.

In 1956, Baker was at the Democratic National Convention in Chicago as a booster for New York Governor Harriman as the Presidential candidate. Through Harriman headquarters in the Palmer House, Baker became acquainted with Jake More of Harlan, Iowa, an attorney and Democratic state chairman. Baker also met More's beautiful 21-year-old daughter, Carole Ann.

Diminutive and blonde, Carole Ann, then a student of political science at Northwestern University, was impressed by the worldly-wise, 380-pound labor leader.

Baker, who was twice divorced, a twice-convicted felon, was more than twice her weight and more than twice her age. But those facts did not seem to bother Carole Ann. Big Barney was heralded as a sort of hero in the Harriman camp for the primary victory over Kefauver in 1952 in the District of Columbia. Barney didn't let anyone forget his initial contribution to Harriman's political success, and he spoke with seeming authority on matters of labor and civil rights.

The heavy layers of overlapping fat that obscured whatever beauty there had been in Barney's face and figure seemed unimportant to the young girl from western Iowa. A romance developed quickly. The family knew little of Baker's background, and for months accepted Baker's own self-serving (but erroneous) statement that he was a close personal friend of Governor Harriman.

Barney was my nomination as the most colorful figure to dramatize the types of characters that infested Hoffa's Central States organization.

Bob Kennedy expressed some interest in Baker in 1957, but he was centering on other matters. Kenny O'Donnell, Kennedy's administrative assistant, was fascinated by Baker from the start.

In early May, I went to Iowa, and, through some friends in the law enforcement field, learned that Baker had received mysterious envelopes of cash while staying at the Rambler Motel in Des Moines. The money had been sent from the Pittsburgh, Pennsylvania, area.

In Des Moines, Baker had been a constant companion of Luigi Fratto, a Chicago police character who was known in Des Moines as Lew Farrell. Farrell was an old subject of mine from police reporting days. He had been identified before Senator Kefauver's crime committee as a former gambling figure and an associate of the Capone mob in Chicago. Farrell was doing some advising in the labor relations field.

While I was in Iowa, George Mills, the *Des Moines Register*'s state political reporter, broke a story that Barney Baker had married Carole Ann More in Arlington, Virginia, on April 26, 1958.

Back in Washington, I passed what I had picked up about Barney to Kenny O'Donnell and investigator Walt Sheridan of the McClellan committee staff. I also decided to try to contact Baker's two former wives on a chance they might be willing to talk.

I located the first wife in Brooklyn. She had divorced Baker and had regained her maiden name. She was a registered nurse, and she had been in the United States Women's Army Corps during part of her marriage to Baker. They were married in 1940, separated in 1946 and divorced in 1951. This had been during the period of time that Baker had been pals with murderers Squint Sheridan and Cockeyed Dunn before he fled from New York.

Baker had been brutal and had beaten her, I learned. She wanted no more to do with him. She asked that I not use her name or address because she didn't want Baker to find her. She said he had been a tall and attractive man in his younger years, but in her book he was "no good." She said she didn't know anything about his racket connections, and would be afraid to tell me if she did.

After several days of studying court records on Baker's marriages and divorces, I went to New York. On May 16, 1958, I talked with Tom Jones of the New York Waterfront Commission and examined the original testimony of Baker's work as a "collector" for the waterfront mob.

On May 19, 1958, I talked with Captain John Dougherty of the St. Louis Police Department. He told me of arresting Baker in St. Louis in April, 1953. Baker had a gun in his possession at the time. Some Teamsters officials had intervened and the police were unable to get the case prosecuted, Captain Dougherty said. He also knew that Baker's second wife lived in the St. Louis area.

On May 22, 1958, I got a report on the divorce that Mollie Jessie Yates Baker had obtained from Robert B. Baker on October 17, 1955, in St. Louis, Missouri. The record showed that Mrs. Mollie Baker stated in her petition that a child was born to her by Baker in 1950, when she was married to another man. She did not marry Baker until February 7, 1952.[3]

I called Mollie Baker in St. Louis, told her my name and that I was with *Look* magazine and the Cowles newspapers. She was suspicious and bluntly told me she thought I might be someone from the Teamsters or from the St. Louis underworld who was just trying to find out how much she would talk.

"I've got a little girl to look after, and I'm not wanting to have anything happen to me," she said.

I told her that the McClellan labor racket committee was investigating some of Barney's past activities, and that I merely wanted to find out as much as I could from her about his background and what kind of a fellow he was.

She was cautious as she started to talk.

"Barney is no angel," she said. "He didn't tell me everything, but he told me enough that I know what kind of guy he was. I know the kind he had out to the house, and I know some of the troubles he was mixed up with.

"I think I could have straightened Barney out if he hadn't been around with Harold Gibbons and those other Teamsters," Mollie said.

"It wasn't that Barney was such a bad guy, but he was easy

---
[3]McClellan committee, Report No. 621, pages 72-73.

for them to lead into trouble. He liked to give the impression that he was a big operator, but he wasn't."

She said that Barney "could be a real charming guy."

"I really thought he was something when I first met him," Mollie admitted. "He was driving a truck at first, and then he got into the union work."

Barney's first wife was "a nice woman," but Barney had beaten her severely on several occasions, Mollie said. Barney could be mean when he was crossed, but she still thought she could have reformed him if he hadn't been hanging around with the Teamsters crowd.

She didn't want to go into detail about Barney's criminal associates or his political connections, Mollie said. She said that she wouldn't have him back, but that she had received word from one of Baker's friends "in the last few months" that he would like to have her back.

"He knows I'm the best wife he had, or ever will have," Mollie said. "I don't believe I would ever take him back, but if I did it would only be for the little girl's sake."

"Have you heard anything from Barney since his marriage to that young blonde in Iowa?" I said. Mollie was unaware of Barney's marriage to Carole Ann More, and her voice tightened with rage.

"He'd better not let it interfere with keeping up his payments for his little girl," Mollie told me. "If he doesn't keep up those payments, I'll track him down wherever he is, I'll put a gun in his big, fat belly, and I'll blow his guts out."

Mollie wanted to know all about the girl, her age, her looks, her shape, how they met, and how long Barney had been going with her.

She stormed about Baker's deceit in sending word that he wanted to come back to her in the same period of time he was planning marriage to the young Iowa girl.

"That poor girl will live to regret this," Mollie said. "She doesn't know him the way I do. I've been around in some pretty rough crowds in my day, and I knew how to handle him. She won't know what to do when he gets mean. I've seen that man when he was like crazy. He threatened to kill my brother one night when we lived in Silver Spring. He held a knife at his throat."

Mollie was much more free with talk now as she launched into a description of Barney's terror tactics for the Teamsters. She named his associates as Joe Costello and Johnny Vitale—two underworld figures.[4]

She told me of his political work for Governor Harriman of New York and said that Baker had a picture with an inscription of appreciation from Governor Harriman. Mollie had never met Harriman herself, but she relied on Baker's accounts that he was close to the New York governor. Baker had been afraid to go into New York State until Harriman was elected governor, Mollie said.

Then she surprised me by saying that she could blow St. Louis wide open by telling what she knew about the Greenlease kidnap money. Barney had some connection with it, and so did his underworld friends. She talked of it vaguely and refused to be specific. She said she would show them they couldn't push her around because she knew too much.

This was the caliber of a fellow Jimmy Hoffa had hired as an organizer in the Central States Conference of Teamsters.

I called Walt Sheridan the next day at committee headquarters and told him he should get in touch with Mollie Baker quickly. She didn't want to testify before any committee, but she was furious about Barney's marriage and might provide him with some leads.

It was by chance that I bumped into Labor Secretary James P. Mitchell and New York Senator Irving Ives on May 26 at a dinner in the Mayflower Hotel. It was a dinner given by Dan Gainey, a wealthy Minnesota Republican, for Senator Edward Thye of Minnesota.

Ives hailed me, and I dropped by the table to ask him if he knew anything about Baker's connections with New York Governor Harriman.

"I don't know, but I would like to know," Senator Ives said with a smile. It wasn't necessary for him to explain his interest. Harriman had defeated Ives in a bitter campaign for the governorship of New York, and some of that bitterness still

---

[4]McClellan committee, Report No. 621, page 73.

remained. He was eager to learn anything derogatory about Harriman.

I told him of Baker's criminal record, and of Baker's work for Harriman in the Washington, D. C. primary campaign in 1952.

"George Mills, a reporter in Des Moines, had a story on Baker's marriage, and he tells me that Baker has been telling everyone in Iowa he is very close to Governor Harriman," I said.

"Where can I get all the information?" Ives said.

"I know the McClellan staff has been doing some work on it, and I'm sure you or George (Ives) could get it from the files," I said. "I could give you a memorandum on some aspects of it, but it would have to be confidential."

"You send me a memorandum on it," Ives said. "I'll keep it confidential. I'll appreciate it a lot."

"I hope you can ask a few questions of Baker that will help me out," I said.

"You give me the memorandum, and I'll help you any way I can," Senator Ives said.

Walt Sheridan immediately saw the possibilities of ex-wife Mollie as a source of information, and he moved into action. In his first telephone calls, Mollie was cautious. She didn't want to talk because all it would mean would be troubles. If he came to the house the underworld-Teamsters element might see him, and she feared she would be killed.

Later, she agreed to see Sheridan.

It was shortly before 6 p.m. on May 31 that Sheridan went to Delmar Circle in St. Louis. Mollie drove up shortly after 6 p.m. She kept the car doors locked and rolled down the window a few inches for Sheridan to hand her his committee credentials. She studied them for a moment, then opened the door.

That was the first of many meetings over the next few weeks. It took time because Mollie rambled about her personal life. She ran the gamut of emotions in telling of her life with Barney and her fear of the underworld. She did not want to testify, but she would give the committee leads.

"Did she tell you all she told me?" I said to Sheridan.

"She's told that, and a lot more," Sheridan said. "Mollie is a gold mine of information. It takes time, but she knows a lot.

We are finding that much of it can be corroborated, but we need time."[5]

On June 2, I sent a one-page memorandum to Senator Irving Ives. It contained Baker's background on the waterfront. mention of his convictions, his work for Harriman, the work Baker apparently did for Hoffa, and his alleged underworld connections. I also included a note that, when police arrested Baker in St. Louis, they found the telephone number of "Ave Harriman" in his book of private numbers.

"It is my understanding that the F.B.I. has compiled a rather full report on Baker," I wrote. "I would assume that a copy of that report would be available to you through the committee. This would include some detail on Baker's criminal record, and an arrest in St. Louis in the past few years for packing a gun."

I had told Ives that the investigation was going forward at a fast pace, and that it shouldn't be pushed with any public comments at that time. I merely felt he should become acquainted with the record so he could ask questions on it when the case came up for hearing.

On June 6, I was greatly surprised to pick up the newspapers and see that Senator Ives had made a speech before a Republican group in New York, accusing Governor Harriman with being a close pal of a convicted labor racketeer. In the speech, Ives had also indicated that he felt this was the reason Governor Harriman had not taken aggressive steps to investigate the so-called gangster convention at Apalachin, New York.

Ives did not mention the name of the labor racket figure, but he said his source was "a reliable reporter."

I received a call from a Washington correspondent for a Buffalo newspaper, whom I had helped on some earlier background stories on Barney Baker. He asked me if I thought Ives was talking about Barney Baker.

I told him I was sure it was Baker, and that I regretted that Ives had said anything. I wanted the whole thing kept quiet until I could break parts of it. I thought I was dealing with the reporter on a confidential basis as one reporter to another, and I let him see the memorandum I had written to Ives. That did it.

---

[5]McClellan committee, Report No. 621, pages 72-74.

Within a few hours I was being cited on the wire services as the source of the information behind Ives's charges.

I called Senator Ives, who was still in New York. He was apologetic. He said he hadn't meant to bring up the incident, but had made a slight reference to it in his speech and gave out some further information as reporters quizzed him later. He said he realized I had given him the information only as background, and that I had cautioned him to check everything through the committee. I couldn't be too irked over what was done because I'd pulled a boner myself in letting another reporter see my memorandum to Ives.

Bob Kennedy was irritated. He wanted to know if I was afraid the committee wasn't going to go ahead with the investigation because it involved Harriman, a Democrat. He asked if I was trying to light political fires in the investigation.

I told him I knew the investigation was proceeding fast enough, and I saw no inclination on his part to cover up for Harriman or to embarrass Harriman. I told him precisely what had happened, that what I had told Senator Ives on a confidential basis had become a news story because Ives became overly enthusiastic in an extemporaneous speech at a Republican dinner.

Kennedy told me that Baker had already been subpoenaed, as had several other witnesses. He said he didn't want a story on it then because of a fear that someone might shoot Baker if they knew what was being developed on the Greenlease money. He was also fearful of what might happen to Mollie Baker.

I agreed to sit on the story for awhile. I was still sitting on that one on July 8, when the *St. Louis Globe Democrat* broke the story that the McClellan committee had found links between the Greenlease money, Baker and the Teamsters racket figures.[6]

It was not pleasant to be scooped on my own story, but I knew it was for a good cause. The delay had given Kennedy and Sheridan time to develop more angles of the Baker story as an important link between the Teamsters and the underworld from Miami to Buffalo and from Las Vegas to New York.

---

[6]McClellan committee, Report No. 621, pages 70, 73 and 79.

XXVIII

The Old Judge Fools Everyone

The Teamsters were confident in early May, 1958. Union membership was growing. The monitors seemed neutralized, and a steady attack was being conducted to harass the one independent monitor, rank-and-file representative, Godfrey Schmidt. The McClellan committee hadn't fully recovered from the political feuds that accompanied the U.A.W. hearings, and it looked as if it might be permanently adjourned at the end of the year.

Ed Cheyfitz had some friendly advice for me to pass to Bob Kennedy: "You should wise up your friend, Bob Kennedy. He isn't acting like a political pro. He's taking this Hoffa investigation too seriously.

"If he would play this smart, he could have Hoffa and the Teamsters working for Jack (Kennedy) in 1960," Cheyfitz confided.

Cheyfitz said that if Bob would merely study the record of his grandfather, Honey Fitzgerald, he could learn how a real politician operates. Cheyfitz said that Honey Fitz would not have made the mistake of alienating a man like Hoffa.

Cheyfitz accused Bob Kennedy of engaging in a "personal vendetta" against Hoffa and other Teamsters, which could be damaging to Jack's chances for the Presidency.

I told Cheyfitz I would pass the word to Bob. I knew

what the young lawyer's reaction would be.

By the time I mentioned it to Kennedy a few days later, Bob told me he had gotten the word directly from Cheyfitz. They had attended a party at the home of Joe Loftus, Washington labor reporter for the *New York Times*.

Bob related his conversation with Cheyfitz, and it was, almost to the detail, the idea Cheyfitz had planted with me. I was amused at the bold thinking in the Teamsters camp. Bob was a little angry.

"If it means playing ball with Hoffa, I'll never come up to the Cheyfitz standard as a political pro," he said coldly.

The monitors of the Teamsters had made little or no progress by mid-May, when Municipal Judge Cayton suddenly resigned as chairman. It was necessary for Federal Judge Letts to appoint a new chairman before the first monitors' report could be written. The rank-and-file group was concerned. Godfrey Schmidt, attorney for the rank-and-file, had been unhappy about Judge Cayton's leanings toward the Teamsters power center, but he felt a worse condition could be created.

Schmidt and Pat Kennedy (no relation to Jack and Bob), the spokesmen for the rank-and-file group, called at my office. They asked me if I would accept the chairmanship of the board of monitors if it was offered to me.

"I'm not so sure Hoffa or Ed Williams would accept me," I replied.

"Would you object if we suggest you for the monitor chairmanship?" Schmidt said.

"No, I won't object to being nominated," I said. "I'm not sure I could take it. I'd have to do some checking with my editors and publishers on policy."

My name and Bob Kennedy's name were submitted by Schmidt to Judge Letts for the monitor chairmanship.

Schmidt and Pat Kennedy called me a few days later. "We submitted your name, Bob Kennedy's, and Carmine Bellino's," Schmidt said. "Williams and Hoffa went through the roof. Williams said you are antiunion and prejudiced against Hoffa and the Teamsters."

"I'm not antiunion, but I'm afraid I have developed a little prejudice against the way Hoffa runs the Teamsters," I admitted.

Now, days later, Schmidt and Pat Kennedy were still chuckling over Teamsters reaction to me as the monitor chairman. The amusement gave way to serious concern when I asked who would be appointed.

Schmidt said he was fearful that Judge Letts might name Martin O'Donoghue.

"O'Donoghue?" I exploded. "Do you mean Judge Letts is considering naming a Teamsters attorney as neutral monitor chairman?"

"It sounds that way to me," Schmidt answered. "I don't know what's gotten into the judge."

"The judge is a straight shooter and views this monitorship as one of the most important things he's ever done in his career in public life," I said. "I can't believe he'd name a Teamsters attorney."

A few days later, I decided to drop over and see what Judge Letts was thinking, and let him know I thought any Teamsters lawyer as chairman would be a great error.

As I entered his office in the Federal Court Building, Judge Letts told me he had just named O'Donoghue as chairman. The first thing that crossed my mind was that the Teamsters had somehow hoodwinked this 83-year-old jurist.

"You look disappointed, Clark," the judge said.

"Your Honor, I am disappointed, and I'm sick," I replied. "Judge, if I didn't know you and have confidence in your honesty, I'd say this was one of the worst fixes I've ever come across. As it is, I just feel it is a mistake."

"I'm sorry you feel that way, Clark," Judge Letts said thoughtfully. "I have known Mr. O'Donoghue for some time. He has always been a man of great ability and integrity. I am sure that he will be able to forget his past ties with the Teamsters."

"I hope you're right, Judge," I answered. "I'm not very optimistic."

Bob Kennedy was as upset as I when I dropped in at the Senate Office Building a few minutes later. We had hoped the monitorship would provide some restriction on Hoffa. This decision killed the hope.

"I can't understand how the judge could make such an

appointment," Kennedy said. Neither of us knew O'Donoghue well, but he had been the attorney pleading the International Teamsters' position less than nine months earlier, in the suit from which, in part, the monitor plan evolved.

When I called O'Donoghue before writing my story that night he was pleasant. He didn't bristle when I asked the details of his work for the Teamsters, or of his association with the Teamsters' principal attorney, Edward Bennett Williams. He had taught Williams several courses at Georgetown Law School.

"I suppose you know you'll be on the spot as chairman?" I said it curtly.

"Yes, Mr. Mollenhoff. I expect to have everything I do examined carefully and critically. I'm cutting all my relations with the Teamsters. I hope I won't be criticized too much until I've had a chance to perform."

He sounded like a man who knew he had accepted a difficult post and meant to perform in an honest manner. It was conceivable that Judge Letts had made a good choice, but I was still suspicious. I didn't want to be a sucker on this first impression. It didn't look good, and editorial pages raised the same questions I did on the wisdom of the selection.

Lawyer and public relations conjurer Ed Cheyfitz praised the O'Donoghue selection as excellent. That raised more doubts for me.

Godfrey Schmidt was extremely unhappy about the naming of O'Donoghue when I talked to him a few days after it was announced, but within two weeks he called me to praise the ex-Teamsters' counsel.

"Marty O'Donoghue is perfect for this job," Schmidt said. "Williams and Hoffa aren't going to be able to pull the wool over his eyes. He is honest, and he is bright, and he understands what is needed to clean up the Teamsters."

"It looks like Judge Letts was a lot smarter than we were on this one." I admitted my error with pleasure.

Schmidt said he believed O'Donoghue's background in labor law was particularly beneficial because he would not be subject to attacks for being antiunion.

"This O'Donoghue is the greatest," Pat Kennedy bubbled.

"This guy is a real lawyer. He makes the great Edward Bennett Williams look second rate."

Schmidt had been a thorn in Hoffa's side from the time the monitorship was established. The Teamsters now were getting even with Schmidt by refusing to pay his claim for attorney's fees, or his compensation and expenses as a monitor.[1]

"They know I am not a wealthy man, and Hoffa is trying to starve me out," Schmidt told me.

When O'Donoghue was appointed to the board, he started agreeing with Schmidt. It created a critical situation for the Teamsters for it seemed certain that Schmidt and O'Donoghue would recommend that a number of Hoffa's friends be fired, including his closest pal, Owen Bert Brennan, who had become an international vice president.

Godfrey Schmidt called me to tell me he had been offered $100,000 to resign from the board of monitors. He had rejected it, but he said he wanted to tell me just how far some of the Teamsters would go to get rid of him.[2]

The offer was made to his attorney, Bartley Crum, Schmidt told me. Crum was handling Schmidt's claim against the Teamsters for legal fees and monitor's fees. Schmidt provided me with the reports Crum had made on the incident, and I wrote the story.

The monitors and the McClellan committee came under nearly every type of attack in the summer of 1958. It was as varied as it was shocking.

When investigators Jim Kelly and Jerry Gotch tried to serve a subpoena on Joey Aiuppa, the Chicago labor racket figure, it almost cost Kelly his life. Aiuppa, identified before the committee as a gambler and gunman for the Capone mob, was wanted for questioning about his role as an officer of racket-ridden Local 450 of the Hotel and Restaurant Workers Union.

Aiuppa raced his car directly at Kelly, and the committee investigator barely jumped aside in time to avoid being hit.[3]

The Hotel and Restaurant Employees and Bartenders Union in Chicago presented no political problem within the McClellan committee. It did present other problems. The committee was

---

[1]McClellan committee, Report No. 1139, pages 615-617.
[2]McClellan committee, Report No. 1139, pages 615 and 726.
[3]McClellan committee, Report No. 621, pages 603-604.

down to the job of fighting for testimony on the operations of a group of the old Capone mobsters, including Tony Accardo, who were using a union gimmick to shake down hotels, night clubs and restaurants. But some witnesses were frightened and refused to talk. Others were threatened but talked anyway. Gunmen calmly walked into the restaurant owned by a key witness, Gustav Allgauer, held customers at gun point while they poured an inflammable liquid around, then set the place afire. The $1.4 million Fireside Restaurant was destroyed.[4]

On July 18, two Chicago women testified that they were threatened with broken bones if they didn't join the Hotel Employees and Restaurant Workers Union.

"I was told not to come to Washington—that I should get sick—or I would be sicker when I got back," testified Mrs. Beverly Sturdevant, an employee of Embassy Restaurant.[5]

But there were other, less physical approaches by witnesses with political connections. Abraham Teitelbaum, a former lawyer for the Capone mob, was subpoenaed to testify and was being questioned by Bob Kennedy in advance of the hearing.

"I know your brother's in politics, and I've got a lot of good connections," Teitelbaum said. "If you go easy on me, I can do him some good."

The chief counsel had to suppress a smile of amusement as he declined the deal. It was pretty routine for witnesses or their lawyers to make some subtle gesture in the direction of a political deal, but there had been only a few who were as blunt as Abraham Teitelbaum. It was not a coincidence that another rather blunt political approach had been made to Senator Kennedy on behalf of an employer.

With no political deal possible, Teitelbaum took the Fifth Amendment on questions dealing with his relations with racketeers Tony Accardo and Jacob (Greasy Thumb) Guzik and the Hotel Employees and Restaurant Workers Union.[6]

On July 23, investigator Joe Maher served a subpoena on Rolland McMaster, a Teamsters business agent, at Hoffa's Detroit headquarters. McMaster, a hulking, 245-pound convicted thug

---

[4]McClellan committee, Report No. 621, pages 611-615.

[5]McClellan committee, Report No. 621, pages 619-620.

[6]McClellan committee, Report No. 621, pages 599, 625, 641-644.

and thief, grabbed the slim committee investigator by the throat with one hand and drummed the other against Maher's face and chest. Then Maher was tossed bodily out of the Teamsters conference room. Maher, a 38-year-old former F.B.I. agent, was surprised and shocked. He had assured himself that not even in Hoffa's headquarters would there be such arrogant disregard for a Federal investigator.

Between July 9, 1958, and the end of the month there were three threats to an important woman witness. Mrs. Nancy Dawson, an attractive young owner of a laundry, received the first threat a few days after she talked with committee investigator Pierre Salinger. She had cooperated by relating to Salinger how a group of Teamsters and gangsters were intimidating the customers of her firm, Dawson Industrial Laundry, to try to force them to give business to a gangster-backed firm. The first threat was general, but the others were to disfigure her or harm her family. The committee arranged to put the woman under an F.B.I. guard.[7]

Amidst these problems a personal tragedy hit John Mc-Clellan on July 23, 1958. James, the last of his three sons, was killed in an airplane crash in Arkansas. Crushed by the tragedy, McClellan appeared to be a broken man for several days. Bob Kennedy said he wasn't sure the hearings would continue in early August, but McClellan set his jaw and told Bob that he felt the best thing to do was to get back to work. He gave notice that hearings on the Detroit Teamsters and James R. Hoffa would start on July 31. Within two weeks after his son's death, McClellan was again at work on the biggest undertaking of his career.

John McClellan and Bob Kennedy had no clear and certain idea of how Hoffa and his racketeering friends would be eradicated from the labor movement. They only knew they had a job to do in informing the Congress and the people of the nature of the danger Hoffa presented to the country.

They hoped that further demonstration of Hoffa's degraded union operations would create more public pressure for enactment of the Kennedy-Ives labor reform bill that was then pending in the House of Representatives.

---

[7]McClellan committee, Report No. 621, pages 680-682.

There had been indications that some newspapers were losing interest in the Teamsters story of greed, viciousness and crime. I was afraid that some editors would start to cut the story to a few meaningless paragraphs, then bury it. That was what the Hoffa crowd wanted. I hoped the nation could again be shocked to attention by the latest cases of arrogant defiance of all government and morality—the burning of the restaurant owned by one witness, the choking of a committee investigator, and the threats to disfigure a woman witness.

There seemed to be nothing to which some of these union gangsters wouldn't stoop to quiet witnesses and obstruct justice.

XXIX

Light from a Human Torch

It was shortly before 11 p.m. on August 3, 1958, when Frank Kierdorf and a companion entered the Latreille Cleaners on the eastern edge of Flint, Michigan. Burning a dry cleaning establishment was not a particularly exciting venture for the 56-year-old Teamsters business agent of Flint Local 332. Arson and violence were an old story to him. He had served two penitentiary terms for armed robbery before his Uncle Herman introduced him to Jimmy Hoffa ten years earlier. Hoffa had arranged for Frank Kierdorf to become a Teamsters business agent and he teamed with Jack Thompson, another convicted armed robber turned business agent.[1]

Union "work" had become a good racket for Frank Kierdorf, much better than the old independent armed robbery game that twice had put him behind bars. A Teamsters business agent had power and political influence. If there was trouble with the law, Kierdorf knew the Hoffa organization provided high-priced lawyers, paid the fines, and even paid a salary if the worst happened and a union official was sentenced to jail.

Frank had used the Fifth Amendment before the McClellan committee in October, 1957, when he was questioned about violence and taking payoffs from employers.[2] Frank wasn't

---

[1] McClellan committee, Report No. 621, pages 4-5.

[2] McClellan committee, Report No. 1417, page 295.

worried, because Uncle Herman had also taken the Fifth Amendment before the McClellan committee a few days earlier. Uncle Herman had once been convicted of armed robbery and impersonating a Federal officer, and it hadn't hurt his stock with Hoffa.

Frank Kierdorf was typical of the robbers and thugs who held office in the Teamsters union. He had faith in the power of the Teamsters, and in Hoffa's loyalty to the ex-convicts who surrounded him. George Meany's plea for an uprising of honest union members brought only a sneer from Frank Kierdorf and his kind. They had nothing but contempt for rank-and-file union members and for the employers.

Kierdorf wasn't worried about Federal Judge F. Dickinson Letts or the monitors. Nothing could go wrong while Hoffa was at the helm, and Hoffa seemed to be getting stronger every day. Hoffa had beaten two Federal indictments, he had defied the A.F.L.-C.I.O., and he was planning a huge transportation union that would control all ships, planes, trains and trucks. Kierdorf believed it when Hoffa said that there was no force in the United States that could stop the mighty Teamsters union.

This was just another chore the night of August 3 for Frank Kierdorf. He spread a wick of papers, poured inflammable fluid across the floor, and prepared to start the blaze. Suddenly, something went wrong. In a few frantic seconds he was a screaming torch. He burst from the door of the dry cleaning plant and rolled in the grass. His body was a grisly mass of burns by the time his companion stopped the blaze and bundled him into a car.

It was nearly 1 a.m. on August 4 when two men left Frank on the lawn near the St. Joseph Mercy Hospital in Pontiac, Michigan, and fled. Efforts to treat his burns had been unsuccessful, and this was the only plan they could devise to get hospital treatment for him without answering embarrassing questions.

Frank Kierdorf was true to the gangland code. He lied to protect his criminal accomplices, even though he was so badly burned death seemed certain. "John Doe of Washington" was the only identification he would give the hospital attendants in those first hours.

When Pontiac, Michigan, police were notified of the unidentified human pyre they had one reaction: The Teamsters or barbers union officials had taken care of Bob Scott for testifying before the McClellan committee.

It was 2 a.m., only an hour after Kierdorf reached the hospital, when a police car stopped at Robert Scott's home at 31 Bloomfield Terrace in Pontiac.

"Is Scott here?" a policeman asked when Mrs. Scott answered the door.

"Yes, he's in bed," Mrs. Scott answered in bewilderment.

"Well, I would like to see him," the policeman said.

As Scott entered the room, the policeman grabbed him by the shoulders. "God, I'm glad to see you!"

"Why?" Scott said, amazed at the emotion.

"Well, I thought you just walked into the hospital all burned," the policeman replied. That was Scott's first knowledge of the incident.

The burned and nameless hulk of what had been a man shocked the nation as few Teamsters crimes had in months. Robbery and beatings had become routine, but Kierdorf's refusal to tell who he was led the press and the public to believe for a few hours that this was the ultimate in the Teamsters' brutal efforts to frighten witnesses.

When Kierdorf was finally identified, his Uncle Herman talked with him at the hospital. After Herman's visit, Frank told a tale of being set afire by two men whose names he did not know. Police had immediate doubts about the story, since it could not be corroborated.

Then Herman disappeared, and police found he had left two guns in a bag with a neighbor. One was equipped with a silencer, which is a violation of the law. The hunt was on for Herman.

Frank Kierdorf died at 12:45 p.m. on August 8 without telling the truth, but eventually the police were able to piece together the story of what actually had happened.

Despite his silence, during the last three days of his existence, the robber turned Teamsters official unintentionally dramatized the fact that Hoffa's criminal associates hadn't changed colors. Kierdorf and his arson and his flaming death were a sample of what Hoffa was trying to palm off as a program for "rehabilitation" of criminals.

Hoffa knew the human torch death reflected on his conduct of union affairs. He had hired Kierdorf, a convicted armed robber. He retained Kierdorf as a business agent despite evidence of dishonesty, brutality and a sell-out of union members.

Hoffa was glum, for the death by burning was the perfect backdrop against which McClellan and Kennedy could show the truth of the Teamsters empire. It focused public attention on the evidence of threats to witnesses and efforts to buy or influence public officials. He knew he was in for at least a month of hearings if Bob Kennedy could get enough witnesses to talk.

Mrs. Nancy Dawson disregarded anonymous telephone threats to her and her family, and told the committee of payoffs and union coercion in the Detroit laundry industry. The attractive 31-year-old mother of four was a nervous witness, but she did not hedge.

Other witnesses showed less courage in talking about old Herman Kierdorf and the Detroit gangsters. Many were reluctant, and some even tried to back away from sworn affidavits in which they had given derogatory information involving Hoffa.

A Capitol policeman testified he overheard Jimmy Hoffa comment after one hearing: "That sneaky little S.O.B. I'll break his back."

"I may have been discussing someone in a figure of speech," Hoffa testified when Kennedy asked him whose back he was going to break. "I don't even remember it."

The day Frank Kierdorf died, a 29-year-old Negro boxer testified he was paid $8,000 from Michigan Conference of Teamsters welfare funds, for which he performed no services except occasionally feeding the race horses of Owen Bert Brennan. Embrell Davidson was a strong, 200-pound man, but he was unsteady as he testified before the McClellan committee a few feet from where Hoffa was seated, cracking his knuckles.

Davidson's boxing contract had been the property of Bert Brennan and Hoffa, and both had been present when he was put on the union payroll, according to his testimony. Hoffa admitted he had "a piece" of Davidson's contract, but he denied knowledge that union welfare funds were used to pay the boxer.

Paying a boxer's expenses with union money was a fraud on the union, Chairman McClellan declared. Bert Brennan slipped behind the Fifth Amendment in the face of this clear evidence of fraud.[3]

Hoffa had claimed Brennan had the answers to questions about the boxer, and about a good many other deals including the mysterious $5,000 to $10,000 a year in miscellaneous "collections" and commissions that appeared each year on Hoffa's income tax returns.

Hoffa said that money had been won in gambling on the horses, but he couldn't give details. Every year, Hoffa said, he gave Bert Brennan money for horse betting. At the end of the year, Brennan very consistently came around and gave him a $5,000 to $10,000 cash payment as his cut.

Bob Kennedy accused Hoffa of using the horse betting as a way of covering up money received from employers for giving them favorable treatment on their contracts. He ridiculed Hoffa's contention that it was simply a matter of steady luck with the horses.

Hoffa admitted he couldn't tell the committee anything about the sure-fire betting system used by his pal, Bert Brennan. He described Brennan as a fellow he had worked with in the Teamsters for twenty-five years, who was as close to him as his wife. He suggested that the committee would have to get its information from Brennan.

Chairman McClellan said the committee would like very much to get the story from Brennan, but that Brennan was invoking the Fifth Amendment. Hoffa shrugged and said he couldn't help it if Brennan felt compelled to take advantage of his Constitutional rights.[4]

The committee's suggestion that Hoffa get an explanation from Brennan and other "Fifth Amendment Teamsters" was rejected. Hoffa said he wouldn't be a party to interfering with the Constitutional rights of Bert Brennan and other Teamsters by questioning them, and in turn having the committee question him.

Monitors Marty O'Donoghue and Godfrey Schmidt con-

[3]McClellan committee, Report No. 621, pages 14-15.
[4]McClellan committee, Report No. 621, page 100.

cluded that the documentary evidence and the testimony of pugilist Davidson were conclusive that Brennan had misused union welfare funds. They decided on a showdown with Hoffa.

On August 15, they filed a report demanding that the International Brotherhood of Teamsters start ouster action against Bert Brennan by August 25. They added that Hoffa should stand aside and let another member of the Teamsters Executive Board file the charge.

Jimmy Hoffa had to decide whether he would allow the monitors to fire Brennan, his pal for twenty-five years, or challenge the power of the monitors. He elected to fight.

His challenge took two forms: Establishment of an anti-racket committee, on which he controlled the appointments; the direct assertion that monitors could only recommend ouster or reform measures, not force compliance.

With assistance of lawyers Ed Cheyfitz and Edward Bennett Williams, Hoffa formed the three-man anti-racket committee to give the public the impression he was an active reformer. The whopping $250 a day and expenses they decided to pay each of the three members was so attractive that they were sure they would be able to hire some well-known and respected political figures to lend their names to the project.

"It is a great gimmick," Cheyfitz told me. "It will help Hoffa investigate the racketeers in the Teamsters, and it will also counteract the bad public reaction from the monitors."

"You mean it will confuse the public to have two committees examining Teamsters' corruption," I said.

"It will do that, too," Cheyfitz agreed smiling.

Hoffa needed public relations plus public confusion to overcome the ugly facts flowing from the McClellan committee. As it turned out, his anti-racket committee was a public relations blunder.

Hoffa named former Republican Senator George Bender of Ohio as chairman of the committee.

The following week, the McClellan committee revealed Bender had been the recipient of political support from two of Hoffa's most trusted subordinates—Babe Triscaro and Big Bill Presser. The minutes of a closed Ohio Teamsters meeting showed that, in the fall of 1954, when Bender had a House subcommittee investigating the Cleveland Teamsters, Presser was full of praise for Bender.

And only a few weeks before he was named to Jimmy's private anti-racket committee, Bender had been hired by Presser to do some legislative work.

Bender was choleric with the McClellan committee. The Buckeye politician charged that Bob Kennedy had pulled "a dirty trick" by putting out information indicating that Bender might not be objective.

At a press conference in the Willard Hotel, Bender said he would not whitewash anyone. He said he had successfully investigated the labor racketeers in Minnesota, and he pulled out a sheaf of thermofax copies of a letter I had written to him in April, 1954, to prove he was a crusader against labor rackets.

As Bender read the letter, I interrupted to ask him to be sure to point out that my complimentary comments were written in April, 1954, and dealt only with his work in exposing the Minneapolis racketeers.

Bender was hurt that I had been so blunt in putting a qualification on my praise. He asked me if I thought he had sold out to someone on this private investigation.

"No, George, I am not saying I think you are sold out," I told him. "I'm just being cautious about general endorsements of anyone under these circumstances. I hope that I'll be able to write you a letter six months or a year from now and tell you I thought you did a great job on Hoffa and the International Teamsters."

"This isn't going to be a whitewash of anyone," Bender repeated to me later. "Hoffa says I have a completely free hand."

"The mere fact that Hoffa named you and is setting the rules for paying you is reason for me to be cautious," I told him. "You don't have to be dishonest to look mighty bad, George. This is a fast league you're playing in, and for your own good you should be extremely careful how you swallow what they tell you at Teamsters headquarters."

"I'm not going to let anyone put anything over on me," Bender said with assurance. "I'm a lot smarter than some of you boys give me credit for being."

"I wish you luck, George, but I'm skeptical," I said. "If

you see you can't do any good over there, get out. I appreciated the job you did in Minneapolis, and I'm telling you this because I think it is for your own good."

The Hoffa-appointed anti-racket committee sputtered and quivered for months, but was never any more than a public relations farce.

It was denounced by Federal Judge Letts and the board of monitors, and it was kicked in the teeth by the McClellan committee. Bender was panned by editorial writers, columnists and cartoonists, and the McClellan committee rolled on with more front-page Teamsters scandals.

It was the bulky frame of Barney Baker that provided the best living dramatization of what was wrong with the Teamsters. The roster of Barney's friends included the worst underworld characters from coast to coast: Meyer Lansky in Florida, Trigger Mike Coppola in New York, Gus Zapas in Indianapolis, Bugsy Siegel in Las Vegas and Los Angeles, Lew (Luigi Fratto) Farrell in Des Moines, Angelo Meli in Detroit, John Vitale and Joe Costello in St. Louis, and Paul Dorfman and various Capone mob tigers in Chicago.[5]

There were a dozen witnesses to sing of the fascinating career of Barney Baker. None was more devastating than his divorced wife, Mrs. Mollie Baker. In addition, a former girl friend, Mrs. Ruth Brougher, a tired-looking 44-year-old blonde, was on leave from the Florida Women's Reformatory to testify.

Baker was unsuccessful in 1955 in trying to spring Mrs. Brougher from a manslaughter conviction involving the death of her former boy friend, Murray Dubois, a Miami union organizer and dope peddler. But the testimony of Mrs. Baker and Mrs. Brougher pictured Big Barney as one of the most versatile labor gangsters in the nation.

According to testimony: Baker had a good arm with stink bombs in New York theaters, served two prison terms, lost his parole because he and four others beat up a waterfront reformer, and he had been wounded twice in gangster shooting scrapes.[6]

Barney was a strong-arm and collector for the waterfront mob. He had been a bouncer in Florida for a big-time racket

[5]McClellan committee, Report No. 621, pages 78-80.
[6]McClellan committee, Report No. 621, pages 70-80.

group that included Meyer Lansky, Frank Costello, and Joe Adonis. He had hired out to Bugsy Siegel shortly before Siegel was cut down by machine-gun fire and died on a divan in his Los Angeles home.

Initially Mollie Baker told committee investigator Sheridan that she would not testify because she feared retaliation by the underworld or the Teamsters. She did testify, however, with no trace of nervousness. Her story bubbled forth as freely as when she had told it to me four months earlier. Baker knew about the $300,000 missing from the Bobby Greenlease kidnap ransom, Mollie said, and so did Joe Costello, the convicted racketeer who ran a St. Louis taxi firm.[7]

With a nudge from Senator Irving Ives, Mollie told of Baker's support of New York Governor Averell Harriman, and she testified that Baker was "very close" to Harriman. This was apparently only Baker's bragging to her, for she had never met Harriman, and both Harriman and Baker denied there was any close association. Baker had been an enthusiastic political supporter of Harriman and was prominent in the Governor's headquarters at the 1956 Democratic national convention.

Ruth Brougher testified that Baker and Trigger Tom Burke, another of Hoffa's organizers from Detroit, had entertained her royally during the months before she went to jail. The plush apartment and the luxurious estate that Baker provided for her cost $20,000 to $25,000 a year, which she assumed came from the Teamsters funds—or from the payoffs Big Barney was engineering. Mrs. Brougher gave dates, names and figures of payoffs and attempted extortion by Baker, and there was some corroboration of these. She also told of Baker's dealing in mysterious diamond transactions. Other witnesses told of seeing Baker and Trigger Burke in possession of handsful and jars packed with diamonds, estimated to have a value of at least $75,000 or $100,000.[8]

According to testimony at this hearing, Baker was a party to shaking down a Pittsburgh trucking firm for several thousand dollars. Part of the payoff money was the $1,000 in cash he had received in an envelope at the Rambler Motel in Des Moines,

---

[7]McClellan committee, Report No. 621, pages 33-34 and 72-73.
[8]McClellan committee, Report No. 621, pages 74-77.

the same month that Hoffa was before the McClellan committee for the first time—August, 1957.[9]

Barney ate gargantuan meals—as much as thirty or forty dollars worth of groceries at a sitting—at Teamsters expense. When he had swollen to between 350 and 380 pounds he would tap the Teamsters welfare and insurance funds for hospital costs so he could reduce. He also used hotel credit to obtain un-explained cash advances of several thousand dollars, and his telephone credit account showed charges amounting to thousands of dollars spent on calling girl friends.

Harold Gibbons, the St. Louis Teamster, called Baker "one of the great speakers in the American labor movement." Jimmy Hoffa said Baker was a "great organizer," who had made "some mistakes" in his early life, but Hoffa wasn't going to hold it against him.[10]

Barney Baker's oratory did as much for that phase of the McClellan hearings as Frank Kierdorf's mysterious silence be-fore and beyond the grave. Barney was color, comedy and tragedy roughly molded into one fat ball. His serious-faced efforts to explain his actions were ludicrous. He had spectators and re-porters broken up with laughter.

There were those persons in the Hoffa camp who believed Big Barney could talk his way out of anything, but after he had been in the committee's witness chair a few days they changed their minds.

"We've got to shut this guy up," one Teamsters lawyer told me. "He's killing us with the members. The members will excuse a lot of errors, but this is making the Teamsters leadership a laughingstock."

On August 27, Baker was due to return for further testimony, but he was reported to have suffered a heart attack. I was sur-prised, when I talked to the doctor, to find it was a real heart attack. Big Barney was in serious condition. The heart ailment claim had been used so often in the labor racket hearings that investigators called it "the subpoena flutters."

Harold Gibbons, executive vice president of the Teamsters,

[9]McClellan committee, Report No. 621, pages 81-84.
[10]McClellan committee, Report No. 621, page 68.

had to take the responsibility for hiring Baker.[11]. Hoffa had to accept the responsibility for retaining him. Hoffa was tough and belligerent, and he was still confident he could whip the McClellan committee.

That United States Supreme Court decision on the Benanti appeal stopped the committee from using recordings of Hoffa's telephone conversations. He admitted the business agents and officers in the Teamsters included a lot of convicted thugs, robbers and extortionists, but he said he would handle these problems his own way. He didn't consider a criminal record a bar to union office.

Hoffa said he had called in a few of these convicted racketeers and asked them if they were stealing union funds, engaging in violence, or taking payoffs from employers.

"They denied it," Hoffa said, as if the denials meant he could not have fired them.

Harold Gibbons conceded he told his subordinates in St. Louis that, if they were arrested, they should give police their names, addresses and no further information.[12]

This was no conspiracy against law enforcement, Gibbons said. It was necessary because St. Louis police often framed labor officials.

A pretty brunette woman testified she had been used by Gibbons as a decoy to lure a taxi driver to a place where he could be ambushed and his taxi wrecked. Miss Mary Lou Bledsoe said Gibbons was present at the meeting where the orders were given. When she and a group of Teamsters were arrested, she said she had refused to testify about Gibbons' involvement because of Teamsters threats to her and her family. Gibbons testified he could not recall the meeting of which the girl spoke.[13]

Politics were a big part of those particular hearings. Jimmy Hoffa admitted he had contributed Teamsters union funds to candidates for governor in at least five middle western states— Michigan, Kentucky, Ohio, Kansas and Iowa.

The Teamsters put $17,500 into the 1956 campaign of Governor Herschel Loveless of Iowa, which was about half his total

---

[11]McClellan committee, Report No. 621, pages 68, 72, and 78.

[12]McClellan committee, Report No. 621, page 65.

[13]McClellan committee, Report No. 621, pages 59-60.

campaign cost. In Kansas, the Teamsters used former Republican Governor Payne Ratner as a messenger boy to deliver money on a bipartisan basis. Several thousand dollars went to former Republican Governor Fred Hall, and there was at least as much for Democratic Governor George Docking. Just a few weeks before he testified, Hoffa had put $11,000 of Teamsters money into the campaign of the Democratic candidate for prosecutor in Wayne County, Michigan.

Hoffa testified before the committee that he could see no problem of ethics in his contribution of $22,000 to a public relations campaign fund that paid $100 a week to Wayne County Judge Joseph Gillis and produced television shows to promote the candidacy of Gillis and other judges. It didn't even change Hoffa's view when chief counsel Bob Kennedy called Hoffa's attention to the fact that Judge Gillis had presided over criminal cases involving some of Hoffa's closest associates in the Detroit Teamsters organization during the same period.[14]

Sergeant Bernard Mullins of the vice squad of the Detroit Police Department testified he was present when Hoffa approached Wayne County Prosecutor Joseph Rashid during a trial of Teamsters and criticized him for his vigorous prosecution of Frank Fitzsimmons, vice-president of Hoffa's Local 299. Mullins quoted Hoffa as having told the prosecutor he would spend Teamsters money to defeat him, and Rashid should remember that Hoffa could frame him within 90 days.[15]

Rashid refused to yield to Hoffa's pressure, and later was elected judge over Hoffa's opposition. Sergeant Mullins said Judge Gillis presided in the Teamsters case in which William Bufalino was acquitted. Mullins testified before the McClellan committee that the prosecutor, Rashid, told him "the people of the state of Michigan did not get a fair trial" of Bufalino.

Of all the witnesses before the McClellan committee, Robert Scott told the most sordid story of Hoffa's operations. Scott had been appointed by Hoffa as an officer of Teamsters Local 614 in Pontiac in 1945. Until a falling out with Hoffa in 1952, Scott had been the political arm of Hoffa's Michigan Conference of Teamsters. He had testified in September, 1957, to helping

---

[14]McClellan committee, Report No. 621, pages 92-93.
[15]McClellan committee, Report No. 621, pages 90-91.

Hoffa obtain reports of secret grand jury testimony and of performing other chores for Hoffa in efforts to obstruct justice.[16]

Since that time, McClellan committee investigators had further discussions with Scott, indicating he could expand that testimony. Bob Kennedy also wanted to get into the record the testimony of Scott's harassment by the barbers' union in Michigan since his testimony a year earlier. It became apparent, as Kennedy questioned Hoffa, that Scott would again be an important witness.

"Did you, in fact, instruct Mr. Scott to hide your brother from the police when the police were looking for him?" Bob Kennedy asked.

"I don't ever recall discussing this matter with Scott whatsoever," Hoffa answered.

"Did you or did you not?" Kennedy said impatiently, after Hoffa refused to be specific. "I think most people would answer that question as to whether they asked someone to hide their brother from the police."

"I had no reason to ask Scott to hide my brother," Hoffa answered.

As Kennedy continued to press the point, the Teamsters' chief lawyer, Edward Bennett Williams, declared that he believed Scott was "a wholly unreliable witness."

"My information is that this man, Mr. Chairman, is a narcotic addict," Williams declared.

Kennedy was furious over Williams' unsupported comment that Scott was a narcotic addict, and it was the first subject Bob Kennedy hit when Scott returned to the witness chair a few minutes later.

"At the beginning, Mr. Edward Bennett Williams, the attorney for Mr. Hoffa, has made a statement here, without any proof, that you are a drug addict," Kennedy said. "Will you make any comment on that, please?"

"I would be glad to," Scott replied. "I would like to have Mr. Williams offer some proof to that effect."

"Answer—are you a drug addict or not?" McClellan interrupted.

"No, I am not," Scott said.

---

[16]McClellan committee, Report No. 1417, pages 244-245.

Williams offered no proof. At the recess I asked him if he had any. He blazed with what may have been self-conscious anger and declared he wasn't going to tell me anything.

"You are the director of the American Civil Liberties Union, Mr. Williams," I lashed back. "You are the one who gives speeches on the abuses by unsupported charges—and the smears by Congressional committees."

There was a tense moment or two. Williams still refused to offer proof, and I walked off. After the hearings he stopped me and said he didn't have the proof on Scott with him but could produce some later. He didn't say what it was but said he would bring it to me.

A couple of days later, he told me he could not bring me the evidence but that he had been informed by two reliable witnesses that Scott had been using a narcotic.

"Who are the reliable witnesses?" I asked. It was with some reluctance that Williams said the informants were two Teamsters officials from Michigan—Louis Linteau, who had served time on an extortion charge, and Leaun Harrelson, another agent for Local 614.

Williams said he had no affidavits, so I let the subject drop.

Committee accountants testified that Hoffa had paid out more than $500,000 to lawyers to defend Teamsters criminals, many of whom were convicted of selling out union members.[17]

Counsel Kennedy asked Hoffa if he paid these legal fees and refused to fire convicted crooks because he feared they might expose him.

There was naked hate in Hoffa's eyes as he glared across the committee table at Kennedy, and said, "I was not afraid of being exposed because they have nothing to expose."

Kennedy said it appeared Hoffa was merely afraid of the gangsters and couldn't get rid of them.

"I'm not afraid of anybody," Hoffa chopped back.

Jimmy Hoffa denied he had ever extorted a dime from any employer. He admitted he had a remarkable record for successful borrowing. Truck-line operators, labor relations consultants and union business agents and officers happily loaned him anything from $1,000 to $25,000, for the asking. Usually it was with-

[17]McClellan committee, Report No. 1417, pages 237-239 and 253-254.

out a note, without collateral, and with no date specified for repayment.

He sometimes borrowed directly from the union funds. Often, he loaned union money to others, then would borrow from the borrowers. There was $5,000 he borrowed from Jack Bushkin, a labor relations man;[18] $5,000 from Joe Holtzman, Bushkin's partner; $25,000 from Henry Lower, a former Teamsters business agent who was promoting the Sun Valley project in Florida with help from the Teamsters treasury; $4,000 from Herbert Grosberg, the Teamsters accountant who had borrowed at least $75,000 in Teamsters funds to finance a construction company, and $25,000 from Harold Mark on May 15, 1956, exactly a week after Hoffa's local 299 loaned $25,000 to Mark.[19]

In all, Hoffa admitted to borrowing at least $110,000 in his own highly unusual way. And he said he still owed about $70,000 of this money at the time he was testifying.

The record indicated that Hoffa had misused millions of dollars in union funds for the benefit of himself, his lawyers, his accountants and his racketeering cronies, Chairman McClellan declared as he recessed the hearings on September 18. He stated that Hoffa had engaged in "willful perjury" and in "arrogant disrespect for members of the union, the general public and the United States government."

"This situation even now is critical for the nation," Senator McClellan warned. "All our lives are too intricately interwoven with this union to sit passively by and allow the Teamsters (under Mr. Hoffa's leadership) to create such a super-power in this country—a power greater than the people and greater than the government."

---

[18]McClellan committee, Report No. 621, page 14.
[19]McClellan committee, Report No. 1417, pages 227-229.

XXX

Contests and Conquests in Court

There was a smirk of contempt on Jimmy Hoffa's face as he completed his testimony the afternoon of September 18, 1958. When he left the huge Senate caucus room he was accompanied by attorneys Edward Bennett Williams, George Fitzgerald and David Previant. If he was embarrassed he didn't show it.

The McClellan committee could expose and condemn his activities, but the swaggering little labor Napoleon from Detroit knew the limitations of Congress. Chairman John McClellan had charged him with being a liar, a cheat and a thief—but condemnations by a committee chairman were not a conviction.

Congress had only two weapons in forcing testimony: A contempt of Congress recommendation, and referral of the record to the Justice Department when perjury was indicated. Hoffa knew the United States Supreme Court had, in recent years, cut sharply into these two weapons. It had become difficult, if not impossible, to obtain a prosecution that would stand up on appeal.

It mattered little to Hoffa that McClellan had accused him of misusing millions of dollars in union funds and had branded him as thoroughly corrupt—"a cancer" in the American labor movement. As long as Hoffa had control of the Teamsters union treasury he could fight back.

Chairman McClellan had warned the nation that Jimmy Hoffa was welding together a transportation alliance that included the racket-infested International Longshoremen's Association of the East Coast and the Communist-tainted International Longshoremen's and Warehousemen's Union of Harry Bridges on the West Coast. Hoffa had learned long ago that the public had a short memory on such things. He was confident that he could coax or coerce the other transportation unions into an alliance if he had the time. He knew he had the money—more than forty million dollars in the international treasury.

He had the tremendous economic power of the Teamsters, and Hoffa didn't need John McClellan or Bob Kennedy to tell him how to whip employers and other unions into line.

McClellan and Kennedy had compiled a list of 141 Teamsters officials who, testimony indicated, were involved in "improper activities." Probers had pointed out that 73 Teamsters officials had exploited the Fifth Amendment on each question dealing with misuse of union funds, brutality or violence.

On such problems Hoffa had a standard explanation for publication in the Teamsters magazine: Everyone had a constitutional right to take the Fifth Amendment.

It would always be possible, Hoffa had learned, to find some naive priest or minister to lend his name to a statement on "rehabilitation" that would explain the employment of convicted thieves, robbers, extortionists and other criminals.

James R. Hoffa did not intend to get rid of Barney Baker, Bert Brennan, John McNamara, Joey Glimco or John O'Rourke simply because Senator John McClellan had said, "Hoffa . . . and his chief lieutenants had consorted with major racketeers and gangsters . . . from New York to California, from Florida to Michigan."

Hoffa's second wire-tapping trial in New York City had ended with an acquittal. He was full of confidence in his ability to make a convincing explanation of any of his actions. He had a record to back such confidence: two acquittals and one hung jury in less than a year.

Now that the Benanti decision from the Supreme Court kept the McClellan committee from using recordings of his telephone conversations, Hoffa felt he was completely adequate to deal with all that Bob Kennedy or McClellan could throw in his direction.

The McClellan committee had found that Hoffa was a hard man to trail. He was reaping the benefits of twenty-five years of carefully planned operations. His financial path was difficult to trace. He dealt only in cash. He had had no bank account prior to 1957, he told the committee.

Telephone toll records on Hoffa's most interesting activities were sparse. He carried a pocket full of change and made a habit of using pay telephones on an irregular basis to lessen the possibility that someone would put a tap on the telephone he was using at the moment. He wrote few letters, and he periodically, systematically destroyed the financial records of his local union.

At that point where Dave Beck had mourned the loss of respectability, Jimmy Hoffa had only narrowed his eyes and made plans to launch a full counter-attack against the United States Government. Now he paced the floor of his plush burl walnut and glass office on the third floor of the International Teamsters Building in the nation's capital, glared across the Capitol Plaza at the Senate Office Building, and snapped out orders for a far-reaching campaign against McClellan, Kennedy, Meany, the Justice Department and the relatively innocuous board of monitors.

There were persons who had tried to stop Jimmy Hoffa before. He had found ways to coerce them, coax them to his side, or simply overpower them. Hoffa now seemed convinced he would eventually pack the same wallop of influence in Washington, D. C., that he had in Wayne County, Michigan.

Control of the union magazine, the *International Teamster,* was an important weapon to Hoffa. It could be used to tell rank-and-file members that McClellan's charges were not true. Hoffa ignored the documented record and tried to picture McClellan and Kennedy as engaged in an attack on the wage scale of the truck drivers and dock workers who made up the bulk of the union membership.

"The McClellan committee, big business and its political stooges in the Federal government have gone all out to destroy us," Hoffa wrote in the *International Teamster.*

When he went before the Central Conference of Teamsters on September 23, 1958, he charged that McClellan used "rumors, falsehoods and deliberate perjury" to "smear" him. He accused Bob Kennedy of "trying to destroy this wonderful organization," and made fun of the "young millionaire who has never done a day's work." He pictured Meany as a "stuffed shirt," and said Senator Kennedy was "a reactionary" who would not get a dime of Teamsters support in his bid for the Democratic Presidential nomination in 1960.

At the same time, there was one move after another by Hoffa to undermine and destroy the effectiveness of the three monitors. An action was filed in Federal District Court on September 29, 1958, seeking the ouster of monitor Godfrey Schmidt, the most outspoken Hoffa critic.

It was claimed by Hoffa that Schmidt had worked for a trucking firm, and that this created a "conflict of interest." Schmidt said his work for various employer groups had been known at the time he was named a monitor. He accused the Hoffa group of "trying to ditch me because they can't frighten or buy me off."

John Cunningham, one of the original rank-and-file Teamsters who had hired Schmidt, had switched to the other side and engaged in a series of law suits to harass Schmidt. Cunningham's expenses and his lawyer's fees were paid with money obtained from Moss Herman, a Teamster who was a Hoffa booster. The McClellan committee investigators developed testimony that Herman received part of the money from Hoffa.[1]

Monitor chairman Martin O'Donoghue ran into a stone wall in his effort to make Hoffa comply with recommendations from the monitors. In desperation, he took the problem to Federal Judge Letts. O'Donoghue and Schmidt told the judge that Hoffa paid little or no attention to their recommendations, and they asked that authority be clarified.

Edward Bennett Williams spoke for Hoffa and the Teamsters. He told Judge Letts that, in his view, the monitors had "only advisory" power and could not force action by Hoffa. But Williams added that he believed Hoffa had acted in "reasonable compliance" with the monitors' recommendations.

[1]McClellan committee hearings, Part 43, pages 16131-16178.

O'Donoghue said Hoffa flew into shouting rages and treated the monitors "as if we were defendants." False reports on monitors' actions were printed in the *International Teamster* magazine, and Hoffa refused to print retractions, O'Donoghue told Judge Letts.

O'Donoghue declared it was ludicrous that Hoffa was willing to pay $750 a day to the anti-racket committee that he himself appointed, but refused to pay the salaries and expenses of court-appointed monitors.

The monitor chairman portrayed Hoffa as a violent little man who tried to browbeat the monitors and was evasive and arrogant in his defiance of the Federal court. O'Donoghue said that if the monitors had no more than a "purely advisory" function then the whole effort to clean up the Teamsters was futile.

Judge Letts took the dispute under advisement, but while he was studying the matter the Hoffa organization in Ohio was able to raise the question of monitors' power in a more friendly forum.

On December 2, 1958, Federal Judge James C. Connell of Cleveland became the hero of the International Brotherhood of Teamsters. He ruled that three rank-and-file Teamsters members were ineligible to run for office in Youngstown Local 337 because the union dues checked off by the employers had reached union headquarters a few days late. Judge Connell's decision upheld a ruling by Hoffa, and overruled a decision of the court-appointed monitors.

The Connell decision meant the rank-and-file group, headed by truck drivers Joseph Lawrence Carelly and Joseph Sammartino, had to give up their efforts to displace Joseph Blumetti, a convicted white slaver who was a favorite in the Hoffa organization.[2]

It was a controversial decision, but Judge Connell was accustomed to controversy. Prior to his appointment to the Federal bench in 1954, Judge Connell had been an attorney for the Teamsters locals in Cleveland. The American Bar Association's committee on judicial appointments had protested the

---

[2]McClellan committee, Report No. 1139, pages 714-715. Also see hearings, Part 54, pages 18817-18820.

nomination because of Connell's "arbitrary attitude" as a Common Pleas judge in Cleveland.[3]

The Bar Association in its report to the Senate Judiciary Committee declared that, "in this instance, the office of United States judge is being used for political purposes and not to enhance the more perfect administration of justice."

The nomination was confirmed in August, 1954, despite this adverse report, after several prominent Cleveland attorneys and Republican Senator John Bricker had praised Connell.

The Connell decision in the Carelly-Sammartino case was in complete agreement with the views of Hoffa on the powers of the monitors.[4]

"Their (the monitors) capacity under this consent decree . . . is in an advisory capacity only," Judge Connell wrote. "They are there to help him (Hoffa) . . . . After they make a recommendation and he disagrees with it, and he makes a decision, they have no right to negative his decision . . . ."

Judge Connell accused the monitors of intentionally trying "to embarrass" Hoffa and the Teamsters executive board. In making the decision, the judge had first barred two rank-and-file members from making an appearance in the suit, then ruled against them without hearing their story.

Members of the McClellan committee were outraged. Senator Barry Goldwater, the Arizona Republican, declared that Connell was "totally biased" in his ruling. "It is too bad the committee isn't empowered to investigate the Federal courts," Goldwater said.

The McClellan committee did take testimony that William K. Bronstrup, secretary for Judge Connell, had two side jobs with the Teamsters. While serving as secretary for Judge Connell he received $100 a month from an Ohio Teamsters lawyer, Robert Knee, in connection with some duties on one Teamsters fund, and he received $30 a week for work for the Cleveland welfare fund. It was testified that Judge Connell knew of this arrangement and approved it.[5]

---

[3]Transcript, Senate Judiciary Committee hearing on the nomination of Judge Connell, July 15, 1954, pages 7-8.

[4]McClellan committee, Report No. 1139, pages 714-715.

[5]McClellan committee hearings, Part 54, pages 18817-18820.

On December 11, 1958, Federal Judge Letts ruled that the Teamsters union and Hoffa must comply with all reasonable recommendations from the monitors he had appointed. It was a flat rejection of Judge Connell's philosophy. "The Court does not subscribe to the view that the duties and privileges of the monitors were merely advisory," Judge Letts ruled. The monitors "are empowered to exert every known method of achieving the basic purpose set forth in the consent order, to wit: that a new convention would be free of corruption and in recognition of the rights of the membership."

Judge Letts also ruled against Hoffa's plan for a convention in February, 1959.

Letts's decision held that the monitors had the power to oust any corrupt forces in the Teamsters, including Jimmy Hoffa. In stern words he criticized Hoffa and his group for attempting "to frustrate and block" the monitors' efforts to clean up the union. He warned Hoffa and the executive board that they were only temporary officers, and that his court had all the power it needed to remove them if they did not carry out in good faith the recommendations of the monitors.

Letts said members of the Teamsters should not be barred from seeking office simply because their dues, collected under the checkoff system, were delivered to union headquarters a few days after the first of the month. Otherwise, the judge said, officers of the union who were not subject to the checkoff would have a favored position and could arbitrarily manage union affairs to limit the number of persons eligible to run for office. Letts added: "Because of such discrimination it (the dues rule) is contrary to public policy and void."

Hoffa and Williams said Letts's order would be appealed.

Ultimately, the Court of Appeals for the District of Columbia reversed Judge Letts with respect to the power of the Board of Monitors, holding that, like Masters in Chancery, its power was advisory only and its recommendations need not be followed until approved by the Court and embodied in a court order.

The same day of the Letts decision, the McClellan committee made public a shipping bill for $538.59 which indicated Ohio Teamsters had ordered nine champagne dispensers at $57 each to be engraved for delivery to "Dave Beck, John English,

James R. Hoffa, B. Brennan, Hon. James C. Connell, Senator Geo. Bender, R. Bliss, P. Dorfman, The Pressers."

Judge Connell claimed he had never received the gift from the Teamsters. He declined Chairman McClellan's suggestion that he appear as a witness before the Senate investigating committee.

Committee investigator Walter Sheridan testified he had examined Teamsters records that disclosed the names of persons for whom the champagne dispensers had been bought. He said he then gave the records to Big Bill Presser, Ohio Teamsters boss, to have them photostated. The investigator testified that when the records were returned to him, the section bearing the names of Beck, Hoffa, Bender, Connell, Dorfman, English, Bliss, and Presser had been removed.[6]

On December 19, the McClellan committee voted to cite Presser for contempt of Congress. The committee asked the Justice Department to "determine whether Presser has been guilty of perjury and the willful destruction and mutilation of records under subpoena."

Bender also claimed he had not received the champagne dispenser that was engraved with his name. He also declined McClellan's invitation to appear before the committee.

Chairman McClellan reported to the court-appointed monitors that the Teamsters had paid $24,800.58 to Bender for heading the so-called cleanup commission for less than three months. Bender had received $15,750 in fees at the rate of $250 a day. The rest was for expenses.

Bender was angry at McClellan, and he issued a press statement asserting that he had intended from the outset to give all his fees to charity. "I'm not in this for the money," Bender blustered to me. "I think it is a dirty trick for McClellan and Kennedy to put out how much money I received, and indicate that it was not a proper expenditure."

From a Teamsters executive council meeting in Florida, Hoffa announced that he had received a report from Senator Bender that the Hoffa-appointed "anti-racket" committee had found the Teamsters union "free of corruption."[7]

---

[6]McClellan committee, Report No. 621, pages 26-27.

[7]McClellan committee, Report No. 1139, pages 717-720.

Almost immediately, the two other members of Bender's committee—F. Joseph Donohue, a Washington attorney, and retired Judge Ira W. Jayne of Detroit—disassociated themselves from the Bender report.

I asked Bender how he could make a report that there was no corruption in the Teamsters in the light of the McClellan committee hearings. He replied that "the hearings were one-sided." He said he had written to every one of the Teamsters locals, and to prosecuting attorneys all over the country, for reports on any Teamsters locals. He insisted he had also asked prosecuting attorneys all over the country for reports of Teamsters racketeering. He said he had received reports from officers of various locals indicating there were no racketeers in the union.

Bender's explanation was as ludicrous as his investigation.

With a clean bill of health from Bender at least, Jimmy Hoffa announced he was stepping up a drive to organize ten million city, county, and state employees. He also said he would back a drive to organize the policemen in New York City and in other metropolitan areas in the nation.

The specter of Hoffa and his Teamsters influencing promotions, assignments and discipline in police departments resulted in editorial anguish and public indignation.

Hoffa now carried his menacing program one step further. He said he would back a New York local in its picketing of public buildings to shut off fuel, gasoline and other products to the New York Police Department—"to show the commissioner (Stephen P. Kennedy) the union's economic power."

Police Commissioner Kennedy declared that a police strike was against the law, and that it was a violation of the law for police to join the Teamsters union. He was ready to fight the Hoffa forces.

I called Hoffa to get his reaction. Jimmy was mighty chipper. Contrary to some stories, he said he had no intentions of backing down on his efforts to organize police and municipal employees. "We are just going about it in a little different way."

"Our position has been misrepresented," Hoffa said. "We aren't going to do anything illegal. We have smart lawyers, and we are going to stay within the law."

"Jimmy, why in hell are you sticking your nose into all this police organizing?" I protested. "Haven't you enough problems if you really mean what you say about cleaning up the Teamsters?"

"We are doing it as a public service," Hoffa replied with what was probably a straight face. "We want to take the security of these people out of the hands of the politicians."

"You actually believe that putting the police of this country in the Teamsters is in the public interest?" I said.

"Unionization of the police is in the public interest because it allows the police to support their families without taking side jobs," Hoffa replied. "Police who take side jobs get obligated to people outside the police department. I don't think the police should be obligated to any of these business interests." He scoffed at my suggestion that the Teamsters union might be a bad influence on law enforcement if it controlled jobs in the police departments.

I asked Hoffa if he was worried about the McClellan committee.

"You know me better than that, Clark," he replied. "I take it as it comes. That committee isn't going to be around forever. They'll be going for another nine₊ months, and Bob Kennedy will be running off to try to elect his brother President." Hoffa said he thought he could stand on his head until the McClellan committee folded. He talked with the utmost confidence in his ability to outlast the Senate committee and emerge on top.

In late December, the Senate Internal Security subcommittee charged that Hoffa's proposed alliance of all transportation unions was a "menace to national security." "This alliance includes among its directive forces two categories which are notorious for their defiance of law, namely Communists and racketeers," the subcommittee report stated.

It pointed out that although Hoffa talked as a foe of Communists, he was willing and even eager to do business with Harry Bridges, head of the International Longshoremen's Warehousemen's Union (I.L.W.U.) of the West Coast. The subcommittee report noted the number of Communists and former Communists who had dealt with Hoffa's Teamsters in recent years, and it warned that a strike by the transportation alliance "could strangle the military force of the nation in the event of war."[8]

The juke-box hearings before the McClellan committee had demonstrated the Teamsters' connections with many of the biggest underworld figures in the nation—Abner (Longie) Zwillman, top-ranking gangland figure in New Jersey; Vito Genovese, head of an international narcotics ring; Tony Accardo, an old Capone mobster from Chicago, and Carlos Marcello, identified as a gambling czar and Mafia hoodlum in the New Orleans area.

But the underworld connections of his Teamsters were not as devastating to Hoffa's prestige among the union members as was new testimony in February, 1959, that the International Brotherhood of Teamsters under Hoffa did business with a man who was a Communist at least as late as 1956.

The testimony showed that a man expelled from the C.I.O. for Communist activity had been receiving financial help from Hoffa and Harold Gibbons as late as 1958.[9]

That man was identified as Gus Brown, operator of an independent furniture workers' union in Los Angeles. Robert Savage, a business agent for Teamsters Local 208 in Los Angeles, testified he was one of several union men who were told to walk a picket line to help Brown. Savage testified that the instructions came from John Filipoff, the burly secretary-treasurer of Los Angeles Teamster Local 208 and a Hoffa favorite.

"I like to pride myself on being an American citizen," Savage told the committee. "I don't choose to be helping those who are seeking to overthrow the U. S. Government." He said he walked the picket line because he would have been without a job if he had refused to carry out Filipoff's instructions.

The McClellan committee used letters and financial records to show that Hoffa and Gibbons had expended at least $11,166 in Teamsters funds to finance the operations of Brown's Furniture Workers Local 123.

Meyer (Mike) Singer, a swarthy 250-pound Los Angeles Teamsters boss, answered with the Fifth Amendment on questions dealing with certain California Communists. He also took the Fifth Amendment on a long series of questions dealing with

---

[9] McClellan committee, Report No. 1139, pages 701-704.

[8] McClellan committee, Report No. 1139, pages 726-727.

his spending of union funds and allegations that he extorted money from employers in the Los Angeles area.

The McClellan committee heard testimony that union funds were used to pay the expenses of a beautiful, buxom woman traveling companion for Singer. According to the testimony, the woman accompanied Singer to all parts of the country on organizing drives for Hoffa.[10]

In spite of all the information turned up by the McClellan committee, it was difficult for the Justice Department to get court action to clean up the stables.

A special Federal grand jury started an investigation of Teamsters officials in northern Ohio and encountered the opposition of Federal Judge James Connell in Cleveland. He quashed subpoenas calling for the appearance of 13 union leaders and their records. The judge charged the grand jury investigation was "a fishing expedition." He called it illegal search and seizure and forced the Justice Department to beat a retreat.

In Washington, D.C., Federal Judge Joseph R. Jackson acquitted Clyde Cardinal Crosby, the Portland Teamster, of a perjury charge arising out of his testimony before the McClellan committee. Judge Jackson ruled it was immaterial whether Crosby told the truth under oath before the McClellan committee, because, in the judge's opinion, the questions were not closely enough connected with obtaining information for labor legislation.

Federal District Judge Richard B. Keech directed acquittal of bakery union president James G. Cross on another perjury charge. Cross denied taking part in the beating of a man and his wife in a San Francisco hotel to intimidate the opposition in a bakery union convention. He was indicted after several witnesses testified he was present and took part in the beatings. Judge Keech ruled that it was immaterial whether Cross lied, because the question was irrelevant to the legislative function of the labor racket committee.

Chairman McClellan declared that the rulings were "ridiculous." Justice Department attorneys were in despair. If the rulings of Judges Keech, Jackson and Connell were to stand, it

---

[10]McClellan committee, Report No. 1139, pages 671-672.

would be almost impossible to follow up the McClellan committee with investigations or perjury prosecutions.

It was also being demonstrated that local law enforcement officials were equally ineffective in dealing with the money and political power of the alliance of gangsters and union leaders in such areas as New York, New Jersey and Chicago.

The McClellan committee was grinding out the evidence of the crippled or corrupted law enforcement that allowed an underworld-union alliance to grab monopolies in the operations of juke boxes and other coin-machine devices.

But the picture wasn't all black. On February 19, 1959, a Federal Court jury in Tacoma, Washington, convicted Dave Beck of evading $240,000 in income taxes from 1950 through 1953, and for failing to file returns. Federal Judge George H. Boldt thanked the jurors, fined Beck $60,000, and sentenced him to five years in prison.

Beck said it wasn't the first time an innocent man had been convicted, and he gave notice that he would appeal.[11]

The Beck conviction didn't jar Jimmy Hoffa's confidence. He said he would not fire Joe DeGrandis, the twice-convicted head of a New York Teamsters local who had been organizing the juke-box business. Nor would be take action against Joseph (Joey) Glimco, the Teamsters boss in Chicago who was linked with Capone mobsters and the juke-box monopoly.

Hoffa said he was going ahead with his organizing drive in Puerto Rico despite comments by Governor Luis Munoz Marin that the Teamsters were a corrupt organization that was not wanted there.

He was more confident than ever about his battle with the

---

[11]Beck was convicted on four counts charging tax evasion and on two counts charging that he had taken part in the filing of false income tax forms for the Teamsters union for 1950 and 1952. He was sentenced to pay a $10,000 fine and five years on each count, with the prison terms to be served concurrently. The United States Court of Appeals for the Ninth Circuit sustained the convictions on the two counts charging that Beck had taken part in the filing of false union tax forms, but it reversed the four counts charging tax evasion following an earlier court precedent that "embezzled" funds were not taxable as income. On June 11, 1962, the United States Supreme Court declined to review the Ninth Circuit decision. This left standing a five-year jail sentence and a $20,000 fine. Beck entered prison at MacNeil Island Federal Penitentiary in Puget Sound on June 20, 1962.

A.F.L.-C.I.O. president, George Meany. The A.F.L.-C.I.O. decision not to oust the Carpenters union was amusing to Hoffa.

"They've got a double standard," Hoffa said. "There was no difference between the Carpenters' case and the Teamsters' case, but they knew they couldn't oust the Carpenters or all the building trades would walk out. Meany and the rest of the A.F.L.-C.I.O. are businessmen. If the Carpenters and the building trades unions walk out, the A.F.L.-C.I.O. will be operating at a deficit."

Hoffa boasted that his Teamsters had more money and more members than when they were kicked out of the A.F.L.-C.I.O. He said frankly he would like to get back into the A.F.L.-C.I.O., but that he wouldn't return under any agreement to give up autonomy of the Teamsters.

"It will be on my terms," Hoffa declared.

I wasn't sure that he was wrong. After everything that had been exposed about his operations, he still had important people kow-towing to him. They included employers as well as politicians.

That was made brutally clear on February 26, 1959, at a testimonial dinner for Raymond Cohen, president of Philadelphia Teamsters Local 107 and a trustee of the International Teamsters. Hoffa was an honored guest. The McClellan committee had exposed fraud and misuse of funds in Local 107, as well as the use of convicted criminals as business agents.[12] Cohen's operations of Local 107 had been condemned by the court-appointed monitors, and still he was given a testimonial dinner.

In the light of the testimony, and Cohen's Fifth Amendment plea, I wondered how municipal judges from Philadelphia could attend the dinner. I wondered why the former Pennsylvania attorney general, Thomas McBride, would allow his name to be used as an "honored guest" on the Cohen dinner program.

Perhaps it was the voters' fault for being so complacent about these things. They would be enraged if their officials attended or sponsored a testimonial dinner for a Communist. Why weren't they just as angry when the same officials attended functions honoring persons who had recently been proclaimed dishonest by the McClellan labor racket committee?

---

[12]McClellan committee, Report No. 621, page 10.

XXXI

J.F.K. Goes All the Way

By the summer of 1959, the McClellan committee hearings had established Jimmy Hoffa as the villain of organized labor in America.

There were a few leaders in the A.F.L.-C.I.O. who felt compelled to deal with him and say a good word for him, but most of labor agreed with A.F.L.-C.I.O. President George Meany who called Hoffa an "outlaw." A few political figures were still willing to take Teamsters campaign money and some cautiously tried to play Hoffa's game on labor legislation, but most politicians felt compelled to avoid public identification with the little renegade from Detroit.

Senate and House debates on labor reform legislation were liberally sprinkled with derogatory comments about Hoffa. Some legislators, still obviously carrying the ball for the Teamsters, went out of their way to assure the Congress that they were not protecting Hoffa.

Most newspaper editorials and cartoons dealt with the labor reform proposals in an overly simplified manner, interpreting them as "stop Hoffa" measures. Every section of those proposals was discussed from a standpoint of how it would apply to Hoffa, Barney Baker, Johnny Dioguardi, Tony Ducks Corallo, or other equally notorious figures in what the McClellan committee called Hoffa's "hoodlum empire."

Chairman John L. McClellan and the Kennedy brothers, Jack and Bob, emerged as the heroes in the labor reform drama. Lack of Presidential aspirations permitted Chairman McClellan to stay above the partisan political squabbles in the hearings and on the Senate floor. His awesome reputation for fairness and non-partisan objectivity made him feared and respected by both sides.

Senator Kennedy's obvious Presidential ambitions became the natural target for most of the Republican barbs, but on the issue of Jimmy Hoffa few quarreled with the young Massachusetts Senator. No one wanted to appear to be a defender of Jimmy or the Teamsters.

Senator Kennedy piloted the labor reform bill through the Senate. He was a key figure in the compromises that were finally signed into law in September, 1959. This bill was the first significant legislative record for the junior Senator from Massachusetts. It was personally important from the standpoint of Senator Kennedy's drive for the 1960 Democratic Presidential nomination, but it was far from a total victory. The legislation did not carry the Kennedy name as the Kennedys hoped it would, but was referred to as the Landrum-Griffin Labor Management Reporting and Disclosure Act of 1959.

The new law was not as tough as Senator McClellan wanted it to be, but he accepted it as a substantial step forward. Tighter reporting on union finances and tighter administration of union elections were required. In general, the legislation was an effort to protect the rights of rank-and-file union members in their dealings with union bosses. Efforts by labor lobbyists, including the A.F.L.-C.I.O. and Hoffa's Teamsters representatives, to weaken the legislation would have been more successful if it had not been for stubborn insistence by Senator McClellan on a "Bill of Rights" for union members.

Senator Kennedy and Majority Leader Lyndon B. Johnson, both seeking A.F.L.-C.I.O. political favor in connection with the 1960 Democratic convention, accepted compromises against Senator McClellan's objections.

Even with all the A.F.L.-C.I.O.-sponsored compromises, the new labor reform legislation presented problems for the loose-spending and free-wheeling Teamsters. It required a tighter accounting of funds, made the financial reports public, and guaranteed union members the important right to go into court and force an accounting on the handling of union business.

Most important to Hoffa and his associates at that time were the new law's provisions designed to limit the use of union money for lawyers to defend dishonest labor leaders or for "paying, directly or indirectly, the fine of any (union) officer or employee convicted of any willful violation of the Act."

The new labor reform law, if tightly enforced, spelled real trouble for the Teamsters. Jimmy Hoffa and his racketeering associates needed lawyers and funds to pay the lawyers. The tighter reporting provisions of the law made it difficult to hide what had been common—expenditures for bail bonds, lawyers, fines and even salaries for men who were convicted and sent to prison.

Hoffa's problems now were legion. The court-appointed monitors were on his back, the McClellan committee was still prying into Teamsters' dealings in every part of the country, and a dozen state and Federal grand juries were in action and had already indicted many of Hoffa's closest associates. Also, the A.F.L.-C.I.O. was exerting pressure to try to force its member unions to abandon pacts with Hoffa.[1]

Perhaps most serious to Hoffa was the danger he faced in revelations of his Sun Valley real estate project in Florida. As one of the trustees, Hoffa was barred by law from making direct use of several hundred million dollars in the Teamsters Central States Southeast-Southwest Area pension fund. Therefore, he denied that the interest-free deposit of $400,000 of funds from Local 299 was serving as collateral on a $395,000 loan from the Florida National Bank at Orlando. Detroit Teamster Owen Bert Brennan and Hoffa had a major financial interest in the Sun Valley promotion scheme, and the bank was preparing to foreclose. In that event Hoffa would be exposed as having pledged union funds for a personal real estate venture. Hoffa needed $400,000 in a hurry. His pal, Benjamin Dranow, suggested a solution.[2]

Dranow's plan was simple and bold. He suggested to financially pressed contractors and real estate developers an easy way

---

[1]McClellan committee, Report No. 1417, pages 448-449.

[2]McClellan committee, Report No. 1417, pages 225-227.

to obtain huge loans on some high-risk projects. For a ten per cent commission he indicated he could arrange multi-million-dollar loans from Teamsters pension funds through Jimmy Hoffa. Working with an accountant and several promoters, who he said handled the details, Dranow advised asking for a bigger loan to cover the ten per cent commission. He did not seem concerned about the size of the loan nor how poor the collateral might be. One thing he did specify—the payoff had to be in cash.

Some builders balked at the suggestion of a cash payoff. A cancelled check would give them a record of the transaction for business expense deduction, but Dranow wanted no checks. He insisted on cash in small, old bills to be available for delivery when he desired it.

Dranow and his associates arranged millions in loans from Teamsters pension funds. Payoffs of as much as $400,000 were made. Dranow tucked the cash into a black bag, or slipped it under his shirt, with the comment that he was taking it to "the boss" in Washington.

With Dranow's help, Hoffa was bailed out of the $400,000 problem at Sun Valley, the bank released the $400,000 in funds of Detroit Local 299, and it appeared that for the moment the Sun Valley problem was settled. However, as later events showed, Hoffa's trouble with Sun Valley really was just beginning.[3]

Monitor chairman Martin F. O'Donoghue and Federal Judge F. Dickinson Letts were demanding that Hoffa begin to take steps to rid the Teamsters of the racketeers, the robbers, perjurers, and extortionists who continued to hold union office. Even as Hoffa maintained he was cleaning up the Teamsters, he named a convicted perjurer, Frank Matula, as one of three trustees who had the responsibility for the honesty of the accounts on the multi-million-dollar International Teamsters treasury.

Only a few months earlier, Matula, treasurer of Los Angeles Teamsters Local 386, had been convicted of lying to a California investigative body about a garbage collection racket. The ludicrous result of this appointment was that in January, 1960,

[3]Transcript, U. S. v Burris, Hoffa *et al.,* in the United States District Court for the Northern District of Illinois, Eastern Division (Chicago), 63 Cr.-317.

Matula obtained leave from his jail term in order to go to Washington, D.C., to perform his function as a trustee of the International Teamsters.

The Matula case was symbolic of Hoffa's continued use of convicted Teamsters, so O'Donoghue decided it was necessary to initiate steps to remove Hoffa from office. Ouster action started against him resulted in a mammoth attack by Hoffa on the whole monitorship concept. Teamsters lawyers stalled all action against Hoffa and filed dozens of petitions to load the desk of Judge Letts and inundate the court with work.

Teamsters lawyers were so numerous that Marty O'Donoghue referred to them in court as "the Teamsters bar association." It became a full-time task simply to read the complicated motions that immobilized the monitorship. Mountains of paper swamped the 80-year-old judge and forced O'Donoghue to hire a large Washington law firm to fight through the maze of legal jockeying. There were more than sixty pages of docket entries, compared with the normal case that can be handled on one page. An extremely long case seldom takes more than two docket pages. More than 1,200 docket entries, more than thirty hearings, more than thirty appeals made the monitorship case the bulkiest record on file in the Federal District Court in Washington.[4]

"They are trying to harass us with litigation and smother us out of existence so we cannot perform the function for which the Federal court monitorship was established," O'Donoghue said.

Routine work was handled by lawyers Herbert J. (Jack) Miller and John Cassidy, as Judge Letts and O'Donoghue ignored threats and subtle bribe offers from shadowy Teamsters sources to push forward with a few of the actions that might result in actual removal of Hoffa.

The McClellan subcommittee concluded "that Hoffa . . . used every means available to him to thwart bona fide attempts

---

[4] For an account of the harassing action by the Teamsters union see the testimony of Monitor Chairman Martin F. O'Donoghue on January 24, 1961, in the hearings on "James R. Hoffa and continued underworld control of New York Teamster Local 239." The hearing was before the Permanent Subcommittee on Investigation of the Senate Government Operations Committee. Also, see Report No. 1784 issued by the same subcommittee on July 25, 1962, pages 28 through 40.

on the part of the U. S. district court appointed monitors to accomplish a cleanup of corrupt and criminal elements within the Teamster movement."

"The matter relating to Raymond Cohen and other officers of Local 107 provides a classic example of the extremes to which Hoffa will go to maintain corrupt elements within the Teamster movement and to 'acquit' officers concerning whom there was readily available evidence of forgeries, misappropriation of union funds, and other improper activities."

As the months passed, it became apparent that O'Donoghue and his legal associates were engaged in an exercise in futility. Letts and O'Donoghue were able to keep abreast of all of the Teamsters maneuvers and the misrepresentations and perjury by Teamsters witnesses. However, the Appeals Court seemed to miss the implications inherent in the ocean of paper the Teamsters filed. It represented a serious challenge to the Federal courts. I hoped Judge Letts and Marty O'Donoghue would be successful, but by mid-1960 I was not optimistic.

The McClellan committee and the Federal and state grand juries continued to create persistent irritations for Hoffa and his associates, but he was one of the first to recognize that his major problem was the political aspirations of Senator John F. Kennedy. The anti-Hoffa drive of Jack and Bob Kennedy had made the Kennedy brother act familiar in every household in the nation. Identified as opponents of the gangsters and racketeers who infested organized labor, they were associated with the drive to break Hoffa's power. No doubt existed that Bob Kennedy was doing all he could to jail Hoffa and free labor from Jimmy's stranglehold.

Bob Kennedy, as chief counsel for the McClellan committee, was a threat to Hoffa even though he had no power to prosecute. Under a Kennedy Administration, Jimmy Hoffa knew the full pressure of law enforcement would be used against him.

In his determination that there would be no Kennedy Administration, Hoffa was not as naïve as some who believed that John Kennedy had no chance. He devoted issue after issue of the *International Teamster*, the union's magazine, to attacks on Senator Kennedy and Bob Kennedy. In speeches before labor groups he called them "anti-labor" and blamed them for passing the Landrum-Griffin labor reform bill. Each attack on either Bob or Jack Kennedy proved to be helpful to Senator Kennedy's drive for the Democratic Presidential nomination.

Hoffa's activity against the Kennedys in the Democratic primaries backfired. In the crucial Wisconsin primary, Bob Kennedy seized on Teamsters support given to Senator Hubert H. Humphrey, the Minnesota Democrat, as an indication that Humphrey was Jimmy Hoffa's man.

When John Kennedy was victorious in the crucial tests in Wisconsin and West Virginia, Hoffa went all out to back Majority Leader Lyndon B. Johnson as the man most likely to block the Kennedy drive. Hoffa and his lobbyists were friendly with Robert G. (Bobby) Baker, then secretary to the Democratic majority in the Senate and a leading Johnson-for-President organizer.

In the last frenzied moves before the Democratic convention, Bob Kennedy rapped Lyndon Johnson as the Teamsters' candidate.

Hoffa was furious when John Kennedy was nominated on the first ballot as the Democratic Presidential candidate. Johnson as the Vice-Presidential candidate was no solace. The idea of any administration with Bob Kennedy in it was pure poison to Hoffa. He swung his support to Richard M. Nixon, the Republican candidate. Bitter anti-Kennedy propaganda was distributed to the Teamsters by Hoffa, but it is certain that many of them rejected it. Hoffa's anti-labor charges against the Kennedys seemed ludicrous in the light of the warm endorsement Kennedy received from the A.F.L.-C.I.O. where the only real displeasure was with the naming of Johnson as the Vice-Presidential candidate.

In Jimmy Hoffa's eyes, the tragedy of November, 1960, was that John F. Kennedy was elected President of the United States. Within a few weeks Robert F. Kennedy was named Attorney General of the United States, with direct control over investigation and prosecution of Federal crimes. Hoffa knew he was in for a rough time.

XXXII

Pincers on Hoffa

Jimmy Hoffa forced the surrender of the federal court-appointed monitor in February, 1961, but he realized a long, hard battle for survival was in the offing. As Judge F. Dickinson Letts reluctantly brought the monitorship to an end, a Justice Department team was being assembled to devote full time and attention to Hoffa and his associates.

Herbert J. (Jack) Miller, who had served as lawyer for the monitors, was named by Attorney General Kennedy to be Assistant Attorney General in charge of the Criminal Division. Steeped in two years of study of Teamsters activities, Miller needed no adjustment to his new job.

Walter Sheridan, a 35-year-old former F.B.I. agent and an investigator on the McClellan committee staff, was named a special consultant to the Attorney General. It was never officially stated that a "Hoffa unit" was established, but it existed and its headquarters was Sheridan's unpretentious office in room 2509 in the Justice Department. The out-of-the-way office on an inner corridor, with no name on the door, permitted visitors to slip in and out with little possibility of being observed.

John Cassidy, a young lawyer who had worked for the court-appointed monitor, became Sheridan's assistant. Accountant Carmine Bellino, a special assistant to President Kennedy, had a small office nearby, in addition to his White House office.

Sheridan and Miller had a free hand in hiring lawyers or in shifting career Justice Department lawyers to this unit that was concentrating on Hoffa and his associates. From outside, they recruited James Neal of Nashville; Charles Shaffer, a former assistant United States Attorney in New York; Charles Smith of Seattle, Thomas McKeon·of New York, Thomas Kennelly of San Francisco, and Paul Allred of St. Louis. Career Justice Department lawyers who were moved into the unit included Abe Poretz, a veteran trial attorney who had been working on a number of Teamsters cases; William French, an aggressive and able young Notre Dame graduate; Thomas J. McTiernan and James Canavan, two former F.B.I. agents; William Ryan, a former Marine colonel, and Robert Peloquin, whose background included legal work with the Federal Communications Commission as well as the Justice Department.

The "Hoffa unit" was given top priority. Sheridan had a close personal relationship with Jack Miller and William Hundley, head of the section dealing with organized crime. Special liaison was provided through Courtney Evans, a longtime friend of Sheridan, who was an assistant to F.B.I. Director J. Edgar Hoover. Sheridan's personal rapport with Attorney General Kennedy made the Attorney General's office accessible day or night.

The men of that unit believed, as Bob Kennedy believed, that successful prosecution of Hoffa was essential to the preservation of any respect for law and order. They had no doubt about the existence of the crime and corruption. It was simply a matter of able and persistent investigators having the necessary backing to help them obtain the evidence necessary to prosecute Hoffa and his racketeering associates.

Jimmy Hoffa was not flattered by the creation of this special unit. It would have been difficult for him to have been unaware of its existence as Sheridan and his crew of specialists popped up in all parts of the country to investigate or to coordinate F.B.I. investigations, to handle federal grand juries, or to serve as special prosecutors. In the first six months, grand juries were working on Hoffa-associated cases in Florida, California, New York, Detroit, Chicago, Minneapolis, St. Louis, and Washington, D. C.

For the first time, Hoffa and his million-dollar stable of Teamsters lawyers faced a superior force. F.B.I. investigators followed every Hoffa trip that seemed of consequence, observed Hoffa's associations with racketeers, and obtained records of Hoffa's long distance telephone calls. There were government lawyers to meet every legal trick the Teamsters lawyers could devise. Most important, Sheridan, by direct contact with Robert Kennedy, could obtain immediate help from President Kennedy at any point it was needed.

Sheridan and Bob Kennedy were only mildly concerned in June, 1961, when Federal District Judge Joseph Lieb of Tampa, Florida, dismissed the mail fraud indictment against Hoffa that had been based on the Sun Valley real estate project. Lieb ruled that the federal grand jury which returned the indictment was not properly selected under the terms of the 1957 civil rights law.

Bob Kennedy commented that Judge Lieb's decision "did not go to the merits of the case against Hoffa," but only to the technical problem of the selection of the grand jury which had returned the indictment on December 7, 1960, which was the last month of the Eisenhower Administration.

A few important convictions had been obtained prior to January, 1960. By the first six months of 1961 the pattern was unmistakable. Justice Department lawyers were getting tough with lower-rank Teamsters and others who were helping to hide crimes by giving false testimony or destroying records. Witnesses must be convinced that it would be less dangerous to cooperate with law enforcement officials than to risk conviction for perjury or obstruction of justice.

The perjury conviction of Frank Collins helped make the point. Collins, former secretary-treasurer of Hoffa's Detroit Local 299, delivered false records on Local 299 to a New York grand jury. He was tripped up and sentenced to a three-year prison term because records he said he signed in 1953 were written on a typewriter manufactured with a type face which was not invented until 1955. Destruction of union records by William (Big Bill) Presser, chairman of the Ohio Conference of Teamsters, resulted in his conviction and a prison sentence for contempt of Congress. The records he had destroyed were under subpoena by the McClellan committee.

Mrs. Sally Hucks, who had been chief telephone operator at the Woodner Hotel in Washington, D.C., paid a big price for her association with the Teamsters. She was convicted of perjury, conspiracy, and obstruction of justice for destroying and altering records of telephone calls made from the Woodner by Hoffa and other Teamsters.

Mrs. Hucks insisted she had never received more than a smile from Jimmy Hoffa, and there was no proof to the contrary. But testimony showed that she lied about her role in destroying records that were under subpoena by the McClellan committee, and that she lied in denying that Ben Dranow gave her a mink stole and financed a month-long trip she took to Honolulu, Hawaii. Hoffa told her only that the Honolulu Teamsters would see to it that she was properly entertained, she insisted.

Although she was queen for a month, Sally Hucks lost her $65-a-week job at the Woodner, and the court sentenced her to twenty months to five years in prison.

Pressure was also on the shakedown racketeers. Robert B. (Barney) Baker, one of Hoffa's Central States organizers, was sentenced to two years in prison after conviction of taking money from an employer in violation of the Taft-Hartley labor law. Also convicted on a similar charge was Edward F. Weinheimer, former Teamsters official in the New York area, who was sentenced to one to three years in the federal penitentiary.

These were not big names in the Teamsters operation, and the convictions seldom received more than local notice. But the message was getting across in important places. Only Collins and Weinheimer had been actually imprisoned because appeals were still pending on the other convictions. The full impact was not to come until appeals were exhausted and the perjurers, obstructors, and shakedown artists finally were behind bars.

Walter Sheridan made Hoffa a 24-hour-a-day project. He knew where Hoffa was nearly every hour of the day or night, or he could find out within a matter of minutes. Through informants in the Teamsters union, Sheridan knew most of Hoffa's schedule in advance.

Daily reports of Hoffa's speeches at local Teamsters meetings, or at secret meetings in the Teamsters headquarters, reached Sheridan. He was aware of Hoffa's reactions to the indictments, convictions or other government moves to tighten the pincers on the Teamsters.

Across the country, men walked into F.B.I. offices to volunteer confessions or cooperation in hopes of immunity from federal prosecution.

Certain of the Teamsters lawyers, convinced that Hoffa would eventually fall, tried to cooperate with Justice. Rarely did one informer know the identity of others, because Justice was wary of exposing them to men who might be serving in a double agent role.

Obviously, in some cases Hoffa men were pretending to cooperate with the Justice Department while in fact seeking information for Hoffa's use against Sheridan or Bob Kennedy.

Hoffa was aware that some of his close associates were talking, but he didn't know who they were. He was worried and angry, but he fought to demonstrate that he was not on the run and did not intend to flee from Bob Kennedy or the Justice Department.

Evidence of the strain was showing on him as he dealt with his associates, but publicly he gave no indications of fear or weakness. If Hoffa had doubts about his ability to defeat the Justice Department, the doubts were not evident. Hoffa only reached out for more power and more money.

As long as he controlled the Teamsters' mighty tentacles and the Teamsters' treasury, Hoffa knew he was a formidable adversary for the United States Government. Though cracks showed in his power structure, he believed he could hold it together with a show of strength. When signs of wavering or weakness could have been disastrous, Hoffa held his grip with a dramatic display of strength and confidence.

Hoffa called a Teamsters convention in July, 1961, to dramatize his contempt for the government, the press, and public opinion. He made plans to use that convention to seize more power, boost his salary from $50,000 to $75,000 a year, and push through a boost in union dues as a means of forcing the members to finance his all-out war on the Kennedy Administration.

Several days prior to that convention, Sheridan had a complete summary of Hoffa's convention tactics, including the plan to elevate Frank Fitzsimmons, a Detroit Teamster who had taken the Fifth Amendment before the McClellan committee, to a position as an International Teamsters vice-president.

Also, it was reported that Hoffa planned to make a slight switch in the membership of the three international trustees. William Presser, twice-convicted Ohio Teamsters boss, was slated to replace John Rohrich of Cleveland. Apparently Rohrich's error was that he had not been criticized in the McClellan committee reports or by monitor chairman Marty O'Donoghue. Rohrich probably was the only one who had not been, since the other two members were Matula, the convicted perjurer, and Raymond Cohen, who took the Fifth Amendment before the McClellan committee on a series of questions dealing with misappropriation of Teamsters union funds. At the time of the convention, Cohen was under indictment on Pennsylvania state charges of misappropriating large sums of money from his local union treasury. (Cohen was convicted on June 3, 1963, and sentenced to a one- to two-year prison term and fined $500.)

Hoffa adopted a public-be-damned attitude. He to'd the 2,000 delegates to the convention he didn't care what the press, the public or the Kennedy Administration thought about his actions. This attitude was against the advice of close associates who felt it was only courting more trouble.

It obviously was Hoffa's belief that he couldn't be in more trouble, and that any sign of weakness could be fatal. He explained to the convention that he was boosting the union dues by one dollar a month, with sixty cents of this amount going to the International Teamsters treasury and forty cents staying with the local unions. This would amount to another one million dollars a month in the international treasury on the basis of nearly 1,600,000 dues-paying members.

An additional twelve million dollars a year would bolster the "legislative machine" which Hoffa told the delegates "will be second to none in the United States."

Hoffa lashed into President Kennedy as "anti-labor," and accused Robert Kennedy of assigning 150 F.B.I. agents to that Teamsters convention.

In a meeting with the Michigan Teamsters delegates on July 3, Hoffa told them that they should be wary of "Mata Haris" in their midst. He warned the Michigan Teamsters that the union's counterspies had discovered that the F.B.I. had sent "dozens of women agents" to Miami Beach to lure delegates into compromising positions in an alleged plot to divulge confidential Teamsters information.

He declared that Bob Kennedy was using F.B.I. agents in Miami Beach to seek grounds for challenging Hoffa's re-election. Many law enforcement officials were, in fact, assigned to keep track of the racketeers among the delegates as well as those who merely congregated around Hoffa's Teamsters with no official status, but Sheridan said Hoffa's figure was many times too high.

Sheridan and John Cassidy stayed at the Hotel Patricia, a small and ordinary sort of place away from the Deauville and the Monte Carlo, those two lavish hotels which were the centers of most of the union's convention activity. I stayed at the Hotel Patricia as a safety measure, for it was headquarters for Federal law enforcement officers during the convention, and it was unlikely that any of the Teamsters hoodlums would appear there. I tried to eat one meal a day with Sheridan and Cassidy to keep pace with the espionage and counter-espionage that were taking place. However, it wasn't always possible, for Sheridan often was out at odd hours, meeting with informants from the Teamsters union at 1:30 a.m. or 2:30 a.m., or bouncing out to take early morning calls that informants were making from pay telephone booths where it was unlikely their calls would be intercepted.

An editorial in the *Miami Herald* struck sharply at Hoffa's salary grab and the dictatorial framework he was establishing for handling the power and funds of the Teamsters union. Hoffa was fighting mad as he went before the convention to denounce the Knight newspapers, and to speak contemptuously of editorials which he said were "written by men employed at wages less than earned by Teamsters truck drivers."

Even as Jimmy Hoffa said he didn't care about public opinion, he tried to increase his own stature with the Teamsters delegates and to win approval of activities that had been criticized by the McClellan committee.

On July 5, Teamsters general counsel Edward Bennett Williams stirred the convention with the charge that Chairman McClellan and his chief counsel, Robert Kennedy, had engaged in "guilt by accusation" in the investigation of the Teamsters.

Williams avoided specifics but created the impression that the McClellan committee produced no evidence of misuse of union funds or union power, yet the committee had accused union officers of wrong-doing by "rumor, hearsay and innuendo."

Lawyer Williams spoke of six acquittals of Teamsters in the courts, but made no reference to any of the convictions.

In his turn, Hoffa praised Williams, then cautioned the delegates that they should not "go around chuckling while someone else is on the front page or in the cartoons."

"Tomorrow it may be you," Hoffa warned.

It was already apparent that some of Hoffa's closest associates were missing. Barney Baker, thrice-convicted labor racketeer, had been jailed after violating a court's travel restrictions while awaiting the result of an appeal on a criminal charge of taking money from an employer. Benjamin Dranow had been arrested in Miami a few days before the convention and taken back to Minneapolis to stand trial on federal mail fraud and bankruptcy charges.

No one had to remind the delegates that many other Teamsters had been convicted or were under indictment. Anthony (Tony Pro) Provenzano, an international vice president from Newark, was on the platform with Hoffa despite an indictment charging him with being a central figure in an extortion scheme. Louis N. (Babe) Triscaro of the Cleveland Teamsters remained a constant companion to Hoffa and a convention functionary despite a conviction for armed robbery and evidence that he had a large interest in a trucking business.

The Teamsters convention could boast a roster of unusual characters, but it sorely lacked an air of respectability. The attempt to achieve this culminated in Edward Bennett Williams escorting John Roosevelt to the platform.

John Roosevelt, Republican son of the late Franklin D. Roosevelt, was a partner in an investment consultant firm that handled about twenty-five per cent of the one hundred and sixty million dollars in the Central States Southeast-Southwest pension fund.

The son of the former President agreed to address the delegates, and he went all out for Jimmy Hoffa.

"If I were a delegate there would be no question in my mind that I would vote for Jimmy Hoffa," John Roosevelt said. "I hope that in the years to come Jimmy will have more time to work for the affirmative side of your aims, rather than to be under the continual harassment of certain agencies of the government."

Hoffa used the John Roosevelt speech in a sort of "affection by association" maneuver to capitalize on the esteem for the late President Roosevelt and his wife in the minds of many of the delegates.

"Great people are not by accident; they are born," Hoffa intoned. "It is too bad there isn't another Roosevelt in the White House today."

The ovation for John Roosevelt was deafening, and as the smiling financial adviser came off the platform I asked him his reason for coming to the convention and supporting Hoffa.

"My firm serves as adviser to Teamsters pension funds," he said. "I am down here to attend the convention the same as I would attend a bankers convention or some other convention."

On July 7, 1961, Hoffa was re-elected president of the International Teamsters for a five-year term. He became the highest paid and most absolute ruler in the history of American labor. His only opponent, Milton Liss, president of Teamsters Local 478 in Newark, New Jersey, received only fifteen votes of the 1,875 cast.

John F. English, secretary-treasurer of the International Teamsters, led the tributes to Hoffa in a speech to the cheering delegates.

"Hoffa fought everybody in this country," English said. "He fought judges, lawyers and everybody."

The aging secretary-treasurer stressed Hoffa's defiance of the federal court-appointed monitors. "No matter what the monitors said to us, no matter what our lawyers said to us," English boasted, he and Hoffa had done as they pleased until they broke the monitorship and forced a call of this special convention.

Hoffa displayed his contempt for his critics as he told the cheering delegates, "I care not what people say about me, only you."

Delegates to the convention were, for the most part, the paid officers and business agents of local unions, totally uninterested in the views of Congressional committees, the A.F.L.-C.I.O., or the newspapers.

They lambasted "trouble makers" such as James Luken, head of Teamsters Joint Council 26 in Cincinnati, who had given a five-minute speech for Liss for Teamsters president.

Luken carefully avoided attacks on Hoffa, but the speech was loaded with indirect jibes.

"My candidate (Liss) would come home to the A.F.L.-C.I.O. with clean hands, with a clean record, with a clean name and a genuine desire to do what is best for all labor unions," Luken said.

The pro-Hoffa delegates wanted the reference to "clean hands" expunged from the record because it might be considered as critical of Hoffa. They resented comments by Luken and a few others about the lack of democracy in the convention.

Delegate Ray Schoessling of Chicago Teamster Local 744 summed up the views of many of Hoffa's most ardent supporters:

"I don't think that I have witnessed, nor have I ever observed, a chairman of a convention that has been more democratic, that has allowed more democracy to creep in here, and that has been fairer (than Hoffa)."

Delegate George Leonard of Los Angeles Local 203 spoke caustically of Hoffa's opponents who "would like to see us go out of here confused, mixed up and divided."

"Jimmy, this is my sixth convention," Leonard said from the microphone on the floor. "I don't know of any man that has the patience of you, unless I read about him in the Bible."

The gaudy Teamsters convention ended as everyone had suspected it would, and the display of Hoffa's power had been overwhelming. Delegates and the general public gained the impression that Jimmy Hoffa had a charmed life—a power against which even the United States Government was helpless.

Attorney General Kennedy and Walter Sheridan were disgusted with the spectacle of the Teamsters convention, but they were not disheartened. The investigations and prosecutions were moving ahead steadily and in a methodical manner which they were certain would pay off in a few months. As the indictments and convictions fell on Hoffa's associates, a few became disenchanted and provided the testimony Kennedy and Sheridan needed on the cases which were being developed.

The direct action against Hoffa centered on three major cases:

1. The Sun Valley real estate project in which Hoffa and Bert Brennan had a large financial interest. A mail fraud indictment against Hoffa was dismissed on technical grounds involving the grand jury panel selection, but Kennedy planned to reinstate it and probably broaden that charge.

2. Benjamin Dranow was a key figure in more than twenty million dollars in loans from the Central States Southeast-Southwest pension fund, and there was evidence that he was demanding a ten per cent cash fee for getting these loans approved. There was some evidence that Hoffa was receiving benefits from these payoffs to Dranow, but there wasn't a clear enough case for an indictment.[1]

3. Hoffa's wife, Josephine, continued to share in profits from the Detroit truck-leasing firm that had been set up for Mrs. Hoffa and Mrs. Bert Brennan by executives of a Detroit trucking firm that had dealt with the Teamsters union. Justice Department lawyers believed the evidence would establish that Hoffa received part of the money and that this constituted a conflict of interest and a violation of the Taft-Hartley labor law.[2]

The major question at the Justice Department was whether they wanted to seek an indictment in Detroit, where the truck-leasing firm operated, or in Nashville, Tennessee, where Mrs. Hoffa's truck-leasing firm was incorporated. There was understandable reluctance to bring an indictment against Hoffa in his home territory of Detroit. While Bob Kennedy and Sheridan did not believe that Hoffa was invincible in Detroit, they had gained

[1]McClellan committee, Report No. 1139, pages 634-635.

[2]McClellan committee, Report No. 1417, pages 229-232.

considerable respect for his glibness and his ability to wiggle out of tight corners.

Jail doors had started slamming on key Teamsters. Appeals had run out and Dave Beck and Barney Baker were in prison. Ben Dranow had been convicted on bankruptcy fraud and had been indicted for Federal income tax evasion. More than a dozen convictions had been chalked up against Teamsters in Cleveland, Miami, New York and Louisville. Rumblings of discontent in many areas now were combined with signs of open revolt against Hoffa in Cincinnati, Chicago, Los Angeles, New York and Philadelphia.

The Justice Department, with help from informants, had stepped up the pace of its investigations. More than thirty new indictments were returned against racketeering Teamsters, including a half-dozen of Hoffa's most intimate cronies in Detroit and Pontiac, Michigan. In October, 1961, the Justice Department obtained a re-indictment of Hoffa and a Detroit banker in connection with the Sun Valley project. It was the only direct step against Hoffa, but it would prove to be the least significant and least exciting of many moves launched in the following months to break Jimmy Hoffa's power over American labor.

XXXIII

Jury Tampering in Tennessee

The Kennedy Administration started its second year in full swing. Two dozen more indictments were ready against Teamsters officials. There was increasingly better cooperation from informants among Jimmy Hoffa's most trusted associates. Some of the latter saw an opportunity for more power if Hoffa was removed. Others were disgusted with the abuse to which they were subjected when Hoffa went into one of his frequent temper tantrums.

The pressure of the investigations was beginning to tell on Hoffa in those first months of 1962. Every week brought bad news to Jimmy in his war with Bob Kennedy. Occasionally, he could boast of some little victory, but Jimmy was a realist who could see what the Justice Department was doing to the legend that he was invincible. He could see the doubts growing among his associates as the net tightened and one after another of his henchmen was indicted or convicted.

Herbert L. Grosberg, long-time Teamsters accountant, resigned following a dispute with Hoffa over union financial records. Hoffa had ordered Grosberg to give him all of the records. Grosberg refused on the grounds that it was "unethical" and a violation of the accountants' code which required that he keep copies. Herb Grosberg had handled all the union accounts and Hoffa's personal income tax returns. Hoffa was furious about the resignation, and the reasons were obvious as to why he might be concerned.

The Internal Revenue Service was squeezing Hoffa for $14,427 in back taxes for 1957. It was not a large amount, but it involved a ruling ▸that the $22,500 the Teamsters had paid to Edward Bennett Williams, who had represented Hoffa in the bribery trial, must be treated as taxable income to Hoffa. It meant there would be tax troubles in the future if union funds were used to pay for lawyers who defended Hoffa on criminal charges.[1]

Even as indictments fell on Teamsters in Kansas City, Birmingham, New York, Chicago, and Detroit, Hoffa bragged that he would be able to thwart the Federal investigators. But all of Hoffa's boasting of the Teamsters' "billion-dollar organization" didn't stop the tide. It did, in fact, stir Senator John McClellan to suggest that perhaps the Congress should make the mighty Teamsters union subject to the antitrust laws.

The bitterness that was brewing around Hoffa broke into the open briefly on May 17, when Teamsters organizer Sam Baron called Walter Sheridan and said that Hoffa had beaten him severely during a temper tantrum typical of Jimmy. That afternoon, Baron filed a criminal complaint of assault against Hoffa in the municipal court in the District of Columbia.

The slight, 59-year-old organizer told the prosecutor that he had been slugged by Hoffa, knocked down, beaten and kicked before he was rescued by other employees in Hoffa's international headquarters. The witnesses, represented by Teamsters lawyers, told the prosecutor that the muscular, 190-pound Hoffa had only defended himself. With no witnesses to support his story of what took place in the International Teamsters headquarters, Baron later withdrew the charges.

The Sam Baron incident was inconclusive, but it was indicative of the atmosphere of tension and bitterness that prevailed within the Teamsters union in mid-May, 1962.

Two days after Sam Baron filed those assault charges against Hoffa, a Federal grand jury in Nashville, Tennessee, returned an indictment charging that Hoffa and the late Owen Bert Brennan,

---

[1]James R. Hoffa, petitioner, v. Commissioner of Internal Revenue, United States Tax Court, January 8, 1962, No. 163-62.

a Detroit Teamsters official, had been paid $242,000 by a Detroit trucking firm in violation of the Taft-Hartley labor law.

The indictment grew out of the operations of a truck-leasing firm which had been organized in 1949 by Commercial Carriers, a Detroit trucking firm. Representatives of Commercial Carriers incorporated the truck-leasing firm in Nashville and registered it in the maiden names of Mrs. Hoffa (Josephine Poszywak) and Mrs. Brennan (Alice Johnson). Mrs. Hoffa and Mrs. Brennan had little to do with the truck-leasing firm except to collect substantial profits through dealing with Commercial Carriers, according to a Congressional report.

The broad outline of the arrangements was exposed by Wint Smith's House Labor Subcommittee in 1953. Scoffing at criticism of the "conflict of interest" involved in the income his wife received from the trucking firm, Hoffa disregarded advice to end the truck-leasing arrangement.

It was an old case, and yet it was a new case because the payments had continued through 1960. Payments of more than $1,008,057 to the truck-leasing firm meant more than $242,000 in profits flowing to Mrs. Hoffa and Mrs. Brennan.[2]

The Justice Department made the decision to seek an indictment in Nashville to avoid the Detroit political jungle that Hoffa knew so well. In addition, the *Nashville Tennessean* had just hired a new editor—John Seigenthaler, who in 1961 and 1962 had served as administrative assistant to Attorney General Robert F. Kennedy. That was assurance of understanding editorial support in the trial area.

Protecting the Hoffa jury from improper approaches was a major concern for the Justice Department, and Sheridan was installed in a suite of offices across the hall from Judge William E. Miller's courtroom in the Federal Building in Nashville in October, prior to the trial. A background study was conducted on the members of the jury panel, and as the trial date approached F.B.I. agents moved into Nashville to guard against jury tampering.

Efforts to tamper with the jury panel were made even before the Hoffa trial started in October, 1962. Anonymous tele-

---

[2]U. S. v. James R. Hoffa and Commercial Carriers, United States District Court for the Middle District of Tennessee (Nashville), Cr. No. 13241.

phone calls were received by men and women the government considered to be among the best jury prospects. Persons contacted in this manner had to be dropped as prospective jurors, for the mere contact made it unlikely that they could start the trial with the necessary objectivity.

Equally disturbing were reports that flowed to Sheridan that some of Hoffa's associates were actually trying to bribe prospective jurors. The initial reports came from informants who could not be identified at that time, so it was impossible to obtain the necessary corroboration.

The government team was a strong one. James Neal, a 34-year-old graduate of Vanderbilt University Law School in Nashville, was the chief prosecutor. He had convicted Ben Dranow in Minneapolis and had the advantage of a Tennessee drawl in working with the jury. His top assistant was Charles Shaffer, a brilliant young trial lawyer from New York. They were backed in research by two bright young legal scholars— James Durkin and Nat Lewin.

Equally important was the Sheridan team that worked outside of the courtroom and carried the major responsibility for protecting the jury from improper contacts. From the first days of the trial it was apparent that the latter job was as important as the prosecution itself, perhaps more important.

To bolster Sheridan's staff additional F.B.I. agents were moved into the Nashville area to provide surveillance of the Teamsters racketeer contacts who invaded Nashville.

On the surface, this was just another trial. But when one looked closely, the bitterness and power of the underlying struggle was obvious. Hoffa tossed whispered threats and profanity at government lawyers Neal and Shaffer when court was recessed. My presence sent him into a rage, which was revealed in the profanity he loosed on me at recesses. Caustic comments and baleful looks were aimed at Walter Sheridan when the two men passed in the corridor.

Sheridan wisely avoided direct contact with Hoffa, but it was impossible for Neal and Shaffer to escape the insulting harangues Hoffa launched .at them as soon as the judge left the bench.

The court was still in the process of selecting a jury when

Judge Miller was suddenly jolted with clear evidence of an attempted jury fix. Until that morning of October 24, he had believed the Justice Department was overly concerned about the possibility of jury tampering.

Shortly before 9 a.m., Judge Miller's secretary called him to tell him that a Mr. James C. Tippens, one of the prospective jurors, wished to speak with him.

Judge Miller realized it was more than a family problem when the tall and powerfully built, grey-haired man stepped through the door. His face tense with worry, Tippens spoke cautiously, as if unsure of his course. Normally, Tippens displayed the friendly voice and jovial attitude that had promoted the success of his general insurance business in Nashville, but events of the last day had changed his entire bearing. He was frightened.

Tippens had been seated in chair number 12 in the jury box when court recessed on Tuesday, October 23, and he appeared to be a likely selection to sit in judgment on the Hoffa case.

Tippens nervously told Judge Miller that, within two hours after leaving the Federal Building that day, he had been contacted by an acquaintance who had offered him $10,000 in "easy money."

Tippens was mindful of Judge Miller's warning that prospective jurors must avoid any discussions that might prejudice them either for or against Hoffa, but, he told the judge, there had seemed no reason to be wary of going for a car ride with an old acquaintance—his neighbor, a man he regarded as his friend. There was no reason to believe this man would have any interest in the outcome of the trial of the president of the International Brotherhood of Teamsters.

Tippens told Judge Miller that the first comments of his neighbor had not directly linked his offer of $10,000 in $100 bills with the Hoffa case, but Tippens had asked the direct question, "You are referring to being a prospective juror in the case?"

The man had acknowledged that the offer was connected with the Hoffa case, and he had urged Tippens to take it.

Tippens said he had insisted he wanted no discussion of the matter.

Tippens worried about that conversation all night, he told Judge Miller, but he resolved to do the one thing he was certain was right: he had to tell Judge Miller about it even if it meant trouble for his friend.

Calm and stern-faced, Judge Miller questioned Tippens briefly about the $10,000 offer. The 55-year-old Federal judge assured Tippens he had acted properly in reporting the incident. In quiet tones, he instructed the insurance man to say nothing about the affair to anyone until he could be questioned by the Federal Bureau of Investigation.

Walter Sheridan was not surprised to hear that an effort had been made to bribe a juror, but he was surprised that such an attempt was taking place before the jury had been selected. He passed the information to the F.B.I., which immediately began to investigate this first solid evidence of jury tampering.

Judge Miller summoned government and defense lawyers to his chambers and told them he had never heard of such a bold attempt to subvert the jury system in his twenty-seven years as lawyer and judge. The judge carefully avoided any contention that Hoffa or Hoffa's lawyers had any knowledge of the contact with Tippens, but Miller explained that Tippens must be released from jury service. It was agreed that any juror would have a difficult time being objective after such an experience.

Prosecutor Neal commented that the number of improper and illegal telephone calls made to prospective jurors had made it necessary to eliminate the most responsible people from the jury panel.

It had been impossible to identify the callers, and Neal said: "I am personally becoming very disturbed about this situation. . . . It seems the people who are contacted are otherwise good jurors.

"I am inclined to suggest at this point that the jury be locked up," Neal said. "I realize how onerous that is on everyone."

Z. T. (Tommy) Osborn, Jr., one of Hoffa's defense lawyers, objected, "It is an awful long time, and if there is any way to avoid it Your Honor should avoid it." Osborn suggested that the telephone calls to jurors were probably the work of "crackpots and do-gooders."

Prosecutor Shaffer said he did not like to inject "an acrimonious note" at an early stage in the trial, but added: "I have no way of relating this to the defendant, Hoffa, but . . . the government does know and it is a public record that jurors have been approached before (in cases) in which he was on trial."

There was a vigorous protest from defense lawyer William E. Bufalino, who jumped forward: "That is not so. . . . I have been in every one of those cases that you have been referring to. I was in the Washington case, the New York cases, and when Bobby Kennedy makes statements (about approaches to jurors) . . . in his book, The Enemy Within, (it) does not make it a fact."

Shaffer snapped back that he was familiar with the Washington case in which Hoffa had been acquitted on charges of trying to bribe an investigator for the McClellan labor racket committee. He said he was also familiar with the two trials of Hoffa in New York on Federal charges of illegal wiretapping. The first trial had ended in a hung jury with one juror holding out against conviction. Hoffa had been acquitted in the second trial on the same charge.

"In a second trial before Judge Murphy . . . a juror was approached, and she was excused, and it is in the court record that the reason that she was excused by Judge Murphy is that she was approached," Shaffer said.

Bufalino was indignant. He declared that the incident was no reflection on Hoffa, for there was no evidence that Hoffa had had anything to do with it.

"I say I don't have any proof to relate it to defendant Hoffa," Shaffer replied. "If we did, Mr. Hoffa would be prosecuted."

The decision on "locking up" a jury was a difficult one, and Judge Miller commented that it could be a great hardship on twelve jurors and four alternates. It could mean virtual imprisonment for the six or eight weeks the trial was expected to last. It would mean that all sixteen persons would remain in the custody of U. S. Marshal Elmer Disspayne and his deputies,

with no opportunity to lead normal lives. It would mean radio
and television programs would be censored, newspapers clipped
of stories dealing with the trial. Communications with family
members would be monitored by representatives of the court.

Judge Miller was concerned over the Tippens incident, but
he said he believed that the discussions and his warning made
further tampering unlikely. It appeared to the judge that only
a fool or a totally corrupt scoundrel would attempt to contact
the Hoffa jurors now in the face of such warnings.

The jury would not be locked up at this time, Judge
Miller ruled. He proposed stiff warnings to the jurors, and
informed the defense lawyers about the F.B.I. investigation that
was being started. He said he hoped that would settle the jury-
tampering issue for the duration of the trial.

In the next nine weeks, Judge Miller was to realize that he
was not dealing with the normal attitudes of society toward the
courts and juries. Day after day, his patience was tested as he
fought to maintain the decorum of a Federal court—to avoid the
atmosphere of a circus.

Even as the Tippens investigation was starting, Walter
Sheridan was told of other specific efforts to fix the Hoffa jury.
An informant had called Sheridan the night of October 23 to
relate conversations with Hoffa and Ewing King, president of
Nashville Teamsters Local 327. The informant had said that
Hoffa had called him into a room, slapped his back pocket, and
said that he might want the informant to pass something. The
informant told Sheridan that Hoffa had frankly boasted that it
was his plan "to get one juror or try to get a few scattered jurors
and take their chances."[3]

The informant told Sheridan that Ewing King had commented that "they had a meeting set up on the jury that night."

The information was spotty, and Sheridan wasn't certain of
the reliability of this informant. There was no way of obtaining
firm corroboration for the reports, and until there was solid

[3]U. S. v. James R. Hoffa *et al.,* United States District Court for the Eastern
District of Tennessee (Chattanooga), Cr. Nos. 15876, 15877, 15878, 15879. (Essentially all of the account of Sheridan's contact with the informant "Andy" is
from the transcript of the Chattanooga trial.)

corroboration, the reports had no value in making a criminal case.

Sheridan was highly enthusiastic about the possibility of making great use of this new informant, a man who had only recently decided to break with Hoffa and cooperate with the Justice Department. There was a bright twinkle in Sheridan's eye when he first told me that he had an informant "right on Hoffa." He didn't identify the man at the time, for it was a dangerous game with big stakes. In reports and in staff conversations the informant was known by the code name of "Andy." I didn't want to know the identity of informant "Andy," although by some simple reasoning and familiarity with the Teamsters entourage it was possible to narrow it down to three or four possibilities.

"Andy" seemed almost too good to be true, and Sheridan was eager to obtain some reports that could be tested and corroborated. The opportunity popped up sooner than Sheridan could have expected.

"Andy" called Sheridan the evening of October 25 to report a conversation with Hoffa on the Tippens affair. He reported that Hoffa was furious over Tippens's report to Judge Miller, and quoted Hoffa as saying: "The dirty bastard went in and told the judge that his neighbor offered him $10,000. We are going to have to lay low for a few days."

The next day "Andy" called Sheridan to relate a conversation with Nashville Teamsters boss Ewing King. "Andy" said that King was making efforts to contact a woman juror whose husband was a state highway patrolman. King was going to contact the patrolman, and "King also said he knew some lady who was a good friend of (juror) Mrs. (Betty) Paschal, and that he was going to try to have the lady sway Mrs. Paschal toward Hoffa."

Sheridan knew that Mrs. Betty Paschal, a pretty 35-year-old brunette juror, was the wife of Tennessee Highway Patrolman James Paschal of Woodbury. Andy reported that King had told him that he was going out to a place where the highway patrolmen "hang out" and talk to one of Paschal's closest friends. The informant also related that he had had a conversation with King outside the courtroom in which King had pointed out a heavy-set, dark-haired lady.

"King said that the lady was the one that came up to see if she could go home with Mrs. Paschal and talk to her," Andy told Sheridan. "After court recessed, King (said) the lady had gone home with Mrs. Paschal."

It was possible to corroborate some of this information from Andy, for it jibed with independent information Sheridan was receiving from the F.B.I. He was elated, and the reports from Andy became better.

Andy reported he had been in Hoffa's hotel suite, and that the Detroit Teamsters boss had been upset because of the testimony of a banker which he felt had hurt him. "Hoffa then said he would pay $15,000 or $20,000, whatever it cost to get to the jury," the informant told Sheridan.

On October 31, Andy left Nashville for four days. Sheridan missed those intimate inside reports from the Hoffa camp, but he had the F.B.I. agents busy trying to corroborate every possible detail. He didn't tell prosecutors Neal and Shaffer of the information he was receiving, for there was no point in taking their minds off the trial.

The courtroom itself was a lively place, with the Tippens affair being only one of many incidents. There were constant, loud harangues in court, and when court adjourned Hoffa and two of his lawyers continued their arguments. There had been a rowdy series of disputes between Hoffa and U.S. Marshal Disspayne, in which Disspayne finally maintained order by threatening to eject Hoffa's followers from the court.

On November 4, Andy returned, and the next day he phoned Sheridan. He quoted an irate Hoffa as complaining: "King keeps telling me he can get the patrolman but he don't get to him. He keeps talking about it and fumbling around."[4]

King was reported to have told Andy that he believed patrolman James Paschal would try to influence his wife, and that King was supposed to meet the patrolman the following Sunday at a spring back of a farm near Woodbury, Tennessee.

"They were going to take coon dogs so if anyone came upon them they could say they were coon hunting," Andy told Sheridan. The meeting was to take place at midnight.

The next trial day was a bad day for Hoffa, and Andy said

---

[4]Transcript, U. S. v. Hoffa *et al.,* Chattanooga trial.

he had told Hoffa he thought so. He told Sheridan that Hoffa replied:

"Well, don't worry about it too much. Because I have got the colored male juror in my hip pocket. One of my business agents, Campbell, came into Nashville prior to the trial and took care of it."

Andy reported that Hoffa told him Teamsters business agent Larry Campbell "was kin to the (Negro) juror, who wouldn't take any money but he wouldn't go against his own people." Andy said Hoffa had described the juror as "an old retired railroad worker."

Hoffa reportedly said that it looked like his best bet was a hung jury, and added, "If they have a hung jury, it will be the same as acquittal because they will never try the case again."

In leaving Nashville on November 7, Andy called Sheridan to say Ewing King was complaining and that Hoffa was "on King" for not making contact with patrolman Paschal "for insurance" of a hung jury.

This was Sheridan's first opportunity to put Andy's reports to a thorough test. He alerted the F.B.I. to keep Teamsters boss King under tight surveillance. The F.B.I. set up a blind near the spring and installed an infrared camera to be used to photograph the expected "coon dog meeting" between King and Paschal.

It was a disappointing experience. An F.B.I. agent was perched on a hill near the spring from early evening on Saturday night, November 10, until the morning of Sunday, November 11. It was a miserably rainy night, and neither King nor Paschal appeared. Sheridan was more disappointed than the F.B.I. agent who had endured the rain.

However, the F.B.I. had at the same time started to work cautiously to determine the background and travels of Larry Campbell, a business agent for Hoffa's Detroit Teamsters Local 299. Campbell had come from Nashville, and he still had relatives in Nashville. But Campbell was not related to the one colored male juror, Gratin Fields. This investigation did develop the fact that Campbell had an uncle, Thomas Ewing Parks, who worked in Nashville and who had had some contact with the family of Gratin Fields.

The F.B.I. investigation had to be sharply restricted. The jury was not locked up. Fields and Mrs. Paschal were going home each night, and it would be improper and prejudicial for the F.B.I. to question relatives of jurors under these circumstances. Such an F.B.I. investigation could be considered "improper pressure" on the jurors if they learned about it.

Andy was back in Nashville on November 14 and 15, and he reported to Sheridan that Hoffa was now "cursing and calling King a stupid S.O.B. for thumbing around and not getting the job (of contacting Paschal) done."

Indications were that Hoffa now had pressure on King, and the F.B.I. surveillance of King continued.

On Saturday night, November 17, an F.B.I. agent trailed Ewing King as he drove to a restaurant on the edge of Nashville, swapped cars with George Broda, another Teamsters official, and drove off in Broda's blue 1959 Ford in the direction of Woodbury. The car swap temporarily lost the trailing F.B.I. agent.

It was 1:07 a.m. on November 18 when another team of F.B.I. agents noticed Broda's Ford parked at the Paschal home. Paschal, dressed in his highway patrol uniform, was standing in a drizzling rain, talking to the driver of the car.

It was later discovered that Oscar (Mutt) Pitts, a Teamsters friend of Paschal, had driven the 1959 Ford over to make arrangements for Paschal to meet with King at 1:30 a.m. at a place called River Spring.

F.B.I. agents Francis Norwood and Willis S. Turner had noted the time, and then, because they did not wish to be conspicuous in that little town of 1,600 people, they drove on past the Paschal home. They recognized the uniformed patrolman as James Paschal, husband of the juror.

The two F.B.I. men swung back past the Paschal home at 1:35 a.m. and found both the 1959 Ford and the highway patrol car gone. They continued their patrol of the little hill country town, and at 2:12 a.m. they noted that the highway patrol car was back in the Paschal driveway.

Other F.B.I. agents also reported that Paschal and King had met at that desolate, wooded spot known as River Spring, three miles south of Woodbury. Instructions were radioed to agent Warren L Walsh to go to the vicinity of Lebanon Pike and the old Lebanon Road and wait there until he saw Ewing King drive past in the 1959 Ford.

Walsh parked as instructed at 2:20 a.m. and remained there until 4:12 a.m. when the Ford passed him. He saw it briefly in his headlights and identified the driver as King. Walsh followed King to the Teamsters official's home at 112 Benson Drive, where still another agent, Harry T. Posey, was parked in a manner that prevented King from parking.

Posey got out of his car, walked to King's car, and excused himself with: "Sir, I will be out of your way in a moment." In that moment of close conversation Posey assured himself that the man in the car was Ewing King.

This was the first solid corroboration of the many reports that Andy had been making. Sheridan was elated with the night's work, but there was still much work to do.

On December 5, Sheridan got another break, though it hardly seemed like a break at the time. A bloody altercation broke out in the courtroom when a young mental patient walked in and fired a pellet gun at Jimmy Hoffa. Fortunately, the jury was out of the courtroom or the incident could have been grounds for a mistrial.

The pellet did not injure Hoffa, but the free-swinging fists and gun butts that felled the intruder created momentary chaos in the court. I was seated near the front of the courtroom, and within seconds after the fighting broke out I found myself in the middle of the fracas, trying to protect the bleeding young man who had been slugged and stomped by Teamsters business agents and U. S. marshals who jumped to defend Hoffa. I did not see the pellet gun at the time it was fired. I realized only that a seemingly defenseless, bleeding man was being beaten.

Judge Miller restored order within a few minutes, and the mental patient was taken to jail by the U. S. marshals. A bigger problem remained. If the jurors found out what had happened it might be grounds for a mistrial. Judge Miller had no alternative but to lock up the jury. With the jury sequestered for the duration of the trial, Walter Sheridan was free to broaden the jury-tampering investigation, with court approval. Investigations into the efforts to fix Gratin Fields and prospective juror

Tippens still had a long way to go, but now there were reasons for trying to force the issue of the efforts to contact Mrs. Paschal.

On December 6, government attorneys James Neal and Charles Shaffer asked for a secret hearing on King's efforts to contact juror Mrs. Paschal. When the courtroom had been cleared of all spectators, Neal revealed the barest outline of King's contact with patrolman Paschal and questioned several F.B.I. agents to establish that point.[5]

"These facts create compelling, suspicious circumstances indicating an improper approach," Neal said in asking for removal of juror Paschal.

Daniel Maher, one of Hoffa's lawyers, said Neal's revelations were of little consequence. "All that he (Neal) has said is that a juror's home was visited and a person who has been in the courtroom (King) was observed talking to the spouse of the juror," Maher asserted.

"What do you think about the head of the Teamsters union in Nashville swapping cars with someone else and going to the home of a juror?" Judge Miller responded to Maher.

"I think it is a circumstance," Maher replied.

"I think it is a shocking state of affairs," Judge Miller said, biting off the words.

U. S. Marshal Elmer Disspayne was instructed to bring Ewing King and highway patrolman James Paschal to the court. King, taken into custody in the courthouse corridor, entered the court with Disspayne, surveyed the scene momentarily, and predictably took the Fifth Amendment on all questions about the early-morning meeting with Paschal.

Prosecutor Shaffer complained that the Nashville Teamsters president invoked the Fifth Amendment after receiving a five-finger sign flashed to him by Jimmy Hoffa. Defense lawyer William Bufalino loudly denied Shaffer's claim. He declared that the Teamsters boss only had his hand on his chin, as he frequently did during the trial.

"Take your hands down so there won't be any question at all," Judge Miller instructed Hoffa.

Mutt Pitts, a Teamsters union member, also took the Fifth

---

[5]Later, the transcript of this secret hearing was made a part of the public trial record of the Nashville trial.

Amendment when questioned on reports that he had put King in touch with Paschal.

The last witness was patrolman Paschal. At first, he denied that he had ever talked to King. In later questioning, however, he told Judge Miller that Mutt Pitts, a long-time friend, had told him King wanted to see him.

"I told . . . (Pitts) I would meet him (King) up by what we call River Springs," Paschal said. "He (King) just more or less asked me if I would like to get a promotion on my job, that there had been some boys that know me who drive a truck and we are all friends, and they were interested in helping me get a promotion, and if I was interested in it, he would be glad to help," Paschal said.

"What else was said at this time?" Judge Miller asked.

"Well, I just don't recall every little thing that was said," Paschal answered.

Paschal insisted that King had never tried to discuss Jimmy Hoffa with him, and he said he had never mentioned to his wife the strange circumstances of the offer of a promotion.

"Did it occur to you that he was trying to reach you so that you would influence your wife?" Judge Miller bored in.

"Nothing was said about it," Paschal again insisted.

"Wasn't it funny to you that a complete stranger would offer to help you get a promotion?"

"I didn't know," Paschal replied.

Judge Miller ordered Mrs. Paschal excused from the jury on the basis of reasonable evidence that an effort had been made to improperly influence her decision.

With Mrs. Paschal off the jury, Walter Sheridan concentrated on the gathering of evidence that indicated some Detroit Teamsters were attempting to reach juror Gratin Fields. Justice Department lawyers Thomas McKeon and William French, with Bernard C. Brown, special agent in charge of the Detroit F.B.I. office, went to work on the records of Teamsters long distance telephone calls and travel out of Detroit headquarters to Louisville and Nashville. Justice Department lawyer Paul Allred worked with Ian D. MacLennan, special agent in charge of the Louisville F.B.I. office, in an around-the-clock sorting of more than 100,000 long distance calls from public pay booths in the Louisville area.

The trial was drawing to a close in the week of December 16 when French and Allred delivered results of the telephone toll-call studies that appeared to support the story informant Andy had told Sheridan. Detroit Teamsters business agent Larry Campbell had made contacts in Louisville with his uncle, Thomas Ewing Parks, and Parks in turn had reached persons in Nashville. The Nashville persons had then contacted a son and a daughter of juror Gratin Fields. There was no evidence of an improper contact with Fields, but Sheridan did not feel he could take a chance in the light of the story Andy had told.

On December 19, Sheridan asked Andy if he would be willing to make an affidavit affirming that Jimmy Hoffa had said, "I have the colored male juror in my hip pocket." Andy's identity was to be kept secret from everyone except Judge Miller and the prosecutors. The notary public called to witness the affidavit at Sheridan's apartment would have no knowledge of the contents of the affidavit and no knowledge of the identity of the persons with whom he was dealing.

Testimony in the case was completed, and on December 20 government lawyer James Neal requested a secret session. In that session he asked that Gratin Fields be removed from the jury.[6]

"We have submitted to the court certain . . . documentary evidence enclosed in a sealed envelope which, because of confidential nature of its contents the Government requests . . . be sealed after the court reads and considers it," Neal said.

Judge Miller read the secret papers and immediately ordered the clerk to reseal them. The judge said: "It is very evident . . . from reading the sealed documents why they should not be released. It is also very evident from the contents of the documents . . . that there is every reason to believe that an effort has been made, if not actually accomplished, to influence this jury improperly. It is an astounding situation."

Defense lawyer Daniel Maher objected to dismissal of Fields. "There is nothing to even suggest a contact of a juror," Maher said.

---

[6]Later the transcript of this secret hearing was made a part of the public record of the Nashville trial.

"I am frankly astonished at the history of attempted jury fixing in this case," Judge Miller replied.

Defense lawyer James Haggerty complained that the sealed letter was "a pig in the poke" and contended that it placed the defense in "a ludicrous position."

Judge Miller replied that "this is the most astounding, most amazing set of circumstances that I have ever seen."

"If an appellate court . . . should say that I have done wrong, that I have been in error in excusing these jurors, then they will just have to say it. I don't intend to sit here timidly and see efforts made almost before my very eyes to influence this jury improperly," the judge declared.

Juror Fields was excused over the objections of defense lawyers, and the case was submitted to the jury the next day. Four times the jury was reported "hopelessly deadlocked," and on December 23, 1962, Judge Miller gave up and declared a mistrial. It was impossible to learn what influenced the decisions of individual jurors. The vote was seven to five for acquittal.

Although the grueling nine-week trial yielded only that inconclusive, hung jury, there were some rather conclusive comments by Judge William Miller on jury-tampering efforts that had shocked his sense of ethics.

He ordered an immediate investigation of the jury-tampering charges. He said that his order was not intended to reflect on the honesty or integrity of any person who had served in the Hoffa trial. He declared that the evidence presented at the secret court sessions indicated "illegal and improper attempts were being made by close labor union associates of the defendant (Hoffa) to contact and influence certain members of the jury."

Strong action was needed "to protect the court as an institution of government," Judge Miller said.

"The right of a defendant in a criminal case to be tried by a jury of his peers is one of the most sacred of our constitutional guarantees," the judge declared. But, he went on to say, "The system of trial by jury . . . becomes nothing more than a mockery if unscrupulous persons are allowed to subvert it by improper and unlawful means.

"I do not intend that such shameful acts to corrupt our jury system shall go unnoticed by this court," the judge said in quiet fury. He ordered a Federal grand jury convened to investigate.

Nashville Teamsters boss Ewing King was among the Teamsters and Teamsters lawyers who flocked around Hoffa to offer congratulations after the trial. Hoffa's supporters regarded the hung jury as a victory, but their enthusiasm was cooled by Judge Miller's order for the broadest possible investigation of jury tampering.

Jimmy Hoffa had the hung jury he wanted on the charge against him of violating the Taft-Hartley Act—an indictable misdemeanor with a maximum one-year prison term. But now he was under investigation for alleged jury tampering—a felony charge with a maximum five-year prison term.

Perhaps Hoffa felt it was a good bet that he would win. But he didn't know about the steady stream of information that the government's informant, Andy, was giving to Walter Sheridan. And if Hoffa's espionage system could have gained access to Justice Department reports, he still wouldn't have known that the man identified only as "Andy" was Edward Grady Partin, a Louisiana Teamster who had accompanied him to court day after day during the Nashville trial.

XXXIV

Guilty Verdict and an Assassination Plot

In May, 1963, a Federal grand jury in Nashville returned an indictment charging that James R. Hoffa and six others had tried to bribe members of the jury that had tried Hoffa a few months earlier.

Jimmy Hoffa had reason to believe that the whole power of the federal government was being used to put him in jail. Robert F. Kennedy had emerged as the second most powerful man in that government. He was more than the Attorney General and the nation's top law enforcement officer. He was also an intimate adviser to the President. All who opposed Bob Kennedy knew that his power could not be broken as long as John F. Kennedy was President. It was not possible to use the political power of certain corrupt big-city political machines, or the backstage belligerence of influential Senators and Congressmen, to undermine this Attorney General.

The Kennedy Administration seemed destined to continue for many years.

Then suddenly, it was ended on November 22, 1963. Bullets from the gun of Communist-indoctrinated Lee Harvey Oswald resulted in immediately weakening the power of Robert F. Kennedy.

A few days after President Kennedy was assassinated, Jimmy Hoffa gloated that now Bob Kennedy "is just another lawyer."

"He (Bob Kennedy) is not going to be able to guarantee patronage, or advancement to the Court of Appeals, or the Supreme Court, because the passing of our President by assassination makes him just another lawyer," Hoffa said in a taped interview with WSM-TV in Nashville while he was in that city to promote the re-election of Ewing King as president of Teamsters Local 327. "He (Kennedy) is not going to be able to promise —as he has many times—promotions if (he) could secure convictions, disregarding all the ethics that normally is practiced in court cases."

Hoffa was bitter in those days—and allowed his bitterness to show through. Only two days before the assassination, the Federal court in Nashville had taken action to disbar one of Hoffa's attorneys, Z. T. (Tommy) Osborn, Jr., on the grounds that Osborn had conspired to give a $10,000 bribe to a prospective juror in connection with the pending jury-tampering trial.

It was a shocking development that a former United States Attorney in the Middle Tennessee district, and a prominent local lawyer in line for the presidency of the Nashville Bar Association, should be involved in an attempt to corrupt the Federal judicial system. Two United States District Judges—William E. Miller and Frank Gray, Jr.—stated that Tommy Osborn had admitted making an arrangement with a Nashville policeman to bribe one of 36 prospective jurors in the new Hoffa trial slated to start on January 6, 1964.

Judges Miller and Gray stated that Osborn first denied making the deal with the policeman, but that Osborn later admitted it. The two Federal judges stated that questionable activity by Osborn had been reported to them early in November and they had authorized F.B.I. agents to obtain evidence by strapping a concealed recording device to the body of an informant.

Hoffa was in a rage over the disbarment of Osborn, and he stormed about the unfairness of the government tactics.

"I feel that it's a travesty on justice that the government, the local officials and the judges should have any part of a setup (to) entrap him (Osborn) and be able to take away from me a competent lawyer to represent me in this case," Hoffa said. "I believe it is the full intention of those who have perpetrated

this crime—and it is a crime, and should be treated as such—
in entrapping the attorney that I had hired."

On December 7, 1963, a Federal grand jury in Nashville
returned a three-count indictment charging that Tommy Osborn
had tried to bribe three jurors to acquit Hoffa. Two counts
dealt with allegations that the 44-year-old Nashville lawyer had
tried to bribe jurors in Hoffa's 1962 trial, and the remaining
count dealt with the alleged effort to bribe a juror in the Hoffa
trial scheduled to start in January, 1964.

The indictment of Osborn coincided with more unrest in
the Teamsters union, where for a few weeks it appeared there
was a possibility of a revolt against Hoffa's rule. Even with
dissension in the ranks and trouble all around, Hoffa managed
to keep a steady hand on his $75,000-a-year job and maintain
his control over the $40 million Teamsters treasury and the more
than $200 million in welfare and pension funds.

While Hoffa fought to survive, it was apparent to lawyers
in the Justice Department that Hoffa's analysis of the results
of the assassination of John Kennedy was cruel but accurate. The
special Hoffa unit in the Justice Department could no longer
count on the fervent interest of the Attorney General, and they
were no longer sure of the backing they would receive at the
White House. Bob Kennedy was in deep grief, and even if that
subsided there was a long-standing antagonism between Bob
Kennedy and the new President Lyndon B. Johnson, which
would seem to bar any real support.

Nevertheless, the Hoffa unit moved forward with previously
made plans and an impetus which would carry for some months
without new power from the top.

The jury-tampering indictment was returned against Hoffa
and six others on May 9, 1963. The five-count indictment
charged Hoffa with "aiding, commanding and inducing" several
attempts to influence two jurors—Mrs. James M. Paschal and
Gratin Fields—and a prospective juror, James C. Tippens. Those
indicted were Ewing King, president of Nashville Teamsters
Local 327; Allen Dorfman, the Chicago insurance broker and
close friend of Hoffa; Larry Campbell, a business agent for
Detroit Teamsters Local 299; Thomas Ewing Parks, Campbell's
uncle from Nashville; Nicholas J. Tweel, a Huntington, West

Virginia, businessman, and Lawrence W. Medlin, a Nashville merchant.

It appeared that there was a strong case with direct evidence against King because of his approach to the state patrolman husband of Mrs. Paschal. Equally strong was the evidence that Lawrence Medlin had contacted his neighbor, James Tippens, with the offer of "easy money." However, the evidence against Hoffa and the other defendants did not appear to be strong, and, in fact, links to Hoffa and those others seemed largely circumstantial.

Hoffa's lawyers had reason to be optimistic, for Jimmy had a record of demonstrating that he could be extremely effective in talking a jury into acquittal or a "hung-jury" verdict. The defense lawyers did not expect that substantial evidence could be obtained from informants, nor did they believe it would be possible to corroborate an informant if one was obtained. Hoffa was careful about not having too many witnesses to important conversations, and he seemed to be a master in using the flat denial of conversations he was alleged to have had in earlier years with potential informants.

If Hoffa now was worried about an informant, it was not about Edward Grady Partin of Baton Rouge, Louisiana. If there was one Teamsters official who seemed to have more problems than Hoffa, it was Partin. Ed Partin had led a rough life that included a burglary conviction, a number of jail terms, and the general rough stuff that goes with running a rough union. Even as he attended the Nashville trial, Partin still was under indictment on a state charge and a federal charge involving alleged mishandling of Teamsters union funds.

It appeared that Partin was thoroughly loyal to Hoffa. He had been selected by Hoffa to serve as a guard outside Hoffa's door at the Andrew Jackson Hotel in Nashville when important conferences were in progress. When the grand jury started the jury-tampering inquiry, Partin told Hoffa that he had been subpoenaed, and, following advice from one of Hoffa's lawyers, Partin took the Fifth Amendment before that grand jury.

Hoffa and his lawyers were unaware that Ed Partin had been in almost daily contact with Walter Sheridan throughout the earlier Nashville trial. They were unaware that it was on

Sheridan's advice that Partin went along with the suggestion that he use the Fifth Amendment when questioned by that Nashville grand jury.

Sheridan knew that certain of Hoffa's associates had arranged "leaks" from grand juries in the Detroit area in earlier years. If there had been a "leak" from the Nashville grand jury the report would have indicated that Ed Partin was true to the Teamsters' code and was following a conspiracy of silence.

I knew there was a key witness who could give strong testimony involving Hoffa, but I knew only his code name. I was aware he was such a valuable witness that Sheridan considered it highly dangerous to have him identified, even in the most secret reports with the Justice Department and the F.B.I.

Even without inquiry, I had this informant-witness pegged as one of the three men I knew had been close to Hoffa during parts of the first Nashville trial. Inadvertently, I stumbled into almost total identification of the key witness while talking with Sheridan about men who continued to hold office in the Teamsters union despite indictments and convictions.

On the surface Ed Partin appeared to be just another one on the list of convicted Teamsters, but Sheridan's reaction to my inquiry about this was unusual. There was a momentary twinkle in Sheridan's eyes, a slight grin, and a comment that perhaps it wouldn't be fair to place Partin in the same category with Barney Baker, Babe Triscaro, or Tony Ducks Corallo.

Ed Partin was special, even though the cold record did not show it. I didn't ask Sheridan to explain because I didn't want to put him on the spot with a direct question. I let it drop for the time.

Even in the turmoil following the disbarment and indictment of defense lawyer Tommy Osborn, Ed Partin was regarded as one of the Teamsters who would remain loyal to Hoffa in the face of rebellion. The Hoffa-Partin relationship seemed to remain that way as preparations were made for the trial.

The jury-tampering trial was shifted from Nashville to Chattanooga because the two Federal judges in Nashville, Judge Miller and Judge Gray, felt that their experience in handling the sordid jury-tampering evidence might make them much less than objective with regard to the whole matter. At his request, the charge against Lawrence Medlin, the Nashville merchant, was severed from the body of the charges, to be tried separately in Nashville.

The jury-tampering trial started on January 20, 1964, in United States District Judge Frank W. Wilson's court in Chattanooga. There was the same bitterness that had permeated the Nashville trial, but there were a few major cast changes. The government had hired John J. Hooker, Sr., one of the great trial lawyers in Tennessee, to team with James Neal of Nashville and United States Attorney John Reddy. It provided a team of Tennessee lawyers to argue to the jury about these outlanders who had corrupted the jury system in Tennessee.

The prosecution's strategy decision was made. The government planned to hold its secret witness, Ed Partin, until near the end of the case. F.B.I. agents and other witnesses, most of them corroborative of Partin's story, were to be used to weave the major story in what would appear to be a circumstantial case until Ed Partin was suddenly called.

From the outset, the Justice Department recognized that there were two problems in using Partin:

First, his police record made him vulnerable to tough cross-examination by defense lawyers and made it possible to raise doubts about his motivation and his credibility.

Second, the whole set of circumstances under which Partin had decided to cooperate with the government had to be kept from the jurors. If the government dealt with Partin's reason for becoming an informant in any but the most careful manner, it could result in statements that might be regarded as highly prejudicial to Hoffa.

The second problem was by far the greater. Defense lawyers were entitled to pry into Partin's relationship with the Justice Department, and yet somehow the court had to stop this prying at a point somewhere short of bringing out prejudicial testimony.

The story Ed Partin told of why he became an informant was more chilling than the tale of Teamsters jury-tampering. It started on a morning in late September, 1962.

Captain Thomas T. Edwards, warden in Louisiana's East Baton Rouge parish jail, had heard much of criminal conspiracy in his sixteen years in the sheriff's office, but nothing had been more astounding to him than the story Ed Partin told the morning of September 29, 1962. Partin told him of a plot to assassinate Attorney General Robert Kennedy with "plastic explosives." It was a story that seemed too fantastic for belief, but Partin insisted that it was true.

"This is something for the District Attorney's office to handle," Captain Edwards said. "I don't want to know any more about it."

Partin was a prisoner in the Baton Rouge jail, held on a kidnapping charge that had grown out of a friend's domestic squabble. Captain Edwards called the home of William H. (Billy) Daniels, an assistant to District Attorney Sargent Pitcher. Within an hour, Daniels arrived at the courthouse and took the elevator to the fourth-floor jail.

Alone with Daniels, Partin poured out his story. A few weeks earlier, he said, when he had been in Washington at the International Teamsters headquarters, he had been called into an office there and asked about obtaining plastic explosives for the assassination of the Attorney General.[1]

"Something has to be done about that little S.O.B., Bobby Kennedy," Partin quoted Jimmy Hoffa as saying. "He'll be an easy target, always driving around Washington in that convertible with that big black dog. All we need is some plastic explosives tossed in with him, and that will finish him off."

Partin said he had been told that day that some thought was also being given to using the plastic explosives on the Robert Kennedy home at McLean, Virginia.

The muscular Louisiana Teamster said he assumed he had been approached because those involved in the plot believed he was in so much trouble over federal criminal indictments that he would find the plan acceptable. He explained to his Baton Rouge listeners that some of the top Teamsters also knew he was a gun fancier, with a private gun collection, who might have convenient access to sources for explosives. Partin said he was asked to obtain plastic explosives from sources far enough away

---

[1] The story of Partin's contacts and conversations with law enforcement officers is from the transcript of the Chattanooga jury-tampering trial, supplemented by interviews with Partin, Daniels, Pitcher, Duffy, Grimsley and Sheridan.

from Washington that they could not later be traced back to those who would use them.

Daniels doubted the story of the assassination plot, despite Partin's insistence that it was true. Billy Daniels knew the Justice Department was engaged in a comprehensive investigation of the Teamsters in every part of the country, and he was aware that only three months previously the investigation had resulted in a twenty-six-count indictment against Partin on charges involving alleged embezzling from union funds of Baton Rouge Teamsters Local Five.

Why was Partin talking now? Partin explained that he had been concerned about the operations of the International Teamsters for some time but had felt he had to go along with them. He claimed to be irritated with the lack of local autonomy under Hoffa and said that the whole union was becoming too much of a one-man dictatorship.

Ed Partin had been in the Teamsters union for a long time, and he was not inclined to be critical of the rougher elements. In his twelve years as business manager and secretary-treasurer of Local Five, Partin had become accustomed to some flexible handling of union funds and the condoning of a bit of minor violence when that was necessary to make a point in a union-management dispute. But the idea of assassinating anyone—and particularly the Attorney General of the United States—was too much for him.

A plastic bomb plant at the Robert Kennedy home in Virginia would also endanger the Kennedy children, and Partin had small children of his own. He said now that he had hidden his shock when the plot was mentioned, but, he told Daniels, he had tried to contact Attorney General Kennedy and another top official. He had been brushed aside by subordinates. He emphasized that he didn't want to tell his story unless it was to go to the top people. He didn't want to take a chance that word might leak out of the Justice Department to the International Teamsters headquarters. He didn't want to jeopardize his job as a Teamsters official or his safety by being tabbed as a "squealer."

Billy Daniels told Partin he thought he could arrange a talk with top Justice Department people, but that it would be necessary to discuss this with District Attorney Pitcher first. Daniels said he would try to return later with Pitcher.

That evening, Daniels and Pitcher returned to the East Baton Rouge Parish Building. Partin repeated his story of the assassination plot. Pitcher called New Orleans, where he reached Assistant United States Attorney Peter Duffy. Pitcher did not want to discuss the subject on the telephone, and he told Duffy only that Partin had related a story of a "grave matter involving national security."

Duffy made an immediate call to A. Frank Grimsley, a Justice Department lawyer from Atlanta, who had been working with the United States Attorney's office on several Teamsters matters, including the investigation that resulted in the indictment of Partin a few months earlier on a charge of misuse of union funds. Partin's name and background were familiar to Grimsley. Certainly, the subject matter was vague, but Grimsley had learned that all possibilities should be covered on the theory that only a small percentage might check through.

Grimsley called Walter Sheridan's home in Bethesda, Maryland, and without hesitation Sheridan told him to leave for Baton Rouge as quickly as possible. Whatever Ed Partin wanted to talk about would be worth the trip, for Partin had been close to Hoffa and several other key officials in the Southern Conference of Teamsters. Sheridan's unit had already cultivated a half-dozen informants among the men trusted by Hoffa, but another informant could always he helpful.

Sheridan's strongest interest at the time was the trial of Hoffa scheduled to start in Nashville only three weeks later, and at the time he did not associate this meeting with Partin and the Nashville trial.

On Monday, October 1, at the F.B.I. office in the Baton Rouge Post Office Building, Pitcher and Daniels outlined the alleged assassination plot to Grimsley and Assistant U. S. Attorney Duffy. Daniels explained that it would be best not to talk to Partin during the day. Too many people might know that Partin was talking with federal officials. It might get back to the Teamsters. A jailer who could be trusted to keep his mouth shut was to come on at the midnight shift, Daniels explained.

Grimsley approved the plan, stepped out to an anteroom,

called Walter Sheridan and outlined the suspected plot before returning to the Capitol House Hotel for dinner and a rest before the night meeting.

It was after 2 a.m. on October 2 when Grimsley and Duffy returned to the East Baton Rouge Parish Building. At 3 a.m., Partin was brought from the jail to the District Attorney's office. From 3 a.m. until 6 a.m., he talked and answered questions. Grimsley, Duffy and Daniels reviewed the details over and over, and cross-examined the Louisiana Teamster on every aspect of his story of the assassination plot. Partin cooperated fully, and he seemed to be telling the truth.

Grimsley called Sheridan with the full details of the alleged assassination plot. "Do you believe him?" Sheridan asked.

Grimsley said he had first been inclined to discount the story as too incredible for belief, but he admitted that the cross-examination of Partin had convinced him that Partin was telling the truth. Partin had volunteered to take a lie-detector test, Grimsley said.

Sheridan was still skeptical. However, there were some routine things that had to be done. He notified Assistant Attorney General Herbert J. (Jack) Miller, head of the Criminal Division, Attorney General Kennedy, and the F.B.I. Some basic security measures were urged with regard to the Attorney General and his family, including temporary abandonment of the convertible Robert Kennedy often used. The F.B.I. was to arrange for a lie-detector test for Partin. If this indicated that Partin was truthful, then a number of additional security measures would be taken.

In five years of investigating corruption and racketeering in the Teamsters union, Sheridan had learned to use caution with informants. He knew of Teamsters efforts to plant double agents with the McClellan labor racket investigating committee and even with the Justice Department.

The F.B.I. report on the lie-detector test confirmed Grimsley's view that Partin was telling the truth. There was still no indication that Partin would be helpful in the major problem at hand—the trial of Jimmy Hoffa in Nashville.

On October 8, Ed Partin called Hoffa in Washington to tell him he was out "on the street again," having been released on bail. (The state kidnapping charge then pending against Partin was later dropped.) Partin recorded the conversation with a device given to him by Daniels as Hoffa joked about Partin's jail time and warned him to be careful.

Later in October, Partin reached Hoffa again at a Newark, New Jersey, telephone number, to complete arrangements for seeing the Teamsters president about union business.

"The twenty-second (of October), I'm going to be there (in Nashville) ," Hoffa said.

"Will Sunday or Monday be all right?" Partin replied.

"All right, Ed, either Monday or Tuesday at the Andrew Jackson Hotel," Hoffa said. Again Partin recorded the conversations.[2]

On October 20, Partin called lawyer Frank Grimsley in Atlanta, told him he was going to Nashville, and asked if there was anything the Justice Department wanted him to do.

"Just keep your eyes and ears open for any evidence of jury fixing," Grimsley said. He gave Partin the unlisted telephone numbers of Walter Sheridan's office in Nashville and instructed him to call Sheridan on a pay phone when he had anything to report.

On the afternoon of October 22, Partin arrived in Nashville and checked in at the Andrew Jackson Hotel—temporary Teamsters headquarters during the trial. While in the coffee shop waiting for Hoffa, Partin talked with Chicago insurance man Allen Dorfman, one of Hoffa's associates, and a dark-faced man he could not identify when he made his first telephone call to Sheridan.

Partin and Sheridan's first face-to-face meeting was in a room at the Noel Hotel. Partin told Sheridan then that he had been able to identify the dark man with Dorfman as Nicholas J. Tweel, a Huntington, West Virginia, businessman. He reported that Tweel had said Dorfman had asked him to "come down to Nashville and help him set up a method to get to the jury." (During the trial, Tweel and Dorfman both denied knowledge of any jury-fixing efforts by Hoffa or anyone else.) Partin told Sheridan that Hoffa himself had identified Nicholas

---

[2]From appellee's brief, page 26, filed with the Sixth Circuit Court, in connection with the appeals from the Chattanooga convictions.

Tweel as a friend of Allen Dorfman who was "up here to help me."

Partin reported that Hoffa had called him into his hotel bedroom and told him "to stick around a day or two"—that Hoffa might have one or two people for Partin to call.

"He (Hoffa) said that they were going to get one juror, or try to get a few scattered jurors, and take their chances," Partin told Sheridan.

Partin said he had met Ewing King, president of the Nashville Teamsters local, and King then told him "they had a meeting set up on the jury that night."

On Tuesday, October 23, Partin left Nashville, but before he left he again called Sheridan. Hoffa, he reported, had "called me into his room and told me when I came back he may want me to pass something for him."

"He (Hoffa) put his hand behind his pocket like that and hit his rear pocket," Partin told Sheridan.

That was Partin's story of how he decided to cooperate with the government and how he relayed to Sheridan the first information of jury tampering that was later to be corroborated by F.B.I. agents and other witnesses. It was a story unknown to Hoffa and the defense lawyers in the first two weeks of the trial, when it seemed that a circumstantial case was being constructed and it appeared that Hoffa was adequately insulated against direct involvement.

For the first two weeks of this second trial, Hoffa was his usual cocky self and his attorneys were highly optimistic. Then, at 1:50 p.m. on February 4, Ed Partin, who had been hidden on the outskirts of Chattanooga for three days, stepped through the rear door of the courtroom as the principal prosecution witness.

Hoffa glowered with shock and rage. Partin was one of the last Teamsters he had expected to talk. Within a few minutes after Partin was given the oath, his testimony had implicated Hoffa, Ewing King, and Larry Campbell as having knowledge of the jury tampering in Nashville. Thomas Parks was the only defendant whose name was not brought into the testimony by Partin. With Hoffa prodding them, the nine defense lawyers made a frantic effort to suppress Partin's testimony.

Judge Wilson overruled the defense motions to bar testimony from Partin, and Special U.S. Prosecutor John J. Hooker brought out Partin's story of his talks with Hoffa and others and the passing of information to Sheridan. It was this testimony that linked Hoffa to the jury tampering that had been explained earlier by other witnesses.

Two of Gratin Fields' children—Carl Fields and Mrs. Mattie Leath—testified about the $10,000 bribe offer from Parks to Carl Fields. Fields admitted accepting $100 cash, but he said that there had been no contact with his father. He admitted he had lied to the F.B.I. when first interviewed and that he had signed a false affidavit in the office of one of Hoffa's attorneys in Nashville.

State patrolman James Paschal and Teamsters official Mutt Pitts then testified that King had tried to get Paschal to influence his wife to acquit Hoffa, promising the patrolman a promotion in the highway patrol. "I am sincerely sorry I furnished false information to Judge Miller (in Nashville) and the F.B.I. agents on December 6 . . . I had heard they (the Teamsters) were a rough bunch, and I thought I might wind up floating in a river with a log chain tied around me if I told anyone about this contact," Paschal said as he sought to justify his initial false statements.

The prosecuting attorney avoided questioning Partin about the assassination-plot conversations that had been a part of Partin's first contact with the Justice Department. Hooker and Neal argued that details of the assassination plot were immaterial to a trial involving jury tampering. They wanted to bar information that might be considered as simply inflammatory and prejudicial to the rights of Hoffa and other defendants.

The prosecution's efforts to avoid those first conversations between Partin and Federal Attorney Grimsley only made the defense lawyers more eager to explore those talks.

Prosecutor Neal objected to their repeated efforts to do this. He asked for a closed session to explain the talks, away from the jury. In that closed session, he warned, "This man (Partin) reported a threat by James R. Hoffa to kill the Attorney General."[3]

"We have no objection (to the testimony)," attorney Harry Berke said for Hoffa. "We think it is so fantastic and unbelievable we are not trying to suppress it."

Judge Wilson ruled that talk of the plot was immaterial to the jury-fix trial and not to be explored. However, the defense persisted in open court. Harvey Silets, lawyer for Dorfman, pressed Partin with questions, and Partin said, "It concerned something that I've been instructed not to say."

"Now in your course of meeting with (Daniels) . . . Mr. Hoffa's name came up?" Silets said.

"In a manner not related to this (case), sir," Partin replied.

Federal lawyers Grimsley, Daniels, and Pitcher were called to testify as defense lawyers sought evidence of inconsistency or grounds for a mistrial.

Frank Grimsley insisted that the first calls from Assistant United States Attorney Duffy sketchily mentioned a "security" matter.

"Wasn't the name Hoffa mentioned at all?" Silets asked.

"No, I don't believe the name Hoffa itself was mentioned," Grimsley replied.

Grimsley testified that he had been given details on the plot just prior to his meeting with Ed Partin.

"Tell us what that was?" Silets coaxed him.

"It doesn't pertain to this case," Grimsley replied.

Judge Wilson cut in to comment: "I will allow him to tell the subject matter of it, but it would not be appropriate to go into the details of it, gentlemen."

"Mr. Partin stated that in a conference with Mr. Hoffa—," Grimsley started to say but was cut off by Judge Wilson, who said, "Don't go into the details of it."

"Well, Mr. Partin stated that Mr. Hoffa told him that he would like—" and again the judge cautioned Grimsley against going into the details.

"An assassination plot," Grimsley testified.

"What is the date of that?" Silets probed.

---

[3]Later, this closed session was made a part of the public record of the Chattanooga jury-tampering trial.

"That would be September or October, 1962," Grimsley said, believing that Silets had reference to his October 2 meeting with Partin.

"I'm inquiring about this conversation—reputed, alleged conversation between Hoffa and Partin," Silets corrected him. "When was that to have taken place?"

"Sometime in the summer of 1962," Grimsley replied.

"Well, did you ever check it (the Partin story) out?" Silets asked.

"Yes, someone did," Grimsley answered.

"And what did you discover?"

"He (Partin) stayed somewhere in Washington," Grimsley replied.

"Did you discover whether he had seen the defendant, Hoffa?"

"That I'm not certain of," Grimsley replied.

"As a matter of fact, he never did see the defendant, Hoffa, isn't that true? . . . Specifically in the summer of 1962, all your report discloses was that he was in Washington. You have no specific information of his being with the defendant, Hoffa, isn't that right?" Silets pressed.

"I wouldn't know," Grimsley told him. "I haven't read the report lately."

Silets then tried to characterize the assassination plot as a "contrived circumstance" and "unsubstantiated wild charges" to hide improper schemes of wiretapping involving the Justice Department.

On cross-examination, Prosecutor James Neal tried to refute comments by Silets that tended to discredit Ed Partin and his story of an assassination plot.

"Mr. Silets talked about a wild rumor and so forth respective to an assassination"—Neal started his question. Then he said, "Did you or someone give Mr. Partin a lie-detector test on that?"

"The F.B.I. gave him one, yes," Grimsley replied.

"And what were the results?"

"That he was telling the truth," Grimsley said.

Then Louisiana lawyer Billy Daniels was grilled by Silets on the alleged assassination plot.

"He (Partin) indicated to me that he had sought to make contact with a law enforcement agency that he could trust in order to divulge what he termed a plot," Daniels explained.

Daniels then said that, in the subsequent investigation, the Baton Rouge District Attorney's office had recorded some of Partin's conversations with Hoffa in October, 1962. Daniels testified that one recorded conversation "had its origin in a newspaper story that had appeared locally, either in the latter part of September or the first part of October, with the theft of a plastic explosive in the New Orleans area.

"Mr. Partin placed a call to Mr. Hoffa to apprise him of the fact that he had access to a supply of this plastic, as he termed it," Daniels testified.

"Did Hoffa actually speak to him, do you know?" Silets said.

"This I don't remember, sir," Daniels replied.

"This conversation, did you hear Mr. Hoffa's voice on that recording?"

"I don't recollect that I heard Mr. Hoffa's voice on that recording," Daniels said.

Lawyer Frank Grimsley then was called back to the witness chair to clarify a point for the jury.

"Mr. Grimsley, you stated that one of the recordings had to do with an assassination plot," Prosecutor John Hooker began.

"Yes, sir," Grimsley answered.

"Did it have anything to do with the assassination of President John F. Kennedy?" Hooker inquired.

"No sir, it did not," Grimsley answered.

Walter Sheridan, who then was called by the defense, testified: "I was furnished a report concerning this specific (assassination) matter. I believe it was turned over to the court."

Sheridan said, "Instructions were given to the F.B.I. to pursue the matter further . . . they took certain action as a result of that."

He testified that he had not planted Partin in the Hoffa crowd, but added: "I was glad that he was there when he was there. In fact, he left many times when I wished he could have stayed there . . . . Each time I got information, it was turned over to the F.B.I. They conducted an investigation to corroborate the information, did corroborate it, at the time action was taken."

There was a defense effort later in this trial to use testimony of convicted criminals and disreputable women to discredit Partin as a "narcotics addict," but such testimony was contradicted by medical experts. Two doctors who were specialists on narcotics testified that tests they had given to Partin indicated he had never been a narcotics addict.

Hoffa, usually a smooth star witness on his own behalf, was now a snarling and argumentative witness under the cross-examination by stentorian-toned Prosecutor Hooker. Hoffa denied discussing jury fixing with Partin. He said he didn't know what Ewing King and others among his associates had been doing.

In the prosecution's argument to the jury James Neal gave a careful analysis of the F.B.I. testimony supporting the information Ed Partin had passed to Walter Sheridan. He and Assistant U. S. Attorney John Reddy left the dramatic close to John Hooker.

"Yours is a great responsibility," that big-voiced Nashville lawyer told the jury in his distinctive drawl. "Hoffa is the head of the largest labor union in the world, but that don't give him a license to fix a jury, and I say to you with all the sincerity at my command, that Chattanooga, after more than a hundred years, has survived Chickamauga and Missionary Ridge but Chattanooga can never survive the acquittal of those who have been proven to be guilty of contaminating, tampering with, fixing a jury in the courts of justice in this state."

The jury returned its verdict on March 4, 1964, finding James Riddle Hoffa and three of the other defendants—Ewing King, Larry Campbell and Thomas Parks—guilty of obstructing justice. The jury acquitted Allen Dorfman and Nicholas Tweel. One defense lawyer, Jacques Schiffer, was cited for contempt of court, sentenced to a sixty-day jail term and fined $1,000. (He appealed the conviction.) [4]

Judge Frank Wilson sentenced Hoffa to eight years in the

---

[4] On July 29, 1965, the U.S. Court of Appeals for the Sixth Circuit (Cincinnati, Ohio) affirmed the jury-tampering conviction of James R. Hoffa, Thomas Parks, Larry Campbell and Ewing King. It was a unanimous decision. An appeal to the Supreme Court was indicated.

Federal prison and a $10,000 fine. It was three-year prison terms for King, Campbell, and Parks.

Hoffa shouted he was "innocent," but Judge Wilson declared that the evidence clearly sustained the guilty verdict.

"You stand here convicted of having tampered, really, with the very soul of the nation," Judge Wilson said. "You stand here convicted of having struck at the very foundation upon which everything else in this nation depends . . . that is the administration of justice."

The conviction of Hoffa and his three associates in the Chattanooga trial was the first of several moves to punish the jury fixers.

Lawrence W. (Red) Medlin, the 53-year-old Nashville merchant, was convicted on April 3, 1964, on a charge of trying to influence prospective juror J. C. Tippens. He was sentenced to eighteen months in prison.

Henry F. (Buster) Bell, vice-president of the International Longshoreman's Association, was convicted a few days later on a charge of attempting to bribe another juror in Hoffa's Nashville trial. He was sentenced to five years in prison and fined $5,000.

Z. T. (Tommy) Osborn, in the year he had planned to be president of the Nashville Bar Association, was convicted and sentenced to a three-and-one-half-year Federal prison term and fined $5,000.

All three of these men appealed their convictions, but there was more trouble ahead for others in the Hoffa entourage involving still more charges of jury tampering.

This drama was indicative of—and a result of—the attitude in Hoffa's "hoodlum empire," where it was believed that "every man has his price."

In Tennessee, Hoffa had outsmarted himself. He had been on trial in Nashville in 1962 on an indictable misdemeanor charge that carried a maximum one-year jail term upon conviction. He had beaten that rap. But the jury-tampering efforts there had resulted in an eight-year prison sentence. And this man, considered a "smart" fellow by his hoodlum associates, had still more trouble ahead in Chicago.

XXXV

Pension Fund Plunder—Guilty Again

The legend of Jimmy Hoffa the Invincible was destroyed by that jury-tampering conviction in Chattanooga in March, 1964, and the somber union boss went on trial a few weeks later on fraud charges.

The bounce and confidence were gone when Jimmy entered Federal court in Chicago on April 27, 1964, to face trial again. The twenty-eight-count indictment here charged that Hoffa and seven others had engaged in fraud in handling more than twenty million dollars in Teamsters pension fund loans. It alleged that Hoffa and Ben Dranow, a former Minneapolis businessman, and their associates had diverted more than one million dollars from the union pension fund in loans for their own use. The indictment asserted that more than $100,000 was used to help bail out Hoffa's Florida real estate scheme, Sun Valley.[1]

This indictment was most damaging to Hoffa's reputation with his own union members, for it charged abuse of his position as a trustee of the Central States Southeast Southwest Area pension fund. The fund was accumulated from payments by employers for the pensions, life insurance and disability of more than 200,000 rank-and-file Teamsters in 20 states. By the time the Chicago indictment was returned on June 4, 1963, the money was

[1]U. S. v. George Burris, James R. Hoffa et al., United States District Court for the Northern District of Illinois, Eastern District (Chicago) , 63 Cr. No. 317.

pouring into this huge fund at the rate of more than three million six hundred thousand dollars every month. By trial time a year later, the money was rolling in at more than four million dollars a month.

Annual reports filed by the pension fund showed assets of more than one hundred sixty-nine million dollars on January 31, 1962. At that time, more than one hundred twelve million dollars was invested in real estate loans and mortgages with the approval of the sixteen trustees. The total fund had climbed to more than two hundred million dollars by the summer of 1964.

The Taft-Hartley law required an equal number of trustees from the union and from management, and in this respect the legal requirement had been met. But according to the indictment and trial testimony, the balance of representatives from labor and management had not been effective in guaranteeing careful handling of the pension funds for Teamsters union members. It was claimed that Hoffa dominated the control of the pension funds, and the indictment charged that the tough little Detroit labor leader used "fraud, deceit (and) misrepresentation" to influence the granting of questionable loans. It was charged that he had made false representations and misleading statements to other trustees and professional advisers, and that he had spoken out as an advocate of certain loans being pushed by Dranow.

The trial involved fourteen loans granted by the Teamsters' pension fund to finance construction of hotels, shopping centers and other projects in six states—Florida, Louisiana, Alabama, Missouri, New Jersey and California. It was charged that Ben Dranow had served as collector and that he had demanded commissions of up to 10 per cent of the loans. The payoffs were made in cash, through stock options and through stock interests, according to the indictment.

It was a complicated investigation covering transactions from Las Vegas to New York, and from Minneapolis to Miami. Besides Hoffa, the major defendant was Dranow, who had been convicted of mail, wire and bankruptcy fraud, tax evasion and bail jumping.

Other defendants were:

Abe I. Weinblatt, 67, a retired Miami Beach businessman and former business associate of Dranow;

S. George Burris, 65, a New York City accountant, who was a principal in firms that received pension fund loans;

Herbert R. Burris, 31, son of S. George Burris and a New York attorney;

Samuel Hyman, 69, a Key West, Florida, real estate operator who was a principal in firms that received union pension fund loans;

Calvin Kovens, 39, a Miami Beach builder and real estate operator who had received union pension fund loans and had been convicted on fraud charges prior to the Chicago trial;

Zachary A. Strate, Jr., 43, who had obtained union pension fund loans in connection with his New Orleans building and real estate operations.

Charges were made that Dranow and the Burrises had sought out those persons needing loans, then represented that they were in a favored position to obtain loans from the Teamsters pension funds because of their close association with Jimmy Hoffa. (The charge against the younger Burris was dismissed midway in the trial because of insufficient evidence.)

The eight men on trial and the ten defense lawyers used all the available space at the huge L-shaped table that crowded the front of United States District Judge Richard B. Austin's court.

In numbers, the defense team seemed to overwhelm the two government lawyers, Abe Poretz and Charles Z. Smith. But the two prosecutors were backed by a huge staff of lawyer-investigators in a suite of offices across the street from the Federal courthouse. Walter Sheridan was not on hand, but Tom McTiernan, William Ryan, James Canavan, Don Moore and a group of equally able lawyers were available to rapidly coordinate the investigative work necessary to assure that there would be no tampering with the jury or the government witnesses.

The convictions in Chattanooga had been a warning to jury tamperers, but there was no assurance that it would not happen again in Chicago. In fact, the government decision to go to trial in Tennessee first was based on the supposition that jury tampering was less likely in Tennessee than in Chicago.

Hoffa went out of his way at recess to throw abusive language at me, and when court was in session there was a mean, cold glare in his eyes. He had the same treatment for Prosecutors Poretz and Smith. For the most part, we ignored him, but on a few occasions I couldn't resist the temptation to toss back such a comment as: "Everything is falling apart for you, Jimmy. Your deals are finally catching up with you."

"I'm not done yet," he snarled back, with a crisp prediction that "you'll be six feet under before I'm stopped."

But even as he spoke, with a touch of his old braggadocio, Hoffa was realistic enough to see indications that many of the "smart" people were preparing to drop him.

Edward Bennett Williams, the Washington lawyer who had been on the Teamsters payroll since successfully defending Hoffa in 1957, had told the Teamsters he doubted the legality of using union funds to pay for Hoffa's defense in a criminal case. International Teamsters treasurer John English, who for seven years had been a Hoffa booster, ordered suspension of payment of Hoffa's legal expenses out of the Teamsters treasury.

New York Teamsters boss John O'Rourke, a vice president of the International Teamsters, and John B. Backhus of Philadelphia, another international vice president, requested that no more legal fees be paid for Hoffa pending a meeting of the executive board. The majority of the members of the Teamsters executive board appeared likely to oppose Hoffa because they didn't want to risk personal liability by approving use of union funds for an illegal purpose. It was estimated that more than $700,000 in union funds had been spent on expenses for Hoffa's defense in the trials in Nashville and Chattanooga and in preparing for the Chicago trial.

The Federal labor reform law required that all union funds be expended for union business and the benefit of union members. In the opinion of Labor Department lawyers, the defense of James Hoffa on criminal charges didn't fit that definition. Hoffa's argument that his troubles resulted from carrying out his duties as a union official hadn't impressed the government take the risk.
lawyers and didn't ring true enough for his subordinates to

Facing discontent throughout his union empire, Hoffa now was tied down in what could be a lengthy trial and was no longer free to jump around the country, stamping out fires of discord.

All through Hoffa's camp an air of defeatism was present. At the trials in Washington, New York, Nashville and Chattanooga, Hoffa had been the center of a loudly optimistic circle of supporters. In the company of men who praised and applauded his every move, he found his sustenance and exuded confidence.

By the time the Chicago trial started things were different. Many of his most trusted associates were dead—Owen Bert Brennan, Henry Lower and Gene San Soucie. Many were in jail or were embroiled in so much personal trouble that they wanted no part of Hoffa's troubles. Still others had simply deserted what they felt was a sinking ship. To complicate things more, Hoffa—convicted by the testimony of Ed Partin—had become distrustful of any associates who moved too close to him or tried to know too much of what he was doing.

The scene in the Chicago courtroom was depressing. Instead of the rowdy, rough-voiced but well-tailored men who symbolized Teamsters power and money, Hoffa was confronted with the rumpled and dispirited figure of Ben Dranow.

The once-dapper, big-spending Dranow had become a seedy-looking, gray-haired symbol of defeat. The 56-year-old financial manipulator had started serving twelve years in the Federal penitentiary as a result of his earlier convictions, and he was accompanied to this court by a United States marshal. Gone was the lively living at plush hotels, with the best liquor. Dranow spent his nights in jail and was brought to the courthouse each morning in steel handcuffs.

The handcuffs were unlocked and removed before Dranow entered the courtroom in view of the jury, but the removal of the steel from his wrists did not lift the weight of the long prison term ahead of him.

Although Hoffa and Dranow talked occasionally when the jurors were out, it was not with the warmth and confidence that had marked their relationship before Dranow went to prison.

Jimmy Hoffa, who had never looked down on a man with a prison record, nevertheless disliked the aroma of defeat. Also, there was a practical reason for avoiding contact with Dranow when the jury was present, for much of the evidence centered on testimony of payoffs to Dranow, the promises Dranow had made, and the threats made by Dranow. It was no accident that Hoffa was seated as far away from Dranow as possible when the twelve jurors and four alternate jurors were in the courtroom. He wished to avoid any appearance of the closeness to Dranow that the government lawyers said existed.

Even the presence of Prosecutor Poretz was a reminder of Teamsters' defeats. Poretz, whose experience as a prosecutor traced back to his work as an assistant to Thomas E. Dewey in New York, had obtained one of the earlier convictions of Dranow. Other Poretz victories included conviction of Frank Collins, secretary-treasurer of Detroit Teamsters Local 299, for perjuring himself before a Federal grand jury; Mrs. Sally Hucks, Woodner Hotel telephone operator who had perjured herself before the McClellan committee, and Ed Weinheimer, who had lied before a Federal grand jury when questioned about an alleged payoff to Barney Baker.

From the time the Chicago trial started, Judge Richard B. Austin took the realistic attitude that jury-tampering was a distinct possibility. As the jurors were selected, Judge Austin informed them that he intended to lock up the jury for the duration of what might be a three-month trial. He explained that each juror would be permitted one visit from his family each week and one telephone call each day, which would be monitored by a U. S. marshal.

To accept jury service was almost like volunteering for three months in jail, except that the quarters provided at the Great Lakes Naval Training Center were more comfortable. Few people wanted to serve, and a full two weeks was needed before the jury selection process was completed and the government started to present its case.

There were a hundred ways for the prosecutors to link Ben Dranow to the pension fund frauds, but Hoffa had left fewer tracks. The testimony of Stanton D. Sanson, a Bal Harbour, Florida, real estate investor, provided the first important evidence linking Hoffa to the fraud conspiracy.

Sanson, who had made application for a five million dollar mortgage loan from the Teamsters, testified he was contacted by Dranow. Dranow had said he could assure approval of Sanson's loan from the Teamsters if Sanson would agree to take

over Sun Valley. The real estate man told the jury that Dranow
then put Hoffa on the telephone, and that Hoffa had said Sun
Valley was in considerable difficulty and "he was very anxious
to get a concern such as mine to take over this development and
do something with it."

Hoffa had told him that if he would take over Sun Valley,
then the apartment house loan would go through and further
Teamsters funds would be made available for the proper development of Sun Valley, Sanson testified.

Accompanied by Dranow, Sanson examined the Sun Valley
project, and he now told the court that "the gist of my report
was that the Sun Valley project was hopeless." Dranow did not
want the critical report submitted.

When the Sun Valley deal washed out, Sanson said that
Dranow had met him in a small restaurant in Minneapolis and
told him the five million dollar loan from the Teamsters pension
funds could still be put through for a commission of ten per cent.

"I told him (Dranow) that was ridiculous," Sanson testified.

Sanson said Dranow then came down to five per cent, but
requested that the commission be paid in cash.

"Then I told him that he misunderstood, that the commission would be paid by check, and the check would recite
the purpose," Sanson said.

After he had made it clear that any commission would be
by check only, Dranow dropped the subject and Sanson never
received approval of the apartment house loan. Sanson later
obtained a six million six hundred thousand dollar loan through
the Federal Housing Administration and so had not concerned
himself with further dealings with Dranow. He characterized
the Sun Valley project as "a bad property, handled badly."

O. P. Hewitt, Jr., president and chairman of the board of
the Florida National Bank at Orlando, gave the first firm testimony that Hoffa had deposited $400,000 in Teamsters union
funds in the Orlando bank as security for loans of a like amount
to the Sun Valley project.

"I was loan officer for the bank, and dealt with Local 299
of Detroit," Hewitt testified. He told of the loans to Sun Valley,
his dealings with Hoffa, and the agreement that the deposits

from Local 299 "would remain equal to, or in excess of, any outstanding Sun Valley loans."

In line with this agreement, the bank refused to permit Local 299 to withdraw its money when the Sun Valley project started going bad, Hewitt testified.

The son of Henry Lower, president of the Sun Valley project, gave some of the most important testimony linking Hoffa to a direct ownership of Sun Valley. Hoffa had denied this ownership under oath, and had contended he had only an option to buy. The evidence indicated that Lower simply ran Sun Valley for Hoffa and Bert Brennan.

Frederick Lowe, son of Henry Lower, had changed his name to Lowe by the time he testified in Chicago, nearly a year after his father's death. Lowe identified an agreement between his father and Hoffa that indicated Lower was holding a 45 per cent interest for Hoffa. He said he had found it in a cook book in a drawer in his father's home.

Hoffa's lawyers fought to keep that important piece of paper out of the record, but Judge Austin permitted the so-called "cook book document" to enter the record as evidence.

Lowe testified that Hoffa's signature on the paper was familiar, but he could not be positive that the "J. R. Hoffa" was the signature of the Teamsters president. Later, an F. B. I. handwriting expert, Hilding Dahlgren, stated positively that the "J. R. Hoffa" was the signature of James R. Hoffa, the defendant.

Dozens of other witnesses established the minutes of meetings of the pension fund and identified the records of long-distance telephone calls between Hoffa, Dranow and persons who had received loans from the Teamsters' pension fund. However, Vaughan B. Connelly, a real estate investor, was most important of all Government witnesses.

Testimony by Vaughan Connelly painted the most detailed picture of the activities of Hoffa and Dranow in the big pension fund payoffs. Under oath Connelly admitted that he had borrowed four million three hundred thousand dollars from the pension fund in two loans and had made payoffs of more than $400,000 to Dranow for delivery to Hoffa.

Connelly said he couldn't testify as to how much of that payoff money actually was delivered to Hoffa, but he linked Hoffa to nearly every step of Dranow's manipulations.

Connelly testified he had been seeking the loans in connection with expansion and remodeling of the Everglades Hotel in Miami. He bought the hotel in September, 1957, and was steered to Dranow in 1958 by Cal Kovens, the Miami contractor who was doing the remodeling work.

Kovens had said he would bring a man who could secure Teamsters loans, Connelly related. "He said he was a little man who you wouldn't think . . . could get a great deal done, but he always seemed to be able to deliver the goods."

"He said his name was Grossman," Connelly testified, bringing up the first of many fictitious names Dranow used in carrying out the loan payoff racket.

Connelly said "Grossman" later told him his real name was Ben Dranow. Connelly had advised Dranow he needed about two million to two million five hundred thousand dollars for the project, but he testified that Dranow had suggested he should ask for three million or three million five hundred thousand.

"I said this was far too much," Connelly testified. Then Dranow told him that there would be a ten per cent fee and suggested that he should apply for a three million three hundred thousand dollar loan to provide three million dollars for the construction and the $300,000 fee.

"I followed his advice and got the loan," Connelly testified. Then Dranow had told him the ten per cent fee must be in cash and "under the table," Connelly said.

The first loan of three million three hundred thousand dollars had barely been approved by the pension fund trustees when Dranow and Kovens dropped by to demand the cash fee. When it wasn't paid immediately, Connelly said Dranow had started threatening him.

Connelly quoted Dranow as saying: "I must have that money immediately . . . Mr. Hoffa is raising hell, and he expected it because he had paid the full amount of the loan.

"During this same conversation, Dranow told me he did not want to be the goat on this thing, that Kovens had vouched for me, and that he did not want to see any harm come to me," Connelly said. "He was very abusive.

"Within 24 hours, Kovens telephoned me again and stated again that he was hopeful that no physical harm would come to me but these boys play rough, and he hoped I could get the funds," Connelly testified.

Still later, Dranow had called again, and this time he was conciliatory, saying it would be all right if only $100,000 in cash was given to him immediately, with the balance to be paid later, the real estate investor testified.

Dranow had instructed that the $100,000 should be in small, old bills, Connelly said. He had then called the First National Bank of Miami, spoke to a Mr. Stockwell, the vice president, and arranged to get the cash as directed.

After giving Stockwell a $100,000 check payable to cash, Connelly testified that he had followed Dranow's instructions and taken the bag of cash and walked five blocks to Koven's office.

Kovens and Dranow were present when he arrived, Connelly said. Both were nervous as they counted the money and had to count it "two or three times."

Connelly related that Dranow then burned the bank wrappers that had been around the money, put it in a small, zippered bag, and called in a muscular man who, he had said, would escort him to Washington "to deliver the money to the boss."

Even before the loan finally was approved, Connelly said, Dranow had started draining him of cash. In November, 1958, Dranow had insisted that he arrange to send $3,000 in cash to Sally Hucks, the chief telephone operator at the Woodner Hotel in Washington to pay her costs on a vacation in Hawaii.

Connelly testified that Kovens needed $42,000 for an income tax payment in early 1959, and the Everglades expansion and remodeling were much more expensive than estimated, and that he was in trouble because of a lack of cash.

Dranow had said that he could arrange another $1 million loan through the Teamsters pension fund, but during that same period in the spring of 1959 he had warned Connelly that investigators for the McClellan committee were in Florida, trying to link Hoffa with questionable loans from Teamsters funds.

Connelly testified that Dranow first asked him if the McClellan investigators had seen him, and when he had replied they hadn't, Dranow had advised him "to keep out of sight."

Connelly said he tried to avoid the subpoena services, but in April, 1959, he had been summoned to appear before a Federal grand jury in Orlando.

Connelly testified that Dranow had advised him to give false testimony before the grand jury and had also instructed him that—"I should not take my records up there, and do not implicate either him or Mr. Hoffa in any discussions."

On April 8, 1959, Connelly said, he went before the Federal grand jury, gave false testimony as Dranow had instructed, then went to the Orlando airport. There he met Dranow and assured him that he had not implicated either Dranow or Hoffa.

A month later, again on Dranow's instructions, Connelly testified, he had given a false affidavit to the McClellan committee. In it he had stated that he had never discussed the loan with Dranow, had paid no fee in connection with the loan, and that neither Hoffa nor Dranow had any direct or indirect role in obtaining it.

After giving that statement to the Senate investigators, Connelly said, he had met with Dranow and Kovens at a Miami Beach golf club.

"I told them that I had followed their advice and made a false statement to the McClellan committee," Connelly now testified. He said he had showed them a copy of his statement.

Dranow praised him for his false testimony, Connelly told the Chicago court, and said "that I had stood up for Mr. Hoffa himself."

Then Connelly told of a telephone conversation with Hoffa in which "Mr. Hoffa told me he had heard I had given a fine statement to the McClellan committee, and he appreciated it."

There had been continuing pressure from the McClellan committee, but on July 21, 1959, Connelly stated, Hoffa had pushed through the second one million dollar pension fund loan. Hoffa even arranged for the check to be delivered that same day at the Edgewater Beach Hotel in Chicago. Hoffa had insisted upon issuance of the check despite an attorney's warning: "Jimmy, this will get you in more trouble than anything you have done."

On cross-examination, lawyers for Hoffa and the other defendants pushed to discredit Connelly on the grounds that he was an admitted perjurer since he had lied to the Senate committee and the Federal grand jury.

"I perjured myself," Connelly admitted, and explained, "There was a continuing fear that there would be physical harm to me."

Connelly testified that he had been a multi-millionaire when he started his venture with a Teamsters loan, but that he was "now in bankruptcy" because of the disaster of payoffs and construction costs on the Everglades.

He said he had put more than three million dollars of his own money into the Everglades. The payoffs, confusion and fear in dealing with Hoffa and Dranow had the Everglades in serious trouble within a few months, he said. He had lied because of "fear" and also because Hoffa and Dranow had indicated they would provide enough money from the pension funds to save the Everglades, Connelly related. Instead, they had foreclosed on the Everglades in September, 1959—as soon as Connelly was under oath on a false statement that absolved them of connection with the loans and as soon as it appeared that the Mc-Clellan committee might be going out of business.

Early in this Chicago trial of Hoffa, it appeared the government might have serious trouble when Chief Prosecutor Abe Poretz became ill and finally had to withdraw from the case. Fortunately, William O. Bittman, a dynamic 32-year-old lawyer from the office of the United States District Attorney, was available to try the case. He was young in years but expperienced in the rough and tumble of a trial court. He and Don Moore moved quickly and brought an added vigor to the prosecution.

Bittman and Smith continued to pile up the corroboration of the basic stories told by Sanson and Connelly on Dranow's effort to bail out Sun Valley, the pattern of commissions for loans from the union pension fund, and the cooperation that had existed between Hoffa and Dranow.

Warren Rose, a land developer from the New Orleans area, testified of his experience in acquiring payoff money "in old small bills" for Dranow in connection with a one million three hundred fifty thousand dollar loan from the Teamsters' pension fund.

Rose testified that he had talked with Ben Dranow, but that the actual delivery of the money was by Zachary A. Strate, Jr., who was associated with him in a motel project in New Orleans.

Both Rose and William Sherman, a restaurant operator associated with the motel project, testified that Strate told them of delivery of the cash to Dranow.

"Strate told me . . . he got $165,000 in his suitcase and delivered it to Dranow . . . in Miami," Sherman testified. "When he gave Dranow the suitcase, Dranow opened it . . . and when he was through counting the money he wanted to give Strate back the suitcase. So Strate says: 'The hell with the suitcase . . . you got all the money. Keep the suitcase.' "

Shortly after Dranow took the witness stand on July 13, in Chicago, he threw a screaming tantrum and claimed he could not testify until two government officials left the courtroom. His venom was directed at Miles Lord, the United States District Attorney from Minnesota, and Carmine Bellino, a special assistant to President Kennedy. Lord had prosecuted Dranow in Minnesota, and Bellino had been his nemesis as an accountant-investigator for the McClellan committee..

Dranow's lawyer, Frank Ragano, told Judge Austin that "he (Dranow) can't think clearly and can't testify as he should" while Lord and Bellino were in court.

Bittman snapped back that if the lawyers for Dranow and Hoffa wished to exclude Lord and Bellino, he would insist that Joey Glimco and some of Glimco's labor racketeer associates be removed from the court.

Judge Austin ruled that Lord and Bellino had a right to be in court, and that Dranow and his attorneys would not be permitted to determine who would be present.

Dranow denied everything, as he usually did. He didn't go out looking for borrowers, didn't help put loans through, didn't take payoffs, and didn't deliver payoff money to Jimmy Hoffa, he claimed. On cross-examination, Bittman tore into Dranow's criminal record and emphasized that Dranow was flatly contradicting the sworn testimony and the documented record.

When Hoffa took the witness chair he denied any special power in granting loans. "I'm only one of 16 trustees of the pension fund," he testified. "I have no more authority than any other trustee."

With regard to the loans and payoffs to rescue the Sun Valley project, Hoffa's denial was total: "I had nothing to do with it; no knowledge about it."

Hoffa engaged in his usual skillful denials—and seeming denials when a flat denial represented a risk of perjury. Hoffa insisted that he had received no payoffs. He couldn't deny an interest in Sun Valley, but he questioned whether it was his signature on the bottom of "the cook-book document."

An F.B.I. handwriting expert had given positive identification of the "J. R. Hoffa" as having been signed by Jimmy Hoffa.

Hoffa said he simply couldn't remember ever having signed that document, and he said he doubted that he had because "on a legal document or a letter, I would never use J. R. Hoffa. I would use James R. Hoffa."

On cross-examination, Bittman presented a legal document and two letters relating to dealings with Cal Kovens. Hoffa admitted his signature on the papers. Then Bittman told him to look again and see if he had not signed "J. R. Hoffa" on those documents.

It was a difficult trial for Bittman from the time he entered the arena, for Hoffa used his usual tactics to wear down this replacement on the prosecution team. Often as Judge Austin left the bench each day, Hoffa would approach Bittman, cursing and throwing obscenities and veiled threats.

Although Bittman was young, he was experienced and tough in the battles of a criminal court. He avoided Hoffa, ignored him, and when Hoffa continued to press him, the young attorney would walk into Judge Austin's chambers and ask to make a record of the abuse he was receiving from Hoffa.

Bittman rapped back at the Teamsters boss that he had no need for communication with Hoffa, and that if Hoffa wished to communicate with him it could be done in court or through defense attorneys.

That stopped Hoffa's direct abuse, but it did not stop the growled threats from a little group of Chicago racket figures who waited in the hall nearly every day. The Justice Department assigned two United States marshals as a bodyguard for Bittman through the last five weeks of the trial. Two or more F.B.I. agents were in the courtroom to assist the marshals.

In his argument to the jury, Bittman spent five hours describing how Hoffa had violated his "position of trust" by engaging in a conspiracy with Ben Dranow. He traced the basic loan transactions to the Everglades, the Key West Foundation, the Fontainebleau Motor Hotel, the Good Samaritan Hospital and the First Berkley Corporation.

All the elements of the worst kind of conspiracy to defraud were present, Bittman told the jurors. He pointed to evidence of forgeries, Dranow's use of three or four fictitious names, Hoffa's secret agreement on the Sun Valley ownership, the threatening of witnesses by Dranow and the "huge cash kickbacks and payoffs."

The government had used 114 witnesses to establish the facts because Hoffa and Dranow and their associates had stressed complex transactions for "concealment" of their acts, Bittman told the jurors. He scoffed at Hoffa's contention that he was only one of sixteen trustees and had no special authority to approve loans. He pointed out that Hoffa didn't deny having signed the important "cook-book document," but had dodged a direct answer by saying: "I have no recollection of it. I don't think I signed it, and I just don't recall it at all."

This was a "secret deal" in which Hoffa had a financial interest in promoting land to sell to Teamsters union members, Bittman told the jurors, and when it went into default it was the union's $400,000 deposit which was put in jeopardy.

"Who are you going to believe—Benjamin Dranow or all these witnesses?" Bittman asked the jury. "Dranow—who has been convicted of mail fraud, bankruptcy fraud, income tax evasion and bail jumping."

The young prosecutor declared that he could not recall one government witness out of 114 who had a criminal conviction on his record.

Bittman dramatized the stages of the "misrepresentation by

J. R. Hoffa" to the Teamsters trustees on conditions existing near loan properties. The prosecutor told the jury that the minutes of the trustees' meeting showed Hoffa had claimed "Sears and Roebuck is building a $55,000,000 expansion" near a Florida property involved in a pending loan application.

Although Hoffa had testified he meant only $5 million, Bittman pointed out that this, too, was to be challenged, since the responsible Sears official testified the only money spent in that area was "to paint a wall in their catalogue sales store."

"He (Hoffa) is telling the trustees that Sears . . . is spending $55,000,000 to lead them to grant this loan," Bittman told the jury. "And he (Hoffa) was down there (at the property), and he knew it was a misrepresentation."

Bittman spelled out the frauds in the more than twenty-five million dollars in union pension fund loans, and he lingered over the details of the payoffs and kickbacks which resulted in more than one million, seven hundred thousand dollars being diverted to the personal use of Dranow, Hoffa and their associates.

This was the money of Teamsters union members, Bittman told the jurors, yet it was made a part of "one gigantic scheme to defraud.

"I submit to you that this defendant," he motioned toward Hoffa, "that these seven defendants are guilty beyond a reasonable doubt of the charges in the indictment—mail fraud, wire fraud counts and the conspiracy. And I submit to you that these seven individuals make Jesse James and his gang look like purse snatchers."

Maurice Walsh, one of Hoffa's attorneys, leaped forward protesting. "There is not a train in this case. The prosecution is drawing an invidious comparison, highly prejudicial."

Judge Austin denied Walsh's quickly entered motion for a mistrial.

In his summary for the defense, Walsh tried to portray Jimmy Hoffa as a diligent labor leader, serving as a trustee of the pension fund to protect the funds of union members. He contended that there was no evidence that the Teamsters pension fund had lost money, or that Hoffa had gained any money. In asking for an acquittal of Hoffa, Walsh declared: "He has expended great effort on behalf of union labor. He has served his community in many, many regards." Walsh charged that Hoffa, "a devoted union man," was being "persecuted" for the political ambitions of some unnamed person.

Judge Richard Austin submitted the case to the jury on Friday night, July 25, and it was Sunday afternoon, July 27, when the jury foreman knocked on the door, indicating a verdict had been reached.

The first fraud count involved all seven defendants. All were found guilty. Bittman gave a pleased sigh, but a low growl came from the Hoffa supporters. Several of Hoffa's supporters shouted in rage and rushed from the courtroom. After that it was anticlimactic as the details of the other guilty verdicts were sorted out from among the 21 counts in the indictment.

Judge Austin thanked the jurors for "the contribution you have made to the processes of justice," and then set the sentencing date. A grim-faced Hoffa stalked from the court, barking a "no comment" at reporters.

On August 17, Judge Austin sentenced Jimmy Hoffa to five years in prison and a $10,000 fine on each of the four convictions —one for conspiracy and three for fraud. The prison terms were to be served concurrently, but they were to be served after he completed his eight-year term for jury tampering.

Ben Dranow was sentenced to five more years in prison on top of his four earlier convictions, and he was fined $10,000.

Calvin Kovens and Zachary A. Strate each were sentenced to three-year prison terms and $5,000 fines.

S. George Burris was sentenced to an 18-month prison term and fined $5,000.

Abe Weinblatt was fined $5,000 and sentenced to serve one hour in jail, this as a judicial concession to his grave heart condition.

Judge Austin lectured the defendants:

"The Court is one who feels that the sound of the clanging of the jailhouse door has a salutary effect not only on defendants behind whom it slams, but also those who may be tempted to indulge in the same conduct."

"It may be an old-fashioned idea," Judge Austin concluded, "but it is one that I hold."

ᴊimmy Hoffa was released under $10,000 bond, pending appeal of the conviction, for at 51 years of age, he still wasn't ready to give up and let the jailhouse door shut him away from the power and privileges that went with the presidency of the International Brotherhood of Teamsters. There was speculation among observers that Hoffa would try to run the union from prison, but thirteen years of prison time loomed long and forbidding.

XXXVI

The Teamsters' Corrupting Power

The second conviction of Jimmy Hoffa completed the major job for the "Hoffa unit" in the Justice Department, and dismemberment of that select little group was started within a month after Hoffa was sentenced. In September, 1964, Robert F. Kennedy resigned as Attorney General to become the Democratic candidate for the United States Senate from the state of New York. Walter Sheridan took a leave of absence from the Justice Department to work in Kennedy's Senate campaign. So did lawyer William French.

An income tax prosecution of Benjamin Cohen, a prominent Miami Beach lawyer, was the last important case pending among those connected with the Hoffa unit's work. Cohen, who had served as a lawyer for Hoffa, had obtained large commissions in connection with loans from the Teamsters Central States Southeast-Southwest Area pension fund.

John Cassidy and Charles Shaffer tried the case for the government, and on December 23, Cohen was convicted on a charge of evading $21,000 in federal taxes in 1960. The conviction was for Cohen's failure to report the major part of $60,000 in fees he received in connection with obtaining a one million, one hundred thousand dollar loan from the Teamsters pension fund for a Maryland motel project.

By March, 1965, when Cohen was sentenced to an 18-month

prison term, the entire Hoffa unit had been disbanded, and the job of following up the appeals was handled through regular Justice Department channels. Assistant Attorney General Herbert J. (Jack) Miller resigned and, with Cassidy and Courtney Evans, formed a new law firm in Washington.

Jim Neal was named United States District Attorney in Nashville, and William French joined a law firm in Phoenix. Abe Poretz, Tom McTiernan, Jim Canavan and Bill Ryan moved back into other work with the anti-rackets division in the Justice Department. Charley Smith was named a municipal judge in his home town of Seattle. Bill Bittman and Don Moore were moved from Chicago to Washington, D.C., to take charge of several complicated investigations, including the so-called Bobby Baker case.

The convictions of Dave Beck and Jimmy Hoffa remained etched in the public mind, but most people tended to forget the many other significant convictions that had been won with little more than local notice.

Raymond Cohen, one of three trustees of the International Brotherhood of Teamsters, had been convicted in Pennsylvania on a state charge of defrauding his Philadelphia local union of thousands of dollars.

Anthony (Tony Pro) Provenzano, a vice-president of the International Teamsters, was convicted on a Federal charge that he had extorted $17,000 from officials of a trucking firm that did business in the jurisdiction of his Local 560 in Hoboken, New Jersey. Nunzio Provenzano, brother of Tony Pro and vice-president of Local 522 in Newark, was convicted of attempted grand larceny.

In Detroit, George Roxburgh, a business agent for Hoffa's home Local 299, pleaded guilty to a bribery charge, and Rolland B. McMaster, secretary-treasurer of Local 299, was convicted on a bribery charge. Zigmont (Ziggie) Snyder, a convicted burglar who had been given refuge by Hoffa in a Detroit Teamsters local, was convicted on a Federal tax evasion charge.

Richard T. (Dick) Gosser, vice president of the United Automobile Workers International Union, was convicted in Toledo, Ohio, of conspiracy to defraud the Internal Revenue Service.

James G. Cross, former president of the Bakery and Confectionery Workers Union, was convicted of embezzling $35,000 from that union, and several other top officers were convicted with him.

In all, nearly 200 indictments were returned against Teamsters union officials, their associates in other unions, and the lawyers, accountants, bankers, robbers and petty racketeers who had permitted themselves to become part of the octopus of Teamsters union power. There were more than 125 convictions at the last count in mid-1965, and this was in addition to those won prior to 1961 as a result of the McClellan committee's investigations.

Although it had seemed difficult to convict Hoffa and some others, there were only a dozen acquittals. Of the fifteen cases dismissed, eleven were dismissed upon a government motion. The pending indictments dealt with minor figures involved in those crimes or the cover-up of crimes.

It was an effective job, yet no one could claim that the McClellan committee hearings or the work of the Hoffa unit brought total reform in labor—or even in the Teamsters union. It is unlikely that there ever will be a complete reform as long as such tremendous power is lodged in the huge truck drivers' union. The forty million dollars in the union treasury, the two hundred million dollar pension fund, and the economic force of the one million, seven hundred thousand-member union, each are prizes that ruthless men may find worth great risk. Put these prizes together, and it is little wonder that some of the worst scoundrels and some of the most power-hungry men should seek control over this giant union. The struggle for control of that power will continue as long as the power exists.

Dave Beck, Jimmy Hoffa and many less significant men believed that the might and the money of the Teamsters union gave them immunity from laws that other men must obey. They had a club over every business in America which depends upon truck transportation. It was strength which could be used arbitrarily to strangle the smallest businesses in the smallest towns or to bleed the biggest businesses in our biggest cities.

It was a power which those men used to bring some of the biggest newspapers in the nation to their knees in an exercise of force that the government could not duplicate under our Constitution.

But the power which Beck and Hoffa wielded was not an influence which was confined to dealings with an employer. It was a power which could also be—and was—wielded against rank-and-file union members who tried to dissent from the corrupt and dictatorial leadership. This was manifest in the arbitrary removal of officers who opposed union corruption.

There were cruel applications of that assumption of omnipotence in the brutal beatings of rank-and-file union members who protested against misuse of union funds and in the cancellation of union membership for men who needed a union card to hold a job.

The Teamsters' power was feared in politics. The Teamsters had the money, the muscle and the audacity to find ways to control city, county, state and federal political campaigns. Teamsters funds went into big legal retainers for politically connected lawyers. They went for campaign contributions. They were paid out for public relations fees to judges. From time to time, Teamsters money was involved in direct payoffs.

In the light of this concentration of power, money and labor union immunity, it is remarkable that there ever was a major labor racket investigation. It is amazing that there was a Justice Department with the ability, courage and the aggressive drive necessary to bring about the conviction of either Dave Beck or James R. Hoffa.

No history of American labor can be written that does not include an account of the dramatic nine-year period in which a stern-faced Senator from Arkansas and a boyish-appearing lawyer from Boston rocked the worlds of labor and politics.

John L. McClellan, the cautious Arkansas Senator, and Robert F. Kennedy, an inexperienced young millionaire lawyer, seemed an unlikely pair to succeed in exposing the corruption in American labor. Neither seemed a match for the power of the A.F.L.-C.I.O., and A.F.L.-C.I.O. President George Meany was firmly against any Congressional investigation of labor in early 1957. He claimed that the A.F.L.-C.I.O. executive board, which included Dave Beck, Maurice Hutcheson and several of their cronies, could clean labor's house with no help from Congress.

It is to Meany's credit that, as the first racketeers were exposed in the Teamsters, Bakery Workers and Textile Workers unions, he took a firm stand to try to put the house in order. He frankly admitted that he hadn't known "one tenth" of the problem before the McClellan committee started its hearings.

The A.F.L.-C.I.O. did a far from satisfactory cleanup job in many cases. There were compromises with corrupt forces that proved to be distasteful to those intent on complete reform. The Carpenters and the Operating Engineers were prime examples. But on the whole, it might be said that George Meany did a better job of tackling his problem than had the American Bar Association, local bar associations, and the various employer groups which had had serious ethical questions brought to their attention by the McClellan hearings and the subsequent trials.

But Meany continued to cling to the idea that there was nothing wrong with the tremendous power lodged in the hands of labor union officials. He resisted efforts to curb this power through antitrust legislation or any other means. His is the labor union philosophy that holds it is wrong to cut the unbridled and arbitrary strength in the hands of representatives of organized labor.

The A.F.L.-C.I.O. president, and many other labor leaders who had taken a forthright stand against the corruption in the Teamsters union, would not accept evidence indicating that one of the significant causes was that total power which flowed from the so-called "legal immunities of labor unions." They argued that if they gave up the power, it might weaken their position in some future economic struggle with some employer. Although they were strong advocates of Federal government intervention in nearly every other area of society, they would not trust the government with further power to restrict union leaders in their dealings with union members or in dealing with employers.

President Meany and other high A.F.L.-C.I.O. officials were bitterly resentful of the criticism of excessive union power written in 1957 by the late Roscoe Pound, formed dean and professor emeritus of the Harvard University Law School.

"The labor leader and labor union now stand where the king and government and land owner and charity and husband

and father stood at common law," Dean Pound said in his work on "Legal Immunities of Labor Unions."

He explained how the legal immunities once granted to sovereigns included "the royal prerogative of dishonesty." While the immunities of sovereigns, government officials, persons of rank, land owners, husbands and parents have disappeared through the years, Dean Pound wrote, there has arisen a new species of immunities: "The substantially general privileges and immunities of labor unions and their members and officials to commit wrongs to person and property, to interfere with use of highways, to break contracts, to deprive individuals of the means of earning a livelihood, to control the activities of the individual workers and their local organizations by national organizations centrally and arbitrarily administered beyond the reach of state laws and to misuse trust funds—things which no one else can do with immunity."

While Dave Beck and Jimmy Hoffa finally outstretched those immunities, the point that Dean Pound was making is no less valid, even following enactment of the Landrum-Griffin labor reform legislation.

Conviction of Hoffa came as a result of a massive Senate investigation followed immediately by the full power of a Federal investigation that had the personal backing and interest of the Attorney General and the President. The force needed to bring about those convictions of Hoffa does not mean that he was less powerful but only emphasizes the tremendous strength he held as president of the International Brotherhood of Teamsters.

Hoffa held that power for years after he had been exposed by the McClellan committee. He held it even after he had been convicted of a crime. Despite the great stigma he carried following the McClellan committee hearings, Hoffa wielded a power that had the potential for destroying Meany and the A.F.L.-C.I.O. or any individual union that opposed him. The full force of Teamsters power was never wielded against Meany only because from the time Hoffa took over the Teamsters he was under fire from the McClellan committee or from a Kennedy-directed Justice Department.

The passing of Dave Beck and Jimmy Hoffa from the labor

scene will not end the problem, for there are other corrupt men ready to take their places. Some of these men are in the Teamsters union. And other men will use the Teamsters union and its officers for their own crooked purposes. Many such persons would represent worse elements than either Beck or Hoffa, for there are a few with closer ties to the underworld than Hoffa had.

The tentacles of power of the International Brotherhood of Teamsters will remain a serious problem until that power is restricted. No more evidence should be needed than is available today. Certainly, the gangster elements have been quick to see how the tremendous power of this union could be used to make an industry—both the employer and the employee—pay tribute for the right to do business or hold a job. Mobsters in union office can assume the role of a respected guardian of the rights of the working man—and become more difficult to criticize.

To obtain a real concept of the danger, imagine the power of the Teamsters union falling into the hands of an Al Capone. Then remember that there were officials of the Teamsters union who were working with heirs to the Capone legacy in Chicago. Keep in mind that the tentacles of the Teamsters union stretch into every state and operate with the business and political community through more than 850 local unions.

With this kind of power, an Al Capone would not have needed a gun to install himself in a position of control over the underworld. He could add legitimate businesses to his conquests and spread his evil influence into any locality served by trucks.

The weapon which can crush a business can be as effective as the slaughter of the opposition with a machine gun, and it is far less likely to stir up the anger of the public. The mere possibility of arbitrary revocation of the union membership of the average workingman can be a more insidious way to bring him to his knees than a threat or a beating.

While political figures might feel compelled to take action against overt violence, few aspiring politicians would voluntarily oppose more subtle misuses of union power or take aggressive steps to bring union crooks to justice. Most political figures live in mortal fear of being tagged as "anti-union."

Even political figures who understand the evil inherent in the power held by the Teamsters union will seldom confess it.

They fear the public will ignore the facts and perhaps accept the "anti-union" label. While the public, as well as most union members, may dislike the activities of a Dave Beck and a Jimmy Hoffa, there is often failure to see the necessity for curbing the power and eliminating some of the immunities that made the activities of Beck and Hoffa possible. There often is a failure to understand how intimidation or corruption of employers, union members or government officials can lead to destruction of the civil rights, the property rights or the job rights of almost any citizen.

Conviction of Jimmy Hoffa will have a salutary impact on the labor movement, and specifically on the Teamsters union, but it is no cause for complacency and belief that the problems of labor corruption have been solved. The problems will be there as long as there are no effective legal restrictions on the tentacles of power controlled by the International Brotherhood of Teamsters.

Appendix

While dozens of Congressional investigations and more than 100 criminal trial records form the background for this book, the major documentation can be found in the following list of Congressional hearings and reports and court proceedings:

1. Detroit Juke Box Hearings, known officially as "Investigation of Racketeering in the Detroit Area," by the Joint Subcommittees of the Committee on Education and Labor and the Committee on Government Operations of the House of Representatives. The hearings were in the Eighty-Third Congress, First Session (June 8, 11, 12, and 13, 1953). The report was issued in the Eighty-Third Congress, Second Session. The chairman was Representative Wint Smith (Rep., Kans.).

2. Kansas City Racket Hearings, known officially as "Strikes and Racketeering in the Kansas City Area," by the Joint Subcommittees of the Committee on Education and Labor and the Committee on Government Operations of the House of Representatives. The hearings were in the Eighty-Third Congress, First Session (June 29, 30, and July 1, 2, and 3, 1953). The report was issued in the Eighty-Third Congress, First Session. The chairman was Representative Wint Smith (Rep., Kans.).

3. Detroit Welfare Fund Racketeering Hearings, known officially as "Investigation of Welfare Funds and Racketeering,"

by a Special Subcommittee of the Committee on Education and Labor of the House of Representatives. The hearings were in the Eighty-Third Congress, First Session (November 23, 24, 25, and 27, 1953). The report was issued in the Eighty-Third Congress, Second Session. The chairman was Representative Wint Smith (Rep., Kans.).

4. Minneapolis Racket Hearings, known officially as "Investigation of Racketeering in the Minneapolis, Minn., Area," by the Subcommittee of the Committee on Government Operations of the House of Representatives. The hearings were in the Eighty-Third Congress, Second Session (April 9 and 10, 1954). There was no report on these hearings, but the report on the Detroit Welfare Fund Racketeering included considerable information on the same Minneapolis labor figures. The chairman was Representative George H. Bender (Rep., Ohio).

5. Cleveland Racket Hearings, known officially as "Investigation of Racketeering in the Cleveland, Ohio, Area," by a Special Anti-Racketeering Subcommittee of the Committee on Government Operations of the House of Representatives. The hearings were in the Eighty-Third Congress, Second Session (September 27, 28, 29, and 30, 1954), The report was issued in the Eighty-Fourth Congress, First Session. The chairman was Representative George H. Bender (Rep., Ohio).

6. Los Angeles Welfare and Pension Fund Hearings, known officially as Part One of "Investigation of Welfare and Pension Funds," by the Special Subcommittee of the Committee on Education and Labor of the House of Representatives. The hearings were in the Eighty-Third Congress, Second Session (September 22, 23, 24, and 25, 1954). There was no report. The chairman was Representative Samuel K. McConnell, Jr., (Rep., Penn.).

7. Washington, D.C., Welfare and Pension Fund Hearings, known officially as Part Two of "Investigation of Welfare and Pension Funds," by the Special Subcommittee of the Committee on Education and Labor of the House of Representatives. The hearings were in the Eighty-Third Congress, Second Session (November 29, 30, and December 1, 1954). There was no report. The chairman was Representative Samuel K. McConnell, Jr., (Rep., Penn.).

8. Douglas Welfare and Pension Hearings, known officially

as the "Welfare and Pension Plans Investigation," by a Subcommittee of the Committee on Labor and Public Welfare of the Senate. The hearings (Parts 1, 2, and 3) were in the Eighty-Fourth Congress, First Session. Reports were issued in the Eighty-Fourth Congress, First Session (1955) and the Second Session (1956). The chairman was Senator Paul H. Douglas (Dem., Ill.).

9. McClellan Government Operations Subcommittee Hearings, known officially as an investigation of "Violations or Non-enforcement of Government Laws and Regulations in the Labor Union Field" by the Permanent Subcommittee on Investigations of the Committee on Government Operations of the Senate. The hearings were in the Eighty-Fifth Congress, First Session (January 16, 17, 18, 19, 1957). No report was issued, but this series of hearings set the stage for the establishment of the "Select Committee" also headed by Senator John L. McClellan (Dem., Ark.).

10. McClellan Racket Committee, known officially as the "Select Committee on Improper Activities in the Labor Management Field," with members drawn from the Senate Committee on Government Operations and the Senate Committee on Labor and Public Welfare. This committee was created by the Senate on January 30, 1957, and was composed of four Democrats and four Republicans. The first hearings were on February 26, 1957, and continued through March, 1960. The hearing record includes 58 volumes of testimony. A total of seven reports were filed, and they are No. 1417, No. 612 (Part 1 and Part 2), and No. 1139 (Part 1, Part 2, Part 3 and Part 4).

11. McClellan Government Operations Subcommittee Hearings, known officially as investigation of "James R. Hoffa and Continued Underworld Control of New York Teamster Local 239," by the Permanent Subcommittee on Investigation of the Committee on Government Operations of the Senate, Eighty-Seventh Congress, Fifth Session (January 10, 11, 12, 24, and 25, 1961).

12. Hoffa's Washington, D.C., trial, known officially as U.S. v. James R. Hoffa and Hyman I. Fischbach, United States District Court for the District of Columbia, Cr. No. 294-57. Hoffa was acquitted, the charges against Fischbach were dismissed.

13. Hoffa's New York trials, known officially as U.S. v. James R. Hoffa, Owen Bert Brennan, and Bernard Spindel, United

States District Court for the Southern District of New York, Eastern Division, Cr. No. 3151-18. The first trial resulted in a hung jury. The second trial resulted in acquittal of all three defendants.

14. Hoffa's Nashville trial, known officially as U.S. v. James R. Hoffa and Commercial Carriers, United States District Court for the Middle District of Tennessee (Nashville) Cr. No. 13241. The trial ended in a hung jury.

15. Hoffa's Chattanooga trial, known officially as U.S. v. James R. Hoffa, *et al*, United States District Court for the Eastern District of Tennessee (Chattanooga) Cr. No. 11989. The trial resulted in conviction of Hoffa, Thomas Ewing Parks, Larry Campbell, and Ewing King on charges of attempting to fix the jury in Hoffa's Nashville trial. Two of the defendants, Allen Dorfman and Nicholas J. Tweel, were acquitted.[1]

16. Hoffa's Chicago trial, known officially as U.S. v. S. George Burris, James R. Hoffa, *et al*, United States District Court for the Northern District of Illinois, Eastern Division (Chicago), 63 Cr. No. 317. Hoffa, S. George Burris, Benjamin Dranow, Samuel Hyman, Calvin Kovens, Zachary A. Strate, Jr., and A e I. Weinblatt were convicted on charges of conspiracy and wire and mail fraud. Charges against one of the original defendants, Herbert R. Burris, were dismissed.

17. The Teamsters Monitor case, known officially as John Cunningham, *et al*, v. John F. English, *et al*, United States District Court for the District of Columbia, Civil Action No. 2361-57. See also Cunningham v. English, 175 F. Supp. 764, December 11, 1958, and Milone v. English, 306 F. 2d 814, July 19, 1962.

---

[1]On July 29, 1965, the U.S. Court of Appeals for the Sixth Circuit (Cincinnati, Ohio) affirmed the jury-tampering conviction of James R. Hoffa, Thomas Parks, Larry Campbell, and Ewing King. It was a unanimous decision. An appeal to the Supreme Court was indicated.